Dominic
Di Benedetto J. M. J. †

THE BRIDGE

THE BRIDGE

A YEARBOOK OF
JUDAEO-CHRISTIAN STUDIES
VOLUME II
Edited by John M. Oesterreicher

PANTHEON BOOKS

THE BRIDGE

is published for

THE INSTITUTE OF JUDAEO-CHRISTIAN STUDIES
SETON HALL UNIVERSITY

by Pantheon Books Inc., 333 Sixth Avenue, New York 14, N. Y.

Nihil obstat MSGR. JOSEPH H. BRADY, S.T.D., Censor Librorum
Imprimatur ✠ THOMAS A. BOLAND, S.T.D., Archbishop of Newark
September twelfth, 1956

EDITORIAL OFFICE OF THE BRIDGE: 31 CLINTON STREET,
NEWARK 2, N. J.
COPYRIGHT 1956 BY THE INSTITUTE OF JUDAEO-CHRISTIAN STUDIES
LIBRARY OF CONGRESS CATALOGUE CARD NO. 55-10281
MANUFACTURED IN THE U. S. A.
BY KINGSPORT PRESS, INC., KINGSPORT, TENNESSEE
DESIGNED BY ANDOR BRAUN

CONTENTS

ILLUSTRATIONS

A WORD OF THANKS

IT IS with deep gratitude to God and to our many friends that we enter upon our second year. When the first volume of THE BRIDGE appeared, its editors were hopeful that it would be well received. But none of us dared think that it would be asked for in every continent and that a second large printing would soon be required. Nor did we expect so many distinguished responses, of which I can record only a few.

We are grateful to Eugene Cardinal Tisserant, Dean of the College of Cardinals, who told us how glad he was that THE BRIDGE gave thought to the Jewish tradition of old. Ever since his seminary days fifty-five years ago, he wrote, he has felt that Christians must know the apocryphal and rabbinical literature for the sake of the insights it yields "about the times near to our Redemption." He added that "the findings of Qumran will open a new field of studies where Christians and Jews will be able to collaborate." We are grateful to Archbishop Richard J. Cushing of Boston, who spoke in a broadcast about THE BRIDGE's "high level of scholarship, fruitful of understanding and love and grace"; and to Sister Madeleva, C.S.C., president of St. Mary's College, Notre Dame, who, calling it "magnificent, more than a yearbook," predicted that it would be "something of an encyclopedia."

We are grateful to Rabbi Leo Baeck of London, the venerable survivor of the cruelties of Theresienstadt, for approval that could not be warmer: "It is a wonderful book, both as a whole and in each of its parts. I was greatly inspired and I think it will be really a bridge." We are grateful to Schalom Ben-Chorin, the Israeli thinker, for calling THE BRIDGE a "momentous volume" and for seeing it as a sign "that a new spirit is astir in the United States"; grateful, too, to Sholom J. Kahn, for his words in the *Jerusalem Post:* "This superbly edited volume sets out to 'span an abyss,' 'open a road for communication,' and be 'an instrument of peace.' But it does so frankly from the point of view of the Catholic Church." Having underlined this limitation, as he sees it, he nonetheless declared: "We can praise without reserve the scholarship and sensitivity of its execution. None of its score of essays is superficial or unrewarding."

When we declared it our purpose to serve the never resting dialogue of Christians and Jews, some Jewish critics asked whether a presentation in which "one party speaks but indirectly" can be called a dialogue. We think it can. Wherever the "other" is met not as an object but as a "thou," a living and loved being, there is dialogue. Again, to serve a dialogue is something deeper and more fruitful than to enter into a discussion. We could not in conscience, that is, in the love we bear for Christ, open our pages to a dispute on the basic tenets of our faith. We are committed, and gladly so; and it is precisely this commitment that binds us to the Jews. Our bond to them is not against or apart from our faith, but of it. When we call them "our separated brethren," we seek to express the authentic mind of the Church, for in *Mystici Corporis,* Pius XII pleads that genuine love for the Church must know no limits or borders. Not only her members, he says, but also those who are not yet one with us in Christ's Mystical Body, must we "recognize as brothers of Christ according to the flesh, destined together with us to eternal salvation." This being true of all the sons of Adam, it is most certainly true of the sons of Abraham, "the father of our faith."

Thus we should like to reiterate our stand in the words of Monsignor John J. Dougherty: "It is in the name of the One God that THE BRIDGE seeks a meeting of Jews and Christians. This name, however, is for us ever wedded to the name of Christ, a name that keeps Christians and Jews apart. THE BRIDGE, then, desires to make understood Him who separates, and those whom He separates. For as prejudice feeds on ignorance, love requires understanding and understanding knowledge."

As we restate our intention, we give thanks. The many encouragements we have received from our readers, both Jewish and Christian, give us assurance that what we called a "venture of love" was indeed so welcomed, and give us hope that this second volume too will serve a loving encounter.

JOHN M. OESTERREICHER

STUDIES

Alexander Jones

THE WORD IS A SEED

OF EVEN the richest languages it is true that for every million ideas there are only a thousand words. The color range may serve as an example: no one will ever fit words to every shade of the spectrum— not a tongue is called for but a paint brush.

Now if this were the whole of it, we might well despair of expressing all but our most simple thoughts. But in truth there is no such thing as a pure note in the scale of human tongues; or, rather, each note summons its family of overtones, born to it in its years of history. The word the mother teaches her child was already venerable when she herself received it. It had grown old in the service of her ancestors; it had been sent on this errand and on that; at one time it had toiled in the cellars of literature, at another it had shone in its courts, adroitly adapting itself to all changes of fortune. After the experience of a hundred lifetimes this word, old but very vigorous, remained still itself but became so much more. And now it wears on its face the pain and the joy of its long story. We ourselves give it something, too; because having served with us it outlives us who seemed to be its masters. We pass. The word remains.

I

Now what if God should choose to take the word into His service? Supposing God were to use the tongue of man—what then? Plainly, no word will outlive Him; nor did it exist before Him. God foreknows the fortunes of His word. No part of its story (what we call past and present and future) is hidden from Him. He sees it, therefore, with eternal eyes and knows it wholly—seed and flower and fruit. Should He send it to do His bidding, He already knows what will become of it. Man learns the varying power of the word only as generation succeeds generation; but God is aware of it from eternity. Or, if we may change the image yet again, the word that first appeared naked will reappear—since it is for man that God intends it —in the fashion of the generation to which it is revealed.

If, therefore, through the medium of written sentences God elects to reveal Himself to man in one favored millennium of history; and if—since God is a wise God—that revelation is tuned to the reception of its hearers; and if—because God is a God of truth—that revelation can never contradict itself as it increases in volume but must now cry aloud the selfsame thing that once it whispered, then the thousand years of revelation is a period to be considered in its entirety, to be savored only when it is complete. Then and then only can its first beginnings be seen as beginnings and the innate but latent power of the Word acknowledged. I do not know the acorn until I have seen the oak.

II

THE Bible, then, is not a granite block of equal density throughout, immovable, undeveloping, dead. It is not like a coral reef growing in bulk through the years by the mere juxtaposition of homogeneous matter. It is the living word of the living God. It is a thing that grows from within, vitally. At no stage of its growth, therefore, can it be justly appreciated. We must wait until it has achieved full stature. After all, we can no more make an exploratory incision into living things without destroying the tissue than we can give ourselves time to admire the water's flow by freezing it. I say this with regard to the theme of the present essay but dare add, in passing, that it has wider application in a wider context. So much distortion of God's Word is born of the monstrous parentage we may call the static outlook. So often it is the Bible's misfortune to be taken for a series of adjacent oracles, each independent of the other and all independent of their setting, snatched out to vindicate the perpetuation of some passing stage of man's relationship with God. There is no more fundamental error in the whole range—and it is an alarmingly wide range—of exegetical absurdities. In this way a man could even justify the desert law of vendetta in our modern cities, could build another Ark of the Commandments according to the pattern shown to Moses on the

Mount, could make the thousandth year of revelation look no different from the first.

For if the Word was not spoken idly to the fathers, neither was it spoken only to the fathers. It was spoken also for our instruction "upon whom the final age of the world has come" (1 Cor 10:11). That the Word still lived was the basic conviction of the Church's earliest days. It has been very justly said, indeed, that "the application of prophecy was probably the earliest form of Christian theological thought." [1] This theology, which precedes and underlies our New Testament writings, is therefore a biblical theology in the fullest sense of the phrase. The first duty of the disciples was, no doubt, to inform the world of the facts—of the suffering, death, and resurrection of Jesus of Nazareth, "a prophet mighty in work and word" (Lk 24:19). But they had also to show their Jewish brethren that this new Thing was no foundling in Israel's cradle but the heir of all the prophets. To the Gentile they had to show that the wisdom of Providence had not been silent before and had spoken freely now. Old and New Testaments had to be brought together; the Word must be shown to be consistent with itself—the Word at no time destroyed and now at last fulfilled.

III

WHATEVER the New Testament writers meant by the term "fulfillment," they did not mean some mathematical equation of past promise and present performance. Far from it. For them the reality transcended the promise: Israel had expected a king; it had received a king of kings. With this in mind we may well hesitate before some popular forms of what is called "the prophetic argument"—forms that would persuade us that the prophets wrote the gospel before the gospel. No, the vision of the prophets was obscure; they could hope only for a vague outline, peering out, as through a fog, to catch some sight of the period and pattern of messianic days. [2] This is why Christ

1. C. H. Dodd, *History and the Gospel* (London: Nisbet, 1938), p. 60. Dr. Dodd's statement is adequate as long as we remember that the theological argument does not consist of an alignment of texts selected from Old and New Testaments. The argument implicit in this present essay is of a very different kind.

2. Such is the clear impression left by St. Peter when he speaks of the prophets' "earnest inquiry and search" into the grace that was to come (1 Pet 1:10).

could bless the eyes of His disciples, which looked upon the things "many prophets and just men had longed to see" (Mt 13:16–17).

Even the formal assurance of prophecy, therefore, had its short-comings. But we have more than this, much more. For it is the whole record of Israel's story that is God's word to man—an acted word, as truly conveying His meaning as does the visible universe. The pattern of this history not only recurs within itself but reappears in the full-ness of time. And when it thus reappears it is not, as it were, larger; rather is it resumed on a higher plane, becoming more refined, assum-ing a spiritual nature.[3] It was thus that the Hebrew always looked upon his history. Unlike the Greek he never saw time as a series of wheels, each period powerless to grow beyond its own circumference, impotent to do aught but imitate its predecessor in rise, decline, re-turn. For the Hebrew, as for the Christian, a driving Providence bears history along toward a goal. The movement is real and forward, not frustrated and cyclic.[4] Nevertheless, as we have said, it is repetitive: the ascent goes on and the same obstacles recur to be conquered, though on a higher level. The summit is above the clouds.

About the Old Testament there hangs an air of something unfin-ished, and one feels that the Hebrew mind should be the first to sense it. In his heart's heart the Jew, son of patriarchs and prophets, cannot believe that God should halt where the Old Testament ends, and so he lives on deferred hope. Neither can the Christian believe it, but for him the New Testament provides insuperable climax. For the Christian the Old Testament and the New are movements of one great symphony, the one movement calling for the other. Without the New Testament the Old is a chain of melodies of great beauty— of melodious hints leaving us with a sense of loss, of lovely sounds cut off in their childhood. But without the Old Testament the New bursts upon the ear almost brutally, the ear being not yet attuned to the key or to the mode; the music is heard, but its great motifs are not fully recognized; its several parts are wondered at, but are not under-

---

3. One example is the "March in the Desert" theme, taken up by the prophets and gathered into the New Testament. See J. Guillet, "La marche à travers le Désert," *Recherches de Science Religieuse* (1949), pp. 161–181; also Barnabas M. Ahern, C.P., "The Exodus, Then and Now," *The Bridge*, I, 53–74.

4. C. N. Cochrane has reminded us again of St. Augustine's repugnance for the theory of cycles, for history's moving like a wheel, which so utterly contradicts the Judaeo-Christian conviction that time and also space are not causes but op-portunities, "not gods but gifts." See Cochrane, *Christianity and Classical Culture* (New York: Oxford University Press, 1944), pp. 483–484; *De Civ. Dei*, XII, 14–21 (PL 41:360–372).

stood as the parts of one majestic whole. For the Christian the thin
and separate melodies of the Old are in the New brought together,
given richer tone, contrapuntally interwoven, discovered to have belonged all the time to one musical composition. And as foolish as it
would be to deliver judgment on the sole witness of preparatory bars,
so foolish does he hold it to pronounce upon either New Testament or
Old without its fellow.

This sensation (for it is more than an impression) has a cause
which is capable of literary proof. All the great themes of the Old
Testament—and they are all "words" of God: we might name at
random the themes of the Presence, the Sacrifice, the Temple—work
toward a sublime maturity they do not find except in the New.[5] Of
such themes we shall examine one: the theme of the Word of God
itself. It is the very term we apply to the Scriptures. If we pursue this
theme to its end, it should be clear how, not in fantasy but quite exactly, we can say: "The Bible is Christ."

Scripture grows, ripens into Christ, *is* Christ, for the Word of God
is a seed. This agricultural image is common to both the Testaments;
though the actual phrase belongs only to the New, its spirit is that of
both. What in one is life-giving water is the very germ of life in the
other:

> *As the rain and the snow come down from heaven,*
>   *and return no more thither,*
>   *but soak the earth and water it,*
>   *and make it to spring*
>   *and give seed to the sower and bread to the eater:*
> *So shall my word be,*
>   *which shall go forth from my mouth:*
> *It shall not return to me void,*
>   *but it shall do whatsoever I please*
>   *and shall prosper in the things for which I sent it.*
>   (Is 55:10–11)[6]

5. See A. G. Hebert, *The Authority of the Old Testament* (London: Faber and
Faber, 1947), p. 218; cf. pp. 199–238; H. H. Rowley, *The Re-Discovery of the
Old Testament* (London: James Clarke, 1945), pp. 14–23, 202–215; and Albert
Gelin, *The Key Concepts of the Old Testament* (New York: Sheed and Ward,
1955). A short essay on the Temple theme from this point of view may be found
in A. Jones, *Unless Some Man Show Me* (New York: Sheed and Ward, 1951),
pp. 136–145.
6. In the Word of God infallibly executing His will, man is blessed. Hence
Isaiah likens the Word to rain, so needed by the dry land, so obviously not under

The sower went out to sow his seed. . . .
Now the parable is this:
The seed is the word of God.

(Lk 8:5, 11)

IV

WHEN we speak of the "history of religion," what do we mean? By "religion" we mean the acknowledgment of a relationship between the human and the Divine, between the finite and the Infinite. Now, to establish such a relationship, infinite power is necessary. But have there not been many attempts by man to bridge the infinite abyss between the finite and the Infinite? Indeed; yet even these human gropings, the pagan religions, would not have been possible had not the infinite Hand moved first. Strictly speaking, then, the history of religion is not so much, nor essentially, the story of man's quest for God but of God's for man.

The story begins with man's creation—the making of the bond between man and God. It proceeds with man's growing recognition of this basic fact and of its consequences for himself. Whence comes this recognition? From reason, we say. True, but not the whole truth. It is reason indeed but reason working on something intelligible. That intelligible thing is man himself and the creation around him—contingent things through which human reason attains to the existence of the Necessary. In other words, by the fact of creation God has *communicated* with man; creation is a Word of God to man—the first Word of God to man.

The act of creation is therefore an act of speech, of speech in a tongue understood by all who would hear, a standing witness against all who would not:

human control, so clearly a gift—a blessing, then, for field, beast, and man. The thought of rain as a gift is stressed in the Jewish prayer book. In the second of the Eighteen Benedictions, the devout Jew prays: "Thou, O Lord, art mighty forever, thou revivest the dead, thou art mighty to save." From fall till spring, from the day after the feast of the Rejoicing of the Law till the eve of Passover, he adds: "Thou causest the wind to blow and the rain to fall." See *The Authorised Daily Prayer Book,* trans. and ed. J. H. Hertz (New York: Bloch Publishing Co., 1952), p. 133. In connection with this Benediction, the Talmud speaks of three keys that are God's: the key of rain, the key of birth, and the key of the rising of the dead —a beautiful thought even though the Talmud adds that these keys are not entrusted to the hand of any messenger (Ta'an. 2a; cf. *The Babylonian Talmud,* ed. I. Epstein, London: Soncino, 1938, *Ta'anith,* p. 3).

For from the greatness and the beauty of created things
their original author, by analogy, is seen.

(Wis 13:5)

And again:

The heavens declare the glory of God,
and the firmament proclaims His handiwork.
Day pours out the word to day,
and night to night imparts knowledge.

(Ps 18:2–3)

The created universe, then, is a revelatory Word to man; it is a thing that speaks to him, and in this the two meanings of the Hebrew term *dabar* ("word" and "thing") come together.

So much for man. But as it proceeds from God, the Word not only speaks; it is also creative. When God "utters," an effect is necessarily produced. The Greek *logos* and the Hebrew *dabar* may agree in their dictionary meaning; in reality, since the two terms are children of opposed mentalities, they are poles apart.[7] For the Greek, the "word," *logos,* is an instrument and expression of thought even if the thought

---

7. Thorleif Boman, in *Das hebräische Denken im Vergleich mit dem griechischen* (Göttingen: Vandenhoeck & Ruprecht, 1952), sums up this difference well. The noun *dabar* comes from the verbs *dabar* and *diber,* "to speak." But the root-meaning is "to thrust forward" and in consequence—picturing, as it were, the act of speaking—"to let words follow one another." Because of the basic meaning of the verb, *dabar* means "deed" as well as "word." Eliezer's telling, for instance, "all he had done" (Gen 24:66) is in Hebrew his telling all the "deeds" or "words" he had done. But to say that the Hebrews made no sharp distinction between word and deed is not to say that they did not know words that promised much but were never acted on. In such a case, the fault, as they saw it, was not that the speaker brought forth *only* a word, and no deed. What he had brought forth was an evil, empty, lying word, a word that lacked the inner power and truth for realization. Never could a Hebrew have burst out contemptuously, as Hamlet did: "Words, words, words." Never could he, with Goethe's Faust, have called words *Schall und Rauch;* they were reality. To the Hebrew, then, the "word-deed" is that which is highest and noblest in man. The Greek *logos,* on the other hand, derives from *legein,* "to speak," the basic meaning of whose root, *leg,* is "to collect, to order." Hence *legein* comes to have such diverse meanings as "to count, to think, to say." *Logos,* having nothing to do with the function of speech, the dynamics of being-spoken, or the articulateness of speech, has to do with meaning, the ordered, rational content. And in this sense it represents to the Greek the highest human function. Compared, the two "words" show what each people held most important in the life of the spirit: for the Hebrew it was the dynamic, lordly, majestic, powerfully creative; for the Greek it was the ordered, measured, carefully planned, and meaningful (pp. 52–54).

remain unuttered. But when the Hebrew speaks of the "word," *dabar,* he always thinks of something strangely operative; when he speaks of the Word of God, *debar Yahweh,* he is thinking of the expression of God's sovereign will and also of the vehicle of His irresistible power. This creative aspect of God's Word is never far from the Hebrew mind. Hence the book of Wisdom:

> *God of my fathers, Lord of mercy*
> *you have made all things by your word.*
>
> (Wis 9:1)

And the Psalmist:

> *By the word of the Lord the heavens were made;*
> *by the breath of His mouth all their host.*
>
> (Ps 32:6)

Those two facets of God's Word, the revelatory and the creative, will never be separated in Israel's literature—an ancient and momentous concept which the Christian revelation takes to itself, giving it climax and sublimity.

V

THE act of creation, then, is the first stage of God's revelation to men, the initial epiphany of His "Word." But it is only a beginning.

When God chose to shape a single people as the organ of His message to the world, the Word became more articulate. The voice of God sharpened, as it were, into a series of specific commands addressed to a nation: into the Sinaitic code which, in the most ancient legislative texts of the Bible, is called "the words." It is said, for instance, that the Lord would write upon the Tables "the words"; and again, that He wrote upon them "the words of the covenant, the ten words," *dibere ha-berit ʿaseret ha-debarim* (Ex 34:1, 28). The Word written in the created heavens now comes to earth. And though it commands, yet it is a kind, beneficent word, for obedience removes all obstacles to the Word's creative power, which will carry Israel to its destiny. This is why Israel is bidden to follow the voice of the angel of the Exodus—God's own mouthpiece—if it would reach the Land.

Israel's fortune will always lie in following the Word, whatever form it may assume.

The Word of the Law is more articulate than the Word of creation; nevertheless it bears the same message of God's nature and demands. If the creative Word already implied a divine law for man— a law founded upon man's intrinsic dependence—it is no less true that the legislative word is likewise creative. It brings forth a light as real as, more real than, the light that came when "God said: 'Let there be light,' and there was light" (Gen 1:3). Hence the Law is a light to the mind:

> *A lamp to my feet is your word,*
> *a light to my path.*
>
> (Ps 118:105)

It does not surprise us, therefore, when the Psalmist passes without apology from praise of the sun to praise of the Law. Sun and Law are each a Word of God:

> *He has pitched a tent there for the sun*
> *which comes forth like the groom from his bridal chamber*
> *and, like a giant, joyfully runs its course. . . .*
> *The law of the Lord is perfect,*
> *refreshing the soul . . .*
> *rejoicing the heart . . .*
> *enlightening the eye.*
>
> (Ps 18:5, 6, 8, 9)

Here creation and legislation are side by side, products of the Word which is light to the outer and to the inner eye. Again, the same Word that rules the universe rules God's people:

> *He sends His word and melts [the frozen waters];*
> *He lets His breezes blow and the waters run.*
> *He has proclaimed His word to Jacob,*
> *His statutes and His ordinances to Israel.*
>
> (Ps 147:18–19)

But the Word is not exhausted in the ten words of the Decalogue nor confined to the restrictive "Thou shalt not!" On the contrary.

Long before the Exile, "the Word" had come to stand for God's great favor to His people—His self-manifestation by which each might live. There is nothing cold, narrow, or legalistic about it; rather is it an abundant source of life:

> *It is something very near to you,*
> *already in your mouths and in your hearts;*
> *you have only to carry it out. . . .*
> *It means your very life.*
>
> (Deut 30:14; 32:47)

So much is the Word the life of the people that the silence of Yahweh is, for the earliest of the prophets, the most dreadful of all the punishments that could befall it:

> *I will send forth a famine into the land:*
> *not a famine of bread,*
> *nor a thirst of water,*
> *but of hearing the word of the Lord.*
>
> (Am 8:11)

How could the absence of His Word not have been the dread punishment it was, since Israel's God is the "God who speaks"? And as sacred history goes on, the Hebrew idea of the Word grows warmer and richer so that one begins to wonder what divinely intended goal can satisfy this almost unconscious thrust. The 118th Psalm, which has so often been most unjustly taxed for "its legalistic spirit," is in reality radiant with love: it is perhaps *the* glorification of the Word in the Old Testament, its highest praise. "I hope in your word" is its keynote. For "your word, O Lord, endures forever; it is firm as the heavens"—a phrase that recalls Jesus' own: "The heavens and the earth pass; my word shall not pass." And the Word which is promise and precept is "sweet to the palate; sweeter than honey." "How deeply do I love your word!" is like a refrain which, in many variations, runs through the whole psalm.[8] It is important to note the entrance of this element of affection, of profound love, because if

8. Ps 118:74, 89, 103; and many other verses of the same psalm. An excellent vindication of the truly devotional spirit of Ps 118 (in the Hebrew Ps 119) will be found in A. Robert, P.S.S., "Le Psaume CXIX et les Sapientiaux," *Revue Biblique,* XLVIII (1939), pp. 5–20.

ever the Word is to be "fulfilled," Israel will surely expect it to be supremely lovable.

VI

As THE "Word," this medium of God's contact with Israel, runs its course, it gradually becomes an object of worshipful reverence—not indeed for its own sake but because it is God's. The very fact that it has assumed two forms, creation and the Law, demonstrates that it is independent of either and is free to assume a third. Certainly we are far from Stoic philosophy, in which the *logos* was no more than the inner pattern, the intrinsic order and intelligibility, of the self-revealing cosmos. The Hebrew *debar Yahweh* is quite clearly detached from any created thing; is it in any sense whatever distinct from God? There is no doubt at all that such an unexpected distinction confronts us in the inspired poetic literature. And, in truth, this process of personification is far from alien to the concrete mode of Hebrew thought. Though it does occur notably in the hellenistic period and reveals a certain Greek influence, the process is authentically Hebrew, for already in the Psalms the attributes of God are poetically endowed with personality. God's attributes of mercy and justice, of kindness and truth, are pictured as two soldiers of the royal guard stiffly marching:

> *Kindness and truth go before you.*
> (Ps 88:15)

Justice and peace are said to kiss, truth to spring out of the earth, and justice to look down from heaven (Ps 84:11–12). The Word is similarly endowed, and since it can scarcely be described as an "attribute," its personification becomes all the more striking. Thus it goes forth as a messenger, not an idle one, but one that fulfills the errand that sped it on its way:

> *So shall my word be,*
> *which shall go forth from my mouth;*
> *It shall not return to me void,*
> *but shall do whatsoever I please.*
> (Is 55:11)

Even more significantly, it reappears in the book of Wisdom as a warrior of God destroying the firstborn of the persecutor:

> *Your all-powerful word from heaven's royal throne*
> *bounded, a fierce warrior, into the doomed land,*
> *bearing the sharp sword of your inexorable decree.*
>
> (Wis 18:15–16)

The process goes on when Israel begins to identify *debar Yahweh,* in which are all the treasures of wisdom, with the wisdom so eagerly sought in the Greek world. Indeed, long before, in the book of Proverbs (about the fifth century B.C.), Israel had identified the Word—which is the Torah—with the Wisdom the sage so perseveringly commends. In the much later book of Wisdom (middle of the first century B.C.), this identification is explicit:

> *You . . . have made all things by your word*
> *and in your wisdom have established man*
> *to rule the creatures produced by you,*
> *to govern the world in holiness and justice.*
>
> (Wis 9:1–2)

But it should be noticed that this Word-Wisdom of the Hebrew is not, as it was for the Greek, the achievement of man but the gift of God. True Wisdom dwells in heaven; if it is to come to earth God must send it. What man has gone up to heaven to bring it down from the clouds? asks Baruch (3:29).

Because of the identification of the Word with Wisdom, the frequent personifications of Wisdom in the books of the inspired scribes of Israel are pertinent here, for they are personifications—however poetic—of the Word itself. This Wisdom-Word appears in public like a prophet preaching in Jerusalem's streets:

> *On top of the heights along the road,*
> *at the crossroads [Wisdom] takes her stand;*
> *by the gates at the approaches of the city,*
> *in the entryways she cries aloud.*
>
> (Prov 8:2–3)

Wisdom claims eternal companionship with God before the world was, claims fellowship with Him in the work of creation, claims to hold within itself the very sources of life:

> *From of old I was poured forth,*
>   *at the first, before the earth. . . .*
> *When He made firm the skies above,*
>   *when He fixed fast the foundations of the earth. . . .*
> *then was I beside Him as His craftsman,*
>   *and I was His delight day by day. . . .*
> *He who finds me finds life.*
>
>   (Prov 8:23, 28, 30, 35)

This life it offers to men; the Wisdom-Word offers its own self as the ever-sustaining food:

> *Come, eat of my food*
>   *and drink of the wine I have mixed.*
>
>   (Prov 9:5)

The fathers of Israel were ever being reminded that "not by bread alone does man live, but by every word that comes forth from the mouth of the Lord" (Deut 8:3). Their children too were ever being assured that this Word would never cloy but would give increase of appetite:

> *He who eats of me will hunger still,*
>   *he who drinks of me will thirst for more.*
>
>   (Ecclus 24:20)

Are not these words somehow heard again on the lips of Him who sorrowed: "You are not willing to come to me that you may have life" (Jn 5:40); who stood and cried out:

> *If anyone thirst,*
>   *let him come to me and drink.*
>
>   (Jn 7:37)

On His lips there is also the claim, couched in the very terms of
Ecclesiasticus and yet infinitely bolder:

> *He who comes to me*
> *shall not hunger,*
> *and he who believes in me*
> *shall never thirst.*

(Jn 6:35)

When a man comes who says: "I am the bread of life" (Jn 6:35), it
is evident to the Hebrew mind what he is claiming to be.

VII

WE HAVE witnessed a tendency in Israel's sacred literature to contemplate the Word of God as in a way distinct from God; to consider
it, with poetic—no, more than poetic—imagination, as a person. The
post-biblical Jewish tradition went further still on the way toward the
personification of the Word. The author of the book of Sirach had
written that the Word which came "from the mouth of the Most
High" was created "before all ages, in the beginning" (Ecclus 24:3,
9). He was speaking of the everlasting Wisdom. Rabbinical tradition
took up the theme. The Torah, it said, was made before the world
was made, the working tool of the Holy One for its creation; God's
perfect daughter, it was light, life, and truth.[9]

A no less honored place was given to the Word by the Targumim,
the Aramaic renderings of the Old Testament, whose oral tradition
dates back to long before Christ, though their final redaction was not
made till centuries after Him. Now the Word is called *memra.*[10] At
first glance, Memra would seem to be but a respectful synonym for
God. It is, as we shall see, much more than this; yet it is indeed a literary device to safeguard the divine transcendence, a "buffer word,"

9. References in Gerhard Kittel, *Theologisches Wörterbuch zum Neuen Testament* (Stuttgart: W. Kohlhammer, 1933), IV, 139, lines 14–27.
10. To be more specific, the Targumim use two terms for "word": *pitgama*
where the Hebrew Scriptures have *debar Yahweh,* "the word of the Lord," be it
revealing, prophesying, or commanding; and *memra,* which the Aramaic translators
introduced into the text to take the place of Yahweh, of God Himself. See R. D.
Middleton, "Logos and Shekinah in the Fourth Gospel," *Jewish Quarterly Review,*
XXIX, 2 (Oct. 1938), pp. 107–108.

as George Foot Moore has called it.[11] Thus it is no longer God who
feels and tastes and handles, who is angered and takes offense; it is
His Memra that does and suffers all these things. So the Targum to
Gen 3:8 does not read: "They heard the sound of the Lord God walking in the garden"; rather: "They heard the sound of the Memra
walking in the garden." In the Targum to Deut 9:3, it is not the
Lord God, it is His Memra, that is called "a consuming fire." Again,
it is not Yahweh, the Lord God, it is His Memra, that regrets having
created man, that smites all the firstborn of Egypt, that is offended by
Israel's grumblings in the desert.[12]

In these and other instances, Memra may well be a literary device
to avoid speaking of God in too human terms. Yet there is a startling
rabbinic insistence on the Memra's mediatorship between God and
man. "The Memra brings Israel near to God and sits on His throne
receiving Israel's prayers," reads the Jerusalem Targum to Deut 4:7.
Other targumic passages speak of the Memra as God's agent in the
creating of the earth, in the administering of justice, in the ruling of
man's destiny. Still others see the Memra as the shield of Noah and
of Abraham, as the guardian of Jacob and of all the house of Jacob.
Again, the Memra works the wonders of Egypt, goes before Israel in
the desert, blesses the people and battles for it. It is called "comforter"
and "witness" and "like a father to Israel." In the Memra "redemption will be found." "My Memra," says the Lord God, "shall be unto
you like a good plowman who takes off the yoke from the shoulder
of the oxen." [13] These beautiful passages leave no doubt that the targumic literature regarded the Word as a mediator between heaven
and earth. Here, clearly, is an attempt to build a bridge between the
finite and the Infinite, and we receive the impression that something
new has been seen. Or better, the vision of God seems somehow
fuller and richer; He is the God utterly transcendent and yet utterly

11. George Foot Moore, *Judaism in the First Centuries of the Christian Era*
(Cambridge: Harvard University Press, 1944), I, 419.

12. Targ. to Gen 6:6; Targ. Pseudo-Jon. to Ex 12:29; Targ. to Ex 16:8.

13. The locations of the Memra passages are as follows: On creation, etc.—
Targ. to Is 45:12; Targ. Jer. to Num 33:4; 27:16. On Noah's shield, etc.—Targ.
Jer. to Gen 7:16; Targ. to Gen 15:1; 28:20-21; 35:3; Targ. Jer. to Ex 12:23,
29. On the wonders of Egypt, etc.—Targ. Jer. to Ex 13:8; 14:25; 20:1; Targ. Jer.
to Num 23:8; Targ. to Jos 3:7; 10:14; 23:3. On the comforter, etc.—Targ. to
Is 66:13; Targ. Jer. to Jer 29:23; 31:9. On redemption—Targ. to Zach 12:5.
On the good plowman—Targ. to Os 11:4. For a fuller treatment see "Memra,"
Jewish Encyclopedia, VIII, 464-465.

immanent,[14] very far and very near. Moreover, the work of mediation between God and man is a divine work, given to the divine
Word, the Memra, which issues forth from God.

Certainly the way is paved here for St. John's presentation of
Christ as the Word and for St. Paul's presentation of Him as the Wisdom of God (see 1 Cor 1:24, 30; Col 2:3). A Christian would suspect that here Jewish tradition was under a wondrous pressure from
revelation.[15] At the least the targumic use of Memra was a psychological preparation for the shock of Christ's newness; in this sense too
Memra may be called a "buffer," but a "buffer idea" rather than a
"buffer word." Quite evidently, and understandably, Jewish faith in
the one living God—a faith so often imperiled by the polytheistic
world around it and by the people's temptation to compromise with
that world—would have been affronted by a brusque "I am God"
from Jesus' lips. But the Memra might well say: "I and the Father
are one" (Jn 10:30), or: "Philip, he who sees me sees also the Father" (Jn 14:9).

Yet an anxiety to combine God's remoteness above the universe
with His proximity to His people Israel does not account for all the
uses of Memra. This anxiety may well have led to the adoption of the
term but scarcely explains its subsequent expansion—I mean its use
in cases where no anthropomorphism is to be feared. The Targum to

14. Well worth recording is J. Abelson's view that the chief reason behind the
use of Memra is the desire to express God's immanence. "The view commonly
taken that the Memra is an expedient for avoiding the ascription of anthropomorphism to the Deity is only half the truth," he writes, for "the Memra has a
deep theological or mystical significance," entering "into the relations between the
human and the Divine, between God, man and the world, to an even greater extent
than the Shechinah." The Memra, Abelson states, "is the expounding of the
'Word' from the Jewish point of view. All things exist by virtue of the word (i.e.
Memra) of God. It permeates everything, brings everything into the realm of
being, conditions everything. It is the immanent manifestation of God in the world
of matter and spirit. Divine wisdom, Divine power, Divine love, Divine justice,
all these do not abide in the highest heavens, isolated, unapproachable, unknow-
able. They are imbedded in the scheme of things that we can see and feel and
touch and know. They are a part of the constitution of man and the world. Man
and the world are a fragment of them. The Memra comprises and expresses these
teachings" (*The Immanence of God in Rabbinical Literature*, London: Macmillan,
1912, pp. 150–153).

15. L. Bouyer rightly calls attention to the importance of this post-biblical tradition in *La Bible et l'Evangile* (Paris: Les Editions du Cerf, 1953), pp. 245–251.
See also L. Hackspill, "Etude sur le milieu religieux et intellectuelle contemporain
du Nouveau Testament. 3. La Parole de Dieu," *Revue Biblique*, XI (1902),
pp. 58–66.

Deut 33:7, for example, reads not: "Hear, O God," but "Hear, O Memra of God, the voice of Judah's prayer." Or again, the Jerusalem Targum to Num 10:35–36 which had Moses plead: "Arise, O Memra of the Lord. . . . Return, O Memra of the Lord." Memra, then, is more than a literary device, more than a "buffer."

To say, as Moore does, that Memra "is purely a phenomenon of translation, not a figment of speculation,"[16] is perhaps to offer too sharp an alternative—an alternative which takes little account of the psychology behind a growing tradition. It would surely be rash to contend that the rabbinic tradition was setting up, side by side with the one God, a distinct creative and law-giving Person, itself divine in nature, even though the Targum to Gen 28:20–21 has Jacob vow, on the morning following his vision at Bethel: "If the Memra of the Lord be my help . . . the Memra of the Lord shall be my God." On the other hand, the insistence and persistence and extension of the extraordinary use of Memra seem to betray a need in Israel's soul comparable to the yearnings of the prophet that God would rend the heavens and come down (Is 64:1). Hence, for instance, the repeated angelic interventions in the Jewish apocalypses of the same period. After all, it was that epoch of Greek speculation which sought intermediaries between finite and Infinite; the Jewish mind must have felt the influence. Further, it seems highly probable that the loving use of Memra in the targumic literature was later thought to come too close to Christian teaching—this would explain its suppression by the rabbinic commentaries on Scripture, the Midrashim, which followed the Targumim.[17] If this suggestion is valid, then the Memra must have stood on the threshold of personification. I do not contend that Jewish tradition really knew whither it was tending but rather that there may have been a half-conscious thrust toward an unseen goal.[18]

16. Moore, *op. cit.*, I, 418.

17. Such is the view of Kaufmann Kohler, who ends his article on "Memra" in the *Jewish Encyclopedia* by saying: "Possibly on account of the Christian dogma, rabbinic theology, outside of the Targum literature, made little use of the term 'Memra'" (VIII, 465).

18. This position is midway between the two extremes: Memra a mere synonym for God, a device of translation devoid of all theological content; or Memra a person intermediary between God and man. In support of "mere synonym," see Moore, *op. cit.*, I, 417–419; and "Intermediaries in Jewish Theology," *Harvard Theological Review*, XV (1922), pp. 53–54; Strack-Billerbeck, *Kommentar zum Neuen Testament* (München: C. H. Beck, 1922), II, 303–304; W. F. Albright, *From the Stone Age to Christianity* (Baltimore: Johns Hopkins, 1940), pp. 286 ff:

To sum up: The Word of God in biblical thought reveals. It reveals whether by creation or by more direct instruction, which breaks in upon man from without. For the Greek, the Word, *logos,* was the inner order and reason determining the self-revealing cosmos, whether a personal God was to be thought of or no. It was not so, it could not be so for the Israel of old with its deep sense of the otherness of God, a sense we Christians inherit. Pantheistic thinking was as alien to the ancient people of God as it is to us. The Word, we have seen, became more and more articulate: the voice of creation was reinforced by the voice of the Law, the voice of the Law by the tongues of the prophets and of the inspired scribes. Finally, the notion of the Word reached a stage beyond which it could not go unless in truth it appeared in person upon earth. At this stage Israel stops, the Church goes on.

VIII

IN THE first chapter of the fourth Gospel, the final step in the long march is taken: "And the Word was made flesh." The Word that had spoken to man from rock and river; the Word that had alighted on Zion and spoken to Israel through the Law; the Word that had been spoken by the lips of the prophets; the Word that Israel's scribes and rabbis had reverenced as its guide and protector; this same Word—said the Evangelist—had this time, this end of time, taken to itself a human body.[19]

In a certain sense this Word had taken to itself many human bodies when it spoke through the prophets,[20] but now by a unique, permanent, and personal union it had assumed a human nature as its instru-

J. Bonsirven, S.J., *Le Judaïsme Palestinien* (Paris: Beauchesne, 1934), I, 216–217; J. Lebreton, *History of the Dogma of the Trinity* (London: Burns Oates, 1939), I, 121–123, 162–163; and V. Hamp, *Der Begriff "Wort" in den aramäischen Bibelübersetzungen* (München: Filser-Verlag, 1938), a complete examination of the targumic literature dealing with this subject. Against this position, see Middleton, *loc. cit.,* pp. 107–113; Bouyer, *op. cit.,* pp. 35–37; W. J. Phythian-Adams, *The People and the Presence* (London: Oxford University Press, 1942), p. 177.

19. I use "human body" here the same way the Evangelist uses "flesh," for the whole of human nature, soul and body, with the emphasis on what is its infinite distance and difference from God: its mortal frailty.

20. In the books of the prophets we read: "The word of the Lord came to Isaiah, saying . . ." (38:4), or "to Ezekiel" (1:3), or "to Hosea" (1:1). But nowhere in the New Testament do we read that "the Word of the Lord came to Jesus, saying . . . ," because it is *in* Him.

ment, as the new vehicle of revelation, speaking as neither creation nor Law nor prophet could ever speak.

It is needless to say that we men are incapable of understanding God's Word as it is in Him. It must be mediated through the words of a human intelligence. Hence the humanity assumed by the *Dabar,* the *Logos,* is a true human nature, not an appearance only, and its intelligence functions in truly human fashion—otherwise the Incarnation is not the link between God and ourselves. Nevertheless "the Word was God" (Jn 1:1). The Word was no second God any more than the "Word" of Jewish tradition had been, but the Godhead was now seen to bear within itself a mystery of plurality in unity—plurality of relation, unity of essence—or, in the formula of a Christian theology no less tenacious of monotheism than the Jewish: one in nature, more than one in person.[21]

IX

IT WAS, if I may call it so, the paroxysm, the climax, of divine effort that brought the Word in the flesh. The creative Word in the cosmos had been ignored by the Gentile, "who from the good things seen," the author of the book of Wisdom mourns, "did not succeed in knowing Him who is" (13:1). The revealing Word in the Law had so often gone unheeded; that Israel had not heard had so often been the lament of the prophets (Is 1:3; 30:12; Jer 6:10; Ez 3:7; Os 9:17; Soph 3:2). And so the Word that spoke through the prophets speaks again, this time through the Son, speaking truly with human lips but most poignantly in deeds. Of old, God had repeatedly declared His love for His people, repeatedly shown it in Israel's history. Yet it was

21. Without discussing here certain of his misinterpretations of St. John's Gospel, it is interesting to note that Abelson (*op. cit.,* pp. 161–165) finds nothing in St. John's theology to counter ancient Jewish tradition. To the Evangelist, who, according to Abelson, echoes "the Jewish apocalyptic as well as the Palestinian rabbinic teachings in the first century A.D.," the truth that God is one, that there is no "dualism of Deity," is an "unassailable stronghold." In the passage, "The Word was with God, and the Word was God. He was in the beginning with God. All things were made through Him, and without Him was made nothing that has been made," Abelson sees but a firm insistence on the divine unity. I fear, however, that he did not discern the full meaning of his own words when he spoke so rightly of the unity of God as "unique," "incomparable." For the oneness of God is a oneness which breaks open our everyday thoughts and terms, a unity absolutely above any unity to be met in the world of finite creatures; it is a unity on an infinite plane.

still possible for men to ask how far that love could go—perhaps
even to begin to wonder what "love" meant at all in an infinite God.
But now, translated into the sacrificing life and sacrificial death of
the Son, God's Word is shown to be a message of love as man understands love. Translated into the resurrection of that crucified flesh, it
is shown to be a Word of triumphant hope and of the promise of
life. For it is the function of the Word-in-flesh to bring life, to create.

This is why the opening phrase of John's Gospel is a deliberate
echo of the first word of the Bible: "In the beginning," *Bereshit*,
which is the very title of Genesis in the Hebrew canon. There "In
the beginning" introduces an account of the creation of the material
universe, and St. John invites us from the outset to identify the Word
which is to take flesh with the creative Word of Israel's tradition:

> *In the beginning was the Word. . . .*
> *and without Him was made nothing.*
>
> (Jn 1:1, 3)

This strikes the Psalmist's note:

> *By the word of the Lord the heavens were made;*
> *by the breath of His mouth all their host. . . .*
> *For He spoke, and [the earth] was made;*
> *He commanded, and it stood forth.*
>
> (Ps 32:6, 9)

And indeed the whole marvelous pattern of John's prologue, which
begins in heaven where "the Word was with God," then comes to
earth where "the Word was made flesh," where it does its work of
grace and creates the new sons of God, urgently recalls the Isaian
description of the Word as the rain coming down from above to water the earth that seeds may grow and men live (55:10–11). Again,
the Word's descent is modeled on the Old Testament hymns to the
Wisdom which is the Word: Wisdom with God from the beginning,
Wisdom taking part in the world's making, Wisdom coming to earth
to bestow its riches upon those who would receive them.[22] Similarly,
according to John, the Dabar is "in the beginning with God"; by
Him all things were made; once more "He came unto His own," to

---

22. Read the hymns in praise of Wisdom in Wis 9:9–12; Prov 8:22–32; Ecclus
24:5–31. See also C. Spicq, "La Siracide et la structure littéraire du Prologue de
Saint Jean," in *Mémorial Lagrange* (Paris: Gabalda, 1940), pp. 183–195.

the chosen people on earth, and gave to "those who believe in His name" "the power of becoming sons of God." [23]

But the prologue of John is more than a prologue; it is in miniature his own Gospel, in which there recurs constantly the theme of the Dabar which creates. We may not agree with those who, on the model of the Genesis account of creation, would arrange the whole of John's Gospel in a seven-day framework [24] but at least it is evident that the motif of new creation underlies every chapter of it.[25] The giving of life preoccupies it: "I came that they may have life," "I am the resurrection and the life," "Unless a man be born again . . ." (10:10; 11:25; 3:5). Forty times the noun "life" occurs in John's Gospel to Mark's four. For John, Christ's is a new world, a creation of higher order than this, an order in which even the material body is glorified. It is the "regeneration" or "second genesis," the *palingenesia,* of which Christ Himself speaks (Mt 19:28), the "new creation in Christ" of Paul (Gal 6:15), the "new heavens and new earth" promised by Isaiah (65:17) and seen near by John (Apoc 21:1). The turning point of history is come: the Word of the Lord, the *debar Yahweh,* has resumed its creative activity on a wondrously higher plane. Its is a destiny worthy of the God from whom it came.

It is not that a stray sentence here or there in the prophets glows more brightly in the light of Christ, but that the total expectation of Israel, increasing in tempo, growing in volume, rising in pitch, could never be thwarted—because it was of God. If there is one datum that stands out in the preaching of the ancient prophets, it is that God would do greater things for His people than the great things already

23. It may be well to remember that John was nurtured not only on the Hebrew Scriptures but on their Aramaic versions as well. Hence the prologue of his Gospel, illumining the mystery of Jesus, has a savor also of the Targumim. For instance, as "all things were made through Him," so, according to the Targumim, the world was created, the earth shaped, and man made in God's image, by the Memra of the Lord (Targ. to Deut 33:27; Targ. Pseudo-Jon. to Is 45:12; Targ. Jer. to Gen 1:27). Again, as the Word-made-flesh "dwelt among us," so according to the Targumim, the divine Presence (*shekinah,* in Aramaic *shekinta*) was to dwell in the tabernacles of Shem and in the midst of the children of Israel (Targ. to Gen 9:27; Targ. to Ex 29:45). And as John saw "the glory as of the Only-begotten of the Father," so the Targum has Moses, Aaron, and the elders of the people see the glory (*kabod,* in Aramaic *yekara*) of the God of Israel (Targ. to Ex 24:10).

24. M.-E. Boismard, *Le Prologue de saint Jean* (Paris: Editions du Cerf, 1953), p. 136.

25. C. H. Dodd, *The Interpretation of the Fourth Gospel* (Cambridge: Cambridge University Press, 1953), pp. 294–296.

done. But since it is of God we speak, the word "great" must not be thought of in terms of size and visibility. In such a context true crescendo is of quality. However invisible its effect, the Word of God that raises creature to supernature is more powerfully active than the same Word when it first constituted creation in its natural being. In this is the Word "fulfilled," that it has established man in the noblest state he is capable of receiving. It has not disappointed Israel's highest hopes in the God whose spirit "renews the face of the earth" (Ps 103:30).

X

THIS, then, is the course the Word of Yahweh runs: from creation to creation, from making to remaking, from the fashioning of the world to the renewal of man, and even of the world in Christ. While marveling at this journey, I am reminded of an old Jewish blessing. Though far from seeing this journey as I have traced it, the prayer speaks most beautifully of the two termini. It is a greeting of the new moon, which the ancient rabbis considered a symbol of the messianic redemption and renewal of Israel. So highly is this blessing valued that, to one of them, the pronouncing of the words which conclude it: "Blessed art thou, O Lord, who renewest the months," was like welcoming the divine Indwelling, the Shekinah.

> *Blessed art thou,*
> *O Lord our God, King of the universe,*
> *whose word made the heavens*
> *and the breath of whose mouth all their host.*
> *Laws and appointed times He gave them*
> *that they should not falter in their parts.*
> *Joyful and glad they are to do the will of their Master,*
> *the true Worker, whose work is truth.*
> *The moon He bade to renew herself,*
> *a crown of beauty for those He upholds from the womb.*
> *In the time to come they will be renewed like her,*
> *and will glorify their Maker for the honor of His kingdom.*[26]

26. The prayer is a talmudic text, Sanh. 42a. See *The Babylonian Talmud,* ed. I. Epstein (London: Soncino Press, 1935–48), *Sanhedrin,* I, 271–272; or *The Authorised Daily Prayer Book,* ed. Hertz, p. 995. For further material on the blessing of the new moon, see *The Jewish Encyclopedia,* IX, 244.

Charles Journet

THE MYSTERIOUS DESTINIES OF ISRAEL

IT WAS at the well of Jacob that Jesus, foretelling a worship new, messianic, not restricted to one place—neither to Mount Gerizim nor even to Mount Zion—spoke the mysterious words: "Salvation is from the Jews." Salvation is from the Jews because the Saviour is a Jew. "I know that the Messiah is coming," said the Samaritan woman, "and when He comes, He will tell us all things." To which Jesus replied: "I who speak with you am He" (Jn 4:21–26).[1] We too know that salvation comes from a Jew. Acknowledged and worshipped by some Jews, rejected and given over to be crucified by others, more vocal then and more powerful, Jesus of Nazareth, in and by His shame, was made the cornerstone of the world redeemed.

Salvation comes from the Christ, and the Christ was born of a virgin of the house of David—a flower on the tree of Jesse, sprung from the patriarchs as root. How mysterious and how little noted: Jesus is the only Messiah, the one Redeemer of all; still, one people, in preference to so many stronger, richer, and more cultivated peo-

---

1. Recently David Daube again drew attention to the *"I am* of the messianic presence." There are several texts in St. John's Gospel, in addition to his account of Jesus' meeting with the Samaritan woman (for instance, 8:24, 28, 58; 13:19; 18:5, 6, 8; see also Mk 13:6 and Lk 21:8), in which the Greek *egō eimi,* "I am," means nothing less than "The Messiah is here." So strong, so awesome, were these words that when the Temple police and the servants of the high priest, who had come to arrest Jesus, heard Him say: "I am He," they were terrified and were thrown to the ground. It is significant, Daube points out, that a similar usage survives in the Passover Haggadah. As it recounts, over the Seder table, Israel's deliverance from Egypt, it enlarges on the words in Ex 12:12: "I will go through Egypt, striking down every firstborn of the land, both man and beast, and executing judgment on all the gods of Egypt—I, Yahweh," and has the Lord say: "I myself and not an angel, not a seraph, not the messenger. I, Yahweh, *ani hu,* I am He. . . ." Whether or not the reference here to "the messenger" implies a combative mood toward the gospel, the "I am He" of the Passover Haggadah emphatically bespeaks the personal presence and intervention of God the Redeemer, as it does on the lips of Jesus. For a further discussion, see Daube, *The New Testament and Rabbinic Judaism* (London: Athlone Press, 1956), pp. 325–329.

ples, was chosen to be bound, by a strange, indeed unique, lot, to the messianic hope and to the drama which is the redemption of the world. So intimate is the link that not only Israel's spiritual destinies —that goes without saying—but even its temporal destinies, with their share of the banal and commonplace, will be forever dependent on the most staggering supernatural mystery it is given us to know.

This solidarity cannot be broken or shaken off. But the way in which Israel is made aware of it, though always divine, varies from age to age with Israel's stand toward salvation. In the first epoch, Abraham's children were made a people, shaped and sustained by the mystery of messianic waiting. God held them like a son; His glory dwelt among them; He swore His covenants with them through the patriarchs and Moses, and made known His will to them in the Law. Theirs was a true worship, theirs the messianic promises, and theirs the high privilege of giving flesh to the Messiah, "who is over all things, God blessed forever" (Rom 9:4–5).

Then came the second epoch, which saw the separation between the "Israel of the spirit" and the "Israel of the flesh."[2] That which was purest and holiest in Israel the Spirit made into the living core of the Church. On the Israel of the flesh, however, there lies heavy the mystery of that redemption it failed to recognize. When Jerusalem refused to come under the wings of the Messiah, it was destroyed, city and Temple, for once Christ was gone its peace was gone (Mt 23:37–38). But even years before Jesus' tears were fulfilled—before the Temple was burned, the city laid in ruins, hundreds of thousands of its inhabitants slain; before the Romans could strike coins that showed a woman bent in mourning with hands chained, coins that bore the inscription *Judaea devicta, Judaea capta,* "Judaea the conquered and captive"—Paul's heart was torn. Toward those of his

---

2. The contrast here between the Israel of the flesh and the Israel of the spirit follows St. Paul's contrasting of the two Covenants (Gal 4:21–31; Rom 9:6–8). The first receives its children by fleshly descendance, the other by the spiritual birth of baptism (Jn 3:5). In no way is the term "Israel of the flesh" intended to label Israel as carnal (in the modern sense of the word) or as sinful; rather does it identify it as an ethnico-religious community which as such remains outside the orb of the Church. Still, the Spirit, breathing wherever He will, can awaken in it saints, true children of God, who, without knowing it, belong, in an initial way at least, to the Israel of the spirit, that is, the Church of Christ (I shall have occasion to speak of this again). And even before the coming of Christ, the Israel of the spirit existed in formation not only within the Israel of the flesh but also within the world of the Gentiles (see Rom 2:10, 14–16).

kinsmen who had not accepted Christ's offer of peace, Paul repeated God's cry in Isaiah that all the day He had stretched out His hands to a people drawing away from Him and walking after their own thoughts (Rom 10:21; Is 65:2). He repeated the cry, for he knew that, though the Israel of the flesh is opposed to the Good News, still it is "most dear for the sake of the fathers" (Rom 11:28).

It is this love, God's fidelity, that in the end will lift from Israel the heavy weight of its resistance. There will be a day, the third epoch, when it will understand and accept the mystery of the Cross and sing hosanna, *hoshi'ah nna,* "Save us we pray!"; when the whole people will once again, and forever, welcome Jesus with the blessing from the ancient liturgy of thanksgiving: Blessed in the name of Yahweh be He who comes.[3] There will be a day when the Israel of the flesh will again be one with the Israel of the spirit—the great ingathering of which the Apostle says that it will be like "life from the dead" (Rom 11:15).

THE ISRAEL OF WAITING

IF ONE searches the Scriptures for the meaning of Israel's existence, this much is immediately clear: Israel was meant to be the servant of the living God. To worship Him and not idols, which are but wind and vanity, things of naught; to give witness to Him in a world that is blind; to live not for its own pleasure but for His glory—these were its given task. If one searches further, one sees, with St. Augustine, that it was not only one or the other in Israel who was prophet of the Messiah but the people as a whole, and that its kingdom was prophetic of the Christian kingdom.[4] Israel was thus chosen to announce the coming of the Christ, to prefigure the world's ransom

3. These words are from Ps 117. There, to the cry of pilgrims entering the Temple: Hosanna, save us, Lord, we pray; prosper us, Lord, we pray! the priests respond with a benediction invoking the name of Yahweh on them as they come to sacrifice. We are accustomed to read this blessing: "Blessed be he who comes in the name of the Lord," but "in the name of Yahweh, in the name of the Lord," should be attached not to "comes," rather to "blessed." How fitting—though they did not know it—that it was in these words that the people of Jerusalem greeted Jesus as He entered the Holy City on the way to His Sacrifice (Mt 21:9)! And how fitting that these same words will, in the days to come, acclaim Him as Saviour and Victor (Mt 23:39)!

4. *Contra Faustum,* XIII, iv (PL 42:283).

by His blood, and to foreshow the messianic kingdom, the kingdom
of heaven now in the garment of a pilgrim but one day to be vested
in glory.

THE ELECTION

We say, for the Scriptures say, that Israel was chosen. What does this
chosenness really mean? While the Gentiles remained under that regime in which the movements of grace—true supernatural grace—
were in some way concealed beneath the best impulses of natural in-
stinct (a regime the theologians therefore call that of the law of nature), Israel was chosen to move, first with the patriarchs, then with
Moses and the prophets, into a privileged regime, that of the covenants and of the Mosaic law. In this privileged regime, Israel was invited to prepare, for itself and for all of mankind, the coming of a
definitive regime of salvation: salvation was to come from the Jews
when the Messiah would appear among them to announce the spiritual deliverance of the world. Israel's election means, then, that it was
chosen not so much to be supernaturally saved itself as to be, in some
measure, supernaturally saviour of the other peoples; not simply to
be itself redeemed but to be, before the Redeemer's merciful coming,
coredeemer of the rest of men.

It would be a fundamental misunderstanding of Israel's singularity were one to forget, even for a moment, that its end was not the
good of Israel only but of the whole human race. "In you shall all
the nations of the earth be blessed," God said to Abraham (Gen
12:3). Great though the privileges were that were granted to his
children, salvation was open to the Gentiles too, and not one of them
was condemned except by his own fault. Even sanctity was mysteriously offered to them. Did not the author of the book of Job make
his protagonist—the just man *par excellence*—a non-Israelite? Salvation was open to both, to Israel and to the nations, because of the
future Messiah; for neither the law of nature, which ruled the Gentiles, nor the much higher regime of the Mosaic law, had of itself the
power to save. Both regimes were provisional, dependent in some way
on the New Covenant, from which their whole significance came and
before which they were destined one day to efface themselves. Still,
by a mysterious anticipation of the fruits of Christ's passion, divine
grace visited with its gentle attentions every soul, whether under one

regime or the other, demanding less of the Gentile, who had received less, demanding more of the Jew, who had been so much more favored, but striving to save each and all of them in view of Him who was to come.[5]

A misunderstanding more basic yet of Israel's election would be to deny its uniqueness, its supernatural transcendence, trying to imprison it within the limits of the general providence by which God governs all creatures according to their structure, or to explain it by the simple play of natural and cultural forces. To Spinoza, for instance, God's guidance is just another word for the chain of natural events, and it is by this, he thinks, that the Jews surmounted so many great perils. All their election means to him is that they enjoyed temporal happiness and the advantages of independent rule, for there is, he says, no other way by which nations are distinguished from one another than by their social organization and the laws under which they live.[6]

Indeed, to pose the question of Israel's chosenness is to pose the very question which divides the modern world so radically and dangerously, the question of the supernatural. To it one must answer either, with the Bible, that the supernatural is a sublime reality or, with Spinoza, Kant, and Hegel, that it is an empty illusion. One must declare either that it is supremely reasonable to believe, if they are attested to, things not against but above reason, or that it is supremely reasonable to treat revelation from the outset as a myth. Finally, one must resolve to believe either in the folly of a God who became man to save men or in the adventure—it will be bloody and catastrophic —of man who undertakes to make himself God.

Supernatural is Israel's vocation: its place in history cannot be fully accounted for by nature, by geographical or sociological forces. Far be it from a theologian to belittle the importance of access to navigable waters, inches of rainfall, acreage of arable land, the size of the population, the map of its migrations, commercial and cultural links to other nations or the lack of them, or any similar factors, for all of nature is God's. But they simply do not add up to Israel's role, which is obviously without parallel.

5. This is the teaching of St. Paul in Rom 2:7–16.
6. *Theologico-Political Treatise.* chap. III, "Of the Vocation of the Hebrews, and whether the Gift of Prophecy was peculiar to them," *passim.*

THE SPIRIT OF RANSOM

Chosen so that the entire world might be healed, lovingly formed by God for His redemptive design, the center of Israel's being must needs have been impregnated with the spirit of ransom. It is this spirit that one day would lead the purest of its children, the Son of Man, to cast His life into that divine commerce in which it would be profitable "that one man die for the people," and more, "that He might gather into one the children of God who were scattered abroad" (Jn 11:50–52). Consequently there must have been present here and there in Israel's history this redemptive spirit, in embryo of course; present too a liking for those pacts with God, those mystical dealings and speculations, which are appeals from God to God Himself, from His punishments to His promises, from the demands of His justice to the demands of His mercy.

There is, for instance, what Léon Bloy calls that "wondrous bargaining, that merciful and lovable Jewishness of the beginning when even the name of the Jews was not yet." He is speaking of Abraham and his "marvelous negotiation for an amnesty for Sodom," [7] of the patriarch who begged that fifty, or forty-five, or forty, or thirty, or twenty, or even ten just be weighed against the townful of wicked; who dared plead with God that He not make His pity prisoner of His wrath, that He, the Judge of all the earth, should not, in His anger against sin, destroy the innocent with the evil, rather spare the evil city for the sake of the innocent (Gen 18:16–33). [8]

We find this same redemptive spirit at work in Moses. When God, having seen the rebellion of His people, having seen them dancing around the Calf as if it were their deliverer, was ready to wipe them out, Moses implored Him to let His blazing wrath die down, to relent and to remember Abraham, Isaac, and Israel, His servants, to remember above all His own great promises. Moses did not halt there: he offered his own life as ransom that the Lord might pardon the idolators. [9]

7. *Le Salut par les Juifs* (Paris: Mercure de France, 1933), pp. 163, 165.
8. *Ibid.,* pp. 166–181; for an English translation, see Bloy, *Pilgrim of the Absolute,* ed. by Raïssa Maritain, trans. by J. Coleman and H. L. Binsse (New York: Pantheon, 1947), pp. 255–261.
9. "If you would only forgive their sin! If you will not, then strike me out of the book you have written," was Moses' plea (Ex 32:31–32). Some take this to mean merely that Moses was so much one with his people that he did not care to

The most towering instance of Israel's God-given sense of ransom, by then manifestly vicarious expiation, is in the 53rd chapter of the book of Isaiah. There is foretold the Servant of Yahweh, who bears our sufferings and is laden with our miseries. That we may be made whole, He is wounded for our sins and crushed because of our guilt. Evidently, Isaiah's prophecy soars far higher than Moses' offer and Abraham's plea; yet of them all can be said what Bloy exclaimed of the patriarch's humble but so daring colloquy with God: "Such are the Jews, the authentic Jews." [10]

It is clear that this spirit of heavenly barter, which, before the coming of the Messiah, when the Church was still in seed, lived in Abraham and in all the true sons of his loins, must now be the magnificent and inalienable privilege of the Israel of promise, the Church now flowered forth. Being the Body of Christ the Redeemer, she cannot but be His coredemptrix; filling up in her flesh what is lacking of His sufferings (Col 1:24), she helps Him ransom the world.

MESSIANIC HOPE

What supremely marks the chosen people is the awakening in them of a living and powerful belief in a God who will not be represented by any image, nor allow any goddess or god beside or even beneath Him; in a word, belief in a transcendent and jealous God. No doubt, human reason can rise to the knowledge of the true God and of His everlasting power (Rom 1:20), but this knowledge cannot remain pure, constant, certain, and trustworthy without an influence from above. [11] Hence if one keeps in mind, first, the cultural and religious

---

live if they had to die. But is this really an adequate explanation? In the days of Ezekiel, when prophets were speaking falsely, priests despising the Law, princes ravening like wolves, and the people wronging the poor, oppressing the stranger, the Lord lamented that He had sought for a man to stand in the breach before Him on behalf of the land, and had found none (Ez 22:26–30). There was then, in the days of Ezekiel, no intercessor like Moses, and Jerusalem was not spared. Jewish tradition too attributes to Moses the spirit of ransom, though the way it pictures his offering of his life is somewhat defective. When Moses realized that the worship of the Calf would mean the death of Israel, since the Law demanded the death of idolators, he deliberately broke the Tables of the Commandments, a rabbinical legend tells. Then the legend makes him say to God: Now I too have sinned. If you will forgive them, forgive me also. And if you will not forgive them, do not forgive me either, but strike me out of the book you have written. (Ex. R. 46:1; cf. *Midrash Rabbah,* ed. H. Freedman and M. Simon, London: Soncino, 1939, III, 527.)

10. *Le Salut par les Juifs,* p. 182.
11. St. Thomas, *Summa Theol.* I, q. 1, a. 1.

background against which Israel's faith stood out so forcefully; then, the effort, so much against the grain, by which it had to assert and preserve itself, always struggling against Israel's own tendencies; and finally, the deeply religious and not just philosophical outlook it elicited—an outlook prayerful, confident, and humble, fleeing sin and begging pardon—one sees that this faith resists a purely natural explanation. Clearly here is a moral miracle.

The God of Israel, so attentive and so demanding, infinitely surpasses the God of philosophy. He is not a God merely thought about; He is the God who has spoken. He has revealed Himself, and His revelation is guaranteed not solely by the witness of the prophets, who are its instruments, but by its own purity and excellence, by the moral context in which it is enshrined, and by the spiritual goals toward which it never ceased to orient Israel.[12]

What one encounters, then, at the bottom of Israel's faith is the inspiration of Moses and of the prophets, who claimed, with unmistakable signs of authenticity, to speak in the name of Yahweh. Their claim and authentication, which do not leave the order of observable facts, are enough to show that here God's might entered into the fabric of history. But why did the one, transcendent God, who created heaven and earth and on whom all mankind depends, reveal Himself in a special way to Israel, rather than to so many peoples more numerous, more powerful, more cultivated? Why, if not because it was His design to use this little nation, nothing in itself, to make Himself known, on the appointed day, to all the great nations of the earth? If God surrounded Israel with such singular care, it could only be to pour out on it the first fruits of a justice and of a love which were

12. That we may appreciate the singularity of Israel's faith in the living God, Hilaire Duesberg, O.S.B., reminds us in his *Les Scribes inspirés* (Paris: Desclée de Brouwer, 1938–39) that Abraham, the father of the Hebrews, sprang from an idolatrous stock. "When one adds the almost irresistible attraction the surrounding world had for them, their continual vacillation between the baals and Yahweh— which Elijah picturesquely called 'limping on both feet' (3 Kg 18:21)—the infidelities of kings, the complicity of sinful priests and false prophets, one understands that their belief in the one and only God was not called for by any psychological tendency, any ancestral recollection, or any intellectual need. Yet this belief was held by them to the exclusion of nations older than they, who long before them had walked the ways of civilization. Far from being the unshared prerogative of a school of thinkers, it . . . aimed to win over people as much as priesthood. . . . No doubt, Israel's unalloyed monotheism was the portion of an elite, but an elite of virtue, not of thought. It is in this sense that it was universal or open to every soul" (I, 487).

bound to reach out from the one people to all men. Here is still another mark which distinguishes this revealed faith as much from simple philosophical monotheism as from the monotheism of Persia or China: seeking all men, it would be, by its very nature, in intention and in the issue—one would like to say on the due date—missionary. Looking toward an imminent expansion of God's kingship over all the world, Israel became the people of messianic hope.

THE EXPECTATION OF THE KINGDOM

There are thus two wonders concerning Israel: that it is unbelievably loved by God, and that it is loved for the sake of others. When Israel was a child in Egypt, the Lord loved him; He took His people into His arms and drew them with cords of kindness, with bonds of love. Even after they had sinned, Hosea declared around 750 B.C., He did not give rein to His anger, but spoke tenderly to them and showed them compassion (11:1-4, 9; 2:23). But prophetic knowledge did not stop with this. It knew Israel had been taken into the Lord's service that through it He might become known to all nations.

Because of these elementary certitudes, the prophets were able in a way to read the hidden meaning of the ebb and flow in Israel's history and thus to run ahead of the course of events. Intuitively anticipating the future, they announced the punishments that were to fall on Samaria and Jerusalem, the deportations, the return from exile, the rebuilding of the Temple. Yet these more immediate predictions never made them lose sight of Israel's supreme destiny, which was to prepare the roads for a vast and wondrous kingdom.

Unlike the empires of earth, the new kingdom would be spiritual and supranational. Hence, on the one hand, only a remnant, not Israel simply as it was, would enter it, and on the other, all the nations would be invited.

> *And all nations shall stream unto [the mount of Yahweh],*
>   *and many peoples shall go and say:*
> *"Come, let us go up to the mount of Yahweh,*
>   *to the house of the God of Jacob,*
> *That He may teach us of His ways,*
>   *and that we may walk in His paths."*

(Is 2:2-3)

Such was the vision of Micah (4:1–2) and Isaiah, about a generation after Hosea. Indeed, the hand of God would be extended even
to Israel's ancient foes. "One of the peaks of prophetic thought"[13]
speaks of Egypt and Assyria as united with Israel and sharing in its
privileges, and tells how Yahweh, the angel-surrounded, would bless
them: "Blessed be my people, Egypt, and Assyria, the work of my
hands, and Israel, my inheritance" (Is 19:25).[14]

Here the vision of the kingdom so widened as to embrace even the
enemy. Ministering to God's ever-unfolding design, the prophets
sought also to deepen the hope for the messianic kingdom. After the
fall of Jerusalem in 586 B.C., Jeremiah, then a refugee in Mizpah,
and especially Ezekiel, an exile in Babylon, started to stress, without
questioning in the least the fact of communal responsibility, the importance of personal responsibility. Stating that each soul shall bear
the burden of its sin and that each shall be judged according to its
ways, crying too that the sons of Israel must cast away their transgressions and make themselves a new heart and a new spirit, Ezekiel
insisted on a division that cut right through the community of Israel:
the just and the sinners.

Then there is Daniel, also taken captive to Babylon at the time of
the sack of Jerusalem by Nebuchadnezzar.[15] In the book of Daniel,
the division within Israel is drawn more strongly yet, prefiguring even
here below the lasting separation of the good and the wicked: those
who have forsaken the Covenant shall see everlasting horror, while
the saints of the Most High shall receive the kingdom and possess it
forever and ever (12:2; 7:18).

What Père Lagrange has said of the book of Daniel, that, as to the
fulfillment of prophecy, "history was not clearly distinguished from
eternity,"[16] can also be said of the other prophetic writings: earth and

13. J. Chaine, "La Révélation de Dieu en Israël," in *Israël et la foi chrétienne*
(Fribourg: Editions de la Librairie de l'Université, 1942), p. 49.

14. The authenticity of Is 19:16–25 has been challenged, and conjectures as to
its date vary. But surely, whatever the scholarly conclusions about the actual pen-
man, the thought is clearly Isaianic.

15. The book of Daniel, though not gathered together till the days of the
persecution by Antiochus Epiphanes (168–164 B.C.), no doubt contains a true
Danielic nucleus. Cf. M.-J. Lagrange, O.P., *Le Judaïsme avant Jésus-Christ* (Paris:
Gabalda, 1931), pp. 62, 72. For further remarks on the date of the book of
Daniel, see *A Catholic Commentary on Holy Scripture*, ed. by B. Orchard, O.S.B.,
et al. (London: Thomas Nelson and Sons, 1953), sect. 495a-k.

16. *Ibid.*, p. 69.

heaven are frequently seen together. No doubt, the prospects of national restoration and temporal well-being are not absent from most of the prophecies. They speak of a time when Israel will dwell again in its houses, when Jerusalem will be rebuilt around a marvelous temple, when the land will be fertile and the stars bright, when the pride of the nations will be broken and wars abolished, when the wild beasts will harm man no more, when the wolf and the lamb will go side by side. But here is the main point which, in the eyes of a Christian, illumines the prophecies: from the heights to which the prophets take us that they may show us the sublime works of Providence, we cannot help seeing three truths plainly. First, earthly happiness, of a people or even of mankind as a whole, can henceforth be but secondary. Further, earthly happiness cannot come to man except in a conditional, precarious, and incomplete way, for in this world the law of love has not reached final glory but is still crucified. Lastly, in the mind of God, and even in the mind of the prophets, such happiness is meant to evoke and signify, if not solely at least eminently, the spiritual peace God desires to lodge at the heart of creation that, on the last day, He may remake all things in a harmony as yet unimaginable.

All this becomes clearer yet in those prophecies which have shed any national or material ornament, as, for instance, when Yahweh —in the book of Malachi, which was written in 445 B.C., shortly after Nehemiah returned from exile to begin his work of reform— called for a sacrifice other than that of pitiful and worthless beasts: "For from the rising of the sun even to the going down, my name is great among the Gentiles; and in every place there is sacrifice and there is offered to my name a clean oblation. For my name is great among the Gentiles, says the Lord God of hosts" (Mal 1:11). If anything, then, is fundamental in the prophetic message, it is this vision, without peer in the ancient world, of an all-embracing faith which will gather the entire universe around the God of Israel.

Though it is the prophets who are the great spokesmen of this hope, its light shines in the Torah too. There is, in the third chapter of Genesis, that first ray of hope for fallen man, which means hope for all men. In the twelfth chapter, at the threshold of Israel's history, there is the promise of blessing through Abraham for all the families of earth. Again, near the end of Genesis, we read the farewell of the dying Jacob to his sons, and in it what will befall them and their children's children "in the days to come," that is, in the messianic days. This is the destiny of the sons of Judah:

> *The sceptre shall not depart from Judah,*
> *nor the staff from between his feet,*
> *Until he comes to whom it belongs.*
> *To him shall be the obedience of nations.*
>
> (49:10) [17]

It is the Messiah whose coming is here foretold.

PEOPLE OF THE MESSIAH

Servants of justice that they were, the prophets were of course concerned with the happenings, the right and wrong, around them. But some of their sayings—and these are the most mysterious—give us a glimpse of the King-Messiah, as of lightning rending the web of contemporary events. Of His birth, Isaiah foretold more than seven centuries in advance:

> *Behold the virgin shall conceive*
> *and bear a son*
> *and shall call his name Emmanuel.*
>
> (7:14) [18]

17. Martin Buber, in his translation of the Bible, renders the third part of this verse as *bis erscheint Dems-zukommt,* making "he-to-whom-belong [sceptre and staff]" a single noun, as if it were a proper name. See his *Die Schrift,* I, *Das Buch im Anfang* (Berlin: Lambert Schneider, n.d.), p. 196.

18. Undeniably, the Hebrew word *almah,* which is rendered here as "virgin," means, in its precise sense, "young woman" or "single woman of marriageable age," the technical term for "virgin" being *betulah.* But does it not seem likely that the Jewish sense of chastity often made one tantamount to the other, in very much the same way that the English "maiden" is an equivalent for "virgin," or that the German *Jungfrau* (i.e. "young woman") has come to mean—and this most rigorously—"virgin"? In any case, when, about 250 years before Christ, the Hebrew Bible was put into Greek for the sake of the Greek-speaking Jews of Egypt, its Jewish translators rendered *almah* by *parthenos,* i.e. "virgin." And Matthew, writing for his Jewish brethren, become Christian or not, quotes—without the least fear of being misunderstood—the Isaianic prophecy and claims its realization. None of this implies, of course, that the prophet knew the fullest import of what he foresaw; on the contrary, here as elsewhere, the prophecy does not make obvious what is to come, rather does the fulfillment explain the prophecy.

Rabbinical tradition interprets Isaiah's prophecy quite differently, and, to all seeming, the merest thought of a virgin birth is foreign to it. One wonders, however, whether the thought is really so foreign or whether it was suppressed. For David Daube asks whether the words in the Passover Haggadah, "and God knew" (following, as they do, on "He saw our affliction," which the rabbis interpret as the Israelites' abstention in Egypt from marital union) do not imply the

Im-anu-El, "God-with-us," will be His name, for He is the earnest of God's watching over His own. Lordship will be upon His shoulder and He will govern with authority. He will rule with wisdom and might, with kindness and solicitude; therefore Wonder-Counsellor, mighty God, Father forever, Prince of peace, are among His exalted titles (9:6). And the spirit of Yahweh shall rest upon Him (11:2–4).

At about the same time that Isaiah spoke, Micah foresaw that the Ruler of Israel, the Prince of the messianic kingdom, would spring not from royal Jerusalem but from Bethlehem, a town small and lowly. His going forth was from the days of old, the prophet said (5:2), looking back at the beginnings of David's house, and beyond. "From the days of old" suggests that His were God's mighty deeds in the days of the patriarchs and of Moses, and no less that His origin was in the bosom of eternity. "He shall stand and feed [His flock] in the strength of the Lord," and they shall dwell secure, for He shall be peace (5:4).

The most vivid picture of the Messiah is in those extraordinary passages of the book of Isaiah which sing of *Ebed Yahweh,* the Servant of the Lord.

> *Behold, my servant whom I will uphold,*
> *my chosen one in whom my soul delights.* . . .
>> (42:1)

> *It were too little that you should be my servant*
> *to raise up the tribes of Jacob,*
> *and to bring back the preserved of Israel.*

supernatural birth of Moses, that is, his conception without a human father (*op. cit.,* pp. 5–9). Jean Brierre-Narbonne quotes a significant text from the Midrash Tehillim of Rabbi Moses ha-Darshan. There Rabbi Yudan interprets the words, "Truth shall spring out of the earth, and justice shall look down from heaven" (Ps 84:12), in the following way: "It is our salvation that shall spring from the earth through the immediate work of God. And the two, truth and justice, shall be joined together. But why is it said that truth shall spring; why not that it shall be born? Because its manner of birth shall not be like that of the creatures of the world; rather shall it differ from theirs in every respect. This is the meaning of the verse that follows: 'Yea, the Lord will give what is good, and our land shall yield its fruit' (Ps 84:13). Truly, no one will be able to name his [the Messiah's] father, and much less will anyone know him. But this will be a mystery for the people until he himself comes to reveal it" (*Les Prophéties messianiques de l'Ancien Testament dans la littérature juive,* Paris: Librairie Orientaliste Paul Geuthner, 1933, p. 31).

I will make you the light of the nations,
that my salvation be to the end of the earth.

(49:6)

Behold, my servant shall succeed,
he shall arise and be exalted. . . .
He was despised and aloof from men,
a man of pains and familiar with suffering. . . .
But it was our sufferings that he bore. . . .
Upon him was the chastisement which made us whole,
and by his stripes we were healed.

(52:13; 53:2–5)

In the first verses, "servant" seems to refer to the people of Israel, yet even here there shines through the figure of Him who is the epitome of all that was given to it; Him toward whose coming these gifts had been prepared; Him who is at once Israel's summit and sun. But when the servant's atoning Passion and death are spoken of, the Messiah stands in full sight, He who "takes away the sins of many and makes intercession for the rebellious" (Is 53:12).

Zechariah (around 520 B.C.) also preached the Messiah's might in weakness: His death as a well of grace for His people.

And I will pour out upon the house of David
and upon the inhabitants of Jerusalem
the spirit of grace and of prayers;
and they shall look upon me, whom they have pierced.
And they shall mourn for him as one mourns for an only son;
and they shall grieve over him,
as the manner is to grieve for the death of the firstborn. . . .
In that day there shall be a fountain open
to the house of David and to the inhabitants of Jerusalem,
for the washing of the sinner.

(12:10; 13:1)

Finally, no longer His hidden might but His majesty is told in the book of Daniel. To the Son of Man will be given "power and glory and a kingdom; and all peoples, tribes and tongues shall serve him" (7:14).

Like the prophets, the psalms stirred the hope for the Messiah, some referring to Him in a direct or literal, others in an indirect or typical, way. In Psalm 109, David—whom Israel's tradition always claimed as its author—portrayed the Messiah as king, priest, warrior.

> *Yahweh said to my Lord: "Sit at my right hand*
> *till I make your enemies your footstool". . . .*
> *The Lord has sworn, and He will not repent:*
> *"You are a priest forever, according to the order*
>   *of Melchizedek."*
>
>   (109:1, 4) [19]

The psalmist goes on to tell that, on the day of wrath, the Messiah will crush kings in the might of Yahweh and will judge the nations, heaping up corpses. Here the messianic conquest is pictured with all the cruel fury of battle. Yet is this really anything more than hyperbole for the Messiah's triumph, which will indeed be achieved in blood—not others' but His own? In any case, Israel's vision of Him was purified till the death-dealing Warrior became the suffering and dying Servant.

Psalm 2 also tells that the Messiah will rule with an iron rod and warns kings and nations to serve with fear—the nations that rage and the kings who rise up against Yahweh and His Anointed. Here too the triumphant array but clothes a spiritual center. Seeing Nathan's prophecy about the house of David (2 Kg 7:4–16) as already fulfilled and David's everlasting kingdom as already established, the psalmist made the Messiah say:

> *The Lord said to me: "You are my son;*
> *this day I have begotten you."*
>
>   (2:7)

In all likelihood, the Messiah's sonship meant to the psalmist no more —though this is not little—than His unique dignity as Yahweh's representative, ruling by His authority and standing under His singular watch, for a prophet need not be aware of the fullest content of the revelation he brings.

Great was to be the dignity of the Messiah and great the fruits of His coming. This is how Psalm 71 sees them:

19. Father Bruce Vawter, C.M., has suggested that the Hebrew of this verse would be better rendered by: "You are a priest forever, like Melchizedek" (see his review of Volume III of the Confraternity version of the Bible in *Theological Studies*, XVII, 2, June 1956, p. 240). [Editor.]

Justice shall flower in his days,
    and profound peace, till the moon be no more. . . .
He shall have pity for the lowly and the poor;
    the lives of the poor he shall save.

(71:7, 13)

There is still another psalm which sings the Messiah, but this time not only His glory, His degradation too. It opens: "My God, my God, why have you forsaken me," but rises from lament to praise:

I am a worm, not a man;
    the scorn of men, despised by the people.
All who see me scoff at me.

I will proclaim your name to my brethren;
    in the midst of the assembly I will praise you:
"You who fear the Lord, praise Him;
    all you descendants of Jacob, give glory to Him;
    revere Him, all you descendants of Israel!"

All the ends of the earth
    shall remember and turn to the Lord;
All the families of the nations
    shall bow down before Him.

(21:7–8, 23–24, 28)

Even if one were to assume, with some commentators, that this psalm does not speak literally of the Messiah, that it represents only the suffering of the just man who, apparently abandoned by God, does not totter in his hope, surely his trial is the draft and type of the greater Passion to come.[20]

20. One must insist, writes Père Lagrange, "on the beauty of the soul which reveals itself in this prayer. The psalmist neither speaks of his sins nor invokes, as do so many others, his innocence, which nonetheless shines through. No anger against his tormentors, no curse, no bitterness, no philosophical preoccupation with the problem of pain: only recourse to God and abandonment. Though no other psalm expresses these thoughts with the same beauty, a great many of them never tire of telling the sufferings of the just. At the root of them all is the idea that the true servant of God has no refuge but in Him. Persecuted, vilified, ill used, tortured, he hopes and longs for his own salvation and the salvation of Zion. What, then, must the Servant *par excellence* be like? It is at least in this sense that all these psalms are turned toward the future. And as Israel was more and more wont to attribute these psalms to David, the sufferings of the great king brought close the thought of the sufferings of the Messiah, David's exalted image" ("Notes sur le messianisme dans les psaumes," *Revue Biblique*, XXII, 1, 1905, pp. 52–53).

JESUS THE FULFILLMENT

The few glimpses of the Messiah and His kingdom that I have given from the Old Testament are enough to show a little of the heights toward which Yahweh, patiently and step by step, led His people. The lights He gave His prophets seem to have risen for them one after the other from the dark depth of the future. Hence one must not think of them as having set out intentionally to hide, under the ambiguity of metaphor, a light they themselves deemed too strong for their contemporaries. On the contrary, the prophets strove to free the divine thought from the obscurities, the veils, the images, in which, for them as well as for the people, it remained enveloped. Fully infallible as the prophetic revelation was, still it was one of fragments and parts,[21] trying to stammer a word which was not yet given it to pronounce. The salvation to come was marvelously to transcend the Law and the Prophets, great as they were; hence they could know it only in its preparatory and virtual state, and therefore only imperfectly. "Because the mind of the prophet is a deficient instrument," writes St. Thomas, "even the true prophets do not know all that is intended by the Holy Spirit in their visions, their words, and even their prophetic deeds."[22]

Saying that the contents of the prophecies surpassed the prophets' knowledge of them is the same as saying that the realization of the prophecies was itself a revelation, indeed the greatest of all. Jesus alone could explain the past and give Israel's history its full significance; He alone could put at one what had seemed disparate. He did so when He brought together in His own person the scattered traits of the promised Messiah, and when He announced that the messianic kingdom of glory and power and majesty would begin as a kingdom crucified.

There are various ways in which the Old Testament designates the bearer of the salvation to come. At times it tells that God Himself will come to save His people. On the other hand, it expects a king, son of David, who will mount the throne of his fathers and bring to his own a bliss unheard of. Then there is the Suffering Servant, who

21. Cf. Heb 1:1, which tells of God's speaking "at sundry times and in divers manners." The meaning of the Greek is more clearly that He spoke fragmentarily, in many portions, and by many varied means of communication.
22. *Summa Theol.* II–II, q. 173, a. 4.

will turn the nations to the faith of Israel and whose wounds will be
the healing of our own. Again, a supernatural being will come from
heaven to establish the reign of the saints. Four lines pointing toward
a future light. Will they run forever parallel, or do they meet? No
one could answer till He came who was and is the Answer.

Jesus is God's personal coming in a unique manifestation of goodness,
as He is the fulfillment of the promises to David. He is Daniel's supernatural being, but truly the Son of Man. He must reign as the descendant
of David and as the Son of Man, but only after having preached, suffered,
and died as the Servant of Yahweh. He is come that God's kingship be
recognized on earth, that God be better served and better loved; but it is
through Him that the reign of God over the elect is established above,
for it is by His death and by His grace that the elect are admitted to God's
presence. Thus all the Old Testament prophecies are reality and harmony, and He who is the end of the promises also opens the life to
come. [23]

Without this reconciliation in Jesus of these scattered messianic
traits, the Old Testament would have remained sealed to us, as it still
is—the Christian believes—to the Jews. With Jesus, however, the
Old Testament opens its shell and gives up its meat, so that, with
Tertullian, we may call Him *Illuminator antiquitatum,* the One who
illumines the things of old.[24] He drew forth their light, because He
was their Light.

THE TEMPTATION OF JUDAISM

This is the mystery of Jesus: Servant and King, Man of pain and
Lord of glory, He not only fulfilled the prophecies of old but so il-
lumined them that they yielded their last secrets. Yet not all in
Israel have accepted this mystery; not all have been able to believe
that God so loved the world that He gave His only-begotten Son.
What other key, then, do they offer to the prophecies?

In the description Joseph Klausner, for instance, gives of the Jewish messianic idea, the Messiah pales before the people of Israel.
However beautiful his role, it seems to be secondary, even accidental,
so much so that, according to Klausner, it is quite possible for a Jew

23. M.-J. Lagrange, O.P., *Le Messianisme chez les Juifs* (Paris: Gabalda,
1909), p. 265.
24. *Adversus Marcionem,* IV, xl (PL 2:461).

to conceive redemption without a personal Messiah and still be loyal to his people and his religion. Without the Messiah, Judaism is defective, no doubt, but it survives, for, so Klausner implies, it is really Israel as a people which occupies the forestage of history. "The Jews," he writes, "can and must march at the head of humanity on the road of personal and social progress, on the road to ethical perfection," and so, by repentance and good works, hasten redemption. When the Messiah comes, he will be a just man, indeed the ideal man, filled with the gifts of the Spirit, strong in body, vested in might and valor. For all his greatness, however, Klausner insists, the Messiah will be but flesh and blood, no more than a mortal man. What he will bring is economic and spiritual redemption, eternal peace, material prosperity, and ethical perfection. A triumphant king, he will thus establish the "kingdom of the Almighty," but this kingdom, Klausner stresses time and again, is definitely "of this world," is earthly bliss. Embodying the Jewish longing to shake off the yoke of the Dispersion, he will gather his own people from the four corners of the earth and bring them back to the land of their fathers. And he will govern not only Israel but, in a certain sense, all the nations, who will have been converted to the Jewish belief in the one God, for the restoration of Israel will draw after it the restoration of the whole world. The days of the Messiah, then, will see the end of idolatry and of all the evils it brings about. There will no longer be poverty or pain or war; peace will reign among men and nations. Even nature will be redeemed. Yet, in the picture Klausner paints, the Messiah's first work will be to deliver Israel from political oppression, and only after the ingathering of the exiles, only after national freedom is restored to the Jewish people, will all the nations be leagued in a single band to fulfill God's purpose.[25]

Because of its emphasis on earthly bliss, political freedom, and economic abundance, Judaism's messianic concept has been called materialistic, but this is hardly just, for it also stresses perfection, righteousness, and brotherhood. Yet a Christian cannot help seeing in the dream of a mere kingdom-of-this-world an impoverishment of the prophetic message. It does not do justice to the great texts of Isaiah

25. Joseph Klausner, *The Messianic Idea in Israel,* trans. by W. F. Stinespring (New York: Macmillan, 1955), pp. 520–525, 529–531, *passim.* I quote this author, professor emeritus at Hebrew University in Jerusalem, without wishing to give him the title of an irrecusable witness.

or of the other prophets. What is even more serious, it forces us to assume that God's most immediate concern regarding His kingdom on earth is the political deliverance of the Jewish people and their resettling in the Holy Land; that divine intervention in history has for its final object the temporal and cultural progress of mankind through the intermediacy of an Israel confident in its monotheism and in its good works; [26] and that the supreme end toward which all of God's providential roads converge is a happy millennium on a fertile earth with a political Messiah as leader.

How can an ideal so largely immersed in the things of this world be reconciled with the wondrous outpourings of sanctity and purity passionately predicted by the prophets, who thus anticipated the whole evangelical spirituality of the kingdom that is not of this world? [27] How can such an ideal accord with the astounding adjurations, the "mad" condescensions, the staggering appeals of love, which Yahweh, from the depth of the heavens, addressed through Hosea to his unfaithful and yet ever desired spouse? [28] How can it be in keeping with those mysterious, unfathomed depths of God which Abraham adored when, on Mount Moriah, he could only hope against hope; which Job professed when he was ordered to gird his loins and answer the Almighty; and which were the anguish and the hope of the abandoned Jeremiah? [29] To substitute a kingdom of this world for the kingdom which, though in, is not of, this world is to misunderstand the most hidden, the most divine, the most quickening inspiration of the Old Testament.

It is quite true, however, that the breadth and length of this inspiration could not be grasped till the gospel. For the prophetic message was a living reality, growing with time like a stem growing toward its bloom; and while it grew, no one was able fully to divine what it would be like. Because of this openness toward future revelation, there is a certain indeterminateness about the Old Testament. Hence there was the temptation to read its promises too literally, which

26. Am I wrong in detecting such confidence throughout Klausner's book? At its close, for instance, measured though he means his words to be, he writes: "We can say, without being suspected of undue bias toward Judaism, that the Jewish Messianic faith is the seed of progress, which has been planted by Judaism throughout the whole world" (*ibid.*, p. 531).

27. Is 32:15–17; 44:3–5; 45:8; Ez 11:19–20; 36:26–27; Jl 2:28–29.
28. Os 1:10–11; 2:14–24; 3:1–5; 11:8–9.
29. Gen 22:1–14; Job 38:3; 40:2; 42:1–6; Jer 20:7–13.

meant to break the élan which was carrying them toward their ful-fillment and to cloud their most authentic significance—a temptation into which, alas, Judaism fell. On the other hand, we can show to-day that true fidelity to the ancient promises is that which, by an ad-vance—a going-beyond, no doubt, but without the least violence—leads toward the acceptance of the New Testament.

It was only a remnant in Israel that took this decisive step, while the greater part found the New Testament a stumbling block. Even before the coming of Jesus, there was growing among Jews a move-ment of defense against the contempt and oppression of the Gentiles, a falling back on themselves, which, little by little, stiffened them and made them forget that divine revelation was meant for all and that its wealth was yet uncounted. Even before the coming of Jesus, there was a tendency here and there in Israel to lose sight of the gratuitous-ness of its election, to overlook that it was due not to its own merits but to God's grace, and to weaken the supernatural character of reve-lation. There was a firm resolve to form a nation most faithful to its religion, but to a religion shaped for one people alone; an ever grow-ing zeal for the Law and its punctilious observance which sought to multiply occasions for its diligent service. Further, as a reaction to the Gentile mockery and the foreign rule Jews had to suffer, the convic-tion took deeper and deeper root that the Messiah would be their man, their captain, who would subdue the nations, making the na-tions bow before him and also before them.[30]

To sum up, then: the great hour of grace, the coming in the flesh of God the Redeemer, was prepared by the yearning of the patriarchs, of the prophets, of the many saints of Israel, of all those in whom its true spirit lived. But I sorrow to say that the failure too, the failure to recognize Jesus as the One He is, was prepared from afar, by the misunderstandings and resistances of those who were hard of heart.

THE ISRAEL OF THE SPIRIT

THE Messiah has come; the last, the messianic and eschatological, times have begun. Since Jesus' first coming, the messianic kingdom has been established in the world; but, bearing the likeness of its King, it is a kingdom that, while on pilgrimage through history, must

30. Lagrange, *Le Judaïsme avant Jésus-Christ,* p. 591.

remain crucified. Only at His second coming will His touch of glory unlock the whole fund of love patiently laid up in the course of the centuries; suddenly and awesomely it will burst open in order to pour forth on the universe. But this eternal gladness is not without birth pangs in time.

THE FOUNDING OF THE KINGDOM

With divine sureness, the New Testament claims to be the realization of two thousand years of patriarchal and prophetic waiting. The three canticles of thanksgiving, for instance, which in St. Luke's Gospel surround the birth of the Saviour, the *Magnificat,* the *Benedictus,* the *Nunc dimittis,* tremble with the stupendous certitude that the unbroken line of generations beginning with Abraham and passing through David, always watched over by a heavenly design, have come at last to Him in whom all the seed of the patriarch is summed up (see Gal 3:16).[31]

From the very start of His ministry, Jesus Himself took pains to show Himself the Fulfiller of the things of old. In the synagogue of Nazareth, He read from Isaiah these words:

> *The Spirit of the Lord Yahweh is upon me,*
> *because Yahweh has anointed me;*
> *He has sent me to bear good tidings to the afflicted,*
> *to encourage the broken-hearted. . . .*
>
> (61:1)

Closing the scroll, He declared: "Today this scripture has been fulfilled in your hearing" (Lk 4:21). Later, for example, He identified Himself as David's Lord, the Lord of Psalm 109 (Mt 22:41–46); and again, without the least hesitation, said that Abraham had seen His day and rejoiced (Jn 8:56).

Peter too, interpreting to the multitude of Jerusalem the pentecostal marvel they had seen, proclaimed that in it had come true Joel's prophecy that in the last days the Spirit of Yahweh would be poured forth on all flesh (Ac 2:16–21; Jl 2:28–32). In another dis-

---

31. If one has the good fortune to attend matins at the monastery of La Grande Chartreuse on, for example, the feast of St. Anne, one can hear the monks chant, from an old illuminated evangelary, the genealogy of the Saviour. As their singing rises out of their silence, one not only knows, one feels, how much the Church continues to be fed through her everlasting roots in the Old Testament.

course to his brethren, the "men of Israel," this time in Solomon's Porch of the Temple, Peter announced that with the coming of Jesus, the Just and Holy One, mankind had entered the days predicted by the prophets, days that would be crowned, at His coming again, by a restoration of all things, a renewal of creation (Ac 3:12–26). So He is seen throughout the New Testament: so the disciples understood Him on the way to Emmaus (Lk 24:27), so Stephen portrayed Him to the Sanhedrin (Ac 7), so Philip the deacon explained Him to the courtier of the Ethiopian queen (Ac 8:30–35)—always is He the end and goal of Israel's hope. *O Christum in novis veterem!* Tertullian exclaimed, "O Christ, old are you in your newness!" [32]

To Paul no less was He the focus toward which the Scriptures converged and at the same time the fountainhead from which sprang all the new splendors of the messianic age, for with His birth there began "the fullness of time" (Gal 4:4).[33]

THE FIRST HEARTBEATS OF THE CHURCH

In taking flesh of a virgin of Israel that He might gather the world into His kingdom, the Messiah effected a double mystery, in the one instant crowning the Ancient Dispensation and unthroning it. When He was born, the chain of fleshly descendance that had begun with Abraham was perfected; the prophetic stem of Jesse was all at once brought to bloom. But the same virginal birth broke that chain: what mattered henceforth was sonship of Abraham, not according to flesh and blood but according to the wonder of a hidden, spiritual birth, a birth that could therefore be offered to all nations.[34] Thus St. Paul proclaimed that in Christ Jesus there is neither Jew nor Greek: all are one (Gal 3:28).

True as it is that the message of the Annunciation broke that long and providential chain of generations, that sacred series of links which had led from father to son, it is no less true that the Saviour is of the offspring of Abraham. His mother was of the line of the patriarchs and of David the king. His apostles and first disciples were Jews. He

32. *Adversus Marcionem,* IV, xxi (PL 2:410).
33. For Christ the focus see Ac 13:16–41 and 17:2–3; for Christ the fountainhead see Gal 3:8, 14; Col 1:26, and others.
34. The two births, one of the flesh, the other of the spirit, are, according to the Apostle, announced and prefigured by the two sons of Abraham: Ishmael, child of the loins, and Isaac, child of the promise (Gal 4:21–31; Gen 16 and 17).

Himself declared that He was sent "to the lost sheep of the house of Israel" (Mt 15:24). Consequently, it was from the Israel of the flesh that the Israel of the spirit was first chosen, from the children of Abraham's loins that the first children of the promise were gathered. The light of the prophets had readied them for the redemption; of each of them the poet could have said: "Whose watch is for the Rising Sun, for him nothing is unexpected. For it is precisely toward the unexpected that all his waiting is bent." [35]

Never again, I think, will the Church on earth be so fervent, so loving, so pure, as when she was Jewish; never again in the course of the ages will she find sanctity like that of Mary or even like that of the apostles. One of the reasons for this, her initial excellence, was the task entrusted to her as she came forth from the hands of the Messiah. The great things she did under His immediate influence were perfect, so that they could serve as models to the faithful of every century till the end of the world. Peter's professions of faith at Capharnaum and Caesarea Philippi, the inspired insights of the disciple whom Jesus loved, Mary Magdalene's cry on Easter morn, the martyrdom of Stephen, the conversion of Saul: they all would lend their meaning, ardor, and impetus to the course of future Christians. Thus the first throbbings of the heart of the Church determined the whole rhythm of the Christian life to come. Commenting on the verse, "[Zion's] stones are dear to your servants, and her dust moves them to pity" (Ps 101:15), St. Augustine said of the little Church of Jerusalem:

> From this very dust there came a wall of thousands on thousands who believed, who laid the price of their goods at the apostles' feet. From this dust, then, there sprang forth a human nature perfect and beautiful. Who among the Gentiles can be likened to them? At how few can we marvel for doing as they did, and did in thousands? [36]

But what does it mean that, at the time when her core was being so marvelously formed, the Church was made up entirely of members sprung from the Israel of the flesh? Does it mean that they were exceptional Christians by very reason of their Jewish birth; that in the Church—by its nature above ethnic divisions—racial privileges could

35. Paul Claudel, *L'Histoire de Tobie et de Sara* (Paris: Gallimard, 1942), Act III, scene ii.
36. *Enarratio in Psalm. 101,* 15 (PL 37:1303-4).

be claimed for Jews; that Paul's bitter enemies were right to think that a Christian of Jewish blood was twice a Christian? Certainly not, for, as the Apostle says, "there is a remnant left, selected out of grace" (Rom 11:5). Henceforth it is grace that counts. Jewish Christians who boasted of their ancestry spoke "foolishly" (2 Cor 11:21). Indeed, if they thought of themselves as some kind of superior Christians, they were in peril of falling away from grace itself, so that what, under the Old Dispensation, had been a legitimate title of glory could, under the New, become for them a cause of judgment.

If the miracle of the infant Church does not in the least justify racial pride, what does it tell us? Simply this: we, Christians of Gentile stock, latecomers to the Church, owe to the Jewish people, from whom God chose the Christ, His blessed mother, and His first and fervent followers, an admiration tinged with envy; we owe them admiration, which is radically incompatible with contempt, aversion, hatred, in short, with anti-Semitism. Then, to this admiration we must join an everlasting gratitude toward those first Jews who by grace entered the new faith and were given the mission of carrying with them to the Church the sacred patrimony of the Jewish people, notably its most cherished treasure, the Law and the Prophets.

Having been the bearer of this treasure, Israel's remnant is also pledge and token of the future reintegration of the whole people. Thus it is, within the bosom of the Church, the object of a wondrous choice, which has no equal nor will have. But its privilege is one in whose blessings we all share. With what marvel and thanksgiving they fill us as they come to us on the waves of time! Here then is the royal road, the bridge, by which the Old Covenant passes into the New; here, in Israel's remnant, is the visible continuity between the walled Jerusalem and the Jerusalem whose walls are the ends of the earth—the city henceforth peopled by Jews and Gentiles, by faithful who continually come to her from Jacob's stock and by faithful who come to her from far-off nations, that the two may be one in the Christ, their Peace (Eph 2:14–18).

THE ISRAEL OF EXILE

AT THE moment when the smaller but healthier part of Israel, its remnant, became the Church, identifying its religious destinies with those of the kingdom of God (now, by right and essence, freed of all ethnic and cultural enclosures), the greater part remained aloof. In order to keep their dreams of immediate deliverance, political sovereignty, and earthly happiness, most of the people, under the direction of their official leaders, chose—no, to be correct one should say, acquiesced when those leaders chose—against their true Messiah, against a Messiah too pure and spiritual, too poor and humiliated, too full of pain, too crucified.[37]

To say Yes to God is always, for each one of us, to consent to a Love greater than we can imagine, and to say No is to offend a Love infinite and truly incomprehensible. So it had to be with the people of Israel. Since it had been prepared by the patient and pressing revelation of the prophets to receive its Saviour, its Yes or No had necessarily to express a unique mystery and had to bring about incalculable historic consequences. While the Yes of the remnant gave birth to the Church, the No of the leaders and of all those who followed them gave birth to the Israel of exile. But in that failure they were, as Israel always is, a mirror of the sins of all men.

ISRAEL'S FAILURE

People of God famished for the kingdom, and who would not have it—Israel is in the world and is not of the world; but it is attached to the world, subject to the world, in bondage to the world. One day Israel stumbled and was caught in a trap; it stumbled against God—and in what an encounter, never to be repeated! Israel did not know what it was doing; but its leaders knew that they were making their choice against God. In one of those acts of free will which involve the destiny of a whole community, the priests of Israel, the bad watchers in the vineyard, the slayers of prophets, with excellent reasons of political prudence, chose the world, and to that choice their whole people are henceforth bound—until

37. Vladimir Soloviov well understood that it was the Cross that was the stumbling block for the Jews. But the drama of Golgotha was not, as he was inclined to think, the result of a conflict between two politico-religious messianic concepts, one universal, the other narrowly national; rather was it the result of a clash between Jesus' messianic message of a supra-political kingdom and the multitude's messianic dream of a political kingdom. In his short study on Judaism and Christianity, Soloviov wrote: "The Cross of Christ, which is the gate to the kingdom of God, demanded of the Jewish people a double abandonment of self: first the renunciation of its national egoism, then the renunciation of its striving for earthly happiness" (*Judentum und Christentum*, Dresden, 1911, p. 45). It might be more exact to say: the striving after an uncrucified earthly happiness.

it changes of its own accord. A crime of clerical misfeasance, unequalled prototype of all similar crimes.[38]

How is it possible to say that here was a crime which involved, or, more exactly, burdened, the whole body of Israel? Was the fault not, above all, that of Israel's heads—in the words of Matthew, "the chief priests and the elders of the people" (27:1), or of Mark, "the chief priests with the elders, the scribes and the whole Sanhedrin" (15:1)? And is it not true that many in the crowd gathered before the governor's palace, who had a terrifying part in the crime, did not know exactly what they were doing? [39] Surely when they shouted: "His blood be on us and on our children" (Mt 27:25), they were convinced that they had nothing to fear, that they were only demanding the death of one who, by calling himself the Son of God, had blasphemed, or of one who had not done the people's will, a will they thought was God's.

Still, the spiritual consequences of this dreadful error were bound to continue through the centuries. It was an error that would hurl Israel into religious roads bent from the very start, obscuring for it the pure and authentic significance of the promises of which it had been the bearer. The ways it was thenceforth to walk would gravely hinder the recognition of the Messiah, whose grace, we know, knocks at the heart of every one of Abraham's children. It knocks at their

38. Jacques Maritain, "The Mystery of Israel" in *Ransoming the Time,* trans. by H. L. Binsse (New York: Charles Scribner's Sons, 1941), pp. 152–153. References to Maritain's essay are always to the Scribner edition, though at times the translation used may differ from it slightly. If I quote Maritain so often and so extensively, it is because we owe him so much. Hence I should like to thank him here, in my own name and in the name of all Catholics; for, in the penetration of Israel's mystery, as in many other domains, he has shown us the way.

39. "Brethren, I know that you acted in ignorance, as did also your rulers" (Ac 3:17), said St. Peter in his second discourse after Pentecost, and St. Paul wrote of himself that he too had acted in ignorance (1 Tim 1:13). To this apostolic testimony may be added the penetrating words of St. Augustine: "My brethren . . . we beg you to be on your guard: you who are in the Church, do not insult those who are not; rather pray that they may be in it. 'For God is able to graft them back' (Rom 11:23). It is of the Jews that the Apostle said this, and so it happened to them. The Lord rose and many believed. They did not know Him when they crucified Him. But later they believed in Him, and that great offense was forgiven them. The blood of the Lord, which they had shed, was forgiven to the *homicides.* I do not say *deicides,* 'for had they known it, they would not have crucified the Lord of glory' (1 Cor 2:8). The slaying of an innocent was forgiven them, and the blood they had shed while out of their minds they later drank by grace. Say then to God: 'How tremendous are your deeds!' (Ps 65:3)" (*Enarratio in Psalm. 65,* 5; PL 36: 790–791).

hearts, for even outside the Church's frontiers, grace never ceases to
visit, to run before, and to enlighten all men, trying to turn them to
their ultimate end and toward their true Saviour; consequently, without their always being aware of it, also toward the Church which is
His Mystical Body.

To understand how the stumbling of Good Friday could burden
the whole community of Israel, one must keep in mind two truths,
apparently contradictory. The one, emphatically declared by Ezekiel,
that there is no injustice in the Lord, who judges everyone according
to his works; that only the soul that sins shall die. "The son shall not
bear the iniquity of the father, and the father shall not bear the iniquity of the son" (18:20). The other, proclaimed in Deuteronomy:
that there is the mysterious reality of burdens borne by a whole community. "I, Yahweh, your God, am a jealous God, inflicting punishments for their fathers' wickedness on the children of those who hate
me, down to the third and fourth generation, but bestowing mercy,
down to the thousandth generation, on the children of those who love
me and keep my commandments" (5:9–10). These two revelations,
one about the personal, the other about the social, character of divine
sanctions, are not irreconcilable. The decision of Israel's leaders did
indeed bequeath to future generations enormous obstacles to the recognition of the Messiah. But for the greatest number of souls, these
obstacles may well amount to invincible ignorance.

That the Messiah was denied by the leaders of His own people and
delivered to the Gentiles to be crucified produced, thus, grievous results for all of Israel. But never must we forget—God forbid it!—
that when He was so denied and delivered, the sin was far from resting in equal measure on all Jews. For a great number, the personal
fault was nil, nonexistent. Indeed, it would be the height of injustice
to say that all the Jews of Jesus' day were guilty of His death. As for
the guilty, they were by no means all alike. There were the men of political prudence, who feared that if Jesus were permitted to continue
His work, all would believe in Him, and the Romans would come and
destroy Temple and nation (Jn 11:47–52). There was the Idumean
Herod Antipas, outwardly Jew, inwardly skeptic, who mocked Jesus
(Lk 23:11). There was the fawning Judas, who was used but despised
and for whom it would have been better had he not been born
(Mt 27:4; 26:24).

There were also those who, in a kind of madness, preferred Barabbas to Jesus (Mt 27:20–21; Mk 15:11). But when the pentecostal days came and thousands were baptized (Ac 2:1–41), how many among them must there have been who had cried: "Crucify Him!" and were thus saved by a Lord whom they had sent to His Golgotha. Of how many billions of us were they not the forerunners.

JEWISH UNBELIEF

What kind of fault was it that threw Israel into catastrophe? Was it not a fault against love? One has but to remember the parable of the vinedressers into whose charge a vineyard had been given. When its owner sent servants to receive its fruit, they were mistreated, beaten, or even killed. Undismayed, he sent his beloved son, hoping that he at least would be welcomed, only to see the vinedressers slay him and cast him out of the vineyard (Lk 20:9–16).

We cannot understand the passion of this parable unless we realize that Yahweh—even though men will never know why—is smitten with love for the people He has chosen. He has called it His child, His son, His spouse. He sent prophets that they might show Israel the marvelous dignity of its vocation and ever lead it in the way of its true happiness. However, many refused to hear them; others, irked when the truth was hard to take, called them false prophets and covered them with derision; again others, when the prophetic voices became too strong, tried to silence them with stones. "But the owner of the vineyard said: 'What shall I do? I will send my beloved son; perhaps when they see him, they will respect him.' "

To reason thus, one must love to the point of folly. Indeed, here divine Love seems able to contain its tenderness no longer. The hour had come when what for ages had been hidden would be made manifest: that God so loved all men as to give His only Son that His life might ransom theirs. Many in Israel were now blessed to see what prophets and saints of the days of waiting had longed to see and had not seen, to hear what they had longed to hear and had not heard (Mt 13:17). To these advances of the eternal Lover there was demanded in return a love from which would spring a new gratitude, a tenderness as yet unknown on earth. Instead the "vinedressers" pushed aside the invitation that was so solemn and urgent that, time and again, vast crowds were agitated by it; in order to stifle it, they resolved on the murder of Him who claimed to be the Messiah, the Son of God. What was this resolve if not a supreme offense against the everlasting Love? And if they could have suspected that He who claimed to be the Messiah was truly God, would it not then have been a deicide? But deicide never faces itself: one has to turn one's eyes away, one has to put a veil over God to dare to strike Him.[40] Thus the "vinedressers" could not have delivered Jesus to His death on the cross unless they were blind to His divinity.

So it happened that disbelief in Jesus became the public setting which made possible the woeful moves against Him and the sad catastrophe of Israel's love. In the name of the ancient promises many in Israel rose against their realization and for the love of the stem rejected the flower. Misled by those who should have led God's chosen people to the Messiah, they turned aside, at the supreme moment in their and the world's history, from the full messianic truth. Though in a way Israel continues to know and to profess the messianic truth in so far as it is contained within the shadows of the Old Law, still, in clinging to them, it preferred the promises to the things promised, the preparation to the fulfillment, the figure to the reality. This is its error. Judaism is not a denial pure and simple of the truth of Christ, wrote the Carmelite theologians of Salamanca; it believes in the truth as promised but rejects it as present and manifest.[41]

When the Fathers and scholastic theologians called Israel's failure *perfidia,* disbelief or unbelief, they were seeking to grasp it not under the aspect which led to Golgotha, that is, the aspect which was most passionate and wicked but at the same time most passing and applicable only to a small number. Rather did they grasp it under the aspect which is most nearly universal and most easily definable, that is, the one which applies to the majority of Jews in apostolic days, which has been communicated from generation to generation, and which has thus lasted the longest.[42]

40. As if to show this: When Jesus was before the Sanhedrin, the guards kept striking Him and mocking: "Prophesy, who is it that struck you?" But they could not have done it had they not first covered His face. "And they blindfolded Him," says St. Luke (22:64).

41. Salmanticenses, *Cursus theol.,* ed. Palmé, XI, 416.

42. There is another reason why "unbelief" and not "deicide" is the appropriate term to characterize the erring of the Jewish people. It is simply that deicide is at the bottom of the mortal sins of each of us. We call Jesus "the Lamb of God, who takes away the sin of the world" (Jn 1:29), that is, of the entire world and

Hence Jewish disbelief (the turning from the Christian truth already known and professed, though only under the prefigurings of the Old Law) stands between pagan unbelief (the turning from the Christian truth in so far as it can be known in the glimmers and implications of the natural law) and heretical unbelief (the turning from that truth known and professed in its full, definitive manifestation).[43] In distinguishing these three forms of unbelief, the medieval theologians rank them in two ways. Measured by the gravity of the fault, the act of unbelief which gives rise to heresy is more grievous than that which gave rise to Jewish disbelief; and this is more grievous than that which is at the origin of the various paganisms. If one looks at the truths they preserve, the order is reversed: pagan unbelief, which falls as low as polytheism or pantheism, is incomparably more disastrous than Jewish disbelief, which retains the pure belief in a God, one, transcendent, Maker and Judge of the universe; and there is a vast gap between it and those forms of heresy or schism which keep intact belief in the divinity of Christ.[44]

This twofold comparison of the medieval theologians suggests, and even supposes, a very careful distinction, of which one ought to make constant use, today perhaps even more than in the past: the distinc-

not merely of the Jews. To say, then, that He came to take away sin is the same as to say that sin is the deepest, the most decisive, indeed the final cause of His death on the cross; so much so that it is impossible to place the primary responsibility for it on any cause other than sin, which is common to all men. The part in this universal responsibility proper to the crowd of Jerusalem was in the main that of a ministerial causality, for it was they who, at the instigation of their evil leaders, moved visibly and on the forestage of history. "Human ignorance was at its worst," wrote St. Hilary, "when it refused to accept the Lord of eternal glory clothed in the ignominy of the cross" (*Comm. in Mt.,* XVIII, 3; PL 9:1019). He wrote *"human* ignorance," not *"Jewish* ignorance." Yet it is one thing to say, as the Church obliges us to say, that by their personal sins all men, and of course all Christians, are, behind the scenes but most effectively,"deicides." It is another thing to treat the crucifixion of Jesus as if it were no worse than the killing of Socrates—here a Christian can never compromise. But it is still another thing to turn into a slogan the mystery of sin at work in the condemnation and crucifixion of Jesus, to speak of the "deicide Jews" the way the greed of princes or the ambition of the mighty or the passion of the mob have done in the past so that they might put the Jews outside the law. This a Christian can remember only with sorrow, indignation, and tears. And the Church, never a party to the faults or errors of her children, not even of her best, cannot but deplore and condemn any such abuse.

43. Cf. St. Thomas, *Summa Theol.* II–II, q. 10, a. 5 and 6.

44. Some modern heresies or the Manicheism of old are so utterly removed from anything Christian that they are, of course, far worse than Jewish disbelief. Cf. St. Thomas, *Summa Theol.* II–II, q. 10, a. 6.

tion between the *sin* of unbelief which is at the beginning of paganism, Judaism, or the various heresies, and the *legacy* of unbelief in-
herited by the followers of these religions.[45] Such a spiritual legacy
must needs join truths and errors, and hence it happens that its in-
heritor will, depending on whether he is docile or resistant to the interior light of grace, give his inner attention chiefly to the truths or to
the errors. Thus his personal life will either follow the current of the
original deviation or move in the opposite direction, trying to ascend
from the truths still possessed to their fullness. In this way, such a
legacy of usages and beliefs (even when pagan, much more when
Jewish, still more when heretical but Christian) can, despite its spirit
of dissent and separation, be a vehicle of authentic religious values. It
can, therefore, though not always to the same measure, sustain upright souls—souls open to the secret influences of grace—on their
march toward that fullness which is in and from Christ.

A CHURCH FALLEN

This secret march is not without struggle. Judaism stiffened itself, as
a Christian sees it, against the divine élan which carried the Old Testament toward the New like the dawn toward the day. With all its
power, all its passion, it resisted the gospel and, in a strange fear of
the authentic flowering of the tree of the Old Covenant, has substituted flowers that are not the true flowers. Here then is a Church
which had been divine, which, for all its sinners, had the true sanctity
of its vocation. Seized with vertigo when it heard that the revelations
toward which it had been journeying for ages were imminent, it re-
nounced its future, at last present, in order to fall back on its past.
With the inverted ardor of its first strength, it thenceforth preferred
to the "Jerusalem on high"—which is really Israel itself unfolded and
enhanced—a "Jerusalem of here and now," a city of earthly, unreal
deliverances. This is what I call, with Jacques Maritain, a "fallen

45. This distinction makes clear, I hope, if such clarification is needed, that
when I speak of "Jewish unbelief," it is not as invective but as an objective
statement of facts. Were a Jew himself to describe his own stand toward Jesus as
the Christ, he would call it by the same name. A Catholic cannot help but see
in Judaism a misunderstanding of God's designs, an error, a deviation from the
full truth; but he may not accuse Jews today of infidelity, of the *sin* of unbelief.
For the *sin* of unbelief exists only where there is conscious, deliberate, and perti-
nacious resistance to the known truth.

Church," by no means an "anti"-Church but one fallen from a high place.[46]

Fallen and repudiated as a Church because of its unbelief, and yet, at the same time, loved and ever awaited as a people—for God has never ceased to love it—Israel "is the communion of earthly hope." [47]

Israel passionately hopes for, awaits, wants the advent of God in the world, the kingdom of God *here below*. It wants, with an eternal will, a supernatural and unreasonable will, justice in time, in nature, and in the community. Greek wisdom has no meaning for Israel; neither has measure nor felicity of form. The beauty Israel seeks is ineffable, and Israel wants it in this life of the flesh today.

A faith which would do violence to the whole order of things that a man may receive today, tangibly, the substance for which he hopes and the accomplishment of the desire which God has planted in him, and hence would have him regain everything—such is the faith of Israel. It is such a faith Israel is burning to have, and at the same time doubts it has (for if Israel had it, it would have all justice and plenitude). . . . Only on the day it possessed the world would Israel be assured that it had, and had had, faith. Till then, anxiety and doubt will remain at the heart of the Jewish faith.

Jewish charity is also a virtue fallen from a high place. I do not mean a false love; far from it! Divine charity can be present in it, as it may be absent from it. Nor is it Lutheran pity, nor Slavic pity. It is an active and, on occasion, a relentless love of the creature as such; it grapples the creature, torments it, never lets it go, so as to oblige it to become aware of its evil and deliver itself from its evil.

Of earthly hope the Jews have an excess; and of this virtue many Christians have not enough. The basic weakness in the Israel of exile is its failure to understand the Cross, its refusal of the Cross, and therefore its refusal of the transfiguration. The aversion to the Cross is essential to Judaism, in so far as this word denotes the spiritual pattern which shaped Israel's severance from its Messiah. Yet with all Jews in whom grace dwells, as with all souls of good faith and good will, the work of the Cross is present, though veiled and unrecognized, and is involuntarily experienced. Despite himself, and in an obscuring mist, the pious Jew, the Jew of the spirit, carries the gentle Cross, and thus betrays Judaism without realizing what he does. The moment he begins to be aware of this

46. Maritain, *op. cit.*, p. 153.
47. *Ibid.*, p. 154.

mystery of forgiveness and of this putting off of self, he finds himself on the road to Christianity.[48]

In the very bosom, then, of the Israel of the flesh, all who are interiorly attentive to the invitations of grace are, in obscurity and silence, led toward the Israel of the spirit, indeed are already of it: "If you are led by the Spirit, you are not under the Law" (Gal 5:18). And without doubt, there are many who thus belong, in an incipient and salutary way, to the Church universal. One has only to think of the Hasidim of eastern Europe in the eighteenth and nineteenth centuries and their joyous service of God. Groping their way, as it were, they rediscovered something of the coredemptive qualities of Christian love; they sensed that the just man, wrestling to bring sinners back to God by his prayer, at times feels the weight of their temptations pass onto him; they understood too that the just man must go to the utter limit for the sake of those who have recourse to him. As he lay dying, Abraham Joshua Heschel, the rabbi of Apt, said:

Master of the universe, you know that I have no merit at all nor any good by reason of which, after my death, you could have me enter into paradise, among the just. You will have to put me, therefore, into hell among the wicked. Now you know, Master of the universe, that I have hated with a relentless hate all those who offend against your will. How then shall I be able to dwell with them? Thus I entreat you to have all the wicked who are sons of Israel leave hell, for then you will be able to send me there.[49]

What stirs beneath words like these if not those saintly Jewish bargainings dear to Abraham and St. Paul, those bargainings so Christian in meaning?

THE AMBIVALENCE OF EXILE

There is an ambivalence about Jewish unbelief and about the whole destiny of the people of exile. Israel's stumbling, the Apostle tells us, has brought riches to the world (Rom 11:12); Israel's deafness to the gospel made it heard all over the earth; and in closing itself to the Messiah, Israel quickened the conversion of the nations. Though re-

48. *Ibid.*, pp. 154–155.
49. S. A. Horodetzki, *Ha-Hassidout ve-ha-Hassidim* (Berlin: Dvir, 1922), II, 188; as cited by Jean de Menasce, *Quand Israël aime Dieu* (Paris: Librairie Plon, 1931), p. 163.

jected as a Church, it is not rejected as a people; rather does it remain always in a certain way *un peuple consacré à Dieu, un peuple dû à Dieu,* a people set aside for and belonging to God.[50] And as it is dispersed among the nations, it is yet guarded in their midst.

What are the deepest reasons for Israel's dispersion? The first, just spoken of, is Israel's role as the ransom of the nations. Itself unbelieving and unmoved, it hastens, Paul tells us, the salvation of the world by driving away from itself toward the vastness of the Gentiles the divine mercy which—today as then—asks and asks to make its dwelling in Jacob and in Israel its inheritance (Ecclus 24:13). For did not the Lord Himself, when first sending out the Twelve, tell them not to go in the direction of the Gentiles but "rather to the lost sheep of the house of Israel" (Mt 10:6)? But Israel's incredulity is required [51] that it may provoke what we might call the first stage of the world's conversion.

This is not all. For Israel must one day come back to its Messiah, so that the nations, enlivened and enriched by its return, may at that moment enter the second stage of their conversion. As long as Israel fears and flees its reintegration into the everlasting Church, that wondrous moment is put off. Here, then, is the second point made by St. Paul. Israel holds back the supreme outpouring of grace on the world and thus the course of redemptive history—which, however, in being held back is exalted. In the words of Léon Bloy: "The history of the Jews obstructs the history of mankind as a dam obstructs a river, in order to raise its level." [52]

To raise history's level—this is to say that Israel's unbelief is accompanied by luminous corollaries. The unbelief of Abraham's children stirs up the Church to desire them, and to pray. Never forgetful of what she owes them, that she received from them the Saviour, the Virgin, the apostles, the Law and the Prophets and the marvelous psalms she never tires of singing, she asks again and again that the veil be lifted from their hearts. For this she knows, though, alas! her children have not always understood: in permitting that the Jews do

50. M.-J. Lagrange, O.P., *Epître aux Romains* (Paris: Gabalda, 1916), p. 279.
51. I say "required" the way the Apostle dares to say, in a sense related and yet very different, that there "must be" divisions (1 Cor 11:18, 19), a word which scandalizes those who have never reflected on the empire of evil nor on the mystery of a God who makes it serve Him.
52. Bloy, *Le Salut par les Juifs,* p. 44.

not see what she sees, God wants to provoke in her not impatience but love's intercessions.[53] Again, Israel's unbelief urges the divine mercies toward the nations, yet not only to the nations, also—the wonder of it!—toward Israel itself. For if "God has shut up all in unbelief, that He may have mercy upon all" (Rom 11:32), His mercy is on the Jews too. But how? In holding back the supreme out-pouring of redemption which the Apostle calls "life from the dead" (Rom 11:15), in keeping, as it were, Jesus nailed to the cross, Israel's incredulity obliges the Holy Spirit to tokens of infinite patience to-ward this people and draws down on many among them, often through Mary's singular intercessions, strange and marvelous descents of the divine pity. And God's pity seeks among them constant indi-vidual conversions which, without interruption, represent "His peo-ple" in "His Church" so as to announce, prefigure, and prepare its return *en masse*.

If it is true that the Israel of exile blocks the course of history by delaying the full conversion of the Gentiles and the "resurrection" of the world, at present the roles are *reversed*. It is the nations, sluggish toward their own conversion, who stand in Israel's way. By the me-diocrity and all too frequent hypocrisy of their Christian lives, they scandalize the Jews. Far from provoking in them that holy jealousy of which the Apostle speaks, lukewarm Christians seem rather to make every effort to hinder their return to the kingdom. In our day it is the mediocre Christians who shamefully block the march of history

---

53. Fundamentally, the drama of Israel in exile is religious and theological. That it is well above the cultural and political planes cannot, of course, hinder God from using men as His instruments in order to accomplish His designs. Always ephemeral and limited, His instruments are sometimes conscious of serving Him, as Paul was in Corinth, when he left the synagogue to go to the Gentiles (Ac 18:6), but more often unconscious, as was Titus when he destroyed Jerusalem and took its inhabitants into captivity. Yet it would be a monstrous thing, indeed a spiritual catastrophe, if a Christian dared to drag the eternal designs down to the level of men's ephemeral schemes. When men try to replace God's discernment with their own in order to hasten the divine plan, it is usurpation of the worst kind. It is usurpation of the worst kind when men are pretentious enough to make themselves executors of God's justice, imagining that they are thereby authorized to violate God's most sacred laws. So they "justify" the horrible pogroms by invoking the multitude's imprecation that Jesus' blood might fall on them and on their children, or by invoking His warnings to the daughters of Jerusalem (Mt 27:25; Lk 23:28–31). Surely the offense of those who delivered Jesus to the cross is great; surely Israel's estrangement is sad—but to try to avenge the one or to punish the other is the grossest travesty, the very contradiction, of the spirit of Christ.

and "keep Christ nailed to the cross." [54] How high is Israel's dignity and how great its importance in the divine plan if nothing less will suffice to have it turn to Jesus as the Messiah than the first conversion of the nations! Is this not what the Apostle wished to tell the Christians of Rome when he wrote: "For I say to you Gentiles: As long, indeed, as I am an apostle of the Gentiles, I will honor my ministry, in the hope that I may provoke to jealousy those who are my flesh, and may save some of them" (Rom 11:13–14)?

ISRAEL'S RESTLESS SOUL

"Brethren, my heart's desire and my prayer to God is in their behalf unto their salvation. For I bear them witness that they have zeal for God, but not according to knowledge; for, ignorant of the justice of God and seeking to establish their own, they have not submitted to the justice of God," writes the Apostle. A little later he tells that what Israel is seeking, it has not obtained (Rom 10:1–3; 11:7). St. Paul makes a point of using the present tense, "is seeking," for Israel seeks still, seeks always, never rests from striving to be just in God's sight. And yet, as a body, it has not obtained what it seeks.

Rejected as a Church (but never as a people; as a people it is ever loved and protected, for "the gifts and the call of God are without repentance," Rom 11:29), the Israel of exile is devoured by a zeal which is no other than that of a spouse who has been put away— though we cannot expect Israel to agree with us on this. Nonetheless I venture to say that it is this zeal, this jealousy, that unites the whole people. Invisibly, this fiery temperament is communicated from generation to generation, from member to member, and not only to those who venerate the prophets and cling to the worship of Yahweh but also to those who no longer know their Scriptures and have lost the sense of Israel's dignity.[55] Here in this great passion lies the last secret of Israel's unrest but also of its indissoluble unity.

54. It is well to remember here Berdyaev's castigation of the "Christian world," with its wars, its national hatreds, its racial discrimination, its oppression of the working classes. Christians who are "unconverted," whose faith is "formal" rather than real, who lack the love that is Christ's and so are Christians only externally, "thrust themselves," he wrote, "in between Christ and the Jews, concealing the true image of the Saviour from them" ("Christianity and Anti-Semitism," *Blackfriars*, XXIX, 343, Oct. 1948, pp. 463–464).

55. Erik Peterson, in his *Die Kirche aus Juden und Heiden* (Salzburg: Anton Pustet, 1933), makes this interesting observation: "The idea of Israel's becoming jealous is a specifically Jewish concept. In relation to God, Israel knows

Though its origin is in the realm of the spirit, this unrest shows through in Israel's attitude toward the world. I have quoted Jacques Maritain before as saying that "Israel is in the world and is not of the world; but it is attached to the world, subject to the world, in bondage to the world. . . ." He goes on:

The penalty is the working out of the fault; our punishment is our choice. It is terrible to fall into the hands of the living God, for those hands give to each man what his will has settled on. The Jews (I do not mean Jews individually, but the spiritual body of Israel at the moment when it struck against the rock), the Jews at a crucial moment chose the world; they have loved it; their penalty is to be held captive by their choice. Prisoners and victims in this world which they love, but of which they are not, will never be, cannot be.[56]

But what role does their unrest accord them in this world?

Israel is assigned, in the order of temporal history and its finalities, the work of the earthly leavening of the world. Israel is here—Israel, which is not of the world—at the deepest core of the world, to irritate it, to exasperate it, to move it. Like some foreign substance, like a living yeast mixed into the main body, it gives the world no quiet; it prevents the world from sleeping; it teaches the world to be dissatisfied and restless so long as it has not God; it stimulates the movement of history.[57]

Fleeing as it does from a kingdom of the Cross, the Israel of exile is bound to seek after things of this world; and yet all its search covers a deep and persistent sadness which can be felt even in the manifestations of its joy. While speaking of this sadness, I cannot overlook, however, that Israel's having been so long imbued with it has prepared, in those of its children who become truly Christian, an extraordinary sensibility. This sensibility is ever prompting them to suffer as their own the sorrow of their brethren the world over, be they Jewish or not, be they Christian or not; moreover, it predisposes

itself a woman, or, more exactly, His lawful spouse. But when God puts before Israel another woman, Israel becomes jealous. Now God has put the virgin Church before Israel His wife" (p. 57). Again: "Zeal for God is one of the most characteristic features of Jewish piety. Even the Jew who has lost his faith remains a man of zeal. In our day he is perhaps a socialist zealous for justice or a pacifist zealous for a peace which is not of God but of men" (p. 41). Hence the ways of the Israel of today seem best explained by a great messianic élan—its axis, however, gone—, by a mysterious nostalgia.

56. Maritain, *op. cit.,* pp. 152–153.
57. *Ibid.,* p. 156.

them to an intuitive grasp of all the holy and secret anguish of the Church.[58]

Israel is restless. As Péguy sees it, Jewish unrest and Christian unrest are both opposed to that evil calm which is nothing but *patientia non patiendi,* patience not to suffer. For much that calls itself patience, he wrote, is only an anesthetic invention; a defense against pain, trial, salvation, against God; only a gloomy abdication of the very condition of man.[59] But Jewish unrest and Christian unrest are each *patientia patiendi,* patience to suffer. Each having its grandeur, they are yet very different. Jewish unrest is the restlessness of the nomad ready and resigned to abandon his place—an urge to move onward; Christian unrest is the restlessness of the sedentary man—a drive to go deeper.[60]

To carry the analysis further. Jewish unrest is one of movement. It is the restlessness of a people stirred by its deep-seated desire for happiness within time.[61] Not clinging to the soil nor to the present mo-

58. Of my own experience, I can testify that those who come to the Church from Judaism, far from losing their love for their kinsmen on discovering the mystery of the Church, realize as never before the incomparable grandeur of their people's messianic vocation. Their desire for justice keeps alive among us the kind of impatience and violence which was in the prophets. Their dissatisfaction with our provisional arrangements here below; their ardor in hoping and calling for the coming of an order without fault; their, as it were, immediate need for the absolute, are a wonderful lesson, awakening in us the sense of eschatological waiting which always burns in the heart of the Church and of her saints.

59. *Note conjointe sur M. Descartes,* in *Morceaux choisis prose* (Paris: Gallimard, 1928), pp. 94–95.

60. Péguy's thoughts on Jewish unrest are more fully given in his *Notre jeunesse* (Paris: Gallimard, 1933), pp. 73, 108–110. Most of this can be found in the bilingual edition of excerpts called *Basic Verities,* trans. by Anne and Julian Green (New York: Pantheon, 1943), pp. 138–141.

61. Jacques Maritain has shown succinctly the ambivalence of this desire, and I should like him to be heard again: "The will to attain the absolute in the world can assume all forms. It can,—when it confines itself to what is human and contingent, or when it turns to atheism, at least in practice—create that overgrowth of activity in the handling of the goods of the earth and in money making, which finds in capitalist civilization an appropriate ambience; or it can create that revolutionary impatience and that ceaseless agitation which Bernard Lazare and many other Jews liked to point out. When it becomes feverish from wounded sensibility or resentment, it may create a violent pessimism which makes out of bitterness and anger a singularly powerful instrument of discovery, a detector (itself out of gauge) of the self-deceit involved in the pleasure of enjoying a noble soul, of enjoying an orderly existence and a clear conscience. Finally, it can produce, when of the flesh but affecting spiritual things, a pharisaic trend of mind, and the blinding refinements of the harsh cult of the letter, a legal purism.

"But when it is of the spirit, this will toward the absolute brings to flower seeds of true purity, the purity of soul and of morals preserved in the tradition

ment, it turns with a great and insatiable thirst toward the future. Its gaze is toward the messianic bliss which, it has no doubt, its God has prepared for it at the end of history and which will be a re-entry into the first garden of delight. Because of this disregard for the immediate instant and the concrete place, Jewish unrest may be called a non-incarnational unrest. Having ignored the meaning which the mystery of the Incarnation gives to the succession of moment and of place, the Israel of exile has not yet understood that the fleeting instant must be redeemed by turning it toward eternity.

On the other hand, Christian unrest is one of rootedness. It is the restlessness of a people which knows that its temporal condition, however much it may be and ought to be bettered, will never be a paradise; that pure bliss does not dwell within time; that the Son of God descended into history to be crucified in it, and rose in glory not to prolong forever His passing sojourn in time but to await us in a transhistoric abode; that heaven has already come down on earth, not to take away its thorns but to draw forth roses; that eternity has visited time, to fill it not with happiness but with sanctity, not with glory but with love; that there is, right now, a divine task to be done.

Since the Word became flesh at a given time and in a given place, every point in time and space is overshadowed by this mystery; and it is in the *here* that the Christian must set to work and into the *now* that he must plunge to make it bring forth fruits of love. Make the most of time, ransom it, counsels the Apostle (Eph 5:16). One can no more leave the world tranquil than the plant can leave tranquil the soil into which it thrusts its roots. Christian unrest, then, is an incarnational unrest. It knows well that time is on the march, the time of grace and also the time of nature and of culture, and that time is to ripen as a harvest for heaven. It knows no less that the harvest will be according to the seeding, the future glory according to the present

of so many Jewish families. It produces asceticism and piety, love for the word of God and for its sensitive interpretation, uprightness of heart and subtle innocence, and that burning spirituality which is exemplified especially by the hasidic mystics and which shows us the true visage of Israel 'when Israel loves God.' Above all, this will finds expression in the zeal for justice and in the love of truth which is the most exalted indication of this people's election. 'Behold in truth an Israelite, in whom there is no guile,' the Saviour Himself gave witness to the true Israel. . . .

"The love of truth even unto death, the will for truth, pure, absolute, unattainable since truth is that very One whose Name is ineffable,—this is what the best of the Jews owe to Israel and to the Holy Spirit and this is what makes exultant their song in the fiery furnace" (*op. cit.*, pp. 159–160).

love. But the fire which consumes it is that it never quite succeeds in mastering the instant in order to turn it toward eternity. At its very depth, Christian unrest is the unrest of a Church inconsolable that Love is not loved; of the Bride complaining in the name of her Bridegroom that the Father, who had promised to give Him all the nations as an inheritance, has not yet kept His word.

THE INSOLUBLE QUESTION

An intimate part of the redemptive scheme of God, inseparably linked with the salvation of the world, and hence transcending the temporal order, the Jewish problem defies any temporal solution. No political effort, however wise, however just, can ever fully come to grips with a mystery. Still, attempts have been made to end, politically, the tensions and conflicts Israel's existence creates.

There is the "sacral" solution, which—I need not repeat—was, even at its best, no solution. Based on the sacral concept of society, which counted only Christians as citizens and therefore could not incorporate Jews into political life, but based also on a voluntary withdrawal of Jews from the Christian world around them, the medieval status of the Jews was not in itself an injustice.[62] Yet the narrowness and evil passions of many Christians, so unworthy of their high vocation, so far removed from the magnanimity and charity of the saints, at times turned that status into something terrible. Given the constitution of medieval Christendom, it was inevitable that the Jews could be granted only the rights and privileges of strangers; but what was iniquitous was that evil politics so often imposed on them the dilemma of conversion or banishment, or that at the time of the Crusades they were condemned to perpetual servitude. In any case, we must say with Jacques Maritain: "This medieval solution has gone, never to return, as has the type of civilization from which it sprang." [63]

After the trials of the Middle Ages, the French Revolution, with its Declaration of the Rights of Man, seemed to many Jews to be the very age of the deliverance announced by the prophets. Their hard-

---

62. With its respect for spiritual values, such as the significance of baptism, the medieval attempt must never be confused with the treatment of the Jews in Nazi Germany. Not to speak of its bestiality, the Nazi attitude sprang from the utter materialism of racist theories, and if there was one superstition absolutely foreign to the Middle Ages, it was that of race.

63. *Op. cit.,* p. 170.

ships would come to an end, Moses Mendelssohn (1729–86) thought with others, if only the Jews ceased to be a separate entity in any respect other than religion. Having relinquished all jurisdiction of their own in civil or criminal affairs, having renounced past usages such as polygamy, having submitted to military service, in brief, having adopted in many ways the customs of the lands in which they were born, they became citizens of those lands. They ceased to be Jews in the traditional sense of the word and became Frenchmen, Englishmen, Germans, "of the Mosaic confession." Thus to reduce the whole of Judaism to "the Mosaic confession" was the thesis and the desire of "assimilation," which suppressed all difficulties, to be sure, but only at the price of a double suicide. No longer was there to be a Jewish *people.* No longer a Jewish *religion,* supernaturally revealed to patriarchs and prophets by the living God; for it, the partisans of religious emancipation substituted, under the name of "Mosaic confession," a pale philosophical deism.[64]

But Israel refused to die; an irresistible force, surging from the depths of its being, aroused it against this double threat. Its will not to die *as people* led it to work for the recovery of full national life in the land of its fathers. There is nothing in political Zionism to gainsay the prophecies of the New Testament. But will it ever be able to bring "peace upon Israel" (Ps 124:5) and make secure the lives of Jews the world over? Having set out to solve the Jewish problem, does it not rather pose it in all its acuteness? In any case, no matter

64. Using a somewhat different terminology, Maritain writes: "The Jew is lost if he settles down, and by *settling down* I mean a spiritual phenomenon, like the loss of a stimulating disquiet and the failure of a vocation. *Assimilation* involves an altogether different problem, in the social and political, not spiritual, order. An 'assimilated' Jew may be one who is not 'settled.' Assimilation is not the solution of Israel's problem, any more than is Yiddishism or Zionism; but assimilation, like autonomy and Zionism, is a partial accommodation, a compromise solution, good and desirable to the extent that it is possible. Assimilation took place in the past on a large scale in the Hellenistic and Hispano-Arabic periods. Yet it carries with it a risk—as does also Zionism (as a state)—the risk of the Jews becoming settled, becoming *like others* (I mean spiritually). It is the risk of losing the vocation of the house of Israel. Their God then strikes them down by the vilest of instruments. Never had there been Jews more assimilated than the German Jews. They were all the more attached to German culture for its having in part been their achievement. They had become totally Germans, which did not make them either more discreet or more humble. They were not only assimilated, but settled down, conciliatory and well reconciled with the Prince of this world. Jews who become like others become worse than others. (When a Jew receives Christian grace, he is less than ever like others: he has found *his* Messiah.)" (*Ibid.,* pp. 164–165.)

what one thinks of Zionism, even if one believes it "to have a historic importance of the first order," even if one believes that the state of Israel may one day be "the animating center for all dispersed Jewry," one must add at once that it "does not yet represent deliverance from exile." It is at most "a prelude to such deliverance." [65]

In spite of its founders' wishes, *political* Zionism is but an epiphenomenon. Though its partisans hardly ever know it, it is ruled and carried where it would not go by the mysterious, irrepressible Jewish élan toward messianic deliverance. Israel is certain that the dispersion cannot last; that a wondrous return, some unimaginable reintegration, awaits it.

> *Fear not for I am with you,*
> *from the east will I bring your seed,*
> *and from the west will I gather you;*
> *I will say to the north: Give up!*
> *and to the south: Keep not back;*
> *Bring my sons from afar,*
> *and my daughters from the end of the earth;*
> *All who are called by my name,*
> *and whom I created for my glory.*
>
> (Is 43:5–7)

Israel knows that these words, once spoken to the exiles in Babylon, are spoken also to the exiles of today; and it does not deceive itself. The divine promises are true, and they will surpass all its expectations. Hence Israel is right in sighing after the end of the dispersion—this is the truth of Zionism. But Israel is wrong—and this is the error of Zionism—in overlooking entirely the deepest, hidden causes of its dispersion.[66] As soon as a city of peace appears possible for it, the

---

65. *Ibid.,* p. 173.

66. The error of those who offer Zionism not as an accommodation but as the ultimate solution is the same as Israel's first error: tarrying within the limits of the Old Testament instead of passing to the New. But we must not forget that no matter how mistaken Jews as a body may be, each and every Jew is, in the secrecy of his soul, visited by the grace of Christ and urged toward the Jerusalem which is above (cf. Gal 4:26). One has to think only of Rabbi Dov Baer of Mezritch, whose early life was one of dreadful poverty. One day, saddened by the tears of his wife and children, he bewailed his misery. At once a voice from heaven declared that his complaints had lost him his place in the world to come. First he was seized by grief; then on second thought, he was overjoyed. "From now on," Rabbi Baer exclaimed, "I shall be able to serve God with a purer heart, without hope of recompense." But then the heavenly voice was heard again: "Your part

great waters of messianic hope rush into this little opening, rush into
a bed far too narrow for so mighty a torrent. Thus, by an inner dialectic, political Zionism awakens *"messianic* Zionism," only to disappoint
it. But perhaps even these disappointments may serve Israel's redemption, may show it by its pain that it is made not just for figures but
for reality, and may lift its eyes toward the Jerusalem of the spirit
that awaits it.

To say that the Jewish problem cannot be fully solved on the temporal plane is not to say that our only response to it must be idle
waiting. Quite the contrary. In those moments of history when the
Jewish question thrusts itself once more like a thorn into the flesh of
a mankind become materialistic, when the black and suffocating
waves of anti-Semitic propaganda break on the minds of many, Christian love must leap to proclaim right and wrong; and it must speak
clearly, powerfully, surely, with a voice that seems to come from another world. It will not stop to weigh, in newspapers, the merits and
demerits of the Jews, nor to discuss before a wavering crowd, already
biased by covetousness and more than half won by gross slogans, how
the Jews may *differ* from other men, be it religiously, historically, or
politically. No, its first impulse is to cry out their *likeness* to other
men.[67] Never may Christians look on the Jews as an impersonal en-

in the world to come is restored to you, but be on guard not to complain again
when you are filled with compassion for your children. For your compassion is
no keener than God's." (Horodetzki, *op. cit.,* I, 78; as cited by Menasce, *op. cit.,*
pp. 120–121. For a somewhat different version of the same story, see Martin
Buber, *Tales of the Hasidim: The Early Masters,* trans. by O. Marx, New York:
Schocken, 1947, pp. 98–99.)

67. Let us not forget the cry of Cardinal Saliège who, on Sunday, August 30,
1942, had a letter read in all the churches of his archdiocese of Toulouse:
"Jews are men, Jews are women. It is not true that everything is permitted against
them, against these men, against these women, against these fathers and mothers
of families. They are part of the human race. They are our brethren like all the
rest. A Christian cannot forget this." And let us not forget the voice of the since
silenced Archbishop Stepinac who, on the feast of Christ the King, October 25,
1942, a few days after a decree forced the Jews of Croatia to wear a yellow star,
preached in his cathedral that the Church has always condemned, and condemns
today, all violence and injustice committed in the name of racial and national-
istic theories; that she has never countenanced, and does not countenance today,
the extermination of Jews and gypsies on the pretext that they constitute inferior
races, for, he said: "All members of the human race, without exception, are the
creation of God. *Memento homo quia pulvis es, et in pulverem reverteris;* 'Remember, man, that you are dust and unto dust you shall return.' The members of
this race or that may have a higher or a lower culture, may be black or white;
they may be parted by oceans, may live at the North Pole or at the South Pole.
The essential thing is that the Jews who are the object of hatred and the proud

tity, a group one can regard without love or simply pass by. They are persons, creatures made to the image of God and purchased by the blood of Christ. The bond which binds together these persons—these men and women, young and old—into one single community is not first and above all of the temporal order; it is of the theological order, for Israel is a mystery.

The second impulse, then, of Christian love must be to go to the very roots of this mystery. For once the exceptional destinies of the people of God are understood in the light of biblical revelation and particularly of the great Pauline teachings, and are so taught, it will be hard for men to rage against these destinies in stupid and sacrilegious fury. No matter what the faults of the Jews are (and I do not think them any less than those of Christians), true Christian love is impelled to give witness before the world that there is, at the heart of these destinies, a supernatural mystery, as exasperating to the world's materialism as the mystery of the Church. It is impelled to cry out to the world that anti-Semitism and anti-Christianism are two forms of one and the same hatred, the hatred of the supernatural. It is impelled to cry out to the world that to spit on Israel is to spit on the divine decree which made the Word become flesh in Israel, a decree of which that people was for so long the bearer and to which it still owes its existence, being preserved toward the day when it will acclaim the Word that dwelt in its midst.[68]

The third mission of Christian love is to turn to the political plane. If, according to the Catholic position, "there is, till the fulfillment of the prophecies, no solution in the pure and simple meaning of the word, no truly decisive solution" for the Jewish problem,[69] it nevertheless demands of us that we "take part at the temporal level in the constant work of the concrete intelligence which neither definitively resolves nor overcomes antinomies, but at each moment in time dis-

Aryans, all without exception, have an equal right to say: 'Our Father, who art in heaven.' This right comes to them from God, and nobody can deny it to them." (Cf. A. H. O'Brien, *Archbishop Stepinac: The Man and His Case,* Westminster, Md.: Newman, 1947, pp. 19-20.)

68. On the eve of Christmas 1941, when Nazi persecution was weighing so heavily on the Jews of France, Paul Claudel said in a letter to the Chief Rabbi of France: "The Catholic cannot forget that Israel is always the elder son of the promise, as it is today the elder son of sorrow." See John M. Oesterreicher, *Racisme, Antisémitisme, Antichristianisme* (New York: Editions de la Maison Française, 1943), p. 243.

69. Maritain, *op. cit.,* p. 169.

covers whatever is needed to make them bearable and more supple." [70]
Hence I must say a word on the emancipation of the Jews and their
political equality, brought about by the French Revolution. Even
though this emancipation was the result of a "rationalist and bour-
geois-optimist way of thinking, forgetful at once of the mystery of
Israel and of supra-individual realities," and even though its hopes to
end the Jewish problem forever have proved vain, it was in itself just
and necessary, and corresponded to an aspiration truly Christian. Civ-
ilized peoples, to the extent that they wish to remain so, must consider Jewish emancipation definitive. [71]

There is at all times the solution of love, supreme and above politics. It is twofold. On the Christian side: to call attention, again and
again, to the enduring demands of the evangelical law, the natural
law, and the law of nations; to point to the extraordinary destiny of
the people of God in its exile and dispersion; and to remind men that
nothing reveals better the level of their conscience than their relationship to the Jews, that Jews are the touchstone of their Christian
lives. On the Jewish side: always to purify the spirit of earthly hope
by the spirit of sanctity, by that charity so dear to the Hasidim, that
love which, centuries before, inspired talmudic sayings like these:

One must pay the same respect to an aged non-Jew as to an aged Jew,
and offer him a supporting hand. . . . To visit the sick who are not Jews
is to walk in the ways of peace. . . . To bury the dead who are not Jews
and to comfort those who mourn them is to walk in the ways of peace.

He who is merciful to others, mercy is shown to him by Heaven.

Any distress shared by Israel and the nations of the world is a real
distress, but any distress confined to Israel is not such a distress. [72]

THE ISRAEL OF THE REINTEGRATION

HEAVEN and earth await Israel's ingathering. By faith we know that
the day will come, but what it will be like is not given us to know

70. *Ibid.*, p. 150.
71. *Ibid.*, p. 170.
72. The first sayings, from the *Arba'a Turim* by Jacob ben Asher (1269–
1343), may be found in Edmond Fleg's *Anthologie juive* (Paris, 1939), II,
134–135, 469. The second and third are from Shab. 151b; cf. *The Babylonian
Talmud*, ed. I. Epstein (London: Soncino, 1948), *Shabbath*, II, 774; and Deut.
R. 2:22; cf. *Midrash Rabbah*, Soncino ed., VII, 50.

with the same sureness. Hence I shall have to add some conjectures to the certainties of revelation.

PROPHECIES OF THE INGATHERING

That a dispersion prepares a return, and the cruelest dispersion the most beautiful return, is the rhythm by which divine Providence governs Israel. So psalmist and prophets:

> *Yahweh rebuilds Jerusalem;*
> *the dispersed of Israel He gathers.*
> *He heals the brokenhearted*
> *and binds up their wounds.*
>
> (Ps 146:2–3)

> *Hear the word of Yahweh, O nations,*
> *and proclaim it in the islands afar:*
> *He who scattered Israel now gathers them*
> *and guards them as a shepherd his flock.*
>
> (Jer 31:10)

If Israel's captivity in Babylon (brought about by its resistance to the prophets) foreshadowed its even crueler exile among the nations (brought about by its refusal of the Messiah), and if the Jerusalem laid waste by Nebuchadnezzar foreshadowed the Jerusalem laid waste even more terribly by Titus—then the return to the Jerusalem of stone must foreshadow an even more astonishing return to a Jerusalem purer and brighter, spiritual and eternal.

The Saviour Himself gives us a glimpse of this marvelous return at the very moment He announces the imminent ruin of the Holy City:

> *Jerusalem, Jerusalem, thou who killest the prophets,*
> *and stonest those who are sent to thee!*
> *How often would I have gathered thy children together,*
> *as a hen gathers her young under her wings,*
> *but thou wouldst not!*
> *Behold, your house is left to you.*
> *And I say to you,*
> *you shall not see me*
> *until the time comes when you shall say:*
> *Blessed in the name of Yahweh be He who comes!*
>
> (Lk 13:34–35) [73]

73. See note 3.

No sooner, then, does He reproach Jerusalem for having rejected His love than He announces the triumph of God's mercy over its unwillingness. First God will leave the house of Israel to the painful destinies prepared for it by the slayers of prophets: Jerusalem will be desolate. But afterwards an age will come when Israel will at last open its heart to its Messiah and will bless Him in a shout of loving welcome.

It must have been on Christ's promise to Jerusalem that Paul, illumined by the Holy Spirit, based his prophecy of Israel's return to its Messiah.[74] Having alerted Christians of Gentile stock against conceit and false security; having warned them, the wild branches grafted onto the olive tree, against arrogance toward the Jews, the natural branches broken off; having reminded them that only in fear and trembling can they walk the ways of love, he spells out his hope for his kinsmen:

They also, if they do not continue in unbelief, will be grafted in; for God is able to graft them back. For if thou hast been cut off from the wild olive tree which is natural to thee, and, contrary to nature, have been grafted into the cultivated olive tree, how much more shall these, the natural branches, be grafted into their own olive tree!

(Rom 11:23–24)

Do these words imply anything more than that a change of heart is always possible for the Israel of exile? That *if* it does not persevere in its disbelief, *if* it turns to the Messiah, God has, of course, the power to graft it back? But will it ever turn? Can we know that it will? And is this knowledge at all important for Christians of Gentile stock? [75] To all these questions, the Apostle answers forcefully. Just a few lines earlier he asks whether his people in its unbelief had so stumbled as to fall forever, and bursts forth: "By no means!" (Rom 11:11). And now, in one of the most beautiful cries of wonder ever sprung from his heart, he says to his Gentile readers:

I would not, brethren, have you ignorant of this mystery, lest you should be wise in your own conceits, that a partial blindness only has be-

74. J.-M. Lagrange, O.P., *The Gospel of Jesus Christ* (London: Burns Oates & Washbourne, 1938), II, 153.

75. St. Thomas's reply to this is: *Ignorantia hujus mysterii esset nobis damnosa;* not to know the mystery of Israel's return—"mystery" here means God's revealed and manifest design—is a blight to our spiritual lives, a deadly danger to our souls (*Comm. in Rom.* 11:25).

fallen Israel, until the full number of the Gentiles should enter, and thus all Israel should be saved, as it is written:

> *There will come out of Zion the deliverer*
> *and he will turn away impiety from Jacob;*
> *And this is my covenant with them,*
> *when I shall take away their sins.*

(Rom 11:25–27)

Here, quoting from memory according to the Septuagint (Is 59:20–21; 27:9), Paul combines two prophetic passages on the messianic times, but applies them in a new way. He had often proclaimed that the great deliverance, that outpouring of the law of love which the Gospel calls the acceptable year of the Lord (Lk 4:19), will not be for Abraham's children according to the flesh but for his children according to the promise, be they Jews or Gentiles (Rom 9:7–8). Now he proclaims that, at God's chosen time, this great outpouring *will* be for Abraham's children according to the flesh, who will then be also children of the promise. For a special providential design watches over exiled Israel, keeping it distinct in the midst of the nations and leading it on its journey through the centuries to the time of pardon and grace. On that day, decisive for the religious history of mankind, the spiritual fullness promised in the Old Testament will, by a triumph of divine mercy, at long last be opened to the people which was its first trustee.

Thus Israel is not forsaken, being always the people of divine predilection. Even when the majority of its children kept aloof from the gospel, it remained "most dear for the sake of the fathers, for the gifts and the call of God are without repentance" (Rom 11:28–29). But as Israel refused to walk the way of the gospel, divine mercy, thus rejected, lavished itself on the Gentile nations—to make up, as it were, for the loss—and conquered, among others, the Roman readers of Paul's letter, who but lately had been pagans. On seeing this conquest, the Jews will (such is Paul's sure hope) be stirred to emulation, at which God's mercy will, by surprising detours, provoke them to love.

For as you also at one time did not believe God, but now have obtained mercy by reason of their unbelief, so they too have not now believed by reason of the mercy shown you, that they too may obtain mercy.

(Rom 11:30–31)

Bringing, then, these revelations to a daring conclusion, Paul gives the deepest secret of the universal history over which, out of His inaccessible transcendence, God reigns: "For God has shut up all in unbelief, that He may have mercy upon all" (Rom 11:32).

THE TIME OF THE INGATHERING

While the fact of Israel's return to its Messiah is thus unquestionable for St. Paul and for us, its how and when are not so clear. But they will be clearer if we ponder the Apostle's words: "A partial blindness only has befallen Israel, until the full number of the Gentiles should enter, and thus all Israel should be saved" (Rom 11:25–26). The "full number," the *plērōma,* of the Gentiles means here all the nations, not all their members, for, as long as time lasts, the "mystery of iniquity" (2 Thess 2:7) will not cease to operate nor will crosses be lacking to the Church. But there will be a time, according to the Apostle, when all the peoples of mankind (each represented, that is, by a goodly proportion of believers) will range themselves under the law of Christ. It will be in those days that Israel, it too represented by a goodly share of its sons, will at last begin to acknowledge its Messiah. By so uniting with the nations in faith and worship, it will, as it were, set the seal to the manifestation of the Church's catholicity.

Now, must one assume that Israel's reintegration will mark the end of history, giving the signal for the Last Judgment and for the final restoration of the universe? Or may one assume that Israel's return will take place within the very web of historic time, that indeed it is meant to influence the course of the centuries to come after it? [76]

76. It is impossible to accept the chiliastic view of Soloviov, which places Israel's turning to Christ at the end of historic time and at the threshold of a thousand-year reign of Christ with His saints. This is how he sees the last days: The Jews will first favor the Antichrist, who will feign to be one of them and who, under the pretext of establishing their rule over the earth, will install himself in Jerusalem as if he were the Messiah. But soon recognizing him to be a shameless impostor, as one man they will rise against him; and even their enemies will have to admit that the depth of the Jewish soul is not moved by the calculations and cravings of Mammon but by an inner fervor, by the hope and wrath of an age-old messianic faith. There will ensue a hopelessly uneven war, in the course of which the Jews will call on God and the Antichrist will be swallowed up by the earth. Then, as lightning tears the sky apart, Christ will descend to them, clad in royal purple, the marks of the nails in His outstretched hands. From that moment all discord will be gone; the dead will rise and will come from all sides to reign with Christ for a thousand years. See Vladimir Soloviov, "A Short Story of the Antichrist," in *War, Progress, and the End of History,* trans. by A. Bakshy (London: University of London Press, 1915), pp. 224–226.

Both opinions are found within the Church, but the second seems to me to correspond better with the two pertinent texts of St. Paul. Impossible, he declares in the first, that Israel's restoration should not be of inestimable benefit to the other peoples, since even its stumbling marvelously profited them: "If their offense is the riches of the world, and their decline the riches of the Gentiles, how much more their full number!" (Rom 11:12). In the second text, the Apostle is even more precise: "If the rejection of them is the reconciliation of the world, what will the reception of them be but life from the dead?" (Rom 11:15).

What is the meaning of these last words? So much is certain: as Israel's aloofness from Christ was the signal for the world's reconciliation, so Israel's turning to Him will be the signal for the world's consummation and the resurrection of all flesh. But will there be any time between Israel's return and the Day of Judgment? Some think not. For them, Israel's conversion will "unfasten Christ from the cross" and ring the world's last hour. Others think that an indefinite time will elapse between the two events and that history, unceasingly laved by the blood of the redemption, will go on, perhaps for a great many centuries.

According to this second view, Israel's entry will provoke within the Church such a resurgence of love as could be compared to a return of the dead to life. The world, writes Père Allo, will then participate more fully and more brilliantly than before in what St. John calls "the first resurrection" of a thousand years (Apoc 20:4–6),[77] that is, in the life of grace poured out by the Messiah.

If St. Paul's prophecy is understood in this way, it is easier to reconcile the many different sayings of Scripture on the end of ages. After Israel's turning to Christ, after the mighty spiritual resurrection, the great epiphany of the Church's catholicity, it will beget, there will again be terrible persecutions, for the "mystery of iniquity" is always at work (2 Thess 2:7). Vast floods of hate will be loosed, false prophets will rise, and "because iniquity will abound, the charity of the many will grow cold" (Mt 24:9–12). Then will come the apostasy of apostasies, which will pave the way for the triumphant mani-

77. Cf. E.-B. Allo, O.P., *L'Apocalypse de saint Jean* (Paris: Gabalda, 1933), p. cxxxii. The "thousand years" symbolically denote the messianic times, the times that began with the Incarnation and will last till Christ's second coming at the end of ages.

festation of the Antichrist. But at long last the Lord Jesus will appear in the brightness of His coming (2 Thess 2:3, 8).

DEATH FOR THE SAKE OF LIFE

If it is true that, far from putting an end to the unfolding of history, Israel's ingathering will, on the contrary, usher in a future of vast perspectives, it takes on a quite different meaning and raises new problems.

All Israel shall find salvation, the Apostle predicts, and calls Isaiah as his witness that the Deliverer shall come from Zion to rid it of its disbelief, and that this shall be God's covenant with it: to take away its sins. Here a salvation is promised, a deliverance is announced, a covenant is reserved to Israel. Salvation, deliverance, covenant: these great biblical and messianic words have always made Israel's heart tremble—why do they now seem so ambiguous? Why is it that this salvation, this deliverance, this covenant, which for the Israel of the spirit gleams like the promise of an unsurpassed spring, a matchless life, an utter fidelity, held ready by the Lord for the Israel of the flesh —why is it that they appear to this same Israel of the flesh like a mockery, like an odious invitation to consent to downfall, indeed to commit the final treason?

This stumbling block will confront Israel once more, and at the very moment when Israel is about to surmount it. For the grain of wheat must die if it is not to remain alone, but if it dies, it yields much fruit. He who clings to his life will lose it, while he who sacrifices it will save it (Jn 12:24–25). Agonizing paradox: the first covenant must fully die that the second covenant may fully flower.

Like those waters which, along the margin of a river, flow against the current, so the Old Covenant, in a very mysterious way, continues to last and, to this day, to affect the Israel according to the flesh. Ever since the promulgation of the New Covenant, Israel has reversed the movement of life and has fixed its will on its past, thereby betraying that very past with its dynamism. It has invoked the letter of the law against the law's meaning and movement, and is thus judged by the law's letter, whose rigor, as in times past, has thrown it into exile. (I am speaking here, as always, of Israel as a body, for we must never lose sight of the fact that every one of its members is personally visited by the gentle grace of Christ—all grace is the grace of

Christ, aiding those who know Him and also those who do not know Him—and that he is judged in no other way than by his own response to the grace he receives.)

Only when it breaks the dominion of the things of old and throws itself without reservation into the living current of the New Law will Israel attain true salvation, true deliverance. This is the crux: its entry into the new life supposes a death. But—one must say it with a loud voice—it need by no means be the death of Israel as an ethnic group among other ethnic groups; as a people among other peoples; as a nation and country, or, rather, as a group of nations and of countries (of which one may well be the Holy Land) among other groups of nations and of countries. Such ethnic and political structures are perfectly reconcilable with a Christian temporal order. What is required, however, is that Israel die as a "national religion." For the religion of the one true God can no longer be bound to a nation: it was so bound, by His providence, but only for a time; now it is above nations. The people of the one true God can no longer be a particular people: it was that only for a time and provisionally; God's will is that now His people be gathered from all the peoples of the world.

Israel cannot renounce the idea of a nation-bound religion without an agony, without a purification of its memory and its hope so exacting, so painful, that it seems beyond the capacities of human nature. Is this not implied in the Apostle's announcement that the spiritual transformation of the elder people and its entry into the New Covenant will demand an extraordinary outpouring of divine grace over all the earth, an outpouring beyond expectation?

Israel's memory will have to be purified. It is rich with the places of its pilgrimage through the Land of Promise—the sites sanctified by the passage of patriarchs and prophets, by the nation's triumphs or misfortunes; the oak of Mamre and the well of Jacob; Mount Gilboa, where the stricken Saul sought death; the hill of Ramah, where Rachel weeps for her exiled children; the water gate, where Ezra, to the "Amen, amen" of the people, read the Book of the Law; Modin, where the Maccabean resistance began; the beautiful city of Jerusalem; and a thousand places more. Israel will have to learn, not to forget, but to go beyond, this long history, which is, without question, holy and divine, but whose spiritual meaning is somehow thrust into the heaviness of the temporal. Israel must come to value this history, magnificent as it is, less for itself than for what it signifies; to think of it as no more than a stage of its youth, a youth that must give way to maturity. Israel will have to—and indeed will!—see the land of its earthly beginnings in the pure light of Jesus and in the perspective of that great spiritual kingdom which covers the earth.

Israel's hope will have to be purified. It may well be that, at the time of Israel's ingathering, the citadel of Zion will stand again and that the well of Gihon and the pool of Siloam will not be dry. But no matter what is in store for Jerusalem, the world's temporal history will not center around it.[78] For it is in image that it is said: Jerusalem will be built of sapphires and rubies, its gates of crystal, and its borders of precious stones (Is 54:11–12). It is in image that it is said: The nations shall walk in Jerusalem's light and kings in the brightness of its shining, the wealth of the sea shall be turned unto it and the riches of the nations come unto it (Is 60:1–6). These figures have been fulfilled, as far as this aeon permits. The Church is the guardian of the nations' wisdom, the mother of men; sons have come to her from afar and daughters are at her side. She is the radiant Jerusalem of messianic times, even though she still travels through the night of her pilgrimage toward her final glory.[79] Once the children of the patriarchs and prophets recognize this Jerusalem, they must not and will not look back nostalgically toward the splendors of old but will turn toward the eternal, the pure and ineffable, joys to come. They will exult that this aeon has seen the beginning of the kingdom; and they will stretch out for its final, complete, perfect, indeed superabundant fulfillment, which Christ will bring when He returns to make the earth and the heavens new.

But the pain that goes with the cleansing of memory and hope will not be all; Israel may have to undergo an even deeper suffering. If my interpretation of St. Paul's prophecy is right, that even after its ingathering the Jewish people will remain as a people, and if, as I

78. In saying this, I do not wish—God forbid!—to give support to the charge made by some that Zionism is a scheme for a Jewish conquest of the world. What I wish to say is that Israel's very special hopes for an earthly paradise must be cleansed—without forgetting for a moment that the terrestrial hopes of all men and all nations must be cleansed.

79. See, for instance, Dionysius, *Eccles. Hierarch.*, 5 (PG 3:501), as cited by St. Thomas: "The state of the New Law is between the state of the Old Law, whose figures are fulfilled in the New, and the state of glory, in which all truth will be manifested perfectly and without veil" (*Summa Theol.* III, q. 61, a. 4 ad 1).

have said, a deep unrest to go further moves its soul—what will be the unrest of the reborn Israel! Turned toward the service of Christ's kingdom, that unrest will surely be an insatiable desire to spread the kingdom to the ends of the earth, leaving to the fervent sons of Israel no rest of mind or body, no rest from prayer or work, so long as there remains anywhere a single soul closed to the saving Cross and the holy inebriety it brings; so long as there remains a single sheep forgotten, abandoned, or recalcitrant, to be led back to its Shepherd. After its recognition of Christ, Israel—such is the thought of St. Gregory the Great—will preach openly the faith which, in the days of its unbelief, it contradicted. And not content to announce the Redeemer lovingly, it will strive to imitate Him in His Passion; it will expose itself to opprobrium and torture for His sake till it is dyed in His blood.[80]

Is it mere conjecture to think that Israel's saints of the future will be filled with the spirit that made Abraham negotiate with God for an amnesty for Sodom? Abraham's "bargaining" heralded the inexpressible "bargaining" of the crucified Saviour, the ceaseless intercessions of His Mother, and no less the prayers of His true disciples. Is it mere conjecture to say that the purest saints of Israel reclaimed will have a special place among those messengers of the gospel whose anguish and martyrdom will support the unfolding of the Church's catholicity—that great unfolding, after which the great apostasy will come, when the Church, diminished in numbers, will no longer be able to grow save in fire and in beauty? And is it mere conjecture to suppose that the Israel to come, a spouse so marvelously pardoned, will clothe its apostolate in humility, delicacy, and gentleness; that it will array itself in a purity and charm that will be one of the most beautiful jewels of the Church of those days? "Following the Redeemer in His Passion, Israel returned will seek the suffering of warfare, not reward, and to possess Him tranquilly it will gladly wait till eternity."[81]

Once more, this is the marvelous message the Apostle wishes to tell

80. This is taken from the beautiful commentary on 1 Kg 2:26 which figures among the works of St. Gregory the Great (PL 79:108), and whose authenticity is defended by the most distinguished scholars, such as M. de la Taille, S.J. (*Recherches de Sciences Religieuses*, 1916, p. 472), and B. Capelle, O.S.B. (*Revue Bénédictine*, 1929, p. 217).

81. St. Gregory, *op. cit.* (PL 79:109).

the Christians of Rome and all Christians since: On the appointed day, all Israel will be saved and will enter into the kingdom of grace.

It is written in Isaiah that a Redeemer will come for Zion. He did appear *in* Zion to open the gates of messianic times. It was *from* Zion too that He came, being, "according to the flesh, of the offspring of David" (Rom 1:3). It was also *for* Zion first that He came, for "the lost sheep of the house of Israel" (Mt 15:24). But for long centuries, Zion would not know Him.

Yet before the desired and terrible hour of His glorious parousia, before the last judgment of all the world, the Deliverer will come again in Zion. Not visibly, to be sure, as in the days of His earthly life, but mystically, by the sovereign power and hidden light of His love. He will take away Jacob's sins, bless the Israel of the flesh and at last gather it into the messianic kingdom, granting it that, by its fervor, it may ransom the tardiness of so many centuries. "This is my covenant with them, when I shall take away their sins" (Rom 11:27).

And if it is true that a covenant can only be mutual, the hour will have come when Jesus' brethren according to the flesh—conquered by no other force than love—will say and sing: "Blessed in the name of Yahweh be He who comes!" (Mt 23:39).

John M. Oesterreicher

THE COMMUNITY OF QUMRAN

IT MUST be the infinite humor of God that at times disarms our sense
of symmetry. Though He is beyond all question the Lord of order, He
must have smiled at our desire to see cause and effect always neatly
proportionate when He let a fifteen-year-old Bedouin boy make history.
Muhammad adh-Dhib, Muhammad-the-Wolf, with one or more companions, may have been carrying contraband through the Desert of
Judaea or searching for a lost goat; he may have been seeking refuge
from a thunderstorm or, while throwing stones, been startled by the
sound of crashing pottery—as the various stories since grown up
would have it. However it was, early in 1947 he stumbled, in a matter of moments, on one of the greatest discoveries of our time, a discovery for which scholars, had they suspected it, would have toiled
day and night. The young Moslem knew nothing of the intimate bond
between the old Israel and the Church, but in finding by chance a
hidden cave, the shelter of ancient scrolls, he was privileged to un-
earth a never expected confirmation of that unity.

From the moment the Scrolls were found, drama surrounded them;
and no sooner had news of them reached scholars outside the Holy
Land than there was interest and enthusiasm, and then controversy
over their possession, their authorship, their authenticity, their age.
But thus far the battle was confined to the scholarly world. The world
at large knew nothing of the Scrolls, and the few who did know cared
little. It was left to a few men—each of them at odds, for some reason
or other, with the gospel or the Church—to arouse the public's curiosity and to start another battle, whose issues were of more general,
indeed of ultimate, concern. When, in 1950, in his first book on the
Scrolls, André Dupont-Sommer of the Sorbonne implied that Renan
was right in calling Christianity "an Essenism which has largely succeeded"; when, in 1955, the author and critic Edmund Wilson an-

nounced through *The New Yorker* that at last the time had come to do away with "antiquated prejudices" and to regard the rise of Christianity "as simply an episode of human history"; when, early in 1956, John M. Allegro of Manchester University, speaking on the BBC, gave the impression that the Scrolls showed Christ to be merely a representative of a recurring pattern (a position he seems to have since modified); when, in the summer of 1956, the Unitarian minister A. Powell Davies let the cover of his *The Meaning of the Dead Sea Scrolls* state that they are "the greatest challenge to Christian dogma since Darwin's theory of evolution"—millions listened and took sides. These statements have no support in the Scrolls themselves, resting entirely on the bias of those who made them.[1] Yet, by having drawn attention to the Scrolls, they will in the end serve the truth and thus afford another instance of the mirth of God, who enlists in His service even the "critics" of His work.

CAVES, SCROLLS, AND RUINS

FULL of cliffs and crevices, the Judaean wilderness runs for miles along the Dead Sea. Across its northern part cuts the road from Jerusalem to Jericho, which Jesus chose as the obvious setting for the parable of the Good Samaritan and the traveler ambushed by robbers. There, in this bleak and desolate region, a little more than a mile from the west shore of the Dead Sea and a little less than a mile north of a ruin, Khirbet Qumran, which is flanked on its south by a rugged ravine, usually dry, but during the rainy season carrying torrents of water, the Wady Qumran—there, in this stony desert, is the cave where the Bedouins made their first find: earthen jars about two feet

1. Monsignor John J. Dougherty has called Wilson's presentation "mischief" (*America,* Feb. 4, 1956, p. 500), and Professor Harold H. Rowley has spoken of Allegro's claims as "unscholarly" and "immature" (*Time,* April 2, 1956, p. 71). When I charge those who use the Scrolls to empty Christ's gospel of its unique significance with "bias" as well, I must beg the reader's patience, for only as I try to unroll the Scrolls little by little will proof of it appear. I am well aware, too, that Wilson, in his *The Scrolls from the Dead Sea,* repeatedly suggests that it is the religious scholars, Christian or Jewish, who are biased, that it is they who cannot be objective about the meaning of the Scrolls because they are religiously committed. Only a man without religious affiliation can grasp their true significance, he holds—which is like saying that only a man whose taste buds have been destroyed can be a judge of wine, or that only a man whose affections are not engaged can understand love. Besides, is it not really an illusion to suppose that the unaffiliated are in no way committed?

high and ten inches in diameter, some intact, most broken, all but one empty. In it were three mysterious cylinders wrapped in rotting linen, linen of which it was said months later that its odor was "like that of an ancient Egyptian tomb."[2] The cylinders were scrolls of leather, that is, of a coarse kind of parchment, on which the Bedouins could see a strange writing. When they and others to whom they had told their secret revisited the cave, they found yet more scrolls, altogether eleven, representing six "books." After various misadventures, some came into the hands of Mar Samuel, the Syrian Orthodox Metropolitan, at the Monastery of St. Mark in Jerusalem, and others into the hands of the late Professor Eleazar L. Sukenik of the Hebrew University; all are now owned by the University. Professor Sukenik and scholars from the American Schools of Oriental Research were the first to study them.

Because of war conditions, it was not until February 1949 that Père Roland de Vaux, O.P., of the Ecole Biblique et Archéologique Française and Mr. Lankester Harding of the Jordan Department of Antiquities were able to explore the Qumran region scientifically. Thus far, whether by scientists or by Bedouin shepherds, in the Qumran region alone ten more caves have been uncovered yielding jars, broken pottery, phylacteries, and tens of thousands of manuscript fragments.[3] Approximately one-third of these manuscripts are biblical, representing all the books of the Old Testament with the possible exception of Esther. In addition there are fragments from the Septuagint; scriptural commentaries; apocryphal works like Enoch, the Testament of Levi, or the Book of Jubilees; a page of "Testimonies," that is, of messianic passages from the Old Testament; liturgical texts; and others, above all, duplicates of the so-called Damascus Document[4] and of books found in what has since come to be known as Qumran Cave One.

The original find in Cave One was two scrolls of Isaiah, only one

2. G. M. Crowfoot, "The Linen Textiles," in D. Barthélemy, O.P., and J. T. Milik, *Discoveries in the Judaean Desert,* Vol. I, *Qumran Cave I* (Oxford: Clarendon Press, 1955), p. 18.

3. There are also the finds from an underground chamber at Khirbet al-Mird, on a hilltop a few miles west of the Dead Sea, and those from the caverns of the Wady Murabaat in the heart of the desert. Valued though these discoveries are, they are outside the scope of this essay.

4. Late in the nineteenth century, there were found in a Cairo *genizah* (a synagogue storeroom for religious writings too worn for further use, too sacred to be

complete; an Aramaic paraphrase of Genesis interwoven with legends; a strange commentary on the book of Habakkuk, which relates its prophecies to a mysterious figure called the Teacher of Justice, to the men of his community, and to his enemies; a document named by Professor Sukenik *Serek̠ ha-Yah̠ad,* the Rule of the Community, by which the followers of the Teacher of Justice lived, commonly referred to as the Manual of Discipline; a collection of hymns modeled after the psalms and beginning, most of them, "I thank thee, O Lord," whence the name given to them, *Megillat ha-Hodayot,* the Thanksgiving Scroll; and, finally, directions, hardly to be taken literally, for fighting what seems to be the impending battle at the end of days, though its military background may be the Maccabean struggle or may perhaps reflect Roman army organization: the War of the Sons of Light with the Sons of Darkness, in which the Sons of Light will be victorious by the power of the great hand of God.[5]

While exploring Cave One, Père de Vaux and Mr. Harding were led to investigate Khirbet Qumran, which for decades had been as-

---

discarded) two incomplete copies of an unknown work. Published by the late Solomon Schechter in 1910 under the title *Fragments of a Zadokite Work,* it speaks of the sons of Zadok "who went out from the land of Judah and sojourned in the land of Damascus" (vi 5), and hence is also known as the Damascus Document. Whether "Damascus" here is symbolic (see Am 5:27) or literal; whether the migration took place at the Community's founding or later; and whether the Document thus represents an early or late stage of the Community's history—questions impossible to answer definitively in the present state of our knowledge—it is obvious that the Damascus Document is intimately connected with the Community of Qumran.

5. Unless the context makes clear which work is intended, the Scrolls will be referred to by the symbols now generally accepted: 1QS = Rule of the Community; 1QH = Thanksgiving Hymns; 1QM = War of the Sons of Light Against the Sons of Darkness; 1QpHab = Commentary on Habakkuk; and CD = Damascus Document. (1Q indicates a scroll found in Qumran Cave One and C one from the Cairo *genizah,* while the remaining letters are derived from the Hebrew titles of the works.) A number of minor problems about the Scrolls will be barely touched on in this essay, and others not mentioned at all; space also forbids the listing of the vast literature on them. A masterfully balanced discussion of many such questions is *The Dead Sea Scrolls* by Millar Burrows (New York: Viking, 1955), a work not only of sound scholarship but of literary quality. A pioneer study of particular value is *Les Manuscrits du Désert de Juda* by Géza Vermès (Tournai: Desclée, 1953), for, more than other works on the Scrolls, it relates them to their general Jewish background. Both works contain excellent bibliographies. Père Vermès's book, with some supplementary material, will be published in English in the fall of 1956 by Desclée Co., Inc., New York, under the title *Discovery in the Judean Desert: The Dead Sea Scrolls and Their Meaning.* I am indebted also to Father John F. McConnell, M.M., for making available to me an unpublished manuscript of his, and to Father Roland E. Murphy, O. Carm., for many valued suggestions.

sumed to be nothing but the ruins of a military outpost of Roman times. Several seasons of excavation have shown, however, that caves and ruins belong together, for a monastic establishment has been brought to light which can have served only such a community as the Scrolls bespeak. While in all likelihood the "monks" slept in caves, huts, or tents near by, the unearthed monastery was the center of their common life. The main building of two stories has a fortified tower, a basement for storage, workshops, rooms for study, a large room which seems an assembly hall, another which is most likely a refectory with a reading stand, and by it a pantry containing over a thousand neatly stacked bowls. Interesting is a scriptorium with a plaster writing table more than five yards long, a companion bench, inkwells, one even having some dried ink in it, and shallow basins probably for the ritual washing of the hands required of those who copied sacred texts. No doubt, most of the manuscripts of the caves, if not all, were written here. Interesting, also, are the remains of a potter's shop, certainly the place where the jars for the Scrolls were made, for one just like them was found there. Uncovered too were kitchens, a mill, and a vast and elaborate water supply system with huge cisterns and an aqueduct from high in the Wady Qumran—a system necessary, of course, to sustain the physical life of the Community in the desert, though it may have served its spiritual life as well, so marked by various sacred cleansings. Then there is a large cemetery, with over a thousand austere and uniform tombs, suggesting the stern communal life of those buried there: "Here lie these warriors, these wrestlers of God, after the fierce struggle of their lives on earth!" [6]

In the ruins, coins were found at three different levels, representing three distinct eras: first, from the start of the Hasmonean dynasty to the first years of the reign of Herod the Great (135–31 B.C.), then from the reign of Herod Archelaus to the first Jewish Revolt against the Romans (4 B.C.–A.D. 68), and finally from after the fall of Jerusalem till the second Jewish Revolt (A.D. 70–135). Hence it can safely be concluded that the men of Qumran built their monastery in the desert not long after 135 B.C., and that they remained there either till Herod the Great drove them out or till the earthquake of 31 B.C.

6. This is one of Dupont-Sommer's inimitable phrases from *The Jewish Sect of Qumran and the Essenes,* trans. R. D. Barnett (London: Vallentine, Mitchell & Co., 1954), p. 7. No matter how strongly one may disagree at times with his interpretations, one cannot but pay tribute to his eloquence.

severely damaged this their center. In any case, around the year A.D. 1, the Community returned to the site, restored its monastery, and resumed its life there, which flourished till A.D. 69, when both monastery and community were brought, most likely by the Tenth Roman Legion, to a violent end. Charred palm timbers, which had borne the roof of reed and marl, a layer of ashes, and some iron arrowheads tell silently of the destruction wrought, while the jars in the caves near by show that the end did not come on the men of Qumran unawares. Before they fled or were slain by the Romans, they took that which was most sacred to them, their library, hiding it with reverence and care to save it from desecration. Afterwards—during the third period represented by the coins found in the ruins—Qumran was no longer a monastic house. It quartered first a small Roman military post; abandoned by the Romans, it was briefly occupied by the men of the second Revolt; after the Revolt failed, it remained desolate.

The evidence of the coins, and that of the pottery and potsherds found in the ruins—to ceramic experts, earthenware speaks almost as clearly as if the period of its making were stamped on it in numbers—are supported by what can be learned from the Scrolls themselves about their age: from, for instance, the way the letters are shaped and occasionally connected, from spelling and grammar; also from the cloth wrappings, the fiber used, and how it was spun and woven; and from the jars, their material and style. All these indicate that it was between 100 B.C. and A.D. 50 that those Scrolls which speak of the Community of Qumran were written, or at least copied. But their composition must be dated somewhat earlier, for their historical allusions, cryptic though they are, seem to point to a period from 175 to 40 B.C.

As the Scrolls disclose their age, they open, Professor Sukenik said, "a new door to knowledge of the spiritual life of [the Jewish] people in the last few centuries before the destruction of the Second Temple." [7] They tell of a spirituality that had been largely forgotten or suppressed by rabbinical Judaism, and so reveal Jewish life to have been much richer, more varied, more complex, than has been realized by most. Here was a people at a turning point, a land full of tensions, astir with emotions and passions roused to such a peak that one almost hears the cry for a new outpouring of the Spirit. Thus the Scrolls

7. E. L. Sukenik, ed., *The Dead Sea Scrolls of the Hebrew University* (Jerusalem: Magnes Press, 1955), p. 27.

shed not a little light on "Christian beginnings, in making better known the religious milieu in which the word of Christ sounded and in which the Church grew." [8] In shedding such light, they are a fresh witness to the oneness of the Judaeo-Christian tradition: no abrupt departure but a fulfillment leads from the Israel of old to the Church. Christian monasticism, for example, has been thought by some to be an instance of the Church's frequent adoption of what is good outside her walls, while others have deprecated it as a "pagan accretion"; now that the Bedouin shepherds have broken the two thousand years' silence of the Community of Qumran, it is clear that Christian monasticism is deeply rooted in the Israel of old.

CROSSCURRENTS IN JUDAEA

IT IS true: monasticism in general is a response to one of the deepest natural religious impulses, and can therefore be found in various religious traditions. Yet it was not imported into the Judaea of old from outside; on the contrary, the least glance at postexilic history bears out that it arose as a protest against the pagan influences of Hellenism. For a long time after the return of the first captives from Babylon in 538 B.C., the fervent little nation, gathered around the restored Temple, enjoyed relative tranquillity. Nor was the peace disturbed when Alexander the Great made his mighty conquests, or when, shortly afterwards, in 320 B.C., the Ptolemies turned Judaea into part of their Egyptian empire. Since they did not interfere with the Jewish way of life, there was no movement toward independence, no rancor that the chosen people should inhabit but a small portion of the promised land and be under the yoke of the nations. In 198 B.C., the domination of Judaea shifted from the Ptolemies to the Seleucids, the most outspokenly hellenistic dynasty of the Near East, with their capital in Antioch. At first there was little apprehension among the Jews, for their own high priest remained their head and spokesman, indeed for all practical purposes their ruler, and the Law of Moses remained law.

But stirring times were ahead: foreign rule and trade soon brought in Greek ways. Many rich families and young people were drawn by the theater and the gymnasium, by the plays, the contests, and the races which enlivened Alexandria and Antioch. They would have been

8. De Vaux, *La Vie Intellectuelle* (April 1951), p. 70.

happy to see Jerusalem become like those two gay cities and to see
sport go hand in hand with worship. Jewish life was reserved and
centered in the home; to have it yield to the Greek way, free and
social, lived in street and market place, was the desire of many. Indeed, not a few cultured priests thought the time had come for Israel
to fall in line with the fashion of the day. Let us make terms with the
heathens, let us throw in our lot with them, was the slogan of the
Hellenists (1 Mac 1:12, 16). To strengthen their influence in the
land, they intrigued against the devout high priest Onias III till, in
174 B.C., his own brother Jeshua purchased the pontificate from the
foreign king by stealth and corruption. Though he went so far as to
change his name to Jason, his efforts to hellenize the people seem to
have lacked vigor. In any case, three years later, King Antiochus IV,
known as Epiphanes, the "Illustrious," transferred the pontificate to a
higher bidder. Menelaus, who was not of the Zadokite family and perhaps not even of the priestly tribe, was in every way the king's creature,
all unworthy, with, as Scripture describes it, "the mind of a cruel tyrant
and the rage of a savage beast" (2 Mac 4:25). He stole from the Temple treasure; later he made himself the king's guide in the pillaging of
the Holy Place and his accomplice in the massacre of Jerusalem. Again
at the instigation of Menelaus, the king struck at the heart of the
people: circumcision, the Sabbath, the dietary laws were banned under the severest penalties; worship in the Temple was abolished; the
sacred scrolls of the Torah were burned. To climax all this, in 167 B.C.
there was placed on the great altar of the Temple another altar, dedicated to Zeus Olympios—"the abominable idol of desolation" (1 Mac
1:57).

Years before these frightful events, there had been the beginning
of a religious revival, a new awareness of the unique call of the chosen
people. Jesus ben Sirach, for instance, who wrote his wise counsels between 200 and 170 B.C., had not acquired, despite all his wide travels,
a taste for the new ways. Alive not only to the past grandeur of Israel,
he saw the hidden splendor of Jerusalem. To him Zion was the earthly
habitation of Wisdom, and the Law its wondrous embodiment (Ecclus
24:10; 19:17). There were others, like him in love with the Covenant
and the Law, and thus opposed to the manners of Greece. But some
must have felt that opposition was not enough and therefore banded
together in companies, *ḥaburot.* These brotherhoods may have sprung

up more or less spontaneously, as like-minded men—without, however, leading a common life—sought to encourage one another in the
rigorous observance of their religious duties, especially that of legal
purity. Food, clothing, the very walls of a house, indeed much of daily
life, were subject to the demands of the Law. Thus it was almost impossible to obey it perfectly unless social contacts were severely restricted. How natural, then, to draw closer to those whose companionship was permitted and even helpful. While the *ḥaburot* met a concrete religious need, they were at the same time an expression of the
lasting communal character of Jewish piety.[9]

How soon did the religious impetus which led some to form such
companies lead others to a more complete withdrawal and the establishment of the common life outside the Holy City? We do not know.
However, at the time of the great crisis under Antiochus Epiphanes in
167 B.C., there were "many that sought after judgment and justice
[and, with their families,] went down into the desert" (1 Mac 2:29).
When the aged Mattathias, the father of the Maccabees, cried out that
although all nations obeyed the edict of the king, he and his sons and
his brethren would not obey but would walk in the Covenant of their
fathers (1 Mac 2:19–22), there were the *Ḥasidim,* the "Pious," who
emerged from their caves in the wilderness and rallied to the Maccabean resistance.

But one would misunderstand the Maccabean resistance were one
to think of it as only the valiant struggle of the chosen people against
a pagan oppressor bent on stamping out the true faith. The Maccabean
resistance was no less a civil war, for the efforts of many leading Jews
to plunge little Judaea into the "main stream of civilization" had a
large part in bringing things to a head. It was these who urged Antiochus IV to repeal ordinances which permitted the Jewish people to
live by the Mosaic Law. It was these who proposed building a gymnasium at Jerusalem, and then built it right beside the Temple, lest
the priestly novices lose time in answering the call of the discus. Was
it their doing too that incense was burned in honor of Zeus Olympios
all over Judaea, that the pig was offered in sacrifice, and that the faithful were required to partake of its abominable flesh? Probably not. It
is hard to say how far the hellenistic party was prepared to go; but they
had started a current, and perhaps it became stronger than they had

9. See Vermès, *op. cit.,* pp. 53–57.

expected. In any case, once the Maccabees rose against Antiochus, they were also at war with the Hellenists. It is to these or to somewhat later sympathizers with Greek ways that one of the Qumran psalms may refer:

> *They seek thee with a double heart*
> *and they have not remained faithful to thy truth;*
> *a root bearing gall and wormwood is in their thoughts.*
> *In the stubborness of their hearts they explore*
> *and seek thee among the idols. . . .*
> *With barbarous lips and a foreign tongue,*
> *[they] speak to thy people*
> *that by deceit they may make vain all their works.*
>
> (iv 10–13) [10]

THE TEACHER OF JUSTICE

UNITY among those who were faithful to, and fought for, the heritage of the fathers did not last long. Even during the course of the resistance, the Maccabees and their supporters did not always see eye to eye; relations were often strained between the worldly and power-seeking heirs of Mattathias and the priests among the *Ḥasidim*. A rift was sure to come. When it came, there stood on one side first Jonathan the Maccabee, who, in 152 B.C., took the high-priesthood, indeed took it at the hands of Alexander Balas, a heathen adventurer plotting for the Syrian throne and thus eager for allies; and then Jonathan's brother Simon, who, a decade later, showed not the least scruple about letting the people confer the great priestly office not only on himself but

10. All quotations from the first Hymns to be published are in the translation of George S. Glanzman, S.J., "Sectarian Psalms from the Dead Sea," *Theological Studies*, XIII, 4 (December 1952). For ease of identification, I am preserving his numeration. Virtually all quotations from the other Scrolls follow the excellent translation of Dr. Burrows. Again for ease of identification, I am adopting, wherever possible, particularly in the case of the Damascus Document, the numeration of Père Vermès. The most complete English translation of the Scrolls is Theodor H. Gaster's *The Dead Sea Scriptures* (Garden City, N. Y.: Doubleday, 1956). It is in many ways unique, impressive, and always worth consulting. Even when one disagrees with his interpretation—as, for instance, when he thinks "Teacher of Justice" to be the title not of the Community's one founder but of a number of "correct expositors" of the Law; or when he sees the spirituality of Qumran in terms of the mystical tradition of a Tauler or a St. Teresa; or, again, when he connects the men of Qumran with a nature-mysticism which is hardly Jewish; most of all, when he thinks that the Epistle of St. James "bespeaks the standpoint of men who were neither normative Jews nor normative Christians" (pp. 5, 8, 6, 15)—even when one disagrees with him, one respects him and his true learning.

on his family, the Hasmoneans, with whom it was to remain for more than a century. On the other side of the rift, there may have stood a handful of priests led by that impressive figure who, though without name, dominates the Scrolls of the Desert. It may be that this little group of priests, by calling themselves "sons of Zadok, keepers of the Covenant" (1QS v 2), wished to protest against the Hasmonean usurpation of the high-priesthood, which, since the days of David and Solomon, had come down from Zadok in an uninterrupted line. Such is the intriguing thesis of Père Vermès. Professor Rowley, however, and others with him, identify the Teacher of Justice with Onias III, the high priest deposed by Jason and slain in 171 B.C. by an accomplice of Menelaus. An even greater number of scholars today prefer to see the foe of the Teacher of Justice in the Hasmonean priest and king, Alexander Jannaeus (103–76 B.C.), whose abundance of vices may well have earned him the title of "Wicked Priest," given by the Scrolls to the Teacher's chief opponent.

These are three of the most prominent theories on the Teacher of Justice, and there are others. Will we ever know with certainty who he was and exactly when he began his work? It would seem that the beginning of the Damascus Document offers us a clue:

And now listen, all you who know righteousness and understand the works of God. For He has a controversy with all flesh, and will execute judgment upon all who despise Him. For when those who forsook Him trespassed, He hid His face from Israel and from His sanctuary, and gave them up to the sword; but when He remembered the covenant of the ancients, He left a remnant to Israel and did not give them up to destruction. And in the period of the wrath—three hundred and ninety years, when He gave them into the hand of Nebuchadnezzar, king of Babylon —He visited them and caused to sprout from Israel and Aaron a root of planting to inherit His land and to grow fat in the goodness of His soil. Then they perceived their iniquity and knew that they were guilty men; yet they were like men blind and groping for the way for twenty years. And God observed their works, that they sought Him with a perfect heart; and He raised up for them a Teacher of Righteousness to lead them in the way of His heart.

(i 1–11)

This is how Dr. Burrows renders this eloquent text. Most others translate: "In the period of wrath, three hundred and ninety years *after* He gave them into the hand of Nebuchadnezzar." Even so, it may be doubted that the numbers 390 and 20 are to be read literally. It might well be that the first, obviously taken from Ez 4:5, is symbolic, and that the other is a round or approximate figure, thus leaving us with no more definite answer than before.

Perhaps this is as it ought to be. For what, among other things, distinguishes the Community of Qumran from the Church is that it is almost all expectation: its eyes are on the judgment to come, when God will punish the wicked and comfort His own. Such looking to the future is, of course, very much part of the New Testament too, but there prayer for the kingdom to come is neighbor to prayer for bread for the day. There the yearning for the end of time is side by side with an infinite patience, with a wholehearted attention to little children, even to a lost coin, with a tenderness toward the present moment. Again, one of the characteristic features of the Scrolls is their deliberately enigmatic air, their veiling of persons and dates, while the way of the Gospels is exactly the opposite. The evangelists took delight in being specific, in tying events of sacred history to those of profane history: Jesus was born at the time of a census that Caesar Augustus' passion for statistics had ordered for his empire and vassal states; He was crucified when Pontius Pilate was governor of Palestine, by then a province of the empire. It was not for the sake of embellishment that Luke told who was emperor, who governor, who the tetrarchs, who the high priests, when "the word of God came to John" (3:1–2), nor was it love of ornament, rather a clear vision of sacred history, that made Luke and John give the long line of the ancestors of the Christ.

No such genealogy is given for him who bears the exalted title of *moreh ha-zedek,* "Teacher of Justice." We know neither his origin nor his name.[11] Indeed, we know little for certain beyond that he was a

11. It is but untrammeled lyricism when Dupont-Sommer writes: "Never is he called by his own name. If he is thus anonymous, it is because of the intense veneration of which the person of the Master had become the object: his name was unpronounceable, like the name of Yahweh" (*The Dead Sea Scrolls,* trans. E. M. Rowley, Oxford: Blackwell, 1952, p. 33). Not only is Dupont-Sommer here carried away by his imagination; he is in outright opposition to the text of the Scrolls, which, in their every column, declare the unique majesty of God. On the other hand, Allegro, writing with the flair of a historical novelist, not the soberness of a scholar, tells us that the Teacher's "actual name, real or assumed, seems to have been Zadok." Allegro does not stop with this. He knows too that by his men the Teacher was "regarded as the true High Priest of Israel," and that, in the eyes of his enemies, he merited "a particularly dreadful punishment. . . . This was execu-

priest and that his followers believed God had made known to him "all the mysteries of the words of His servants, the prophets" (1QpHab vii 5). Thus they looked upon him as their master, the true interpreter of the Law (CD vi 7; vii 18). The Psalms of Qumran, most likely, reflect his spirituality, while some, perhaps many, of his teachings are embodied in the Damascus Document and in the Rule, and his passionate partisan exegesis in the Habakkuk Commentary. When Habakkuk is told that if what God wishes to show him tarries, he should wait for it, because it would surely come (2:3), the Teacher of Justice and his disciples took it to mean that since the end is delayed and the last days are stretching out—stretching out even longer than the prophets thought—, they must be "doers of the Law, whose hands do not grow slack from the service of the truth" (1QpHab vii 11–12). Not the least significance the Teacher of Justice attached to the "service of the truth" was the most rigorous practice of all the ordinances of ritual purity, "to make a separation between the unclean and the clean, and to make men know the difference between the holy and the common . . ." (CD vi 17–18). To separate clean and unclean included withdrawal into the wilderness, away from all those who would not heed his words and preferred wickedness to justice, away from the strife-torn Holy City in order to lean "upon God during the period when Israel transgressed and polluted the sanctuary" (CD xx 23). So revered, then, was the Teacher and his teaching by his followers that they thought of all who were outside his Community as unclean, rebellious, and lost, and were convinced that they themselves would be rescued from judgment because of their fidelity to, and their trust in, him.[12]

tion by crucifixion, or the hanging of a man alive from a stake until he died of starvation and exposure. Denied the decency of burial, the body was allowed to hang there until it rotted. . . ." (*The Dead Sea Scrolls,* Harmondsworth: Penguin Books, 1956, pp. 95, 98, 99.)

12. Too much has been made of "God will deliver all the doers of the Law in the house of Judah from the house of judgment for the sake of their labor [or: their sufferings] and their faith in the Teacher of Justice" (1QpHab viii 1–3). Some, following Dupont-Sommer, have interpreted this sentence as if the Teacher of Justice had been regarded by his men in very much the same way that Christ is believed in by His Church. Only recently Charles T. Fritsch wrote: "Salvation for the members of the Qumran community came through faith in the person of the Teacher of Righteousness. Therefore, the Teacher of Righteousness, as the object of saving faith, must have been regarded as more than human" (*The Qumran Community: Its History and Scrolls,* New York: Macmillan, 1956, p. 82). This, I regret to say, is reading into the text, not out of it, for all the text seems to imply is that the men of Qumran felt sure of their salvation because they trusted the Teacher of Justice and obeyed his interpretation of the Law as the only true one.

A man sent by God, the "star out of Jacob" who has come to read and teach the law aright (CD vii 18–19)—such was the Teacher to his "partisans" (1QpHab ix 10); but not to his enemies. And enemies he had many: the Scrolls thunder at the House of Absalom, the "Man of Scorn, who led Israel astray," the Man of the Lie, the "Preacher of the Lie, who enticed many to build a city of delusion in blood and to establish a congregation of falsehood," above all at the Wicked Priest, full of abominations and impurity, who "forsook God and betrayed the statutes because of wealth" [13]—all names concealing, rather than revealing, identities. One of the great issues between these enemies and the Teacher was the liturgical calendar; this indeed was the issue which accounted for so much of Qumran's unbending opposition to the official priesthood and to the rest of the Jewish people, and which therefore gave the Community what is often referred to as its "sectarian" character. God's holy Sabbaths and His glorious feasts were among the hidden things "in which all Israel [had] gone astray," the Damascus Document accused (iii 14). There is a high probability that for centuries, at least since the return from the Babylonian Captivity, the priests of the Temple had used a solar calendar, which so fixed the feasts and sacred seasons that they always fell in the same parts of the year and on the same days of the week. In any case, one of the outrages of Antiochus Epiphanes was his attempt "to change times and laws" (Dan 7:25); yet, in spite of the Maccabean resistance, the Hellenists seem to have had their way, so that the Temple came to follow a lunar calendar, which disturbed the fixed circle of seasons and feasts.[14] This defection from the ancient priestly usage was a crime

---

13. 1QpHab v 9–12; CD i 14–15; 1QpHab ii 1–2; x 9–13; viii 8–13.

14. The Teacher's dispute with the Temple, like other historical disputes over liturgical calendars, may seem to many an argument over trifles—only because nowadays we are so little aware of time as a token and bearer of grace. Yet the "Qumran calendar" is of the greatest importance, for it has prompted scholars to look once more at Enoch and the Book of Jubilees, which present the solar calendar as *the* ancient calendar of Israel and which were, incidentally, among the manuscripts in the Qumran library. This research has suggested a new solution to the problem of the chronology of the Passion, a problem which has always posed considerable difficulty and on which exegetes have long labored. According to the synoptic Gospels, Christ celebrated His Supper, which He had so desired to eat with His disciples before His suffering was to begin, as a paschal meal on the eve of the Passover, "on the first day of the Unleavened Bread" (Mt 26:17; Mk 14:12; cf. Lk 22:7). According to St. John's Gospel, it was on the eve of the Passover, on "the Preparation Day for the Passover" (19:14), that Christ was crucified, so that His Last Supper could not have been a paschal meal. At first sight these two

in the eyes of the Teacher, and he made his Community adhere to the solar pattern, with its round of "appointed seasons." "Not to transgress in any one of all the words of God in their periods; not to advance their times or postpone any of their appointed festivals; not to turn

accounts seem irreconcilable, for in the one Christ appears to have held His parting meal on the 14th of Nisan and to have been crucified on the 15th, while in the other He appears to have been crucified on the 14th. Again, the liturgical usage of the Church places Christ's Last Supper on Thursday, the day before He died, but nowhere is the New Testament this explicit. St. Paul, for instance, places the institution of the Eucharist "on the night in which He was betrayed" (1 Cor 11:23). If the Last Supper really took place on Thursday evening, it is hard, though by no means impossible, to picture how the few hours remaining till noon on Friday permitted all the events that intervened: the agony in the garden, the arrest, the interrogation by Annas, the session of the Sanhedrin under Caiphas, the accusation before Pilate, the appearance before Herod, the second arraignment before Pilate, the scourging and crowning with thorns, the carrying of the cross, and the crucifixion. Both difficulties have been pointed to repeatedly by those who would cast doubt on the authenticity of the Passion narrative; both, however, can be solved by the priestly calendar of Jubilees. While the official lunar calendar of the Temple let the 15th of Nisan fall on any day of the week, the priestly calendar, Père Barthélemy has shown, began each year on a Wednesday and hence had the 15th of Nisan (that is, the first month of the year) also always on a Wednesday, and the 14th of Nisan, the day of the Passover meal, always on a Tuesday. With this as her point of departure, and also with the help of what seems to be the oldest tradition in the Church on the events of Holy Week, in the *Didascalia* of the late second or early third century, Mlle. Jaubert has proposed a chronology of the Passion. In one of the reviews published by the Pontifical Biblical Institute, Father Vogt has found it "supported by the Gospels" and hence "worthy of every consideration." This is the chronology Mlle. Jaubert suggests: Christ ate the Last Supper on Tuesday evening, then went to the Garden of Olives, was arrested that night, and questioned by Annas, at cockcrow being led to the house of Caiphas. On Wednesday the Sanhedrin convened to judge the evidence against Him, and He was kept as a prisoner of the high priest. Early on Thursday morning the Sanhedrin met again to pass sentence; immediately afterwards, Christ was taken before Pilate and then sent to Herod. On His return, He remained a prisoner of the Roman governor and on Friday morning was arraigned again before him. That same morning Pilate had Him scourged; the high priest and the crowd demanded His death; Pilate yielded and condemned Him; He was led to Golgotha and nailed to the cross. Mlle. Jaubert's reconstruction leaves ample time for all the events of the Passion, makes them, indeed, even more vivid. Again, it not only reconciles the Synoptics and St. John but shows what appears to be a discrepancy to be instead full of meaning: Christ ate the Last Supper on the eve of Passover, the 14th of Nisan according to the *ancient* priestly calendar, and it was thus a true paschal meal. He was crucified on the eve of Passover, the 14th of Nisan according to the *official* calendar, and was thus Himself sacrificed as the true Pasch. Mlle. Jaubert's suggestion is one more sign that the discoveries of the Judaean desert, far from casting doubts on the Gospels, bear witness to their authenticity. See D. Barthélemy, O.P., "Notes en marge de publications récentes sur les manuscrits de Qumran," *Revue Biblique,* LIX, 2 (1952), pp. 200–201; A. Jaubert, "La Date de la dernière Cène," *Revue de l'Histoire des Religions,* CXLVI (1954), pp. 140–173; E. Vogt, S.J., "Antiquum kalendarium sacerdotale," *Biblica,* XXXVI, 3, (1955), pp. 403–408; "Dies ultimae coenae Domini," *ibid.,* pp. 408–413.

aside from His true statutes, going to the right or to the left," was an essential part of the Rule of Qumran (i 13–15).

This nonconformism of the Righteous Teacher and his men must have been felt as a constant reproach by Jerusalem. Thus the Habakkuk Commentary tells in its cryptic way of one *Yom Kippur—Yom Kippur* according to the Community's calendar but not according to the Temple's—when the Wicked Priest, in his furious pursuit of the Teacher, insulted him and his followers, trying to make them profane this Day of Awe:

> The Wicked Priest . . . persecuted the Teacher of Rightousness in order to confound him in the indignation of his wrath, wishing to banish him; and at the time of their festival of rest, the Day of Atonement, he appeared to them to confound them and to make them stumble on the day of fasting, their Sabbath of rest.
>
> (xi 4–8)

> For the wrong done to the Teacher of Righteousness and the men of his party, God delivered [the Wicked Priest] into the hand of his enemies, afflicting him with a destroying scourge, in bitterness of soul, because he acted wickedly against His elect.
>
> (ix 9–12)

Falling into the hands of his enemies was the fate of the Wicked Priest, so the Scrolls tell; but the Teacher's death, like his name and birth, they leave entirely obscure. Some scholars have suggested that he met a violent end as martyr for his cause. No question but that this is possible, even probable when one remembers those turbulent times; yet it remains pure conjecture, and to assert it as if it were sure is to wrench the Qumran texts. They speak of no such martyrdom; on the contrary, twice they speak of the "gathering in of the Teacher of the Community" (CD xix 35—xx 1; xx 14), implying thus a natural death. For when the peaceful deaths of Abraham, Isaac, and Jacob are related, the patriarchs are said to have been "gathered" to their kin (Gen 25:8; 35:29; 49:33). While Jesus' death and resurrection are told in the New Testament not once but a hundred times, while Peter and John "cannot but speak of what [they] have seen and heard" (Ac 4:20), while Paul must "preach a crucified Christ" (1 Cor 1:23; cf. 2:2), the men of Qumran chose to be silent about their Master's end.

THE COMMUNITY

Whenever and however the Teacher of Justice came to die, he left behind "witnesses for justice," men who, by their austere lives, wished to "make atonement for the land and render to the wicked their recompense" (1QS viii 6–7). The firm purpose of the "monks of Qumran" cannot but have been his legacy, and their marvelously knit organization, even if it should not be fully his work, is a sign of his genius.[15]

The Community, *yaḥad,* was composed of "Aaron," priests and Levites, and "Israel," laymen: the Rule speaks of it as "set apart, a house of holiness for Aaron . . . a house of community for Israel" (ix 5–6). Further, the lay members were divided and subdivided into "thousands and hundreds and fifties and tens" (ii 21–22), names which could hardly all have represented actual numbers but which recalled how Moses divided the people on its wanderings through the desert (Ex 18:21).[16] The smallest group, that of ten, was, of course, the traditional *minyan* required to this day for corporate Jewish worship. While all members had a voice in the assembly, or "chapter" (to use the vocabulary of Catholic monastic life), there was a definite order of precedence among them. When they assembled, each had his assigned station: the priests were seated first, the elders second, and then the rest each in his order. Nor was any member permitted to speak ahead of the one enrolled before him or until his brother had finished speaking (vi 8–11). It is not entirely clear whether ranks were assigned once for all, or whether, at the great annual assembly, they

15. A number of writers refer to the men of Qumran as the "Essene Community" or the "Essene Order," thus giving the impression that the partisans of the Teacher of Justice, known to us through the Scrolls of the Judaean desert, and the Essenes, described by Pliny, Philo, and Josephus, are identical. No doubt the similarities are abundant, but there are also definite differences. Hence, if "Essenes" is a generic name embracing a variety of related groups devoted to the ascetic life, the Qumranites may be said to be among them. But it will not do to use "Essene" as a synonym for "Qumranite."

16. The safest estimate seems to be that the men of Qumran never numbered more than some two hundred at a time. It is interesting that both Philo and Josephus put the number of the Essenes at about four thousand. Furthermore, while Philo describes them as inhabiting many cities, villages, and settlements, and Josephus speaks of them as dwelling in no one city but rather in every city, concerning the Community we know only of the establishment at Qumran and of a possible sojourn in Damascus. But it is quite likely that it had what could be called outposts, for the Rule speaks of "all their dwellings" (vi 2) and the Damascus Document of "camps" and of "the cities of Israel" (xii 23, 19).

were assigned with regard to conduct during the year past. In any case, the men of Qumran were convinced that without order there could be no true union, no lasting fellowship:

> Let every man of Israel know his appointed position in the community of God for the eternal council. And none shall be abased below his appointed position or exalted above his allotted place; for they shall all be in true community and good humility and loyal love and righteous thought, each for his fellow in the holy council, and they shall be sons of the eternal assembly.
>
> (ii 22–25)

It belonged to the priests, who ranked above all other members, to stand guard over the covenant and to seek God's will for the Community (v 9). Only they, the sons of Aaron, had authority to administer matters of law and property; their judgment shaped the Community's every regulation (ix 7–8). Doubtless, too, it was from the priests that the "Overseer," *mebakker,* was taken, who was probably the superior over all. (Some authors think there were several overseers, with various duties.) In the council of twelve (or possibly fifteen), whose function seems to have been doctrinal rather than administrative or judicial, three were priests. Of them the Rule demanded that they be perfect in all that had been revealed of the whole Torah, and this was the standard they were to set:

> To practice truth and righteousness and justice and loyal love and walking humbly each with his neighbor, to preserve faithfulness in the land with sustained purpose and a broken spirit, and to make amends for iniquity by the practice of justice and the distress of tribulation, and to walk with all by the standard of truth and by the regulation of the time.
>
> (viii 1–4)

All the professed members, *rabbim,* "the many" (which Dr. Burrows translates as "the masters" and Père Vermès as "the great ones"), had a share in the government of the Community, especially when it came to the admittance of recruits or the punishment of members. Offenses over which the professed sat in judgment were, for instance, lying about one's wealth; speaking in anger against one of the priests; answering one's neighbor with a stiff neck, that is, with arrogance, so as to belittle the dignity of his rank; denouncing him without cause; speaking bitterly against him; or bearing a grudge without reason.

Respect for one's confrere was cardinal to the life of Qumran, as it is to that of any monastic community, and so was obedience to its laws. Hence any act of disobedience called for some punishment, but the man who murmured against the authority of the Community, thus rebelling against its very foundation, was dismissed once for all (vi 24—vii 25).

To become "a community in Torah and in property" (v 2), all professed members received the same teaching, followed the same practices, shared their goods in common, and took their food at a common table. "Together they shall eat, and together they shall worship, and together they shall counsel" (vi 2–3). About their common meal, which bound them together and which they held sacred, the Rule has this to say: "When they set the table to eat, or the wine to drink, the priest shall stretch out his hand first to pronounce a blessing with the first portion of the bread and the wine" (vi 4–5).[17] As men of wisdom, the members of the Community were told to pray at the sun's rising, at its height, and at its setting; or, in the language of the Rule, "at the beginning of the dominion of light, through its circuit, and at its ingathering to its decreed dwelling." They were to bless their Maker also at the beginning of months, seasons, and years, at their middle, and at their end; at the time of sowing, ripening, and reaping; and on all the holy days and in all the holy years "in their fixed order" (ix 26—x 8). There is no mention in the Rule of sacrificial worship, probably because the Community had broken off all relations with the Temple, profaned, as they held, by a corrupt priesthood.[18] But till the time came when the Temple would be clean again, life at Qumran was not without offerings:

> *As long as I exist a decree engraved shall be on my tongue*
> *for fruit of praise and for a gift of my lips.*
> *I will sing with knowledge,*

17. The Hebrew word here rendered as "wine" is *tirosh*. Père Vermès points out that while in biblical Hebrew *tirosh* does mean "wine" or, possibly, "new wine," later Hebrew used it rather of unfermented grape juice, "must." He wonders whether this may not mean that the Qumranites, like the Essenes of Josephus's description, abstained from wine (*op. cit.*, pp. 60–61).

18. The Rule's silence on the sacrifices the Torah enjoined on Israel by no means implies contempt. On the contrary, the War Scroll prepared the Community for the restoration of the Temple worship, with its burnt offerings, its sacrifices, the pleasant odor of incense, and the sons of Zadok ministering in the sanctuary again (ii 1–6).

and all my music shall be for the glory of God;
my lyre and harp shall be for His holy fixed order,
and the flute of my lips I will raise in His just circle.

(x 8–9)

Such was the desire of the men of Qumran. Another outstanding feature of their life was the Community vigil, keeping "watch together a third of all the nights of the year"; it was probably in three shifts that they read aloud from Scripture, searched for the right interpretation of the Law, and recited the blessings in common. In each "ten," one was required by the Rule to devote himself entirely, day and night, to the study of the Torah, but not for himself alone, rather that all might be aided in perfection (vi 6–8). Probably this searcher was expected to discover hidden meanings and reveal them to his fellows.

When a candidate "offered himself from Israel to be added" to the Community of Qumran, it was the prerogative and duty of the "Supervisor," *pakid,* to examine him "as to his understanding and his works" (vi 13–14). If he was ready to bear the yoke of communal discipline and "not to turn away from following [God] because of any dread or terror or trial" no matter how long the dominion of Belial lasted (i 17–18), he was admitted to the covenant, that is, to the Community, in a solemn ceremony. First priests and Levites praised the God of deliverance, hailing the great deeds of His fidelity, and all those who were passing into the covenant said: "Amen! Amen!" Then the priests recounted God's mighty works and His steadfast love and mercy toward His people, while the Levites told the iniquities of the sons of Israel, their transgressions, their sins. Whereupon those entering made their confession:

We have committed iniquity, we have transgressed, we have sinned, we have done evil, we and our fathers before us, in walking contrary to the statutes of truth; but righteous is God, and true is His judgment on us and on our fathers; and the mercy of His steadfast love He has bestowed upon us from everlasting to everlasting.[19]

19. This confession is reminiscent of one of the confessions used to this day on *Yom Kippur.* The liturgical formula "from everlasting to everlasting" is prescribed in the Mishnah, as Père Vermès (*op. cit.,* p. 137) has noted. "At the conclusion of the Benedictions said in the Temple," the Mishnah states, "they used at first to say simply 'forever' [in Hebrew *l'olam,* which can also mean 'for the world']. When the Sadducees perverted their ways and asserted that there was only one world, it was ordained that the response should be 'from everlasting to ever-

At the end the candidates were blessed, but if there was anyone among them who entered while keeping "the idols of his heart," shamming conversion, he was cursed with a terrible curse (i 18—ii 18).

Everyone thus accepted was a postulant until the professed, if satisfied with his progress and promise, voted to admit him to the novitiate. During its first year, he was instructed in the Community practices, without being allowed, however, to take part in the common purificatory rites. Nor could he hand over his property, for both he and it were still profane. At the end of this first year, the professed decided whether the novice should draw near or draw away. If they again voted in his favor, he was advanced to the second year, during which the ritual washings were open to him but not the common table. Now he handed over his possessions to the treasurer, but they were kept apart from the Community's property, to be given back to him if he failed to be admitted to full membership. With the expiration of the second year, the novice became a "professed monk"; he was given his assigned position among his brethren for the study of the Torah, for his part in their judgments, their sacred cleansings, and their meals (vi 15–23). Without restriction he shared in the common life, which embodied the perennial monastic ideal of *Ora et labora*. Beside prayers and sacred studies, there was manual work: some would have been assigned to the scriptorium, others to domestic tasks, again others to farming or to herding sheep and goats near by, yet others to the repair of roofs and cisterns.

At first sight this common life would seem to have excluded marriage entirely, for in the Rule as we know it there is no mention of women, and the hope of the Qumranites, as "sons of truth," was to "bring forth seed with all eternal blessings and everlasting joy" (iv 6–7). The Damascus Document, however, speaks of members who "according to the order of the earth . . . take wives and beget sons" (vii 6–7). Again, in the Qumran cemetery a few skeletons of women have been found, and a fragment from Qumran Cave One refers to the Congregation of Israel, to its families, and to the rearing of young people in harmony with the precepts of the covenant.[20] Probably, then,

lasting' [or 'from world to world']." Thus the liturgical formula proclaims the existence of two worlds, this and the next. (Ber. 54a; see *The Babylonian Talmud,* ed. I. Epstein, London: Soncino, 1948, *Berakoth,* p. 328.)

20. 1QSa i 4–16. On the relation of the "Congregation of Israel" to the Community, see Barthélemy and Milik, *op. cit.,* p. 108.

there were, in addition to an assembly of celibates, settlements of families; or there may have been married groups attached in some way to the Community much as, in Catholic religious life, friars have a Third Order Secular affiliated with the First Order.[21]

Beyond doubt, chastity was held in high honor at Qumran; more, it was deemed a singular mark of the men of God's lot. It was with this virtue in view that modesty was rigidly enforced by the Rule. The man who brought out his left hand from under his robe in order to gesticulate was punished with a fine of ten days. The man who laughed a loud and foolish laugh was punished for thirty days; in like manner the man who spit in the midst of his confreres or who uncovered his nakedness. He who indulged in idle chatter was punished with a fine of three months. Even more severe, six months, was the punishment of the man who walked naked before his fellows (vii 9, 12–15). The fine of so-and-so-many days or months was probably a limited fast, the offender being deprived of one-fourth of his food allowance (vi 25).

There were other infractions of the Rule which caused a member to lose his rights, for a time or for all time. In addition to the forfeiting of one-quarter of the food allotment, there was the temporary barring from the purificatory rites, from the meal, and probably from

21. One wonders whether some light is not cast on celibacy among the Qumranites by the injunction of the War Scroll that "no youth or woman shall enter the camps [of the sons of light] when they go forth from Jerusalem to go to battle until they return" (vii 3–4). They thought of themselves as God's vanguard in the eschatological war against the forces of darkness; as having Michael, Gabriel, and Raphael for helpers and all the holy angels at their side. Might it not be, then, that they felt obliged to what ascetic theology calls the "angelic life"? It is impossible to answer, but it is well worth noting that in the appendix to the English edition of his book (see also *Cahiers Sioniens,* IX, 1, March 1955, pp. 43–44), Père Vermès recalls the example of Moses, so revered by the men of Qumran as teacher and guide. The fifth chapter of Deuteronomy records that after God had made His Covenant and given the decalogue at Sinai, the people were commanded to return to their tents, but Moses was bid to stay by Him. In this the rabbis saw God's invitation to Moses to live a life of continence (Ex. R. 19:3; 46:3; cf. *Midrash Rabbah,* ed. H. Freedman and M. Simon, London: Soncino, 1939, III, 231, 529). Time and again Jewish tradition tells that he cut all earthly bonds and separated himself from his wife as a sacrifice to his sacred calling. For God had chosen him to be the singular recipient of His revelations and His messenger to the people; He had set him higher than the angels, showing him what is above and what is below, what was and what is to come; He had willed that he unite himself with His presence. See Louis Ginzberg, *The Legends of the Jews,* trans. H. Szold (Philadelphia: Jewish Publication Society of America, 1940), II, 316; III, 256, 258, 394; and the respective notes.

common prayers. Forever banished, never to return, was the man who pronounced the all-glorious, ineffable name of God; also he who, in the open or in secret, deliberately transgressed a commandment of the Law of Moses (vi 27—vii 2; viii 21–23). This penalty of permanent excommunication was a fearful thing, for it carried with it no release from obligations impossible to fulfill outside: since the excommunicated were not allowed to eat "unclean" food, and since most food other than the Community's was thought unclean, they could well die of starvation. Apart from this threat, the life of those at Qumran—a life separated from the wickedness they saw about them; a life minutely governed by statutes and the word of superiors; a life detached from worldly goods and human pleasures; a life foreshadowing the evangelical counsels of obedience, poverty, and chastity—was not easy. Père Vermès is right, then, when he says that "to share the lot of the 'sons of light,' courage was needed, sanctity, and perseverance." [22]

THE SPIRITUALITY OF QUMRAN

To SAY that Qumran called for sanctity is to ask what kind of sanctity it was, what the Community's idea of perfection. The very first impression is that the awe of God permeated its life, that the center of its thinking was He apart from whose will nothing is done, whose glory none can bear (1QS xi 17, 20). Eternal is His design, His the plan that shall stand, His heart's purpose that which shall abide unto victory, unto everlasting. He is an avenger of evil, full of "power and might and great wrath with flames of fire," yet there is with Him "longsuffering . . . and abundance of pardon to forgive those who turn from transgression" (CD ii 4–5). Stirred by the holiness of the Lord, the men of Qumran sang His praise and their gratitude:

> *Thanks be to God for His righteousness,*
> *to the Most High for His majesty!*
>
> (1QS xi 15)

So unreserved did the Qumranites wish to make their devotion to the will of God as they understood it, so total their dedication of "knowledge and strength and wealth" (1QS i 11–12), that they dared

22. *Op. cit.*, p. 47.

to call it the "following of God" (1QS ii 17). They thought of themselves as doers of truth, and to do the truth was to submit to the Law
of Moses in its interpretation by the Teacher of Justice. "By a binding
oath" they pledged themselves to return to it with wholeness of heart
and of soul (1QS v 8). Theirs was therefore a legal, but by no means a
legalistic, piety. It stayed within the confines of the Law, it demanded
the most meticulous observance of the Law's least letter; yet it was
never satisfied with a merely external compliance. No water of purification could wash the sinner unless he turned from his sin, the Rule
expressly states (v 13–14). No less does the Rule's beginning show
that for the men of Qumran the letter was the expression of the spirit:

> . . . to seek God . . . ; to do what is good and upright before Him as He
> commanded through Moses and through all His servants the prophets; to
> love all that He has chosen and hate all that He has rejected; to be far from
> all evil and cleave to all good works; to do truth and righteousness and
> justice in the land; to walk no longer in the stubbornness of a guilty heart
> and eyes of fornication, doing all evil; to bring all those who have offered
> themselves to do God's statutes into a covenant of steadfast love.
>
> (i 1–8)

A sense of obedience, a respect for order in matters spiritual and corporeal, a view of time as a "sacred trust," [23] the continuous study of
Scripture the better to learn God's will—all these are part of Qumran,
and so round out for us the meaning of its law-linked piety.

For those at Qumran there must have been few moments not filled
with the wonder and the burden of community. Their worship was
corporate, their table was an intimate bond, their daily labors and
their pondering over Scripture were for one another. Not only their
worship and their table but their whole life was liturgical, for they
knew that, both physically and spiritually, man lives not alone but
as part of a body. Indicative, then, of their spirituality is their confidence that they, as a body, knew and walked the right path, that the
Community was the "remnant" spared by God for the last days, that
it alone was the bearer of God's Covenant with His people, that in
fact with it the Sinaitic Covenant had been renewed. Hence the Community spoke of itself as the "New Covenant" (CD vi 19 *et al.*), and
it was axiomatic with the Covenanters that there was no salvation

23. Fritsch, *op. cit.,* p. 68.

outside their ranks. To be born a Jew was not enough; a man had to be given the grace of a call to the Community, and to respond. Adherence to it "was thus a free act, an offering of oneself. It was no birthright: though the brethren were all Jews, not all Jews were brethren." [24] The brethren thought of themselves as an Israel within Israel, as sons of grace, whom God had called by their names; whom He had chosen and to whom He had given wisdom, justice, and glory as their eternal possession; and at the same time as volunteers, as freely dedicated men, communally offering themselves to the walking in His good pleasure (CD iv 4; 1QS xi 7; i 7; v 10).

Freedom and predestination were no contradiction to the men of Qumran, notwithstanding a few of their sayings which, at first glance, seem to exclude free will. Startling and severe some of the Scrolls' passages are; yet it was not pride but humble reliance on grace that made the Qumranites call themselves "the men of God's lot" (1QS ii 2 *et al.*). Conscious of being chosen not for any merit of their own but by divine favor, they prayed:

> *I belong . . . to the company of erring flesh;*
> *my iniquities, my transgression, my sin,*
> *with the iniquity of my heart*
> *belong to the company of worms and those who walk in*
> *darkness. . . .*
> *[But] in His mercy He has brought me near,*
> *and in His righteousness He will cleanse me.*
>
> (1QS xi 9–10, 13–14)

All the Hymns of the Covenanters make clear their distrust of human virtue. They were painfully aware of their weakness, and they were not encouraged to boast about their works, rather trustingly to throw themselves on the mercy of God. Of man's frailty, one Hymn exclaims:

> *I am dry clay and ashes.*
> *What can I purpose, unless thou desire it;*
> *what plans can I lay, without thy good pleasure?*
> *What strength can I gather, if thou dost not support me;*
> *how can I be wise, unless thou dost fashion [wisdom] for me?*

24. Vermès, *op. cit.*, p. 113.

How can I speak, if thou dost not open my mouth;
  how can I reply, unless thou dost instruct me? . . .
Thou, the Lord of every spirit, and the Master of every work!

(v 4–7)

Another of these Psalms of Thanksgiving sings:

Trembling and terror have seized me,
  and all my bones break. . . .
For I remember my guilt
  and the treachery of my fathers.

(iv 29–30)

From trembling, the Hymn mounts to trust:

But when I remembered the might of thy hand
  and the abundance of thy mercy,
I bestirred myself to rise . . .
for I was supported by thy kindness
  and the abundance of thy mercy.

(iv 31–33)

It was on God that the Covenanters depended; it was He who had raised up for them the Teacher who was "to lead them in the way of His heart" (CD i 11), He who permitted the spirit of darkness to rule the wicked and to strive to entrap even the just, but He too who came with His spirit of truth to the help of His chosen ones (1QS iii 18–25). However extreme and at times naïve some of their expressions on the two opposing spirits, the Qumran dualism is by no means altogether new in Jewish tradition.[25] Long before the Community was established, the Book of Moses' Farewell Discourses told of his setting be-

---

25. A great deal has been written on the Covenanters' dualism of the two spirits. It has been likened to Gnosticism, but for the Gnostic the war is always between spirit and matter while in Qumran the battle was between holiness and sin. Its origin has been sought in early Zoroastrianism, which saw the world rent between the two warring forces of light and darkness, truth and deceit. That this view made its way to Qumran is quite plausible when one remembers that even after the Babylonian Captivity many Jews continued to live in Mesopotamia and were thus in contact with Iranian thought. But the genetic approach to ideas, useful as it is, cannot explain the why and whither of their adoption. In the realm of ideas as in that of life, only a healthy body has the power of selective assimilation. Hence, if Qumran adopted the purest of Iranian thought and purified it still more (Zoroastrianism's independent and uncreated forces of light and darkness become, in Qumran, servants of the one Master, God), it is a sign that truth was alive there.

fore his people "life and death, the blessing and the curse" (Deut 30:19), and the Psalter opened with the two ways that are man's choice, "the way of sinners" and "the way of the just"—a vision at its loftiest in Christ's preaching on the narrow road which leads to life and the broad road which leads to destruction (Mt 7:13, 14). There is nothing out of keeping with this inspired tradition [26] when, in the Rule of the Community, the two ways become the lives men live under the influences of the two spirits. The Prince of Light, the Rule tells, enlightens the heart and makes it tremble before the judgments of God; he prompts humility, longsuffering, great compassion, eternal goodness, understanding, insight, and mighty wisdom, a wisdom which puts its trust in nought but God's works and leans upon His abundant mercy. Zeal, a holy purpose, a love for those who obey the Law, a glorious purity loathing all impure idols, are among the counsels of the spirit of truth. But the way of those who follow Belial, angel of darkness, spirit of iniquity, is greediness, slackening in the service of justice, wickedness and falsehood, pride and haughtiness, lying and deceit, cruelty and gross impiety, anger, folly, and proud jealousy. Loathsome works, impure doings, a blasphemous tongue, blindness of eyes, dullness of ears, stiffness of neck, and a hardened heart are the "gifts" of the spirit of perversion (iv 2–11).

To the Covenanters the world was thus divided into two camps, the sons of light and of darkness. Between them there could be no peace: hated and cursed were those who walked by the spirit of untruth. Believing that they lived at the end of days, the Qumranites felt that, as a company of God's warriors, they were called to fight a battle against the hated forces of Belial. This battle, they were sure, would bring to a close the suffering of the just and the arrogance of the wicked, whose end would be shame, eternal ruin, destruction in the fire of darkness (1QS i 10; ii 5–9; iv 12–13). But to the sons of truth there would be granted eternal rejoicing, a crown of glory, the

26. The strength and scope of this tradition is manifest, for instance, in the opening words of the earliest Christian manual of morality, the *Didache:* "Two ways there are, one of life and one of death." The way of life is to love God and neighbor, the *Didache* continues and, unlike the Rule, adds that to love the neighbor is to bless those who curse, to love those who hate, indeed to have no enemy. In Jewish thought this tradition developed into the doctrine of *yeṣer ṭov* and *yeṣer ha-raʿ*, the good and the evil inclinations. For a detailed discussion of the affinities of early Christian writings and the "two ways" passage of the Rule, see Jean-Paul Audet, O.P., "Affinités littéraires et doctrinales du 'Manuel de Discipline,'" *Revue Biblique,* LIX, 2 (1952), pp. 219–238; LX, 1 (1953), pp. 41–82.

raiment of majesty; before God they would stand on the heights of
heaven, and in concert with its angels they would praise His name
forever and ever (1QS iv 7–8). Thus the Rule enjoins the priests of
the Community to bless "the men of God's lot" in this way—an expanded form of the Aaronic blessing:

> *May He bless you with all good*
> *and keep you from all evil;*
> *May He give light to your heart with living wisdom*
> *and be gracious to you with eternal knowledge;*
> *May He lift up His loving countenance to you for*
> *eternal peace.*

(ii 2–4)

QUMRAN AND THE NEW TESTAMENT

How did the Covenanters respond when the good news of Jesus
reached them, as it must have; what did they think of the high priest's
enmity to Him and what of the events of Holy Week? Their deep
spirituality, their feeling for the greatness of hidden things, no less
their conviction that God's appointed time had come, would incline
one to suppose that they welcomed the gospel as soon as they heard
of it, and that they sensed something of the significance of the Passion.
Men of zeal they were: it would be no surprise to see many of them
hastening into the Church. As far back as 1912, when the Qumran
library had not yet been discovered and all that was known of it was
the Damascus Document, Dr. R. H. Charles suggested that the "sons
of Zadok" might account for Luke's joyful report: "A large number
also of the priests accepted the faith" (Ac 6:7).[27] Again, in his recent
commentary on the Letter to the Hebrews, Père C. Spicq, O.P., thinks
it may have been to these priests that the Epistle was written, for its
emphasis is on Christ, the High Priest and Mediator of a superior
covenant.[28] Possibly, then, the "Hebrews" were priests from, or sympathetic to, Qumran, and not the priests in power.

But all these are conjectures, and not likely ones. The men of
Qumran seem never to have been very numerous, and the archaeologi-
cal record shows that they stayed at Qumran until they were forced

27. *The Apocrypha and Pseudepigrapha of the Old Testament* (Oxford, 1913),
II, 786, 794.
28. *L'Épître aux Hébreux* (Paris: Gabalda, 1952–53), I, 226–231.

out by the Romans. There were those who must have left them from time to time, and probably many who did not finish their novitiate; but the Community itself remained rigorously apart even from the rest of the people of Israel. This exclusiveness could not but have been a barrier between it and the Church, whose mission it was to break down the barriers between man and man, between Jew and Gentile. An anthem of the Covenanters' holy war sang:

> *Rise, mighty one;* [29] *bring back thy captives, man of glory!*
> *Seize thy plunder, thou who doest valiantly!*
> *Lay thy hand on the necks of thy enemies*
>   *and thy foot on the heaps of the slain;*
>   *smite the nations, thy adversaries,*
>   *and let thy sword consume guilty flesh!*
> (1QM xii 10–12)

Not only did the Covenanters pledge "eternal hate for the men of the pit," not only did their Levites "curse all the men of Belial's lot"— merely to show mercy to God's enemies was abhorrent to them (1QS ix 21–22; ii 4–5; 1QM iii 5). It was surely, then, with the Qumran-ites in mind that in the Sermon on the Mount Jesus announced: "You have heard that it was said, 'Thou shalt love thy neighbor, and shalt hate thy enemy.' But I say to you, love your enemies, do good to those who hate you, and pray for those who persecute and calumniate you, so that you may be children of your Father in heaven" (Mt 5:43–45). [30] This was a plea; but did the men of Qumran hear it?

To doubt that large numbers of them flocked into the infant Church

29. Probably the "mighty one" is the conquering, royal Messiah. Very much as in the Jewish apocryphal literature, the Community's messianic concepts seem to have been in a state of fermentation. In the Testaments of the Twelve Patriarchs, for instance, Simeon exhorts his children to obey the two tribes of Levi and Judah, "for the Lord shall raise up from Levi as it were a High Priest, and from Judah as it were a King" (7:2). The Community's expectation seems to have been threefold: for the prophet, the kingly Messiah, and the priestly Messiah. Thus the Rule demands that there be no departure from any counsel of the Law "until there shall come a prophet and the Messiahs of Aaron and Israel" (ix 11). Whatever had been cloudy in the people's messianic hope the New Testament brought to a limpid end: the prophetic, kingly, and priestly offices are united in Jesus, the one Messiah.

30. Until recently, Jewish writers often claimed that this saying of Jesus could not be wholly authentic, that only later prejudice could have interpolated the words, "You have heard that it was said, 'Thou . . . shalt hate thy enemy,'" for nowhere in the Old Testament or in the known traditions was such a precept to be found. But now that we have the Scrolls of the Desert, the evangelists are once more proved reliable reporters.

is not to imply that none of them came to her, nor is it to imply that there were no links at all between her and them. It has often been said, and certainly not without reason, that the aged Simeon, Zachary the priest, John the Baptist, and those first apostles who had been the Baptist's disciples, felt the influence of Qumran or of groups in some way like it. It has also been thought that the Baptist, having early lost his elderly parents, was adopted by the priestly Community of Qumran and raised as its ward. Although this cannot be proved, it is not at all improbable, for Luke tells that "the child grew and became strong in spirit; and was in the deserts until the day of his manifestation to Israel" (1:80). If he was indeed reared in the bosom of the Community, perhaps even becoming a professed member,[31] he must have broken with it; in any case, he went far beyond its spirit. Though both the Community and John found their program in the Isaianic injunction to clear in the wilderness the way of Yahweh and to make straight in the desert a triumphant highway for Him (Is 40:3; 1QS viii 14; Mt 3:3), the manner in which they obeyed was quite different. In order to make ready the way by which the Lord would enter, the men of Qumran formed a taut organization which to this day compels our admiration. But all John sought for his work was a simple company of disciples, for he knew and declared his task to be transitory. While the Qumranites saw themselves as the only sharers of the messianic future, the Baptist wanted to be no more than a voice announcing the Bringer of the Spirit's fire, no more than the least servant of the Mighty One to come, no more than the friend of the Bridegroom, soon to step aside (Lk 3:16; Jn 3:29). The Covenanters withdrew into isolation, permitting only such dealings with the rest of men as could not be avoided. John, however, drew to himself the people of "Jerusalem, and all Judaea, and all the region about the Jordan" (Mt 3:5), inviting everyone, even those the Qumranites called "men of the pit," to repent and, in token of repentance, to be baptized. The followers of the Teacher of Justice took it on themselves to practice the Law to the letter, so that they might atone for the sinfulness around them. When John preached *teshubah,* repentance—the change of heart he demanded was simply respect for the neighbor

31. To Wilson, the Baptist's regimen of locusts and wild honey recalls the expelled Essenes, who attempted to live on grass because they had vowed to eat nothing prepared by those not of their brotherhood (*The Scrolls from the Dead Sea,* New York: Oxford University Press, 1955, p. 94).

and brotherly sharing, truth, justice, and love (Lk 3:11–14). But all differences pale beside this one: that he was a finger pointing to the Christ.

Whether or not John the Baptist ever lived at Qumran as one of the *shabey Yisraël,* the "penitents of Israel" (CD iv 2), there was more in his preaching than he could have learned from them, for "the word of God came to John" (Lk 3:2). One must say the same of the whole New Testament: many a phrase in it reads like a phrase from the Scrolls, and yet so much in it one would seek in vain in the writings of Qumran. Still, unhesitatingly and gladly we must acknowledge that in them there has been given us an important element of the "evangelical milieu," [32] of the historical setting into which Christ came, of the frame for His word and work.

There are numerous resemblances between the language of the Covenanters and that of St. John and St. Paul. I can mention only a few.[33] "In the abode of light are the origins of truth, and from the source of darkness are the origins of error," declares the Rule (iii 19). Though part of a far mightier vision, this contrast is one of St. John's great themes. "God is light, and in Him is no darkness" (1 Jn 1:5); "The light shines in the darkness, and the darkness grasped it not" (Jn 1:5). Of the sons of justice, the Rule says that they walk "in the ways of light," and of all the rest that they walk "in the ways of darkness" (iii 20–21). How frequently St. John speaks of those who walk in the light and those who stumble in darkness! There is one passage in particular which, though in a context altogether Christian, combines three expressions dear to the Qumranites, "light," "fellowship," and "practicing the truth":

32. F.-M. Lemoine, O.P., "Les Manuscrits du Désert de Juda," *Lumière et Vie* (1953), p. 119.

33. For more detailed studies of these resemblances, see, among others, W. K. M. Grossouw, "The Dead Sea Scrolls and the New Testament: A Preliminary Survey," *Studia Catholica,* XXVI (1951), pp. 289–299; XXVII (1952), pp. 1–8; Roland E. Murphy, O. Carm., *The Dead Sea Scrolls and the Bible* (Westminster, Md.: Newman Press, 1956); "The Dead Sea Scrolls and New Testament Comparisons," *Catholic Biblical Quarterly,* XVIII, 3 (July 1956), pp. 263–272; Geoffrey Graystone, S.M., *The Dead Sea Scrolls and the Originality of Christ* (New York: Sheed & Ward, 1956); Raymond E. Brown, S.S., "The Qumrân Scrolls and the Johannine Gospel and Epistles," *Catholic Biblical Quarterly,* XVII (1955), pp. 403–419, 559–574; Kurt Schubert, "Bergpredigt und Texte von En Fešha," *Theologische Quartalschrift,* CXXXV, 3 (1955), pp. 320–337; F. M. Braun, "L'Arrière-fond judaïque du quatrième évangile et la communauté de l'alliance," *Revue Biblique,* LXII (1955), pp. 5–44.

If we say that we have fellowship with [God], and walk in darkness, we lie, and are not practicing the truth. But if we walk in the light as He also is in the light, we have fellowship with one another, and the blood of Jesus Christ, His Son, cleanses us from all sin.

(1 Jn 1:6–7)

"Sons of light" was a name cherished by the Covenanters, and St. John tells of Christ's call: "Believe in the light, that you may become sons of light" (Jn 12:36). St. Paul too, in language akin to that of Qumran, urges: "Now you are light in the Lord. Walk, then, as children of light" (Eph 5:8).

There is in the writings of Qumran a strong emphasis on devotion to one's brother, on "loyal love" for one's fellow, but the brother or fellow to be loved is always a member of the Community. Indeed, this commandment of love is linked with the commandment of "eternal hate for the men of the pit." [34] Such a precept of hate is entirely alien to St. John's Gospel, for, he confesses, "God so loved the world [that is, all men] that He gave His only-begotten Son" (Jn 3:16). True, there is a definite resemblance between St. John and Qumran in their stress on brotherly love. "Love one another," Jesus told His little band of disciples at the Last Supper (Jn 13:34); the Evangelist, repeating this command again and again, adds joyfully: "We know that we have passed from death to life, because we love the brethren" (1 Jn 3:14). His look is toward the companions in the faith, and this may make the love he pleads for appear at first as limited as the love of the Covenanters. But the path St. John records is an infinite circle, from God to Christ, from Christ to Christians, and back through Christ to God: "As the Father has loved me, I also have loved you. . . . Love one another as I have loved you" (Jn 15:9, 12). Since love "in Christ" is infinite, there is nothing exclusive about it: all are invited to enter this circle, at once closed and open.

Another instance of similarity is in the Prologue of St. John's Gospel:

> *All things were made through [the Word],*
> *and without Him was made*
> *nothing that has been made.*

(1:3)

34. 1QS ii 24; cf. i 9–10; ix 16–22; x 20–21.

This may well have been an echo of the closing psalm of the Rule:

> *By [God's] knowledge everything comes to pass;*
> *and everything that is He establishes by His purpose;*
> *and without Him it is not done.*
>
> (xi 11)

But if it was an echo, how mighty an echo, greater than the parent sound, for St. John speaks not merely of that Knowledge which is in the heavens, rather of the Word which had become flesh and been seen and heard.

Turning to St. Paul: in his epistles he often writes of God's everlasting design to redeem the world as the "mystery of God." It is the mystery "hidden for ages and generations, but now . . . clearly shown to His saints" (Col 1:26), His mysterious wisdom, unknown to the rulers of this world but revealed to those who love Him (1 Cor 2:7–10). The Hymns and Rule of Qumran also exult in God's decree of salvation as His "marvelous mysteries," His "wonderful counsel" (iv 23–24), as the "mysteries of His understanding and His glorious wisdom," hidden from the sons of perversion but confided to His elect (1QS iv 18). The Covenanters' use of "mystery," *raz,* gives refreshing evidence that St. Paul's use of *mysterion* was not a surrender to the dominance of Eastern mystery cults, as has so often been asserted, but had its deep roots in Israel's tradition. Yet for all the remarkable parallel in words and even content, the two "mysteries" differ: for St. Paul the mystery is Christ crucified and risen, His passion, His triumph— hence mankind's healing and glory.

St. Paul never tires of extolling the grace of God which makes just: not through our own efforts but through His mercy manifest in Christ are we justified. There is a similar insistence on merciful justification among the men of Qumran, quite different from the accent of the Pharisees on works. One of the most beautiful features of the Qumran spirituality, Dr. Grossouw writes, is the consciousness that even the brethren are sinful and that salvation comes from God alone.[35] The Qumran Hymnal exclaims:

> *I know, indeed, that man has no justice,*
> *and the son of man no perfect way.*
> *To God Most High belong all the works of justice. . . .*
>
> (iv 26–27)

35. *Op. cit.,* p. 2.

Here is another classical expression of the Covenanters' teaching that man depends entirely on God's mercy, a teaching which, as often as it broke through the walls of Qumran, must have prepared hearts for the Good News:

> *As for me, if I slip,*
> *the steadfast love of God is my salvation forever;*
> *and if I stumble in the iniquity of flesh,*
> *my vindication in the righteousness of God will stand to*
>   *eternity. . . .*
> *In His mercy He has brought me near,*
> *and in His righteousness He will cleanse me*
>   *from the impurity of man,*
> *from the sin of the sons of man.*
>   (1QS xi 11–15)

There are many other parallels. The "overseer" of Qumran, for instance, and the "bishop" of whom St. Paul writes to Timothy and Titus have certain traits in common; indeed, the term *mebakker* and the term *episcopos* are so much alike that one could be the translation of the other. The Scrolls speak of "the prince of lights" and of "the angel of darkness," the Apostle of Satan's disguising himself as "an angel of light" and of "our wrestling . . . against the world-rulers of this darkness" (2 Cor 11:14; Eph 6:12). His plea, "Put on the armor of God" (Eph 6:11), recalls the Qumranites' warfare against the forces of Belial, the "worthless one"; once his words are so like theirs that they could almost be a quotation: "Do not bear the yoke with unbelievers. For what has justice in common with iniquity? Or what fellowship has light with darkness? What harmony is there between Christ and Belial? Or what part has the believer with the unbeliever?" (2 Cor 6:14–15). Among the works of truth the Rule records are "a spirit of humility, and slowness to anger, and great compassion, and eternal goodness" (iv 3); the Apostle admonishes the Colossians to put on "a heart of mercy, kindness, humility, meekness, patience" (3:12). "To be far from all evil and cleave to all good works," we read among the ordinances of the Community (i 4–5); and the Romans are told by the Apostle to "hate what is evil, hold to what is good" (12:9). Again, how close "I will sing with knowledge"

(1QS x 9) is to "I will sing with the spirit, but I will sing with the understanding also" (1 Cor 14:15)!

There are similarities elsewhere in the New Testament. The Rule's precept on fraternal correction, that no Covenanter accuse his brother before the Community unless he had first rebuked him before witnesses, approaches Christ's urging to show an erring brother his fault first alone, then before witnesses, and then, if he still refuses to listen, before the Church (1QS vi 1; Mt 18:15–17). The canticles St. Luke records in his Gospel of the Infancy—the *Magnificat* and, even more, the *Benedictus*—recall, in certain of their phrases, the Psalms of Thanksgiving. "The Way" is one of the names by which the Covenanters designated their way of life; in the Acts of the Apostles, "the Way" is the road Jesus walked and showed, and hence those who walk it after Him, His little Church (1QS ix 18; Ac 9:2 *et al.*). "The council" and "the many" of the Community have their counterpart in "the Twelve" and "the multitude" of the infant Church (Ac 6:2). There is a resemblance between the communal spirit of Qumran, with its communally owned property, and the life of the Christians in Jerusalem: "The multitude of the believers were of one heart and one soul, and not one of them said that anything he possessed was his own, but they had all things in common" (Ac 4:32). There were sacred cleansings and sacred meals at Qumran, which unknowingly called for a cleansing and a meal to come, indeed for *the* cleansing and *the* meal.[36] "Holy Community," "holy congregation," "holy building," "men of

---

36. As to the cleansings: The ritual washings at Qumran, even though they were not for "all nations" and for "every creature," and were not "in the name of the Father, and of the Son, and of the Holy Spirit" (Mt 28:19; Mk 16:16); even though they did not carry the tremendous promise that Christian baptism does, may well be thought of as among its foreshadowings. For the baptism Christ gave to His Church was not a rite altogether new, rather is it an old rite with a new meaning and a transcendent efficacy. But as one of its foreshadowings, the purifications of Qumran do not stand alone. Not to speak here of the baptism of proselytes to the Synagogue, Jewish tradition has always taught that Israel entered into its covenant with God by circumcision, sacrifice, and baptism, and that it received its baptism when the Lord demanded that the people be sanctified and their garments washed (Ex 19:10). Jewish tradition even goes so far as to teach that "to receive the spirit of God, or to be permitted to stand in the presence of God (His Shekinah), man must undergo Baptism (Tan., Meẓora‘, 6, ed. Buber, p. 46), wherefore in the messianic time God will Himself pour water of purification upon Israel in accordance with Ezekiel 36:25 (Tan., Meẓora‘, 9–17, 18, ed. Buber, pp. 43, 53)" (*Jewish Encyclopedia*, II, 499). Thus the Mishnah tractate on the Day of Atonement calls God "Thou, the *mikweh* of Israel," *mikweh* meaning "hope" and also "pool of immersion" or "fountain." "As the fountain renders clean the

perfect holiness," or "holy ones of the Most High" are some of the names given to the Community; "God's building," "temple holy in the Lord," "saints" are among the early titles given to the Church and its members.[37]

These are by no means all the points on which the Desert Scrolls and the New Testament meet: there are hundreds of similarities. But similarity is not identity. Sameness of expression need not imply sameness of meaning nor bespeak dependence.[38] In fact, where an

unclean, so does the Holy One, blessed be He, render clean Israel" (Yoma 85b; cf. *B. Talmud,* Soncino ed., *Yoma,* pp. 423–424).

As to the meals: The common meals of Qumran were banquets of brotherly love, and in this they can be looked on as an intimation of the Christian Eucharist, but never as more than that. Professor Allegro, however, tells us that "it seems probable that every communal repast was considered to some extent a rehearsal of the Messianic Banquet," and that this was "basically the same act" as the Eucharist (*op. cit.,* pp. 114–115). Professor Frank M. Cross speaks of "the communion meal of the Essenes [*sic*]" and of their "liturgical anticipation of the Messianic banquet" ("The Scrolls from the Judaean Desert," *Archaeology,* IX, 1, March 1956, p. 49). I see no warrant for either assertion. What they refer to is a fragment found in Cave One, the "Two Columns," which begins: "This is the rule for the whole congregation of Israel at the end of days," and which gives the protocol to be followed at the messianic banquet ("the Priest" most likely referring to the priestly Messiah, and "the Messiah of Israel" to the kingly Messiah, as spoken of in note 29) : "[When] they shall gather at the common [ta]ble [or to drink] the wine, and when the common table is set and the wine [mixed] for drinking, [let no one stretch out] his hand for the first portion of the bread or the [wine] before the Priest; for it is [for him to bl]ess the first portion of the bread and win[e, and for him to stretch out] his hand for the bread first. After[wards] the Messiah of Israel shall [stre]tch out his hands for the bread; [and then] the whole congregation of the Community [shall pronounce the bles]sings, each [according to] his rank. This rule shall obtain at every [meal when] at least ten are gathered together" (1QSa ii 17–22). This text would seem simple enough, telling no more than that the Priest-Messiah will have precedence over the King-Messiah, a layman, and, of course, over the whole congregation, and that a similar order in blessing is to be followed at all meals. Not content with so simple a meaning, fitting so well into the Qumran framework, with its reverence for the priestly dignity, Allegro and Cross have weighted the text in favor of their own interpretation by translating "communion table" instead of "common table." In any case, we have the impartial testimony of Dr. Gaster. He does not think that the meal described in the fragment is the messianic banquet, but "even if, for argument's sake," he writes, "this document *did* refer to a divine eschatological Messiah attending a banquet with his disciples, it would still not be a eucharist in the Christian sense, for there is not the slightest suggestion that the bread and wine were regarded as his flesh and blood or that consumption of them had any redemptive power. At most, it would be an *agape,* or 'love-feast.'" Without ambiguity he declares: "There is no Communion [at Qumran]" (*op. cit.,* pp. 19–20).

37. 1QS ix 2; xi 8; CD xx 2, 8; 1 Cor 3:9; Eph 2:21; Phil 1:1.

38. The assertion of identities may betray a writer's lack of depth. On page 89 of his book, Wilson quotes first from the apocryphal Testament of Joseph: "I was beset with hunger, and the Lord Himself nourished me. . . . I was sick and the Lord visited me. I was in prison and my Lord showed favor to me" (1:5–6).

untrained eye might see a dependence of the New Testament on the Qumran writings, there is very often simply a dependence of both on the Old Testament or on the apocryphal literature, which, though not inspired, expressed the hope of the devout that in the end God would right all things. No doubt, Jesus (and later His apostles) often used the Qumranite idiom to convey His message as He (and later they) used the language of apocryphal writings and of early rabbinical interpretations. For instance, when He called Himself the Son of Man, He made His own an expression to which the apocryphal Book of Enoch had given great color and messianic dignity. Or in saying that Abraham had seen His day and been glad, He leaned on a tradition, frequently recorded in rabbinical literature, that the patriarch had been granted a vision of his own times and of the next, that is, the days of the Messiah. Again, in the commission to Simon Peter, son of John, to head the Church, the terms "blessed art thou," "rock," "Church" (*qahal*), "the gates of Gehenna," "binding and loosing" are all terms and images which were part of rabbinical exegesis and law.[39] Thus in Jesus there came to flower, and there is thus alive in the Church, not only holy Scripture but Jewish tradition—all that was true in every segment of the people and of its thought. No stone did He reject that could be built into the lasting house of God, no fruit yielding a seed that could be sown again. There was nothing partisan in Him; rather did He draw apostles and disciples from all "parties." John and Andrew had been followers of the Baptist; Simon Zelotes probably, and certainly the Good Thief, members of the Zealots, the party of national freedom; Nicodemus and Paul Pharisees; while Barnabas had been a Levite. As little, then, as He was a Zealot,

---

Then he quotes the words of Christ: "For I was hungry and you gave me food . . . I was sick and you visited me. I was in prison, and you came to me" (Mt 25:35-36; R.S.V.). Wilson notes the similarity of words but seems unaware of the entirely new dimension in Christ's saying. Whereas the words attributed to Joseph bespeak the creature's gratitude to God, the words Christ promised to utter at the Last Judgment bespeak the ineffable: God's gratitude to His creature. Joseph's words tell of man dependent, Christ's words of God so magnanimous as to accept man's mercies to his fellow man as done to Him.

39. On Mt 12:8 *et al.*, see Enoch xxiv. On Jn 8:56, see Ber. R. 44:22 and Targ. Jer. Gen 15:17 *et al.*; cf. *Midrash Rabbah,* Soncino ed., I, 376, and Ginzberg, *op. cit.,* I, 236–237; V, 229–230. On Mt 16:18–19, see the many references given by Strack-Billerbeck, *Kommentar zum Neuen Testament aus Talmud und Midrasch* (Munich: C. H. Beck, 1922), I, 731–736; or by Alfred Edersheim, *The Life and Times of Jesus the Messiah* (New York: Longmans, Green, 1917), II, 81–85.

a Pharisee, or a Sadducee, was He an "Essene." But He was the Christ of Zealots, Pharisees, Sadducees, and Qumranites—because He was the Hope of Israel and Redeemer of the entire world.

No one can be surprised to hear Christ use the idiom of those He lived with, walked among, and spoke to, His kinsmen according to the flesh, unless he has forgotten that all this was ordained, that God had made the Israel of old the courier of His word, and that the Church has always claimed to have received the Old Testament with the New and to be carrying both toward the day of glory. As Professor Joseph Coppens writes:

No theologian trained in the historic method would ever dream of claiming for the Christian message a total originality, as if God had wanted to write His word on a *tabula rasa,* with materials borrowed from another world, from another planet. Only simplicist minds can so picture revelation, can picture Christianity as descending from the heavens ready-made, all dressed in supernal, transcendent formulas and expressions. If God had spoken to the world in a "language of heaven," no one would have understood. Whenever He addresses His word to mankind, we know in advance that it will be incarnate, and this incarnation is not brought about in concepts and terms entirely new. It is realized with elements borrowed from pre-existent institutions, civilizations, and tongues. This is all the truer of Christianity, since Jesus, His gospel, His Church, regard and present themselves as the heirs of the Old Testament's revelation, beliefs, and hopes, which they came to fulfill.[40]

This fulfillment had to be prepared for in successive stages, and among them, since God likes to make man His helper, were the "reactions of the chosen people, which received this revelation, pondered it, and lived it." [41]

THE TEACHER OF JUSTICE AND JESUS

THE discoveries of the Judaean desert are a blessing to the scholar and to everyone: they illuminate for us the days of Christ's coming and the century or so before it; they stress again, indeed stress in a marvelously new way, the one great bond and the many little bonds between the ancient Israel and the Church. But it is quite another thing to claim, as does Edmund Wilson, that the monastery of Qumran

40. "Les Documents du Désert de Juda et les origines du Christianisme," *Anal. Lov. Bibl. et Orient.,* II, 39 (1953), p. 24.
41. Lemoine, *loc. cit.,* p. 119.

"is perhaps, more than Bethlehem or Nazareth, the cradle of Christianity." [42] In this he leans on Dupont-Sommer, who—though disavowing in a footnote any intention "to deny the originality of the Christian religion"—presents the Teacher of Justice as a Christ before Christ:

The Galilean Master, as He is presented to us in the writings of the New Testament, appears in many respects as an astonishing reincarnation of the Master of Justice. Like the latter He preached penitence, poverty, humility, love of one's neighbor, chastity. Like him, He prescribed the observance of the Law of Moses, the whole Law, but the Law finished and perfected, thanks to His own revelations. Like him He was the Elect and the Messiah of God, the Messiah redeemer of the world. Like him He was the object of the hostility of the priests, the party of the Sadducees. Like him He was condemned and put to death. Like him He pronounced judgment on Jerusalem, which was taken and destroyed by the Romans for having put Him to death. Like him, at the end of time, He will be the supreme judge. Like him He founded a Church whose adherents fervently awaited His glorious return. [43]

Every sentence here is a surface judgment and an oversimplification. The Teacher of Justice is undoubtedly an impressive figure, but he is not of the measure of "the Galilean Master." He and Jesus are incommensurable.

To the men of Qumran, their Teacher was the true interpreter of the Law, but nowhere in the Scrolls does he appear like Jesus who, with His magisterial "I say to you," wished to implant the Law into all men's innermost being, to write it into the heart of His people (Jer 31:33). For the Covenanters, "the Law finished and perfected" meant, among other things, a bar on polygamy and a ban on marriage with one's niece. Can this really be likened to the dignity Jesus gave marriage when He restored it as a lasting bond of love between man and

42. *Op. cit.*, p. 98.
43. *The Dead Sea Scrolls*, pp. 99–100. It is surely not irrelevant to record that the English translation of this long list suppresses the following sentence of the French original: "Like him [the Master of Justice], He [the Galilean Master] mounted to heaven, near to God." Dupont-Sommer's list of likenesses has been seized on by many in defense of their religious liberalism. In his later book, *The Jewish Sect of Qumran and the Essenes*, however, Dupont-Sommer himself has been much more cautious; and later still, in reply to a question by the editors of the *Saturday Review*, he wrote: "I never claimed that the Dead Sea scrolls could strike a blow against the 'uniqueness' of Jesus. . . . I believe that the Dead Sea scrolls do not deny the divinity of Jesus. . . . Viewed as a whole, the originality of the Christian Church seems to me to remain unchallenged" (March 3, 1956, p. 29).

woman, and exalted it as a sacrament, God's lasting pledge of love for them? Again, for the Covenanters, "the Law finished and perfected" meant a Sabbath rest ever more rigorous. No idle words were to be spoken; nothing to be said about the work of the next day; no beast to be struck, even if it balked at doing its master's will; nothing to be carried from the house to the outside, or from the outside into the house; nothing to be eaten save what had been prepared in advance; no vessel to be filled in order that one might drink from it later; no perfume to be worn; no aid to be rendered to an animal in giving birth; and no ladder or rope to be brought to help a man fallen into a pit. Can all this really be likened to the glory of the Sabbath as Jesus saw it, when God is honored but man not forgotten, when rest does not drive out compassion? [44]

There is no doubt that the followers of the Teacher looked on him as their master, uniquely inspired, who had received the true expounding of the Law from "the mouth of God." He was their guide to instruct them about the disaster to come as foretold by the prophets (1QpHab i 2–3; ii 9–10).[45] Quite other was the mission of Jesus. "According to the New Testament, He was plainly conscious that He had come to *fulfill* the prophecies and that it was to Him personally that they pointed. He was the *end,* the primary object, of their foretelling; He knew their innermost meaning, for it was, so 1 Pet 1:11 tells us, His Spirit which had given the prophets their knowledge of the things to come."[46] Never did the Covenanters call their Master "the Elect,"[47]

---

44. CD iv 20—v 11; Mt 19:49; Mk 10:5–12; CD x 14—xi 18; Mt 12:1–13; Mk 2:23—3:5; Lk 6:1–10; 14:1–5; Jn 5:2–17; 9:1–16.

45. If, as several scholars assume, some of the Hymns were written by, or at least in the name of, the Teacher of Justice, then he thought of himself as a "father" given by God to them He held dear, as their nurse; as one who fed God's "eternal planting," for from his mouth came "rain at all seasons, and a fountain of waters unfailing"; as a "banner in the vanguard of righteousness," "a gust of zeal" (1QH vii 20–21; viii 16; ii 13, 15—Gaster's translation). But if this is taken as the Teacher's self-evaluation, then it would be only fair to assume that it is he too who compared himself to a sailor unable to "steer a course upon the waters," he too who confessed: "Confusion and panic beset me" (cf. Gaster, *op. cit.,* pp. 156, 152).

46. Vermès, "Le 'Commentaire d'Habacuc' et le Nouveau Testament," *Cahiers Sioniens,* V, 4 (Dec. 1951), pp. 346–347.

47. 1QpHab ix 11–12 tells of God's punishment of the Wicked Priest "because he had acted wickedly against His elect." The English word "elect" can mean either one or many; and it so happens that—since written Hebrew customarily omits the vowels—the corresponding Hebrew word can be read either as *behiro* (the singular) or *behiraw* (the plural). As it is, 1QpHab v 4; x 13; 1QS viii 6; and ix 14, make the latter, "His chosen ones," a near certainty.

never "the Messiah of God,"[48] as Dupont-Sommer would have us believe; and even if they had, they could never have seen him as the "redeemer of the world," for a world-vision was foreign to them. Nowhere is there any suggestion that the Teacher of Justice was the bringer of salvation, that he had come "to save what was lost." Nowhere in the writings of the Community is there any claim for the Master that even slightly resembles Christ's "I am the light of the world"; "I am the way, and the truth, and the life";[49] "I am the resurrection and the life." Nowhere in the Scrolls is there a word that even faintly approaches the absolute consciousness which could say: "I and the Father are one"; "He who sees me sees the Father."[50]

In no instance is it more obvious how Dupont-Sommer inflates minor affinities than when he calls Jesus and the Teacher alike "the object of the hostility of the priests." A dispute of the kind the Teacher

48. One of the Hymns has for its theme the travail of a woman about to give birth. This may stand for the travail of the soul or for the "birth pangs of the Messiah." If the Community thought of itself as the womb that would bring forth the Messiah, then it could not have thought of him who had founded it as the Messiah; nor is there anything in this Hymn to strengthen the hypothesis that the Community expected the Teacher to return as the Priest-Messiah. See particularly Joseph Baumgarten and Menahem Mansoor, "Studies in the New *Hodayot*—II," *Journal of Biblical Literature,* LXXIV, 3 (Sept. 1955), pp. 188–192. In any case, nothing could be further from the mark than Allegro's reasoning: "As the Sect saw itself as a pregnant woman giving birth to a Messiah through her travail, so Jesus sees himself born out of the sufferings of his people, and suffering with them. All are his kin, 'Behold, my mother and my brethren' . . ." (*op. cit.,* p. 156). The merest glance at the Gospels shows that here, as elsewhere in his book, Professor Allegro indulges in fantasy, if not misrepresentation. For there is no mention of suffering in Mt 12:46–50; Mk 3:31–35; or Lk 8:19–21. What Christ really proclaims there is that He acknowledges as His own, makes His kindred, all who do the will of His Father in heaven.

49. To leap the manifest chasm which separates the Teacher of Justice from Christ, and to sustain his own theological liberalism, which sees in Christianity and, for that matter, in all religion, but a natural phenomenon, Dr. Davies resorts to a string of wild conjectures. Always declaring that he puts forth no more than hypotheses, he writes in regard to Christ's "I am the way, and the truth, and the life," for instance: "This sort of discourse, sonorous and liturgical in tone and entirely different from the language of Jesus in the first three Gospels, would be quite appropriate to the Essenic Teacher of Righteousness . . . and the writer of John's Gospel may have combined some of the Teacher's doctrine with a reconstructed life of Jesus" (*The Meaning of the Dead Sea Scrolls,* New York: New American Library, 1956, pp. 107–108). I need not say that I think these conjectures groundless and in error, but I wish I could say at least that I believed in their author's desire to arrive at the truth. He makes this difficult, for, to give only one example, he goes on to link his conjectures with a statement by Dr. Burrows torn from its context, a statement which gives the impression that Burrows sides with him, which he most certainly does not.

50. Mt 18:11; Jn 8:12; 14:6; 11:25; 10:30; 14:9.

had with the official priesthood of the Temple is entirely absent from, and foreign to, the Gospels. Unlike the men of Qumran, Jesus and His disciples worshipped in Jerusalem. Unlike the men of Qumran, Jesus paid honor to the priests of the Temple—ten lepers He cured by sending them: "Go, show yourselves to the priests" (Lk 17:14). Dupont-Sommer assumes that the Teacher of Justice was the victim of violence; though, as I have shown, the language of the Scrolls suggests the opposite, this is possible, for many holy men in Israel had known such an end. But whether or not he died a violent death, never once do the Desert Scrolls tell of him what the New Testament proclaims again and again of Jesus: that He "died for us," that He "was delivered up for our sins," that His death was the ransom and reconciliation of all men.[51] To the "men of his party," the Teacher was not a saviour. Nor was he, as Dupont-Sommer so eagerly assumes, the "supreme judge." In the Habakkuk Commentary we read: "Into the hand of His elect God will deliver the judgment of all the nations" (v 4). His "elect" here are "the doers of the Law, whose hands do not grow slack from the service of the truth" (vii 11–12), not just their Teacher. For the Covenanters considered it the task of the whole Community as the instrument of God, the Supreme Judge, "to render to the wicked their recompense" (1QS viii 7). Nowhere do the Scrolls say that the Master of Qumran would return as the Messiah; all they proclaim is that in the end of days one would arise to teach justice, that God would send a faithful shepherd (CD vi 10–11; 1Q34 III ii 8).

To bring to a close the argument with Professor Dupont–Sommer: One need not be a Christian to see that the Teacher's foundation and the Church of Christ are not on the same plane, and that not too much ought to be made of the name they have in common. When the disciples of the Teacher spoke of themselves as "those who entered the New Covenant in the land of Damascus" (CD vi 19), they saw themselves as reaffirming the ancient Covenant of Sinai. Theirs was a most earnest attempt to restore what they felt their fathers had abandoned, a fresh and determined will to go back to, and carry out again, the commandments given through Moses. The New Testament, however, did not merely restore or reinforce the work of Sinai; it

51. Rom 5:9; 4:25; cf. Rom 3:25; 1 Cor 15:3; 2 Cor 5:15; Col 1:14, 20, 22; Tit 2:14; Heb 2:9–10; 9:15, 28; 1 Pet 1:18–19; 2:21, 24; 1 Jn 1:7; 2:2; 3:16; Apoc 1:5; 5:9.

went beyond it. To the apostles, the New Covenant was more excellent than the first—not that the Old was not good and noble, but that the New was better and nobler; it was more excellent, for it was sealed not in the blood of wordless, will-less beasts but in the blood of the one Christ (Heb 9:13–15). To them the Old was the beginning of revelation, the New its crown; there was the dawn, here the day.

That there was on the one hand an overwhelming missionary thrust and on the other a complete absence of missionary intention brings into focus the difference between Christ's New Covenant and the New Covenant of Damascus. The followers of the Teacher of Justice had gone to the wilderness, there to await God's judgment, but the desert showed them no far horizon; in a way it threw them on themselves, so that they forgot the prophetic vision that "all the ends of the earth shall see the salvation of our God" (Is 52:10). They considered themselves "an eternal planting" (1QS viii 5), but outside they saw a hopelessly lost world, destined to eternal death, a world they swore to leave to its own devices (1QS v 9–20; ix 21–23). The apostles, on the other hand, were told to go out into the world and preach the gospel to all the nations; to go to the crossroads and plead with the poor, the outcasts, the crippled, blind, and lame, to come in and fill the house of the Lord (Mt 28:19; Mk 16:15; Mt 22:9–10; Lk 14:21–24). Their Master, unlike the Teacher of Justice, made publicans His companions, sinners His friends, and opened the kingdom to harlots. For all the true praise the Community gave to God's mercy, the evil of the world hung like a cloud over Qumran. Not that the infant Church, in its gladness over God's eagerness to forgive, forgot His anger over sin, not that it had any illusions about this world or saw it any less dark. But it was filled with trust in the catholicity, the conquering power, of grace; filled with confidence in God "who wishes all men to be saved and to come to the knowledge of the truth" (1 Tim 2:4).[52]

In contrasting the Community with the Church, I am in no way attempting to lessen the greatness of the Teacher and his men. Quite the contrary, I am led by their Rule, which bids that "none shall be abased below his appointed position or exalted above his allotted place" (ii 23). There was truth and real beauty at Qumran, much that commands respect, much that compels admiration. Still, the Com-

52. Cf. Coppens, *op. cit.*, pp. 33–34.

munity is not the New Covenant. None of its members could possibly have written St. Paul's hymn on love, none said that without love all gifts are vain, all life is empty (1 Cor 13). None could have exclaimed, like St. John, that not to love is not to know God, for God is love (1 Jn 4:8).

> *Thou cause of all good!*
> *Fountain of all knowledge,*
> *Spring of holiness,*
> *Zenith of all glory,*
> *Might omnipotent,*
> *Beauty that never fades!*
>
> (1QS x 12) [53]

So the Qumranites called God. The man who thus inspired them must have been a towering figure. His title bespeaks his greatness, but no less his limitation: he was the Teacher of Justice. He did not plead with the burdened to come to him, nor weep over Jerusalem for not having sought the wing of his care. We do not read of him that he had compassion with a widow who had lost her only child, nor that he spoke of God as a father longing for his wayward son and going out to meet him. He did not see God's love as searching for man the way a poor woman searches for a lost coin, nor could he ever have told the parable of the Good Samaritan in answer to the question: "Who is my neighbor?"

The Teacher of Justice and Christ are incommensurable; Qumran is not the cradle of the Church. Still, for all their shortcomings, the monks of Qumran, poor, chaste, and obedient, penitents of Israel, warriors against the forces of darkness, watchers for God's kingdom, are the Christian's kin.

---

53. The translation is by Gaster, *op. cit.*, p. 117.

Barry Ulanov

THE PAINTER AND THE PROPHETS

THERE has been no dearth of brave and confident generalizations about Michelangelo the man, the painter, the poet, the sculptor, the architect. These estimates speak boldly about his psychology, his aesthetic and poetic philosophy, but rarely, if at all, of his theology. It is difficult to say of any one of these judgments whether it reveals more of its author and his age or of Michelangelo and his. Whatever of the truth may or may not be found in the great spate of words committed to the task of judging Michelangelo's achievement, there is little doubt that we know it as much in terms of the judgments of five centuries as we do in and for itself—perhaps more. For the frame often dwarfs the picture, and when the picture is the Sistine Chapel ceiling, so far removed in physical reality from the viewer's eye, so endlessly complex, so prolific of intimate relationships among its own figures that even a telephoto lens does not make everything clear—when it is such a picture, then it is possible to elaborate almost any sort of judgment about it and to construct for it a frame compounded as much of fantasy as of fact.

The rhapsodies start early with the extraordinary rhetoric of Giorgio Vasari's life of "Michelagnolo Buonarotti of Florence, Painter, Sculptor and Architect," in which Michelangelo is given the status of divinity, or at least of a divine afflatus.[1] By comparison, Ascanio Condivi's *Vita di Michelagnolo Buonarroti*, published in 1553 as a corrective to the exaggerations and misstatements of the first version of Vasari's *Vita,* may at first sound weak and almost unappreciative.

1. See, for example, the opening paragraph, in which the birth of Michelangelo, "a genius universal in each art," is described in terms which rival the creation of Adam, or the narration of the "honoured obsequies, attended by all artists," to which approximately one-seventh of the life is devoted; in Giorgio Vasari, *The Lives of the Painters, Sculptors, and Architects,* trans. A. B. Hinds (London: Everyman, 1927), IV, 108, 179–192.

Condivi calls his master "the unique painter and sculptor"; [2] before he is finished, he has found him without any competition among the ancients, in sculpture at least—a superlative he limits to one art for the sole reason that "of the painting of the ancients there is no memorial." Finally, Condivi praises him as one who "loved not only human beauty, but universally every beautiful thing." [3]

Benvenuto Cellini, who knew Michelangelo fairly well, cannot so much as mention him in his autobiography without the Homeric adjective: almost everywhere that Michelangelo's name appears so too does the description "great" or "noble" or "stupendous," but most of all and highest of all "the divine Michel Agnolo." [4]

The encomia continued to be as ornamental through the seventeenth and eighteenth centuries, although, following the initiative of Pietro Aretino, some exception was taken in the years of the Counter-Reformation to the abundance of nude figures in Michelangelo's work. His offers of friendship spurned by Michelangelo, Aretino had seized the opportunity to attack the nudes in the "Last Judgment" wall of the Sistine Chapel in a letter to Michelangelo which he then had caused to be as "open" as possible, with the consequence that Pope Paul IV had ordered the immediate diapering of the figures.[5] For many in the seventeenth century, Michelangelo ranked somewhere behind Raphael as a painter, but still held title to immortality.[6] In the eighteenth century, the English painter William Hogarth found "the whole mysterie of the art" of painting in a statement attributed to Michelangelo by the late sixteenth-century theorist Giovanni Paolo Lomazzo.[7] And in the same century, in the same country, Sir Joshua Reynolds saw "sublimity" best expressed in the work of Michelangelo, placing him in this respect even before the still rapturously admired Raphael.[8]

2. See the translation by Charles Holroyd in his *Michel Angelo Buonarroti* (London: Duckworth, 1911), III, 3.

3. *Ibid.*, pp. 66, 74–75.

4. See *The Life of Benvenuto Cellini Written by Himself*, trans. J. A. Symonds (London: Phaidon, 1949), pp. 18, 19, 44, 57, 79.

5. See Frank P. Chambers, *The History of Taste* (New York: Columbia University Press, 1932), pp. 47–49.

6. *Ibid.*, pp. 94–95.

7. See *Literary Sources of Art History*, ed. Elizabeth Gilmore Holt (Princeton: Princeton University Press, 1947), pp. 260–261, 491, for the relevant passage in Lomazzo's *Treatise on the Art of Painting* and Hogarth's reference to it.

8. *Ibid.*, p. 510.

It is in the nineteenth century, however, that the descriptions appeared that seem today to hover over any discussion of Michelangelo's work. Following closely upon the first modern biographies in England, Germany, and Italy, Walter Pater, in 1872, identified "the true type of the Michelangelesque" as

sweetness and strength, pleasure with surprise, an energy of conception which seems at every moment about to break through all the conditions of comely form, recovering, touch by touch, a loveliness found usually only in the simplest natural things—*ex forti dulcedo*.[9]

Appreciations by Henry Fuseli and by Stendhal, by Burckhardt (but not in his *Civilization of the Renaissance in Italy,* in which Michelangelo plays a very minor role indeed), and by Michelet, made notable additions to the Michelangelo dossier. At the end of the century, in 1892, the two-volume *Life* by John Addington Symonds filled in the picture sketched by the same writer in his *Renaissance in Italy* and in the preface to his translation of Michelangelo's sonnets. These are the terms in which always thereafter Michelangelo would have to be accepted or rejected: "Michelangelo . . . as Carlyle might have put it, is the Hero as Artist." But this is not mere hero worship:

About the quality of his genius opinions may, will, and ought to differ. It is so pronounced, so peculiar, so repulsive to one man, so attractive to another, that, like his own dread statue of Lorenzo de' Medici, "it fascinates and is intolerable." There are few, I take it, who can feel at home with him in all the length and breadth and dark depths of the regions that he traversed. The world of thoughts and forms in which he lived habitually is too arid, like an extinct planet, tenanted by mighty elemental beings with little human left to them but visionary Titan-shapes, too vast and void for common minds to dwell in pleasurably. The sweetness that emerges from his strength, the beauty which blooms rarely, strangely, in unhomely wise, upon the awful crowd of his conceptions, are only to be apprehended by some innate sympathy or by long incubation of the brooding intellect.[10]

In these same concluding pages of the Symonds biography, another of the central distinctions about Michelangelo is made, one that will

9. Walter Pater, "The Poetry of Michelangelo," in *The Renaissance* (London: Macmillan, 1873), p. 75.
10. John Addington Symonds, *The Life of Michelangelo Buonarroti* (London: Macmillan, 1900), II, 373.

be made again and again, in just these terms: "If we seek Michelangelo's affinities," Symonds asserts, "we find them in Lucretius and
Beethoven, not in Sophocles and Mozart. He belongs to the genus of
deep, violent, colossal, passionately striving natures; not, like Rafa-
ello, to the smooth, serene, broad, exquisitely finished, calmly perfect tribe." [11]

How this rhetoric proliferates itself! In the classic *Abstraction and
Empathy* of 1908, Wilhelm Worringer recalls for his readers "the
incubus, the oppressive dream . . . the tormented, impotent desire
to tear oneself free, which lifts every creation of Michelangelo's spirit
into a realm of profound and gigantic tragedy." [12]

To come to our own day, Erwin Panofsky attempts a scholarly explanation of what has been called "the tense and superb arrogance
of Michelangelo," [13] of his "explosive personality" and "volcanic nature," [14] of his "protest, achieved with obvious difficulty, against beautiful, perfect, immaculate form, a manifesto in the shapelessness
of which there is something aggressive and self-destructive." [15] For
Panofsky, much of the tension, the explosiveness, and the self-
destruction can be explained by "Neoplatonism":

. . . among all his contemporaries Michelangelo was the only one who
adopted Neoplatonism not in certain aspects but in its entirety, and not
as a convincing philosophical system, let alone as the fashion of the day,
but as a metaphysical justification of his own self. . . . While the Neoplatonic belief in the "presence of the spiritual in the material" lent a
philosophical background to his aesthetic and amorous enthusiasm for
beauty, the opposite aspect of Neoplatonism, the interpretation of human
life as an unreal, derivative and tormenting form of existence comparable
to a life in Hades, was in harmony with that unfathomable dissatisfaction
with himself and the universe which is the very signature of Michelangelo's genius.[16]

11. *Ibid.*, p. 374. This is the inevitable treatment of Michelangelo by popular
biographers and historians. See, for example, Egon Friedell, *A Cultural History of
the Modern Age*, trans. C. F. Atkinson (New York: Knopf, 1931), II, 435, in
which the same terms occur in a comparison, once more, of Beethoven and Michelangelo.

12. Trans. M. Bullock (New York: International Universities Press, 1953), p. 85.

13. Martin Johnson, *Art and Scientific Thought* (London: Faber, 1944), p. 143.

14. Curt Sachs, *The Commonwealth of Art* (New York: Norton, 1946), p. 342.

15. Arnold Hauser, *The Social History of Art* (New York: Knopf, 1951),
p. 370.

16. Erwin Panofsky, *Studies in Iconology* (New York: Oxford University Press,
1939), p. 180. Panofsky is too quick to identify Christian commonplace as "Neo-

Finally, among all who make this approach to Michelangelo, smothered in adjectives, there are those who find in him beyond everything else the "mark of the superhuman," for, as Leonardo Olschki says, "Michelangelo's universality consists in his belief in the superhuman as the only worthy subject and motive of artistic creation." [17]

THE SISTINE CHAPEL

TO THE "tormented" creature preoccupied with the "superhuman," "Neoplatonist" by conviction and colossus by achievement, one must add a kind of special pleader in the artist who crafted the Sistine Chapel. In it, Heinrich Wölfflin says, "Michelangelo first advanced the thesis, which became deeply significant for the whole century, that no beauty exists outside the human form." The basis for this statement, sharp and definitive as it is, is the vault itself and the vault alone, for he alludes to no other clarification of purpose by the painter.

On principle, he abandons the decoration of flat surfaces with linear designs derived from vegetable forms, and where one would expect entwined foliage decoration one finds human forms and nothing but human forms, with not a trace of ornamental filling-in where the eye can rest. True, Michelangelo made distinctions and subordinated some of the cat-

platonic notions." Necessarily, Michelangelo spoke the language and painted and carved the figures of his own time, but all his major sources of aesthetic doctrine as cited by Panofsky—Dante and Cristoforo Landino's Commentary upon the *Commedia,* Petrarch, Marsiglio Ficino, Pico della Mirandola—were far more Christian than Platonic or Neoplatonic, no matter what the borrowings from classical materials. When Panofsky says that Michelangelo's "figures symbolize the fight waged by the soul to escape from the bondage of matter" (*ibid.,* p. 181), he is describing a struggle altogether familiar to Christians, and familiar in just these terms. It is unfortunate that Panofsky's skillful but incomplete examination of the iconography of Michelangelo's works should rest so firmly upon a tradition of interpretation so far removed from the obvious origins of all Christian iconography in the Bible and, if one must go beyond primary sources, in biblical commentary. This is a particularly lamentable omission in the case of Michelangelo, for we know of the influence upon him of the Bible and Christian poets with at least as much certainty as we do of the influence of Plato and the so-called Neoplatonists. It should be added here that a similar incompleteness, with heavier overtones of personal conviction, mars the presentation of the poetry of Michelangelo in *Neoplatonism of the Italian Renaissance* by Nesca A. Robb (London: George Allen and Unwin, 1935), pp. 239–269.

17. Leonardo Olschki, *The Genius of Italy* (New York: Oxford University Press, 1949), p. 324.

egories of figures, as well as introducing variety into the color by making
some figures of stone-bronze-color, but this is not the same thing, and,
look at it how you will, the covering of the entire surface with human
bodies betrays a sort of recklessness which furnishes material for reflection.[18]

Perhaps, for all of Wölfflin's seeming logic and for all the seeming soundness of the arguments of others who have made similar
points about the nudes of the Sistine Chapel, it was neither "recklessness" nor the thesis that "no beauty exists outside the human form"
that motivated Michelangelo in the choice of the human figure as the
central symbol, the metaphor, and the subject of the 145 pictures that
make up the vault. We have substantial evidence in Condivi's *Vita*
that Michelangelo was a student of holy Scripture and had a particular admiration for Dante, most of whose works, the biographer tells
us, he knew by heart.[19] We have the witness of Michelangelo's own
work, with the high place accorded biblical subject matter, and particularly Old Testament figures, those surrounding Moses in the Tomb
of Julius II, the David, the Sistine frescoes. We know that the original
plans for the Chapel were simply to surround geometrical ornament
in the center of the great rounded arch with portraits of the twelve
apostles in the pendentives,[20] and that at Michelangelo's own undertaking there was substituted the extraordinary sequence of Old Testament narratives, surrounded by prophets, sibyls, slaves, and ancestors
of Christ—with the prophets and the sibyls specifically replacing the
apostles. And we have, too, the witness of Michelangelo's letters and
even more of his poetry to his philosophical and theological specula-

18. Heinrich Wölfflin, *Classic Art,* trans. P. and L. Murray (London: Phaidon,
1952), p. 50.
19. Holroyd, *op. cit.,* p. 74.
20. A few technical architectural terms must be used to identify various sections
of the Sistine ceiling. A pendentive is an overhanging surface, usually triangular
and curved, which joins a dome or vault (an arched roof) to a wall. The triangular
shape of the Sistine pendentives is unmistakable to a viewer in the Chapel itself,
but is not always clear in reproductions. A spandrel is another triangular form,
formed by the exterior curve of an arch and the enclosing right angle or by the
space between the curves of contiguous arches and the horizontal lines above or
below them. A lunette is a semi-circular window or window-space, partly surrounded by a vault which the wall intersects. The best way to make sense of these
terms and of the descriptions of the Michelangelo paintings to which they are apposite is to consult such a volume as the new Phaidon Press *Michelangelo* or the older
Phaidon edition of *The Paintings of Michelangelo,* or Charles de Tolnay's *Michelangelo, II. The Sistine Ceiling* (Princeton: Princeton University Press, 1949). All
these volumes provide excellent gatefolds of the ceiling as a whole and single reproductions of its major component parts.

tions. All of these activities and articulations—those of the biblical and Dante student and those of the writer and painter and sculptor—suggest a concern with the human form other than that of physical beauty, or at least that the marvel of outward beauty chiefly signified for him the interior depths, serene as well as tormented, and as thoroughly Christian as they are outwardly "Neoplatonist."

In looking for evidence of this thematic material in Michelangelo's poetry, one must clearly restrict oneself to the years up to and including those four, from 1508 to 1512, in which he worked on the vault of the Sistine. This means that one must exclude the late religious sonnets—for all the striking corroboration of a fervent Christian faith to be found in these unusually lucid and straightforwardly orthodox poems. This means too that one must not roam happily in the poems which find in his friendships with Tommaso Cavalieri and with Vittoria Colonna the beauty, the balance, the selflessness, the grace in sum, which is better explicated and defended in Cicero's *De Amicitia* and St. Ailred of Rievaulx's work on holy friendship than in Plato's *Symposium,* to which commentators ordinarily go for explanation of these relationships in Michelangelo's life. This means, ultimately, restricting oneself to a handful of poems and fragments, which can merely suggest the contents of the later, richer, more artfully constructed works. But even in these early pieces, written when he was in his thirties, the themes are the basic ones. In the reproofs to Pope Julius II and the excoriation of the atmosphere of the Curia, there is Michelangelo's typical disgust with the things of this world, expressed epigrammatically:

> *Signor, se vero è alcun proverbio antico*
> *questo è ben quel, che Chi può, mai non vuole.*
>
> *My Lord, if one ancient proverb is true*
> *it is that one which says, He who can never will.*[21]

And he complains, not once, but several times:

> *Qua si fa elmi di calici e spade*
> *e'l sangue di Cristo si vend' a giumelle,*
> *e croce e spine son lance e rotelle;*
> *e pur da Cristo pazienzia cade!*

21. The best edition of the poems is *Die Dichtung des Michelagniolo Buonarroti,* edited by Karl Frey (Berlin, 1897), but the sonnets at least can be consulted in any one of several editions, some bilingual, of the translations of J. A. Symonds.

Here chalices are made into helmets and swords,
and the blood of Christ is sold by the handful,
His cross and thorns are spears and shields;
and even the patience of Christ wears thin.

He describes, as well, the physical misery, the dizziness he encountered on the scaffolding, his body aching from the cramped position in
which he had to lie in order to paint the ceiling above him, *un ricco
pavimento,* a rich covering of paint drops on his face, his eyes squint-
ing and his judgment poor. And there are the early madrigals in
which he laments the unsteady course of earthly love, manic in its
heights, depressive in its depths:

Chi è quel che per forza a te mi mena,
Oimè, oimè, oimè,
Legato e stretto, e son libero e sciolto?

What is the force that pulls me toward you,
Alas, alas, alas,
That all at once draws and ties me and sets me loose and free?

There is in this poetry an unending series of paradoxes and problems,
in which the self, all too conscious of itself, is never sure just who or
what is in possession:

Come puo esser ch'io non sia più mio?
O Dio, o Dio, o Dio!
Chi m'a tolto a me stesso?

How can it be that I am not myself any more?
O Lord, Lord, Lord!
Who has robbed me of myself?

These early poems anticipate almost every one of the major themes
of the poetry to come: the simple and moving last sonnets, prayers
each of them, prayers at the foot of the cross, prayers asking for
strength and purgation and for grace in his last moments, that he
might be brought to see God, and prayers in contemplation of the
precious Blood and the crucified Christ; the poems *in morte,* after the
death of his beloved friend Vittoria Colonna, and those with which
he mourns the death of the exquisite youth Cecchino Bracci, who died
in 1544 at the age of seventeen; all those on the afflictions of love,

love insistently mortal and hence inevitably tainted, whether directed
to Tommaso Cavalieri or to Vittoria; all those poems, of a tolerable
variety, in which desire, concupiscence, of no matter what kind, leads
to death, death physical or spiritual, after which the poet must be-
moan his personal loss. Only the foretaste of the poetry of beauty is
missing, and this is at least implicit in the philosophy of the poems
outlined, however much of the tenderness and the poetic strength of
the later Michelangelo may be lacking.

It is not difficult to see in this poetry, by suggestion at least, the
lines which celebrate heavenly beauty prefigured by earthly loveliness, the lines that mark the evanescent character of beauty in nature
just as in man, the lines which proclaim man's exile here on earth and
look forward to his beatitude in the heaven to come. There are loud
echoes of the Platonic doctrine of reminiscences, or at least of the
conventional vocabulary of this concept of an ultimate reality, a
heaven beyond the heavens, whose archetypes are seen on earth only
in fuzzy reflection and wavering shadow. But here again the outward
appearance of Platonism or Neoplatonism is, like the elusive beauty
Michelangelo pursued so relentlessly in his poetry, painting, sculpture,
architecture, merely suggestive of a greater Christian or Judaeo-Christian reality. The underlying idea is familiar enough to readers of the
Old Testament and the New, to readers of Marsiglio Ficino's *Theo-
logica Platonica* and Pico della Mirandola's *Oration on the Dignity of
Man*, or of any other work in which a pagan cortex is described that a
Christian nucleus may be defined; it is particularly clear to all who
know Dante's poetry well, even if not as well as did Michelangelo.
The personification of love that speaks in that poem of Michelangelo's
written some time in the 1530s—

> *I son colui che ne' prim anni tuoi*
> *Gli occhi tuoi infermi volsi alla beltate*
> *Che dalla terra al ciel vivo conduce.*
>
> I am he who in thy first years
> Turned thy frail eyes toward the beauty
> That leads living men from earth to high heaven.

—this persona is indistinguishable from the one that appears in
Dante's *La Vita nuova*, the destination of his followers is the same in

the later as in the earlier work, nothing less than to come close to the love that moves the sun and the other stars, to beauty bare, to within the presence of God Himself. This is the subject of the Sistine Chapel ceiling—this love whose beauty is not mortal (*Amor,* Michelangelo cries in one of his later poems, *la tua beltà non è mortale,* "Love, thy beauty is not mortal"); this presence he would see wherever he goes (*Deh fammiti vedere,* he pleads with God in one of the last sonnets, *in ogni loco!,* "O Lord, make me see thee everywhere!"). For the sibyls and the prophets were to Michelangelo intercessors with heaven in that central quest of his life just as was the dead youth Bracci, or Vittoria Colonna, or any other in the long line of illustrious ambassadors dispatched from man's earthly dwellings to his heavenly home by poets from Dante's time and Petrarch's to Shakespeare's and John Donne's. To Dante's Beatrice and Petrarch's Laura and the other members of that blessed company, Michelangelo added not only, in a familiar tradition, the beloved dead of his poems, but, in a less familiar one, the great figures that surmount the walls of the Sistine and support the Old Testament histories of its ceiling, the sibyls of Delphi and of Erythrae, Isaiah, Jonah, Daniel, and all the rest.

THE SIBYLS

THE thirteenth-century sequence, *Dies irae,* most probably composed for the first Sunday in Advent, later to become a part of the Requiem Mass, begins:

> *Dies irae, dies illa,*
> *Solvet saeclum in favilla;*
> *Teste David cum Sibylla.*

> *Day of wrath, that day*
> *When the world shall melt into ashes,*
> *As David and the Sibyls say.*

For Michelangelo, this was a testament not lightly to be disregarded; to him, the sibyls were witnesses of more than ordinary significance. He had a whole tradition to rely upon in choosing five of them to sit beside the prophets in the Sistine pendentives. Whether his source was the *Divinae Institutiones* of Lactantius, written at the beginning of the fourth century, or that most curious of the pseudepigrapha, the

Sibylline Oracles, compiled mainly in the course of four centuries from about 160 B.C. to A.D. 240,[22] these ancient pagan prophetesses would serve him well as mediators of grace,[23] figures of ecstatic character, whose messianic predictions had had at least a literary importance for centuries and who had, some of them anyway, convinced not only Lactantius but St. Augustine and other Fathers of the authenticity of their visions of the coming of Christ.

The precise text upon which Michelangelo may have based his conceptions of the sibyls would be difficult, if not impossible, to run to earth. There is little doubt that he knew both the *Institutes* and the *Oracles* and probably selected his five from the same master list of ten sibyls in Marcus Terentius Varro's *Res Divinae* upon which Lactantius had based his brief discussion and characterization of these pagan prophetic women, best identified by their geographical locations. He had the illustrious sanction of Virgil, in the *Fourth Eclogue,* the so-called messianic eclogue, where the Cumaean sibyl prophesies the coming of a redeemer of distinctly Christ-like features,[24] and in the remarkable passage in the Sixth Book of the *Aeneid* in which the same sibyl's

22. The *Sibylline Oracles* grew to their present form from a pagan nucleus. Several centuries before Christ, there existed in Egypt, as elsewhere, a collection of the sayings of various pagan quasi-prophetesses, and as early as the middle of the second century B.C., Jews in Alexandria, wishing to make use of this popular collection for their apostolate among the pagans, inserted in it references to the belief in one God, to the Mosaic ordinances, to events in Israel's history, and to the messianic times. From perhaps the year A.D. 80, Christian interpolators made additions of their own to those of the Alexandrian Jews. Since the messianic references are interpolations, the *Sibylline Oracles* have no theological value; but they do serve as a guide to the temper of the interpolators as well as of their readers. And it is as a guide to Michelangelo's mind that the sibylline books are mentioned here. The real witness of the pagan sibyls, when freed from all accretions, is—like that of the whole world of pagan myths and sages—quite different, of course, from that of the prophets of Israel. While the former voice man's gropings for God, his yearning for redemption, the latter tell of God's search for man and announce the redemption to come.

23. The word "mediators" is used here and elsewhere in this study with strict regard for its Catholic sense. According to Catholic teaching, it is Christ who has broken the chains of sin, Christ alone who is the Saviour of all, the *one* Mediator of justice between God and man. Only in, through, and because of Him can others mediate with God. Therefore the apostle can write: "Pray for one another that you may be saved" (Jas 5:16). It is because of Christ that Mary, the saints of the New and of the Old Testaments, all the blessed in heaven, can be called upon for their intercession. This is the sense in which Michelangelo saw the sibyls as mediators of grace.

24. Some of the "messianic passages" in the translation of John Jackson (Oxford: Oxford University Press, 1921), pp. 11, 12, are more clear than others. For example: "On thee, child, at every turn the unlaboured earth shall shower her gifts.

trance, after Apollo possesses her, is described in a way that foreshadows the mystical union of God and the soul to come through Christ.[25] Twice his master Dante had referred to Cumaea,[26] and there was a vast literature of mythology, of ancient drama and poetry, and of what at least pretended to be history, even of philosophy and the vague outlines of ancient anthropology, to guide him in his use of the sibyl of Delphi. For the others he had a variety of sources to draw upon, if he wanted to use any: St. Augustine's description of the Erythraean sibyl in *The City of God,* where she serves as a prophet of the Last Judgment,[27] and the characters given Persica and Libyca by Lactantius and the *Oracles.* But the abiding impression one receives from any lingering examination of these figures is that they represent a thoroughly original interpretation of the prophetic women of the pagans, different, of course, in temperament and dignity from the uniquely inspired prophets of Israel with whom they alternate in the Sistine pendentives, and necessarily more limited in insight, but each speaking in her own way those clear and precise words of Virgil's Cumaea: *Deus, ecce deus!* [28]

One can see these prophetesses as marking a sequence "determined, first, by their spiritual link with the histories above, and secondly, by the idea of the decrescendo of the prophetic faculties proceeding in the direction of the altar"; [29] one can accept some sort of plan to represent continents and nations; or one can, with more justice perhaps and certainly with greater ease, speculate on the attitudes of the figures and through them on an iconography of grimace and gesture, of drapery and scroll, as Wölfflin does:

What is it that distinguishes the *Delphic Sibyl* from all Quattrocento figures? What gives such grandeur to the action, and endows the whole

. . . Yet shall some few stains of the old-time sin live on. . . . And thou, dear offspring of the gods, mighty seed of a Jove to be—enter thou on thy great office, for the time is all but here! Behold, the world's ponderous sphere bows before thee —earth and the tracts of ocean and the empyreal vault!"

25. See the *Aeneid,* VI, 77 (in the Jackson translation, p. 233): ". . . in her cavern the prophetess, intolerant yet of Phoebus' will, raved in limitless frenzy, straining to exorcize the mighty god from her soul: but all the more he curbed her foaming lips to weariness, subdued her fierce heart, and moulded her to his constraint."

26. In the *Paradiso,* XXXIII, 61–66, and in the *Convivio,* IV, 26.

27. *De Civ. Dei,* XVIII, 23 and 47 (PL 41:579–581, 609–610).

28. *Aeneid,* VI, 46.

29. De Tolnay, *op. cit.,* p. 153.

with an appearance of necessary inevitability? The motive is the sudden attention of the Seer as she turns her head and momentarily pauses, holding up the scroll. The head is seen from the simplest viewpoint, not tilted, and full front, but this attitude is held only under strain, for the upper part of the torso is bent sideways and forward and the arm, reaching across, is another contradiction of the direction of the head; yet, despite the difficulties, it is just this which gives the pose with the head seen from the front its force, and the vertical axis is maintained among opposing elements. . . . The eyes of the prophetess follow the direction of the head by their own movement to the right, and the effect of these searching, wide-open eyes carries at all distances. . . . The hair is blown in the same direction and so is the great sweep of the mantle which encloses the whole figure like a sail.[30]

But all of these alternatives miss a few essentials, simple and obvious, but certainly to Michelangelo's point.

On one side of the ceiling, a perfect symmetry is established among three of the sibyls, the central position being assumed by Cumaea, the venerable prophetess crowned by Virgil and Dante. She is of signal importance because of that similitude in the last book of the *Paradiso* in which the transitory nature of man's perceptions of God in general and of Dante's vision of Him in particular is briefly and beautifully compared to the scattering of the leaves on which the sibyl had written her revelations:

> *Così la neve al sol si disigilla;*
> *così al vento nelle foglie levi*
> *si perdea la sentenza di Sibilla.*

> **Thus does the snow lose its imprint in the sun;**
> **thus in the wind on the frail leaves**
> **does one lose the sibyl's sentence.**[31]

On either side of the Cumaean sibyl are Libyca and Delphica, both of a surpassing youthful loveliness, although the latter seems closer to ecstasy and vision; both, at the moment, free of the book which appears in one way or another with each of the sibyls, although Libyca seems to be reaching for her volume while Delphica has consigned hers to the figures behind her, those tradition calls genii; both, really,

30. Wölfflin, *op. cit.,* pp. 61–62.
31. Dante, *Paradiso,* XXXIII, 64–66.

in poses of the same order, although the Libyan sibyl is much more contorted as she turns toward the book than is the prophetess of Delphi.

Across the vault, the two remaining sibyls, Erythraea and Persica, the youngest and the oldest in appearance of the seers, offer another perfect balance as they face each other, their books and their supporting figures in similar harmonies of place and movement. Behind Erythraea and her book rises the figure of a genius holding a scale, a suitable symbol for one who prophesies the Last Judgment. Behind Persica and the book she is reading with such concentration rests another apparently aged figure, kneeling, perhaps in prayer, fitting attitudes and symbols for the sibyl mentioned first by Lactantius and, by implication anyway, marked as the oldest of the ten he lists.

By their precise symmetry of position, the sibyls point, intentionally or not, to the central panel of the center field of the ceiling, to the Creation of Eve, and then, necessarily, from one side of that central scene to the other: from the Creation of Adam, back to God Separating Sky and Water, the Creation of the Sun and Moon, and God Separating Light and Darkness; from the Fall and Expulsion from Paradise, to the Sacrifice of Noah, the Deluge, and the Drunkenness of Noah; on the one side events that proclaim God's solicitous intervention in human affairs from the very beginning of time, on the other side events that show man's fall from grace and the punishments meted out by a just God, but always with the prefiguration of redemption inescapably present. And if in the ark of Noah's salvation we can see a "type" of Christian baptism [32] and in God's covenant with Noah a prefiguring of God's new Covenant with all men sealed by Jesus, so too in Michelangelo's sibyls can we see forerunners of the prophets. For they are themselves what might be called cousins once removed of Old Testament figures, offering to the meditative viewer of the Sistine Chapel vault a valuable iconography of salvation, incomplete without the prophets, but demonstrating on another level the long reach in time and the vast spread in history of the prevision of the Messiah, who is really the subject of the plastic contemplation in line and color, of the prayer in paint, that is Michelangelo's ceiling.

32. See 1 Pet 3:20–21.

THE PROPHETS

Two themes clearly unite the seven prophets Michelangelo chose to alternate with the sibyls in the Sistine pendentives: their visions or prefigurations of the Messiah and of the Last Judgment. Whether we start with Jonah, who himself prefigured the death and resurrection of Christ, and, following the great arc made by his left hand, move to his left, past Daniel, Isaiah, Zechariah, Joel, Ezekiel, and Jeremiah, or reverse the direction, we are confronted with the same ineluctable and unassailable narrative of prophecy and prediction. Verse by verse, chapter by chapter, seer by seer, we face redemption and apocalypse, we face the Redeemer and Judge. Any attentive examination of the texts must yield these points, these themes, and the unifying Figure who joins together not only those twelve enthroned visionaries who act, in one way or another, as His appointed representatives, but every one of the 343 figures who fill the ten thousand square feet of the Sistine vault.

The revelations of the coming of the Messiah in the writings of the seven prophets are familiar enough not to require extensive rehearsal here; but the close relationship in each of the books between the texts of messianic prophecy and those which reveal divine judgments of that special character we call apocalyptic does require and deserve further amplification if the special roles of the prophets in the Sistine Chapel and in Michelangelo's life are to be more accurately presented.

The least obvious, and yet in some ways the most important, of these relationships is to be found in the book of Jonah. As a "type" of Christ, Jonah is unmistakable: in his being swallowed and, after fervent prayer, being vomited forth from the belly of the whale, the prophet prefigures His passion and resurrection, for "Jonah was in the belly of the fish three days and three nights" (2:1). As one who saw the coming of the Last Judgment, Jonah is not so clear, and yet we know of the destruction ordained of God for Nineveh, that pagan city of "wickedness" to which he has been sent to preach. And we know as well that Jonah's prophecy of destruction, a prophecy in which he merely acts as intermediary for God, is not fulfilled and that God brings mercy to bear upon Nineveh and pardons the repentant pagan people. Jonah is angry at the display of mercy, and yet he knows better, for he says after the pardon: "I know that thou art a gracious and merciful God, patient, and of much compassion, and easy to forgive evil" (4:2). What, finally, we know with Jonah in the last verse of his book is that God's mercy extends beyond the children of Israel to all mankind, indeed to all creation: "And shall not I spare Nineveh," the Lord says, "that great city, in which there are more than a hundred and twenty thousand persons that know not how to distinguish between their right hand and their left, and many beasts?" (4:11).

Michelangelo's Jonah has learned this lesson—in detail. In that great contortion of his body which follows the motion of his arms, he directs his impassioned glance across the whole ceiling, presumably taking in the Creation of Adam and all antecedent events in the making of the universe. Most strikingly, he distinguishes between his right and left hand: his index fingers point down, both of them, perhaps indicating, as De Tolnay suggests, "the abyss from which he came but which he has left behind in this moment of grace and *renovatio*"; [33] more important, he points with the two fingers to the spandrel in which is re-enacted the nailing of Haman to the trunk of a tree [34] and in which Esther appears in two different scenes, one in which she is warned by Mordecai of the attempt to be made on the life of King Ahasuerus, and the other in which she warns the king of his peril. Thus does Michelangelo's Jonah point with the fingers of his two hands to two figures, to Haman, the recipient of God's just wrath, and to Esther, the agent of His mercy. Thus has the Jonah here in the Sistine learned the lesson of the last verse of the last chapter of his book and thus does he point to one who has been delivered, whose prayer to the Lord that He show Himself "in the time of our tribulation" and "deliver us by thy hand, and help me, who have no other helper, but thee" (Est 14:12, 14) has been answered. It is a rich reading of the words of the book of Jonah and a profound parable based upon it that Michelangelo paints, in which many events are linked, all of which prefigure the Last Judgment, as justice and mercy are demonstrated and order in the universe is revealed through a

33. De Tolnay, *op. cit.*, p. 52.
34. For the source of this variation on the biblical text, see Dante, *Purgatorio,* XVII, 25–30.

MICHELANGELO: Daniel

MICHELANGELO: Joel

MICHELANGELO: Zechariah

MICHELANGELO: Ezekiel

prophet who finds his place in this firmament not only as one who saw signs but as one who was himself a sign.

On the lateral wall to the right of the altar (and to the left of Jonah) sit the two prophets who most unmistakably represent the central themes of the pendentives, Daniel and Isaiah. Their roles could not be more clearly defined, the first the author of "the first great apocalyptic work"; [35] the second the great prophet of deliverance, the recorder of so many of the titles of Christ—for example, Emmanuel, mighty God, Prince of peace—and the description of the Messiah as born of a virgin mother, endowed with wisdom and understanding, counsel and might and knowledge, and destined to bring peace and justice to the world.

The first half of the book of Daniel is autobiographical in tone and largely devoted to a series of eloquent tributes to the Lord, ending in chapter 6 with the prescient words: "He is the Deliverer and Saviour, doing signs and wonders in heaven and in earth, who hath delivered Daniel out of the lions' den" (6:27), a majestic description of the Messiah which is repeated almost word for word to bring the book to a close. As much as anything else these words describe the visions which make up chapters 7 to 12 of Daniel; they suggest, at least in part, the high wonder and dramatic portent of a book in which the kingdoms of Christ and Antichrist are set against each other and the angels act as explicators and exegetes in sorting out Daniel's visions for himself and for his readers.

Perhaps the most striking quality of both books is the alternation of the two themes which concern us here. In the rich mosaic which is the book of Isaiah, the elements of sin and chastisement, of rise and fall and rise, of justice and injustice, alternate with the great consoling passages which delineate the marks of the Messiah and lead the writer of the concluding chapters to those passages which recount the final fall and rise of Israel, when the Lord "will bring upon her as it were a river of peace" (66:12). But before this longest of the prophetic books is brought to a close, there is a brief, tightly organized section of four chapters (24–27) of typically apocalyptic character, which, whatever the modern disputes about its authorship, must have struck Michelangelo as further evidence of the indissoluble tie that

35. See H. H. Rowley, *The Relevance of Apocalyptic* (London: Lutterworth Press, 1944), p. 39.

links together Messiah and Judgment and gives motivation and purpose to the Sistine seers.

It is fitting, then, to find in Michelangelo's Daniel and again in his Isaiah as much security without complacency as paintings can convey. The reflective Daniel sits transcribing the momentous messages brought to him, now perhaps by the weighty book held before him by one genius, and later, once more, by the other genius who stands behind him, wrapped symbolically in the prophet's mantle. Michelangelo's noble Isaiah has turned from his book and does not quite pay full attention to the two genii who hold forth new visions to him: this prophet has seen a fulfillment larger than words or gestures can indicate; he is content to rest upon what he knows and to point the index finger of his left hand in a delicate but firm motion that leads the viewer's eye downward, perhaps to the altar, almost certainly to the Chapel itself, and by implication to its *raison d'être,* not simply as a church where Mass can be celebrated, but as the outstanding chapel of the Vicar of Christ on earth.

The remaining four prophets are, as one might expect them to be, old men, Michelangelo's contemplatives, who sift through the evidence for the coming of a Messiah, even as Isaiah did, and look for the likelihood of an exacting punishment and a just reward and the signs of both, just as Daniel and Jonah and Isaiah did. They are grouped together in the Sistine, at Jonah's right and to the left of the altar, Jeremiah, Ezekiel, Joel, and Zechariah, all pondering the significance of what they have seen and are in the process of transmuting and transmitting. Only one of them, Jeremiah, is not engaged in the actual process of examining or communicating part of his text, and he is so engrossed in the meaning of what he has to say in his book of Lamentations that he can be described as engaged in the same process, a central one for these four men in the Sistine.

Michelangelo's Jeremiah may represent him as the author only of the five chapters of Lamentations and not of the fifty-two of the book of prophecy which precedes it in the Bible; or in some other way his significance among the Sistine prophets may be limited to the text of Lamentations, for in a fragment of the scroll visible at his right, in the lower lefthand corner of his pendentive, appears the Latin transliteration of the first letter of the Hebrew alphabet, ALEF, in capital letters, and the Roman numeral V, which together clearly indicate the opening verses of the five chapters of Lamentations, each of which consists of verses which begin, in turn, with each of the twenty-two letters of the Hebrew alphabet. Michelangelo's intention may have been simply to emphasize the book of Lamentations rather than to separate it from the other book of Jeremiah, for the tone and substance of both are essentially the same. The evil doings of his people are spelled out in the one—lying, oppression of the weak, idolatry, giving heed to false prophets, and the persecution of Jeremiah himself—and so too are the punishments that will come upon this people that is, in one of the great figures of Israel and its Creator, as clay in the hands of the potter. In the other, a brief compendium of the misdoings and the misfortunes of the Jews is offered, complete to the destruction of Jerusalem and the Temple, ending with the most moving of Jeremiah's laments, that prayer in which he begs the Lord to "convert us . . . and we shall be converted," to "renew our days, as from the beginning" (Lam 5:21, 22).

That Jeremiah should be the most deeply absorbed in thought of the Sistine prophets is reasonable enough. He is overwhelmed with grief, broken in heart; his is the most prolonged of lamentations and for the most personal of reasons, for the persecution of himself he narrates is so intense and bitter and so completely indefensible as to prefigure graphically the persecution of Jesus. There is, however, as there must be in the words of any of the prophets chosen for the Sistine pendentives, comfort for all in the prediction of the coming of a Messiah in chapters 30 and 33 of the book of Jeremiah, and personal comfort for Baruch in chapter 45, to whom the Lord, Jeremiah reveals, will bring salvation, indicating the kind of renewal of "our days" he pleads for in the last of his Lamentations.

The element of the personal is strikingly present again in Ezekiel, both as he appears in the Old Testament and as he is painted by Michelangelo. This is, after all, the seer of visions so completely his own as to rival the most recondite of mystics. But in the vision of mankind reborn in flesh and bone on Judgment Day (37:1–14) he is also the prophet of the resurrection and, in the course of many messianic prophecies, the most articulate of defenders of God's justice as it will be distributed in the separation of the wicked from the virtuous (chaps. 18 and 33). In the persecutions of Gog, ruler of Magog, which Ezekiel prophesies, there is perhaps as precise an analogy to the book of the Apocalypse of the New Testament as there is to be found anywhere in the Old. And, finally, in the rebuilt Temple of the last nine chapters of his book, there is a vision of the City of God remarkable for its reach across the two Covenants between God and man and for the precision of its name, "The Lord Is There," one which for generations of Christians has accurately described the splendor of the New Jerusalem.

Michelangelo's Ezekiel is a man possessed by the words in the scroll hanging from his left hand, possessed but far from certain of all the consequences of his visions: he looks far into some indeterminate beyond and in the extraordinarily eloquent gesture of his right hand pleads some cause, presumably that of the "children of a hard face and of an obstinate heart" (2:4) to whom the Lord has sent him as prophet, which is to say as intermediary. For it is Ezekiel as no other prophet who is addressed by God, again and again, as "son of man." And if Ezekiel seems, in this company, the most possessed by his prophecies, that too makes sense if one examines the text which must be the source of our understanding of the background of the prophets the painter chose to paint: for it was Ezekiel who was commanded of God to eat the book of "lamentations and canticles and woe" he has been handed from heaven, just as John the Evangelist was commanded later (2:8—3:3; Apoc 10:9–10). And like John, he did eat it and digest it and in the Sistine version of the enraptured "son of man" it has—visibly—become part of him.

With Joel and Zechariah, Michelangelo demonstrates an originality at once arresting and profound, which signifies the use he makes of the prophets. For in choosing these two among all the eleven minor prophets after Jonah, he underscored, although with a measure of poetic indirection and pictorial subtlety, his strikingly personal understanding of prophets and prophecy.

One recognizes with ease the pre-eminent position of Daniel and Isaiah, of Jeremiah and Ezekiel, among the prophets: they are the four major prophets, messianic and apocalyptic by turn in their revelations and so understood by commentators and exegetes for centuries. The place of Jonah in this group is equally self-explanatory: as a figure of Christ he belongs logically to this number, and it is in that special role that he rests above the altar, sitting in review upon all events of the Sistine vault. What about Joel and Zechariah? Why not

the other minor prophets who also, lucidly and persuasively, forecast
the coming of the Messiah? Why not Amos and Hosea, Micah and
Nahum, Zephaniah, Obadiah, Haggai, Malachi? There are many explanations, perhaps, but none so convincing, really, as the great spirit
of rejoicing which fills the rhetoric and swells the poetry of the three
chapters of Joel and of the fourteen of Zechariah. For while in these
books alarms are still sounded and the perils of Judgment proclaimed, the prevailing tone is of jubilation in Judaea, which "shall
be inhabited forever" (Jl 3:20), and of singing in Zion, "for behold
I come and I will dwell in the midst of thee, saith the Lord" (Zach
2:10). The land is now sanctified, in the words of Zechariah (2:12),
and the type of Christ he presents is complete even unto name: he is
the high priest Joshua, the son of Jehozedek (3:1). And Joel's invitation is complete to the last generation:

> *Gather together the people,*
> *sanctify the church,*
> *assemble the ancient ones,*
> *gather together the little ones*
> *and them that suck at the breasts:*
> *let the bridegroom go forth from his bed*
> *and the bride from her bride chamber.*
>
> (2:16)

His prophecy is of complete fulfillment on the Day of Judgment:

> *And it shall come to pass in that day,*
> *that the mountains shall drop down sweetness,*
> *and the hills shall flow with milk:*
> *and waters shall flow through all the rivers of Judah:*
> *and a fountain shall come forth of the house of the Lord,*
> *and shall water the torrent of thorns.*
> *Egypt shall be a desolation*
> *and Edom a wilderness destroyed:*
> *because they have done unjustly against the children of Judah*
> *and have shed innocent blood in the land.*
> *And Judaea shall be inhabited forever,*
> *and Jerusalem to generation and generation.*
> *And I will cleanse their blood which I had not cleansed:*
> *and the Lord will dwell in Zion.*
>
> (3:18–21)

Thus do we move along the far side of the Sistine Chapel, to a middle-aged Joel coming to the end of his scroll, with a fine balance of two genii behind him, establishing the harmony of symmetry— they stand on either side of the prophet—and the poise of completion —the closed book firmly grasped in the hand of one of them suggests termination as clearly as does Joel's look at the last characters on his scroll. This genius, he of the book, points outside the pendentive, past the serene countenance of his fellow genius, to the aged figure of Zechariah who occupies the position opposite to Jonah at the far end of the vault, facing the older generation of prophets (as Michelangelo sees them). Zechariah is not merely an old man: he is the middle-aged Joel turned ancient; no hair on his head, but fully bearded; his nose, his lips, the shape of his head notably cast in the mold of Michelangelo's portrait of the prophet Joel, to whose prophecies his bring more detail and descriptive splendor. Zechariah is shuffling through the pages of his book, coming, at perhaps an old man's pace, to his last words; his happily joined genii looking on behind him with obvious pleasure, relaxed and at ease, in their equanimity entirely different from any of the other genii who accompany the prophets except the composed pair who echo the joyful and consoling meaning of the portrait of Joel.

MEDIATORS OF PEACE

THE central place of the prophets in the New Testament is nowhere better defined than by Jesus in answering the doctor of the Law who wanted to know "which is the great commandment in the Law."

> *Jesus said to him:*
> *" 'Thou shalt love the Lord thy God*
> *with thy whole heart,*
> *and with thy whole soul,*
> *and with thy whole mind.'*
> *This is the greatest and the first commandment.*
> *And the second is like it:*
> *'Thou shalt love thy neighbor as thyself.'*
> *On these two commandments depend the whole*
> *   Law and the Prophets."*
> *   (Mt 22:36–40)*

Thus did Jesus Himself denote the place of the prophets: alongside the Law, they unfold the commandments, they unfold the love and justice of God. And so too does Michelangelo designate the position of the seven prophets of the Sistine Chapel: alongside the histories of the central field and those of the spandrels and the bronze medallions, alternating with the spandrels and the lunettes which present the ancestors of Christ, the prophets—like the sibyls—perform a mediating role in the Sistine Chapel, a work of exposition which is the pictorial analogue of their scriptural duty. But it is not enough to say this, for it leaves unsaid the special words which denote the special grace of the prophets in the life of Michelangelo and which account for the special place—the dominating one—of these particular men of God in the design and execution of the Sistine.

The prophets tell forth the sins and chastisement of Israel, and thus by implication the sins and chastisement of all the children of God everywhere and through all the ages; they also foretell the surcease of suffering which will come through the Messiah at the Last Judgment:

> And all the elect, while they were by their holy living serving as His forerunners, gave promise of Him by prophesying both in deeds and words. For there never was any saint who did not appear as His herald in figure.[36]

But the prophet is gifted with something larger still, larger than foreknowledge and the articulate tongue with which, in his mantic role, to cry forth his prophecies: he speaks well, he speaks boldly, and he speaks, as the Greek word *prophētēs* properly translates the Hebrew *nabi*, for someone, in the name of someone—for and of the Lord. He is, by definition, an intermediary between God and man, who brings upon all who heed his message goodness and understanding and honor: for, as St. Gregory says, "it was meet that all should display that goodness in themselves whereby both all became good, and which they knew to be for the good of all." [37]

The mediation of the prophets is of an exquisite symmetry; its nature is perfectly reciprocal: as the prophet feeds us, we feed him:

> He too feeds the prophet who understands and keeps what is written. Our faith supports him, our advance gives him nourishment; he feeds on

36. St. Gregory the Great, *Moralia*, Preface, IV, 14 (PL 75:524).
37. *Idem.*

our minds and senses, his discourse is sustained by our understanding of it. We give him bread in the morning, in that, placed in the light of the Gospel, we bring to him the establishing of our hearts. By these things is he nourished and strengthened and fills the mouths of them that fast.[38]

Here, in brief, is the motive force in Michelangelo's life, the asceticism which governed not only his personal life but the conduct of his career as an artist. Here is the link between the Scriptures, the prophets, and the sibyls on the one hand, and the poetry, the sculpture, the friendships with Vittoria Colonna and Tommaso Cavalieri, the language of Neoplatonism and of traditional Platonism on the other. The prophets are indeed mediators in Michelangelo's life: they are as logical to him as intercessors in heaven as the saints, for they are members not only in the large sense of the communion of saints but also of the special body of those canonized, whether by *vox populi* or by the positive action of the Holy See, and duly represented in martyrology, missal, or breviary. Thus are the seven prophets of the Sistine traditionally granted feast days, or at least commemorated, in the calendar of the Church. Thus does one pray in the Patriarchal Diocese of Jerusalem:

Lord Jesus, King of the prophets, thou didst foretell by the mouth of thy holy prophet Isaiah thy incarnation, life, death, and glory. Grant, through his intercession, that these sacred mysteries [of the Eucharist] may lead us thy servants to the everlasting joys. Who livest and reignest with God the Father in the unity of the Holy Spirit, God, world without end.

Almighty, everlasting God, in thy fatherly goodness, through the intercession of blessed Jeremiah the prophet, release from the bondage of sin thy servants who plead guilty in thy sight. Let the pain of remorse which is their punishment be outweighed by thy gracious mercy which brings them pardon. Through Jesus Christ our Lord.

O God, thou didst reveal to thy beloved servants the prophets the riches of thy wisdom and knowledge. Grant that, through their intercession, we may never withdraw from the true wisdom, which is Christ, and so in heaven rejoice in the eternal revelation of thy glory. Through the same Jesus Christ our Lord.

38. St. Ambrose, *Epistle LXIII,* 80 (PL 16:1262–1263).

To Beatrice and Laura, then, to Vittoria and Tommaso and young Bracci, and to his sibyls, Michelangelo added the prophets, and did not simply add them, but gave them the place of honor in his personal world of intercessors. This is an artist quite worthy of Cellini's superlatives and Vasari's and Condivi's, but far more important, a man, a poet, a painter of far greater subtlety than the one conjured up by the descriptions of a "deep, violent, colossal, passionately striving" nature, of an "oppressive dream," of a "tense and superb arrogance," of one possessed of "unfathomable dissatisfaction with himself and the universe. . . ." And certainly the beauty allegorized and directly spoken for in the Sistine vault is not that of the human form alone, as Wölfflin and so many others have declared. For the human form is, in general in the Sistine, surrogate for the human soul, and in particular in the configuration of the prophets, deputized to speak for the purpose, the order, and the design—no less—of creation. Far from torment, far from violence, arrogance, or oppression, what Michelangelo communicates in the Sistine Chapel is an understanding of that beauty *che dalla terra al ciel vivo conduce,* that leads living men from earth to high heaven.

Step by step, he moves in the Sistine to the direct contemplation of beauty in the Creator of beauty, uniting, as he does so, the pagan sibyls and the prophets of Israel, the Old and the New Testaments, bringing man from the events antecedent to his creation to the state of the universe when time shall cease and all that shall be shall be forever. And as we contemplate in turn, we are bound to be awed by the realization in time and space of an entity resembling, in some conceptual and plastic way, God the Father, and to be agonized and edified by turns by all the people and places and events that surround and surmount the Creation. The prophets, however, introduce a more personal note, personal to us as well as to the painter: mediators between God and us, mediators by virtue of Him whom they foretold, they bring not so much awe or agony or even edification, but—in all its most honorable meaning—*appeasement.*

Joseph N. Moody

DREYFUS AND AFTER

THE Dreyfus Affair has produced such an enormous literature that there would seem little room for further discussion. It might be argued also that the injustice done to a Jewish captain of the pre-1914 French Army has been dwarfed by the inhumanity of gas chambers, brain-washing, and forced labor camps, with their millions of victims. It might even be alleged that preoccupation with this false charge of treason in the past is unrealistic in our day when such charges seem the normal stuff of partisan politics.

Yet it is these very considerations that sustain our interest in the Affair.[1] The insecurity of the human person in his dealings with the political community, the perennial predicament of the individual faced with the reality of power, these are themes forced upon us by our times. But here we not only have a vivid instance of this confrontation of person and power; we are drawn irresistibly to a case abundantly documented, played out by the most varied characters, and having all the components of a detective thriller. The drama of an individual reveals issues sometimes obscure in abominations committed against a nameless mass, while the still continuing consequences of the Affair imply the tremendous importance of every human being.

Precisely those aspects of the story which add to its appeal introduce also the possibility of distortion. Since the victim is one man, readily identified, we are likely to conclude that the culprit, or culprits, should be equally easy to discover. We should like to settle down as we should with the latest mystery tale and, after an exciting

1. Two volumes on the theme appeared last year: Nicholas Halasz, *Captain Dreyfus: The Story of a Mass Hysteria* (New York: Simon and Schuster, 1955); and Guy Chapman, *The Dreyfus Case: A Reassessment* (New York: Reynal, 1955) —the first excitingly written, perhaps too excitingly; the second far superior in scholarship, scope, and tone.

chase, point an accusing finger at the villain. Not even the complexity of the case dulls our appetite. Though we know that there were three courts-martial and three civilian trials, spread over twelve years, and that there was every possible complication of domestic and foreign policy, we expect this profound drama to be solved, and neatly.

A FIRST SKETCH

IT WAS in the summer of 1894 that the French Ministry of War became aware that some French Army officer was transmitting information to the German Embassy in Paris. There had fallen into the hands of the counter-espionage section[2] of the General Staff an unsigned letter or "list," the famous *bordereau,* enumerating documents the writer intended to send to the German military attaché, Colonel Max von Schwartzkoppen. A precipitate and thoroughly incompetent investigation—featuring disagreements among the handwriting experts consulted—seemed to point to Alfred Dreyfus, a captain of artillery, the only Jewish probationer attached to the General Staff. Arrested for high treason in October 1894, Dreyfus was court-martialed, being convicted in December and sentenced to deportation for life. In March 1895 he was interned on Devil's Island, while his family and a few others continued their struggle to have the verdict revised. The Court of Appeals had already rejected any efforts for revision, for it could deal only with matters of law, not of fact, and, so far as it knew, the law had not been flouted. Not until new facts were available could anything be done.

At last, in March 1896, something new was found. In the wastepaper of the German Embassy, routinely "delivered" to the French counter-espionage section, Colonel Marie-Georges Picquart, the section's newly appointed head, discovered the minute fragments of a letter, a *petit bleu.*[3] Written by von Schwartzkoppen, but never sent, to a French officer on the General Staff, Major Ferdinand Walsin-Esterhazy, it made clear beyond doubt that Esterhazy had a treasonable connection with von Schwartzkoppen. Furthermore, the *borde-*

2. Euphemistically called the Statistical Section. The fact that the case originated in this section, the members of which worked in secret and knew they would be disavowed if their activities became public, had an important bearing on the case.

3. A special delivery letter on thin blue paper, restricted to local Parisian use.

reau, looked at with unprejudiced eyes, could be seen to be in his handwriting. But Picquart's superior officers, General Charles Le Mouton de Boisdeffre and General Charles-Arthur Gonse, the chief and deputy chief of the General Staff, forbade him to pursue his investigations and had him transferred to a remote station in Tunisia.

However, before leaving France for North Africa, Colonel Picquart confided his discoveries about Esterhazy to a friend and lawyer, M. Louis Leblois. Leblois in turn spoke of these grave suspicions to the vice-president of the Senate, Auguste Scheurer-Kestner, who also came to believe in Dreyfus's innocence and began to persuade other senators and men of influence.

At last, in November 1897, a banker discovered by chance that the *bordereau* (of which facsimiles were for sale) was in the handwriting of Esterhazy, with whom he had done business. This crucial discovery was passed on to Dreyfus's brother Mathieu, who in turn communicated with the Minister of War, charging Esterhazy with the treason of which his brother had been convicted. The General Staff could not afford to overlook the accusation, so Esterhazy was courtmartialed. But even less was the General Staff ready to admit its error; hence his acquittal was a foregone conclusion.

Just two days later, on January 13, 1898, Emile Zola, in his famous open letter to the President of the Republic, *J'Accuse,* charged the Ministry of War with contempt for truth and justice, and with letting Dreyfus suffer for a crime he had never committed. The Ministry of War then demanded that Zola be tried for libel. In February 1898 he was convicted and sentenced to a year's imprisonment (though he took refuge in England instead). To stifle the growing demand for revision, Godefroy Cavaignac, the Minister of War in the new cabinet of Brisson, made public in July 1898 a letter, ostensibly from von Schwartzkoppen to the Italian military attaché, Colonel A. Panizzardi. Known as the *"Canaille de D"* letter, that "scoundrel D," it seemed to make Dreyfus's guilt inescapable. But by August it became clear that this letter was a forgery—and only one of many—by the deputy director of the counter-espionage section, Colonel Hubert-Joseph Henry; arrested, he committed suicide in prison.

This suicide marked a new stage in the Affair. The government was forced to act on Mme. Dreyfus's request for a reopening of her husband's case. After several months of investigation, the conviction of 1894 was annulled and a new court-martial ordered. Dreyfus was brought back from Devil's Island to stand trial; in September 1899, a verdict was delivered, even stranger than the first, finding him guilty, though with extenuating circumstances, and condemning him to ten years' imprisonment. Only a few days later, the government set aside this decision by pardoning Dreyfus, who was at once released from custody.

Years later, in 1903, as the full facts were gradually discovered, a new and definitive hearing became imperative. Finally, in July 1906, the Court of Appeals totally quashed the 1894 verdict, and Dreyfus was completely rehabilitated with the rank of major, though he resigned soon afterwards. Recalled to the Army during World War I, he served competently, being promoted to lieutenant-colonel, and then lived in retirement till his death in 1935.

THE BACKGROUND

THE REPUBLIC

THE background of the Dreyfus Affair was nothing less than the calamitous nineteenth-century history of France. It had not been the original intention of the men of the French Revolution to establish a Republic or to suppress the Church. Their aim was a moderate overhaul of the French political and social structure, but their efforts were negated by foreign war, internal opposition, and conflicting views among the reformers. In theory romantic, idealist, and perfectionist, the Republic's actual pursuit of its goals hardened the internal division of France, *les deux Frances,* making deeper and deeper the chasm between the defenders and antagonists of the Republican ideal. The succeeding regimes of Directory, Consulate, Empire, Restoration, and Bourgeois Monarchy might be considered varying, and ultimately unsuccessful, attempts to find a formula that would preserve the basic changes of 1789 while disavowing the more radical proposals identified with the Republic. Yet the extreme spirit of 1792, which, among other things, led to the execution of king and queen, remained alive during this half-century of experiment, to come forth again in the crisis of 1848, when the Bourgeois Monarchy of Louis Philippe was overthrown. The Second Republic that followed failed to retain the loyalty of the conservative majority of the French people, and failed even more lamentably to deal with the needs of the industrial working class.

When the Second Empire (1851–70) collapsed with the defeat of Napoleon III in the Franco-Prussian War, Republicanism was given another opportunity as the "government which divides us least." This new Republic was something quite different from the romantic and revolutionary Jacobinism of its beginnings, placing its trust in a parliamentary regime which contained strong safeguards against the executive power along with equally strong checks upon the direct intervention of the popular will. This conservative Third Republic, pledged to the maintenance of the established social order and of the individual liberties enshrined in the Declaration of the Rights of Man, often showed itself markedly anti-clerical. As the century drew to a close, the Republic slowly won wider support, though it still failed to win the hard core of the traditional opposition.[4]

THE CATHOLICS

The Great Revolution had left a legacy of unsolved questions. First among them was the role of the Catholic Church, to which the overwhelming majority of Frenchmen belonged. Between the First Republic and the Church there was the barrier of blood shed in the name of liberty. In the 1840s the common fight of Catholics and Republicans against the Bourgeois Monarchy led to a *rapprochement,* and for a time in 1848 it appeared that those who had been enemies for so many years had made peace. But when the majority of Catholics swung to the support of Louis Napoleon's Second Empire, the Republican opposition which developed showed strong anti-clerical tendencies. Once the Republicans had gained, in 1879, secure control of the political machinery, they turned upon the Church, which appeared their most redoubtable adversary. The "laic laws" of the 1880s imposed severe penalties on Catholic education, and so greatly intensified the anti-Republican feelings of the majority of Catholics.[5]

4. This background may be found in D. W. Brogan, *France under the Republic* (New York: Harper Brothers, 1940); more analytically in David Thomson, *Democracy in France* (New York: Oxford University Press, 1946); and perhaps most fully in Jacques Chastenet, *Histoire de la Troisième République* (Paris: Hachette, 1952–55).

5. See Evelyn M. Acomb, *The French Laic Laws* (New York: Columbia University Press, 1941). For a survey of the general politico-religious situation, see Joseph N. Moody, "From Old Regime to Democratic Society," in *Church and Society* (New York: Arts, Inc., 1954), pp. 95–186.

A sharp change in the trend of Catholic opinion in France occurred when Leo XIII inaugurated the *Ralliement* with the publication of his encyclical *Au milieu des solicitudes* in February 1892.[6] Having realized that "the cause of the Most Christian King was as dead as that of the Most Serene Republic of Venice," [7] he worked to disentangle Catholics from the Monarchical cause. His encyclical was a clear call to the faithful in France to make peace with the Republic, to rally to its support as the legitimate government, and to work against the anti-clerical laws solely by constitutional means. The Pope's directive met a mixed reception among French Catholics: considerable numbers abandoned Monarchism, reinforcing the tiny group of Catholic Republicans, while intransigent Monarchists stubbornly opposed the papal admonition. The waning support for their cause had already led them to accept the timorous Republican adventurer, General Boulanger, in the '80s; now their despair at this new reverse predisposed them to more risky expedients. This mood of desperation on the Right explains in part some of the more bizarre features of the Affair.

The peace gestures of Leo XIII had an equally mixed reception among the Republicans: the Moderates, frightened by growing social unrest, welcomed the *Ralliés;* the Radicals repulsed them as "reluctant Republicans" who aimed to infiltrate and destroy the Republic as the heir of the Revolution. Yet the *Ralliement* contributed to the improvement of Church-State relations in France, and the period 1891–98 saw a new peaceful spirit, which seemed to promise well for the future.

To bring about such an improvement in the face of the intransigence of a great body of French Catholics tried the wise diplomacy of Leo XIII and his Secretary of State, Cardinal Rampolla. In April 1895 the French Parliament passed a law imposing a tax on the properties of the religious orders, exempting only those engaged in charity and foreign missions. While the justice of such a tax is still a subject

---

6. See Edouard Lecanuet, *L'Eglise de France sous la Troisième République* (Paris: Ancienne Librairie Poussielgue, 1907), II, 377–418 and 513–558. In a succinct summary of the obstacles to the *Ralliement,* Adrien Dansette, in his splendid *Histoire religieuse de la France contemporaine* (Paris: Flammarion, 1951), II, 283–284, wisely notes that it would have taken a generation of peace to eliminate the rooted prejudices of either side.

7. Dominique Cardinal Ferrata, *Mémoires. Ma Nonciature en France* (Paris, 1922); as cited by Robert F. Byrnes, *Antisemitism in Modern France,* Vol. I (New Brunswick: Rutgers University Press, 1950), p. 185.

of debate, specialists agree that it merely revised existing legislation, in some respects bettering it. But the passage of the law brought to the surface the internal split among French Catholics which had been widened by the policy of Leo XIII. The influential *La Croix*,[8] which had given formal adhesion to the *Ralliement* but was always ready to cast doubt and ridicule on the intentions of the Republicans, led the attack on the government in the bitterest terms and demanded resistance by the religious congregations. Openly Royalist journals, such as *La Vérité Française,* seized on the issue to appeal for Catholic support. Cardinals Langenieux and Richard wrote approvingly of defiance. Bishop Fuzet of Beauvais and other exponents of moderation were vilified in the extremist press as apostates. The religious orders themselves were in a dilemma. The five congregations of men authorized by law and all the congregations of women were in favor of compliance, realizing that disobedience would provoke reprisals. But the non-authorized orders decided on resistance. The violent polemic which followed, with the partisans of "resistance" being pictured in the Rightist press as martyrs, made an unfavorable impression on public opinion, which assumed that the orders were able to pay and resented the "pious" protestations which they believed masked political objections. Ultimately the state had its way, but the papal policy of conciliation was seriously weakened. As Bishop Fuzet remarked, the Right would have the ship driven on the reefs to avoid the storm.

THE ARMY

To understand the Dreyfus Affair one must appreciate the role of the Army in the Third Republic. The Republic itself had been born out of defeat in the Franco-Prussian War. The enormous growth of German power after the unification of the German States alarmed the French, and their sense of insecurity was intensified by the isolation to which Bismarck's diplomacy had condemned France—an isolation which had been dramatically broken by the Russian alliance on the very eve of the Dreyfus Affair. Hopes of revenge had withered in the two decades after defeat by Prussia; the Republicans, the party

8. See Lecanuet, *La Vie de l'Eglise sous Léon XIII* (Paris: Alcan, 1930), pp. 221–233.

of national resistance in 1870–71, had even come to accept the loss of Alsace-Lorraine, though their patriotism remained strong. Conversely, it was the Right which adopted nationalism as a creed and sought emotional outlets in Déroulède's League of Patriots. In its demand for revenge against Germany, it unquestionably was seeking to exploit the delicate international situation in order to embarrass the Republic.

Both Left and Right understood the national danger to the East and hailed the Army as the hope of France. Embodying the revolutionary principle of "the nation in arms," it was a citizen army in which all served, a microcosm of the nation. The professional officer class, however, was drawn chiefly from the political Right. The tendency of the aristocratic elements to favor "the honorable profession" had been strengthened as nineteenth-century bourgeois France gradually closed the doors of opportunity to the sons of the old families. Since pay was poor and promotion slow in peacetime, and since France had not developed the social prestige of the reserve officer as had Germany, the bourgeoisie offered no great competition for positions in the officer corps. Approximately one-third of the officers, including the notorious Colonel Henry, rose from the ranks. However, it was the mainly aristocratic graduates from the military academy of Saint-Cyr who set the tone of the service and had the best opportunities for advancement. Most of the Army officers were Catholics, some only nominally, though a majority practiced their faith—a sharp contrast with those in elective office or in certain branches of the administration where the practice of religion was normally a handicap. As a group, the officers scrupulously remained outside of political conflict, and regarded the Army as a thing apart.[9] In the crisis of the '80s, they gave no encouragement to General Boulanger in his aspirations to political power. But their hearts were on the Right, as their background and connections would indicate.

THE JEWS

The Army officers shared the anti-Semitism that came to infect much of French society in the late 1880s. The reason for this relatively

9. Raoul Girardet, *La Société militaire dans la France contemporaine* (Paris: Plon, 1953), notes that officers who were closely connected with civilian groups were adversely noted in their fitness reports.

sudden outburst of ill-feeling toward the Jews is, despite exhaustive
study, something of a puzzle.[10] Never was the remark truer that if the
Jew did not exist, the anti-Semite would invent him, for in France
anti-Semitism was clearly the product of social tensions which had
nothing to do with the Jews.

The Jews were only 0.13 per cent of the French population, num-
bering less than fifty thousand in 1872 and reaching about eighty
thousand in 1900. Before 1871 the only compact body of Jews had
been in Alsace. When this province was lost in the Prussian War, a
considerable number of Alsatian Jews, including Alfred Dreyfus, had
chosen French citizenship. There was also a slight influx from Central Europe in the years before the Affair, but the figures just given
show that it was not very large. Almost all the Jews lived in a few
urban centers. Virtually all were Republicans in gratitude to the Revolution for their emancipation and civil rights. Most of them were
poor, but a few had gained important economic positions. A considerable number had distinguished themselves in literature, the press, the
theater, the professions, and politics. Yet, fantastically, the anti-Semites charged that the Jewish population was four or five or even six
hundred thousand, that its wealth was enormous, and that the administration of the French *départements* had fallen into Jewish hands,
over one-quarter of the prefects and sub-prefects being Jews. Such
was the myth of "Jewish power" in France.

THE ANTI-SEMITES

In 1886, with the publication of *La France Juive* by Edouard Drumont, French anti-Semitism raged into the open.[11] These two volumes were a bitter denunciation of the Jews as the main source of
France's ill fortunes, spiced with scorn for the nobility and upper

---

10. The best study is that of Professor Byrnes, referred to in note 7.

11. To give some notion of the author and his book: early in life Drumont had
fallen away from the Church, and later associated himself with occultist movements.
When he returned, it was without a clear and firm understanding of the faith, rather
with the emotions of what some of his friends, and even he himself, described as a
"historical Catholic"—hardly a reassuring religious career. Not ungifted as a jour-
nalist, he blamed his failure to receive the prominence he craved on the Jewish
owners of his newspaper, on "forces beyond his control." The anti-Semitism of his
book was openly racist: the idealistic Aryan against the materialistic Jew. The Aryan
race alone was the bearer of justice, goodness, and liberty, and the Jews were by
nature spies, traitors, criminals, and carriers of disease. Their fingers were, of course,
everywhere; for instance, every Protestant was half-Jew, and Protestantism merely
a Jewish device for the conquest of Christian society. For further material, see
Byrnes's excellent study, I, 137–155.

bourgeoisie who were vainly seeking to re-establish an anachronistic old regime. The author declared himself in favor of a vague socialism joined to a strong nationalism. His subsequent books and his newspaper *La Libre Parole* encouraged a furious anti-Semitic campaign with leagues, student demonstrations, and various virulent manifestations, all of them sharply divergent from the French tradition.

Drumont's campaign won considerable support in the ranks of French Socialism, which, since Proudhon, had had an anti-Semitic strain.[12] In addition, Drumont's rather bogus working-class sympathies appealed to some Socialists, though others rejected them. He also won a considerable segment of Republicans from the lower middle class, which remained the backbone of his movement. But unquestionably the most vocal support for Drumont came from Catholic publications and organizations. Those of Monarchist persuasion, though resentful of Drumont's criticisms directed at themselves, found in anti-Semitism a potent new weapon against the hated Republic, especially after it was learned that a few Jews had been involved in the notorious Panama Scandal, wherein some legislators had been bribed to obtain permission for a bond issue. Catholics noted that some Jews had been prominent in the political circles responsible for the anti-clerical laws of 1879–84, and, more fundamentally, were bewildered by the disaster that had befallen their cause and so were susceptible to the thesis of a "plot." Unwilling to ascribe to Frenchmen the waning of royalism and the attacks upon the Church, they found it comforting to ascribe them to a "conspiracy of aliens" or "subversives."

Despite honorable exceptions, the extent to which Catholics had succumbed to anti-Semitism in the late '80s is distressing. *La Croix, Univers,* the *Revue du Monde Catholique,* and the violently Royalist *La Vérité Française* were solidly in the anti-Semitic camp. More painful was the concurrence of the venerable organ *Le Correspondent,* once the review of Montalembert, Dupanloup, and Falloux, which could look on so long a record of reasonableness and moderation.[13]

12. To give an example: the most influential anti-Semitic book prior to Drumont's was *Du Molochisme juif* (Brussels, 1884), a posthumously published work by an atheistic Communard of the 1870s, Gustave Tridon. To him the Jews were "parasites" and their religion "idolatrous," and it was their pernicious Semitic spirit, so manifest in both Judaism and Christianity, that was the cause of capitalism and its ills. See Byrnes, *op. cit.,* I, 157.

13. Fairness requires that it be added that moderation was still the temper of this review. For instance, Louis Joubert, its *gérant,* writing the *chronique politique*

Equally sad was the attitude of the Christian Democrats who had received a strong impetus from the *Ralliement*. They already had a penchant for anti-Semitism because of the false identification of the Jews with high finance, an error once frequent among French social reformers. In the period before the Affair they became closely associated with Drumont and accepted his thesis of "Jewish finance-capitalism."

This large-scale surrender of vocal Catholic opinion to the crudities and illogicalities of anti-Semitism is one of the sad chapters of Catholic life in modern France. Even granted the chafing and desperation a nagging anti-clericalism provoked in Catholics of those days, their acceptance of a position so contrary to their faith remains indefensible. It is a commentary on the deficiencies of the religious education of the period and on Maritain's observation that if the meaning of Christianity does not fully penetrate into souls because they have not yet been spiritually purified, then it is indeed easy for human weakness to merge religion with prejudice or with political nostrums.[14] Certainly anti-Semitism contributed to Catholic blindness in the Dreyfus Affair; although Drumont's campaign had slackened by 1894 and he himself had admitted its failure, its passions were readily re-enkindled once the Affair reached its political stage.

A SECOND LOOK

THE background sketched above is necessary for a further elucidation of the Dreyfus Affair. Yet the material must be kept in perspective.

on January 25, 1891 (No. 126 new series, p. 407), quotes approvingly Archbishop Meignan's advice to love those who have "different opinions than ourselves and may be nearer to God than we think." He then praises Lacordaire who wished to place Christian liberty under the protection of civil liberty. "What other source of protection is there?" he adds. On February 10, 1891, he speaks of the two Republics, one moderate, pacific, and conciliatory, the other the Republic of blood, and adds that Catholics can be reconciled to the former. Speaking of the Dreyfus Affair on pp. 605–606 of the issue of November 10, 1897, the same commentator writes: "M. Scheurer-Kestner has said to several persons behind closed doors that he had proof of the innocence of Captain Dreyfus. We do not know if he has, *we would be happy if he had,* but we only assert that if he possesses the secret that would be the salvation of an innocent man, he would be most culpable not to produce it at once."

14. See, for instance, his *Ransoming the Time* (New York: Scribner's, 1941), p. 128; also in *I Believe,* ed. by C. Fadiman (New York: Simon and Schuster, 1939), pp. 209–210.

These predispositions do not warrant the assumption that the case was in its origins a plot to overthrow the Republic. Initially it was a simple error of a military court, anxious to uncover a traitor on the General Staff in an atmosphere fraught with danger to the nation. It showed a humanly understandable desire to reach a quick solution of an embarrassing and explosive problem. Hasty decisions reached in such an atmosphere are not an exclusive fault of the military; civilian courts have given some conspicuous historic examples.

Anti-Semitism played only a limited, and largely unconscious, role in the genesis of the Affair. But it became an increasing factor as controversy developed over the court-martial. Once serious doubt was thrown on the verdict, all the latent passions and tensions in French society exploded, and groups sought to use the case to discredit the enemy on the Left or on the Right. To understand this phenomenon, we need only remember the passions aroused in and by our recent Congressional investigations; yet our post-World War II society, while disturbed, has never been so seriously divided on fundamentals as was the French in the 1890s. The conversation between General Gonse and Colonel Picquart on September 15, 1896, is a frightening illustration of the will to preserve the group at the expense of the individual:

Gonse: "Why are you so concerned that Dreyfus should leave Devil's Island?"
Picquart: "Because he is innocent."
"It is a matter which cannot be re-examined. Both Generals Mercier and Saussier are involved."
"But the man is innocent."
"That is of no concern. There are other considerations which must be weighed."
"But if the Dreyfus family should discover the real culprit what would be our position?"
"If you say nothing, no one will know."
"My general, what you say is abominable. I do not know what I shall do, but I will never carry this secret into the grave." [15]

This dramatic confrontation reaches the core of the issue, as well as the human obstacles to its just solution. After 1896 the problem

15. *La Révision du procès Dreyfus à la Cour de Cassation. Compte rendu sténographique in extenso* (Paris: Stock, 1898), p. 114.

was simply this: Should an innocent man, condemned as a traitor, be retained in prison with his good name traduced in order to shield "the honor of the Army" and to avoid embarrassment to the nation's foreign policy? But while the issue was simple, some were prevented from seeing it because of political conflict or special interest; many more were blinded because the truth was not revealed all at once but was ferreted out piecemeal in circumstances which made it easy for emotions to cloud reason.

THE UNANIMOUS VERDICT

As said before, the case against Captain Dreyfus began with the discovery that certain Army secrets were being passed to the German Embassy in Paris, a discovery alarming both because of the loss of confidential material and because of the fear that the enemy to the East might precipitate a crisis before the newly signed Russian alliance became operationally effective. Panic urged an over-hasty inquiry. Not a member of the old officer caste, an over-ambitious student of military affairs, a little too devoted to his work and too interested in departments not his own, inclined to be boastful and talkative, Dreyfus seemed a likely villain to the heads of one of the divisions of the Ministry in which he had recently worked. But his personal shortcomings did not sum up to a motive, for he was rich, happily married, patriotic, and devoted to the Army. However, three of the several handwriting experts called in, including the famed criminologist Bertillon, identified, or tended to identify, the script of the *bordereau* as that of Dreyfus. The Minister of War, General Auguste Mercier, was having difficulties with the Chamber on other issues—for he had rebuffed an inventor who then betook himself and his invention to Germany; he had ordered the discharge of some sixty thousand soldiers without notifying the Senate, the Chamber, or even the President of the Republic; and he had brought on himself the ire of the Left by insisting that a newly elected deputy, previously excused from military service, now serve in the Army. When his secret order to arrest Dreyfus on suspicion was revealed in Drumont's *La Libre Parole,* which screamed that the case would be hushed up because the officer was a Jew, Mercier and the Cabinet grew fearful and decided on a court-martial.

The court, composed of military men of reasonable probity, did not include a single artillery officer who might have detected flaws in the evidence, for some of the disclosures involved technical matters of that branch. Dreyfus was ably defended by a distinguished lawyer, Edgar Demange, a believing and practicing Catholic. A majority of the officers called to testify as character witnesses voiced their dislike of his manners but spoke well of his work. When the hearing, held in secret, appeared to be going unfavorably for the prosecution, the judges were privately shown a collection of documents assembled by the Statistical Section, none of which was damning to the accused, but which were accompanied by a commentary and a biographical sketch designed to reinforce the case for the prosecution. They portrayed Dreyfus as a gambler deep in debt, and with other discreditable motives for the crime of which he was accused. This file was fraudulent, however, having been "gathered" by the then director of the counter-espionage section, Colonel Jean-Conrad Sandherr. It is more than doubtful that General Mercier knew the file to be a forgery, for he was clearly convinced of Dreyfus's treason. None of the judges was sufficiently versed in procedure to know that the introduction of these documents without showing them to the defense was illegal both in military and civil law. Small wonder, then, that the court returned a unanimous verdict of guilty, sentencing the accused to degradation and deportation for life.

Though there was fraud and illegal procedure, there is no evidence of a plot to convict an innocent man. The majority of the military involved acted honorably, convinced that they were dealing with one of their own who had betrayed his country. The public supported the verdict with near unanimity, relieved that the threat of treason had been lifted. Of the press, only the ultra-Royalist Paul Granier de Cassagnac, in *L'Autorité*, expressed doubts. The great Clemenceau regretted that Dreyfus had not been shot. Jaurès, later to become the founder of the French Socialist Party, declared in the Chamber of Deputies that the traitor had escaped this penalty only because he was a rich bourgeois, and chided the government for protecting cosmopolitan speculators masked as patriots. Beyond his family and intimate friends, only his counsel Demange retained faith in the convicted man who had been sent to solitary confinement on Devil's Island.

THE CASE CLOSED

The second stage in the Affair extends from this trial in December 1894 to the publication of *J'Accuse* on January 13, 1898. The predominant characteristic of this period was the unwillingness of the

Army command or the Republican government to reopen the case. As new evidence was slowly unfolded, those involved in the original trial became conscious of their personal stake in preventing revision. It was this which led to the uncritical acceptance of the fantastic evidence against Dreyfus periodically manufactured by Colonel Henry. Even those Army officers not personally involved were predisposed, on grounds of Army honor, to accept the case as *res judicata,* as a matter already adjudicated and not subject to further litigation. Meanwhile doubts were spreading in some civilian groups on the legality of the procedure, and this led some to believe in Dreyfus's innocence.

The decisive step was the discovery of the true culprit by Colonel Picquart, a practicing Catholic and, like Dreyfus, an Alsatian. In the traditional manner of his province, he did not think too well of Jews. When one of the judges at the first court-martial remarked that he could find no motive for Dreyfus's crime, Picquart is supposed to have replied: "Ah! but you don't know these Mulhouse Jews!" [16] Once the fateful *petit bleu* had aroused his suspicions of Esterhazy— who, inquiries showed, was engaged in all kinds of shady dealings, having been at one time a shareholder in a fashionable house of prostitution and being always hopelessly in debt—, and once he had been struck by the resemblance between Esterhazy's handwriting and that of the *bordereau,* Picquart examined the secret dossier on Dreyfus which had been shown to the judges in the trial of 1894 and recognized its obvious forgeries. But, as we have seen, when he attempted to persuade his superiors that the case against Dreyfus was without foundation and that the real traitor was Esterhazy, he met not only indifference to the truth but the strongest opposition to his continuing his inquiries into the closed case.[17]

At this point the role of his subordinate, Colonel Henry, must be

16. Chapman, *op. cit.,* p. 65.

17. A word must be said here in praise of this hero of conscience. While for most of the defenders of Dreyfus, he was more a means than a person, an issue that served their cause, for Picquart, who had no "cause," there was only an innocent man and justice. James Grossman has put it well: "Picquart was anti-Semitic, disliked Dreyfus, had been an official observer at the court-martial, and had believed him guilty. But he respected a fact, and no prejudice could stand in the way of its logical operation. Many men of genuinely liberal beliefs were helped to the truth about Dreyfus by their prejudices. Picquart is one of the few men who came to the truth in spite of his prejudice, and once he came to it, he never swerved from it" ("The Dreyfus Affair Fifty Years Later," *Commentary,* XXI, 1, January 1956, p. 27).

specially noted. Henry was a professional soldier, up from the ranks, cunning and ambitious, and passionately devoted to the service. He had realized for some time that a revelation of the weakness of the evidence against Dreyfus would react unfavorably on the Army, and also on himself because of his manipulations with the secret file. So all on his own and deliberately, he had set out on a course of forgery, which, although designed to protect his chiefs and himself, actually involved them more deeply. It seems certain that there never would have been that national uproar over revision of the verdict against Dreyfus had it not been for the pernicious intervention of this one man. In deceiving the Army and the public—many, to be sure, were only too willing to be deceived—he prepared disaster for himself and for many others who had no part in his forgeries.

An analogy might be helpful. The French Right, which rejected the Revolution of 1789, has always interpreted it in terms of "plot." The villains vary with the special animus of the investigator—they may be the intellectuals, the bourgeoisie, or the Freemasons—but they are always identifiable, and the causation is reduced to simplest terms. A century and a half of close study of the Revolution and its times has led scholars of every variety to reject the *complot* thesis in favor of what is termed *les circonstances*. By "circumstances" is meant the complex fabric of ideas, internal opposition, foreign and domestic war, human error, *and* dominant personalities, all of which are integral to any satisfactory explanation of the Revolution. On a smaller scale the same is true of the Affair. Henry was neither its cause nor an adequate explanation of its development. But his role was central, and his decisive intervention does not fit any simplicist explanation.

THE MOVE TOWARD REVISION

Sentiment for the captive on Devil's Island grew but slowly in civilian France. The first to denounce the injustice publicly was the courageous and brilliant Jewish writer, Bernard Lazare, who, on November 6, 1896, published a penetrating pamphlet, *La Vérité sur l'Affaire Dreyfus*.[18] Its immediate reception was cool. Jaurès remained indifferent; Clemenceau refused to read it; and Zévaès, of the Socialist *Petite République*, was abusive; most Jews, particularly influential Jews,

18. Péguy pays the highest tribute to Lazare in *Notre jeunesse, Oeuvres complètes* (Paris: Gallimard, 1916), IV, 68–69 and 75–76.

disliked the pamphlet and would have preferred to have the case for-gotten. The Chamber, convinced of Dreyfus's guilt, rebuffed efforts to reopen the case, only five members failing to stand with the government after the debate. But individuals began to drift into the revision-ist camp, the most important being Clemenceau, who found access to the public in the newly established journal, *L'Aurore.* Indiscretions on the part of Henry and Esterhazy and the renewed interest of the press finally brought the case to the general public.

It might be helpful to review the status of the case on the eve of Zola's intervention. It had not yet hardened into a contest between Right and Left, and the bulk of the Republicans were still anti-Drey-fusard,[19] as were most of the responsible Republican politicians in the Chamber and Cabinet. The latter, with the full approval of the Prime Minister, Méline, had definitely closed the door on revision. The Army had not only taken its stand against revision; it had gone too far to turn back without serious damage to several men of high rank. It is important to bear in mind that the Army men involved did not reach this stage by careful plotting—they were notably care-less in consultation—but through a sense of corporate solidarity, which confused Army honor with the reputation of a handful of offi-cers. Catholics in general were inclined to support the Army, and the leading Catholic journal, *La Croix*, was noisily anti-Dreyfusard. The outstanding Catholic leader and *Rallié,* Albert de Mun, vehemently defended the Army, in which he had served in the war of 1870. The hierarchy was discreetly silent, perhaps from fear of unpopularity if they questioned the administration of justice in the Republic, which many of them were known to dislike.[20]

On the other side, sentiment for revision was growing.[21] It was

19. It was still possible to be wrong in good faith, as was the Freemason and Republican Camille Pelletan. See his correspondence with Jaurès, in *La Dépêche de Toulouse,* December 26, 1900. Incidentally, this anti-clerical paper, the leading journal in the Southwest, was anti-Dreyfusard to the end.

20. So declared Cardinal Richard, Archbishop of Paris, when invited by some Parisian professors to lend his name to revision; see Lecanuet, *Les Signes avant-coureurs de la séparation* (Paris: Alcan, 1930), pp. 184–185. Some priests pro-tested against the excesses of *La Croix* but in vain; see Abbé Pichot, *La Conscience chrétienne et l'Affaire Dreyfus* (Paris: Société d'éditions littéraires, 1899), pp. 28–30.

21. Léon Blum in *Souvenirs sur l'Affaire* (Paris: Gallimard, 1935), pp. 45–46, is critical of some features of the handling of the revisionist case in its early stages, especially the failure to bring the ensemble of doubts and counter-evidence to the public in a single, striking form. For his remarks on Zola, see pp. 133–134.

based on a conviction that the proceedings of 1894 were irregular rather than on a belief in Dreyfus's innocence, and had been strengthened by the court-martial of Esterhazy, which, though ending in his acquittal, revealed to the public some of the more suspicious activities in the Statistical Section. What was still lacking was a unifying impulse that would draw together these varied strands of opinion. This was provided by the furor aroused over the publication of *J'Accuse* in *L'Aurore,* which sold two hundred thousand copies in the first twenty-four hours.

A NEW DIRECTION

The year and a half between Zola's intervention and the second court-martial brought the Affair to the center of the stage of French public life, reviving all the basic divisions in the body politic. Zola had charged the General Staff—"that house of Jesuits," as he called it—with the condemnation of a man they had known to be innocent. To him it was all a clerical and reactionary plot, smacking "of unbridled nightmare, of the Spanish Inquisition"; having already struck one victim, it threatened all anti-clericals. However, he had courageously achieved an imaginative reconstruction of the Affair that was correct in major outlines, though inexact in detail and without basis for its wider attributions,[22] and had raised the question of justice for an innocent man to a new political and socio-religious level. He thus enlarged the area from which recruits to revision could be drawn and made the Affair a subject of world attention.

Immediately, however, the impact was not so clear. The ranks of the Army stiffened, for now the whole top level of command was under attack. Violence erupted in the streets, with organized anti-Semitic gangs seeking victims. Still, the mass of the people were unaffected, and even the informed divided on other than strict party lines. An old Royalist like Buffet could speak for Dreyfus, while the leading Freemason, Brisson, and the anti-clerical Republican Berthelot maintained their anti-Dreyfusard positions. The government continued its refusal to reopen the case, in which it had the support even of a substantial part of the Left, for politicians were still concerned about the place of the Army and fearful of civil war.

22. For a critical contemporary estimate, see Francis Charmes, in *Revue des Deux Mondes,* February 1, 1898, pp. 712–713.

But a new direction had been given to the movement, and it was strengthened by Zola's trial, an examination of which reveals how slowly the basic facts of the Affair were available to the public. Clemenceau, for instance, in his defense of Zola, emphasized that he did not know whether Dreyfus was innocent or guilty, but that he was certain the procedure of condemnation had been illegal—a fair measure of the facts then known. The trial of Zola marked the great surge of intellectuals to the defense of Dreyfus. Literary and scientific circles and the faculties of the great Parisian schools, particularly of the *Ecole Normale Supérieure,* had read enough to become convinced of the injustice which had been done. It was from these groups that a substantial part of the membership of the League for the Defense of the Rights of Man and the Citizen was recruited. Organized by the reputable Catholic scholar, Paul Viollet, it grew directly from the Affair.[23]

While the intellectual world had become passionately involved, the general public was still unaffected, so that the elections in the spring of 1898 gave no sign that the Affair had influenced practical politics. The Radicals remained unyieldingly anti-revisionist. The most notable feature of the elections was the effort of the Catholic Right, led by *La Croix,* to defeat the *Ralliés* and the moderate Republicans.[24] The result of this folly was a new Chamber with a somewhat weakened Center and with slightly more strength on the extremes, a shift which was enough to topple the government of Méline, whose attitude toward revision was completely negative, but who had worked for religious peace.

The new Radical ministry of Brisson, with the strongly Republican Cavaignac as Minister of War, showed no disposition to change the policy of its predecessor toward the case. On July 7 Cavaignac admitted in the Chamber that Esterhazy was the author of the *bordereau* and had been wrongly acquitted. But he went on to cite three documents, among them one of Henry's forgeries, the *"Canaille de D"* letter, to justify his conclusion that he was "completely certain of Dreyfus's guilt." The Radicals and Socialists applauded, and the

23. Viollet subsequently resigned when the Committee of the League refused to include religious educators among those whose rights the League should defend. The League went on to become a powerful center of anti-clericalism and within five years was, as Chapman has pointed out, "as fanatic and as treacherous as its enemies" (*op. cit.,* p. 203).

24. See Dansette, *op. cit.,* p. 259, and Lecanuet, *Les Signes,* pp. 122–129.

grateful deputies voted, 545 to 0, with three abstentions, to have his speech posted outside the town hall in the thirty-five thousand communes of France.

Just a month later, things began to change. In August 1898, when Henry's forgeries were exposed and he committed suicide, the Chief of Staff, Boisdeffre, who had played an important role in the Franco-Russian alliance, resigned. The move for revision was now irresistible and the Affair about to become the great political issue. Yet even at this stage the reaction of the government was tardy: Brisson was undecided and Cavaignac was still convinced of Dreyfus's guilt!

THE BREAK AND ITS AFTERMATH

Henry's exposure and suicide were followed by the flight of Esterhazy, who, from the safety of London, confessed his guilt. The case was broken but not the Affair, for too many had gone too far to retreat gracefully. The Army and its supporters, including the bulk of articulate Catholics, had allowed themselves to be deceived by a handful of officers and journalists; unwilling to see themselves as dupes, they refused to change their attitude toward Dreyfus and had added a new injustice—the disgrace of Picquart, who, in January 1898, had been jailed on the specious grounds that he had transmitted confidential papers to a civilian, M. Leblois. As the anti-Dreyfusards became more strident, the increasing number of citizens rallying to the revisionist cause adopted anti-militarism and anti-clericalism almost automatically.

In the fall of 1898, the Criminal Appeals Court agreed to hear the arguments for revision. But the government maneuvered to have them heard before all three sections of the Court of Appeals, hoping that the combined court would reject the plea. However, the parade of witnesses before the tribunal revealed the major outlines of the case to all who would see, and the forty-six judges unanimously decided to return it to another court-martial for retrial. Unfortunately, their judgment was so phrased that the new court would be forced to decide between General Mercier, who had been Minister of War in 1894, and ex-Captain Dreyfus. This was to prove too much for the seven officers who were to sit in judgment on Dreyfus, now returned from four years of solitary confinement. Meeting at Rennes in August 1899, this second military tribunal reviewed (for what was now

a world audience) the confused record of the Affair, and their ver-
dict was—five for guilt and two for innocence! In the minority were
Colonel Jouast, the respected president of the court, and Major de
Bréon, the only member who was a devout Catholic.

More than two months before this verdict, there had occurred a
political change that was to affect profoundly the destinies of the
Third Republic. The six Republican ministries which had governed
France since the arrest of Dreyfus had been either hostile to the in-
nocent man or indifferent to his fate. But in June 1899, the energetic
Waldeck-Rousseau formed a "ministry for the defense of the Repub-
lic." For the first time in the history of the Affair, the issue was posed
in clear political terms between the Right and the Left, between the
Party of Resistance and the Party of Movement. Till this moment,
Republicans had been found in both camps; now they were nearly all
Dreyfusard and were in a position to use the power of government
to punish their old enemies. Significantly, too, for the first time in
European history a Marxian Socialist, Millerand, had taken a port-
folio in a bourgeois government with the approval of the majority of
his party.

It was in this atmosphere that the Affair was finally liquidated. But
not until 1906, seven years after Rennes, was Dreyfus fully vindi-
cated by a decision which completely reversed the verdict of Rennes.
Long before that, however, Waldeck-Rousseau's government of Republican Defense had been succeeded by the government of Combes.
Trained for the priesthood, he had rejected the Church's teachings and
become fanatical in his opposition to her. "He had one and only one
idea, the battle with the Church. For matters of finance, of foreign
policy, of defense, of social welfare, he cared nothing." [25] The religious orders were banned in France, and the Concordat of 1801 was
repudiated. The Church-State problem which had developed in the
course of the Revolution of 1789 had now reached its denouement in
the aftermath of the Affair.

SOME CONSEQUENCES

THE foregoing account makes clear, I hope, that the Dreyfus Case
was not a simple matter of anti-Semitism, but the culmination of a

25. Chapman, *op. cit.,* p. 329.

century of conflict in France. Anti-Semitism was unquestionably present in the Affair; it would be true to say that it permeated every detail. But behind it, and giving it meaning, lay the traditional cleavage in French society and political life. The Affair was not a plot, neither of the Army, nor of the clergy, nor of the Jesuits.[26] In broad terms, it was a mirror of a century of French history, and its conclusion the triumph of much that animated the Revolution of 1789.

This larger significance may be grasped from a summary of the consequences of the Affair.

(1) It wrecked the *Ralliement,* initiated by Leo XIII, and ended a decade in which the Third Republic had followed *l'esprit nouveau,* the new spirit of peaceful relations. True, the *Ralliés* had been relatively weak and had met opposition on the Right and even from *La Croix,* superficially committed to the papal directives. True, too, the spirit of accommodation had been strained by the tax on the property of the religious communities. But the new policy had borne considerable fruit and there had been a serious possibility of a union of conservative Catholics with bourgeois Republicans in the face of the Socialist threat. All this was ended by the Affair which brought the religious conflict to its highest pitch of intensity since 1793–94.

(2) The Affair acted as a centrifugal force on the Republican parties. Though they had been diverging sharply on social policy since the 1880s and, as we have seen, took various positions during the Affair on Dreyfus's guilt, in 1899, after the case was broken, they were able to achieve near unanimity on the proposition that the Church must be punished and the Army brought under Republican control. The first step was the seizure of *La Croix* and the other publications of the Assumptionists, who deserved no sympathy, and received little, even from the hierarchy. Then the campaign moved inexorably to a breaking off of relations with the Vatican. The Army proved more resistant, and the revelation in the Chamber that Combes's Minister of War was using the Masonic lodges and the League of the Rights of Man to spy on the personal opinions

26. That the Affair was not a Jesuit plot must be upheld against those who make too much of a single utterly indefensible article in *La Civiltà Cattolica* for January 1898, which charged that the movement for revision was a plot hatched at the Zionist Congress in Basel. It echoed such rantings of Drumont as that Jews directed all French policy and that the Jew was created "to serve as a spy wherever treason is in preparation." Still, "one foolish anti-Semitic article does not make a campaign." So Chapman, who reminds us that Georges Sorel, no friend of the Church, thought of it as a counterattack and that a few days earlier *L'Univers Israélite* had published a no less violent polemic against the Church (*op. cit.,* p. 201).

of Army officers led to the fall of the Combes ministry in 1905. With it, the Republican bloc broke apart.

(3) The Affair marked the failure to found a conservative party loyally dedicated to the support of the Republic. The consequence of this failure was that French parliamentary life was deprived of a healthy balance between two political tendencies, one in power, the other in opposition. Only such a balance could have kept political divisions in France from periodic degeneration into irreconcilable conflict. The primary responsibility for this failure rested with the intransigents of the Right; but certainly, a share belonged to the Left when, after August 1898, the noble motives of the earlier revisionists were somehow compromised by men who used the Affair for political ends.[27]

(4) The Republic was immensely strengthened by the Affair; some analysts would even say that it was founded in the course of this national crisis. Consequently, the Left became the dominant factor in French politics till the outbreak of World War I. The entrance of Millerand into the cabinet of Waldeck-Rousseau was a decisive event in the history of European Socialism. Of equal importance was the increase in the bourgeois and intellectual components of French Socialism, with all that this implied for the future history of the Left. In addition, Jaurès became a national figure of importance and was able to establish his moderating, democratic influence as the dominant trend in French Socialism until his assassination in 1914. The Affair affected other political groupings too. The record of the Radicals in the early stages of the Affair was somewhat less than notable. But since their strength lay in the provincial centers, which were less responsive to the case, and since their major bond was anti-clericalism, they managed to increase their prestige in the aftermath of the Affair. They became in effect the balance wheel in the subsequent Parliaments of the Third Republic. Personalities were affected as well as political groups. Méline, whose record outside the Affair was excellent, went into eclipse, while Clemenceau returned from political oblivion. These are but two instances of how political fortunes were made or unmade by the case.

(5) Conversely, the Affair marks the end of the old Royalism, and of the old Nationalism as represented by Déroulède. Legitimism had, in fact, ceased to be a political possibility by 1890; but the Affair gave it the *coup de grâce.* Yet, though disappearing as a genuine political force, it survived as a sect, with its unrepentant partisans regrouping in a new formation with a new spirit. Significantly, the spring of 1899 saw the

27. Brilliantly examined by François Coguel-Nyegaard in *La Politique des partis sous la III⁰ République* (Paris: Editions du Seuil, 1946), pp. 98–123.

first issue of *L'Action Française* under the direction of the nationalist Republican Henri Vaugeois and the extreme Royalist Charles Maurras. The facility of the latter in inventing explanations for any aspect of the Affair had established him as the darling of the extreme Right. *L'Action Française* represented a new phase in the Party of Order: its leaders were predominantly agnostic and positivistic, though they "favored" the Church as a force for stability and order, as a link to the past and its culture; instead of a return to the old traditionalism, they were to become godfathers to Fascism. After 1936, they were agreeable to co-ordinating French policies with those of Hitler, and contributed not a little to the philosophical foundations of the Vichy government.

(6) The Affair ended for several decades the possibility of an influential Catholic party left of Center. One of the casualties of the Affair was the Christian Democrats, predominantly anti-Dreyfusard. Marc Sangnier's social movement *Le Sillon* lived on for a while; a remnant of Catholic Republicans survived, but their political influence was negligible until World War II provided the climate for a second try.

(7) The Affair established the reputation of intellectuals for prescience in matters outside their immediate competence, a factor which has been luminously explored in Raymond Aron's *L'Opium des intellectuels*.[28] What Albert Thiebaudet has termed *la République des professeurs*—based on the reputation of the university faculties, and particularly that of the *Ecole Normale Supérieure,* for objectivity and devotion to truth above party spirit—owes much to the Affair.

(8) The impact on the Army is more difficult to weigh. Anti-militarism had been virtually nonexistent before the Affair, except on the extreme Left. Now anti-militarism became common in many Republican circles, particularly among school teachers, though its depth may be questioned in light of the ardent response of 1914. Further, the Army resented efforts to "republicanize" it and there was bitter ill-feeling against suspected informers. Candidates for Saint-Cyr dropped to about forty per cent of the number before the Affair. But again, resentment in the officer corps did not interfere with its performance in 1914, even though efforts to promote Republican officers had not been conspicuously successful.

(9) While the Affair injected new poison into French political life, one consequence was most happy: organized anti-Semitism disappeared as a power, *La Libre Parole* faded after 1904, and Drumont died in 1917 in complete obscurity. It is even more gratifying to note that the Affair was the last instance in French history of anti-Semitism to which any

28. Paris: Calmann-Lévy, 1955.

number of priests succumbed. As Hannah Arendt writes in "From the Dreyfus Affair to France Today": "They [the leaders of Vichy] sought to mobilize the Catholic clergy against the Jews, only to give proof that the priests have not only lost their political influence but are not actually anti-Semitic. On the contrary, it is the very bishops and synods which the Vichy regime would turn once more into political powers who voiced the most emphatic protest against the persecution of the Jews." [29]

CATHOLICS AND THE AFFAIR

A FINAL question must be put. Since the principal victim of the Affair was the Church, to what degree did Catholics bear the moral burden for the retribution visited upon her after 1899? I hope that the following points are justified in light of the narrative above:

(1) The chief moral responsibility among Catholics was the yielding of so many to anti-Semitism during the decade before the Affair.

(2) There is no evidence whatsoever of a sinister "clerical plot" to use Dreyfus to discredit the Jews or to overturn the Republic; but once the Affair had developed, quite a few Catholics tried to use it to these ends.

(3) The overwhelming majority of Catholics were anti-Dreyfusard, some for political reasons, some because of affection for the Army. While the Catholic Dreyfusards were a small minority, they form a list that is imposing, if not in numbers, then in weight. There were the Abbés Pichot,[30] Serres, Frémont, Grosjean, Brugerette, Vignot, Birot, Martinet, de Bréon (brother of the minority judge in the Rennes trial), Jean Viollet, and P. Maumus—to mention only those priests prominent in letters and journalism or in public affairs. Further, intellectuals of the same persuasion united for the defense of justice in *Le Comité catholique pour la Défense du Droit,* founded by Paul Viollet after his resignation from *La Ligue des Droits de l'Homme.* It had two hundred members from univer-

29. In *Essays on Antisemitism,* ed. by Koppel S. Pinson (New York: Conference on Jewish Relations, 1946), p. 179. While admiring Miss Arendt's scholarship, I dissent strongly from some of her conclusions, particularly her imputation of an active anti-Dreyfus role to the Jesuits. While she can cite the authority of Joseph Reinach's *Histoire de l'Affaire Dreyfus* (Paris: Editions de la Revue blanche, 1901–11), to which I, as every student of the Affair, am indebted, she ignores the evidence of Louis Caperan, *L'Anti-clericalisme et l'Affaire Dreyfus* (Toulouse: Imprimerie régionale, 1948), especially pp. 263–276. See also Chapman's discussion referred to in note 23.

30. Author of *La Conscience chrétienne et l'Affaire Dreyfus,* cited in note 20.

sity circles. *La Quinzaine* was the organ of Catholic champions of justice for Dreyfus, and it has already been noted that the contradictory Paul de Cassagnac of *L'Autorité* was the first revisionist. Catholic journalists on *Figaro, Soleil,* and a few provincial papers such as *Salut public de Lyon* defended the innocent man. Even *L'Univers,* which had been the *enfant terrible* of the Catholic press, remained moderate and faithful to the papal plan of conciliation during the Affair.[31]

(4) In spite of this courageous minority, the majority Catholic press succeeded, unfortunately, in identifying Catholics with the anti-Dreyfusards in the eyes of non-Catholics.

(5) No less unfortunate was the malevolent influence this extremist press exercised on Catholic opinion. Much has been made, and rightly, of the three thousand priests who subscribed to *La Libre Parole* and of the three hundred who contributed to the fund for Henry's widow. Indeed, one would be too many; yet it must be borne in mind that there were fifty thousand priests in France, and that three hundred represented but three or four per diocese.

(6) An analysis of the principal figures involved in the Affair breaks down the thesis of a "clerical plot." The governments which, for four years, blocked revision included not a single practicing Catholic; in fact, they were generally anti-clerical in composition. Mercier, the 1894 Minister of War who bears so heavy a responsibility, was no more than a "conventional" Catholic, married to an English Protestant. Henry, the major villain, had only the most tenuous contacts with religion; Esterhazy had none. However, Boisdeffre, Chief of Staff, was a devout Catholic and a friend of the Jesuit Père du Lac. Still other officers in key positions were practicing Catholics, including Picquart. But, contrary to general opinion, few of the officers on the General Staff were trained in Jesuit schools.[32] Hence no particular pattern of the Affair can be drawn on a religious basis.

(7) The hierarchy rigorously abstained from any intervention in the Affair. That is the simple fact. It is possible, however, to give it varying interpretations: Caperan, for instance, argues that it stemmed from a desire not to add to the divisions within the country and from hesitation

---

31. See the article on September 1, 1898, by Pierre Veuillot.

32. De Mun, in a letter to the London *Times,* and again in a Congress at Lyon on May 25, 1894, gives evidence that only nine or ten per cent of the officers on the General Staff were trained by the Jesuits, and that only one officer involved in the Affair was a Jesuit product (Boisdeffre) and he only for two years compared with eight spent at the Lycée d'Alençon; of the others, neither Mercier, Gonse, Henry, Paty du Clam, Picquart, or Esterhazy had any Jesuit schooling. See de Mun's *Combats d'hier et d'aujourd'hui* (Paris: Lethellieux, n.d.), VII, 25–27.

to question the justice of the Republic;[33] others would see the silence of the bishops as approval of the campaign against Dreyfus. Certainly it is regrettable that when the moral issues became clear, the leaders of the Church in France did not speak out. While their conduct might be called correct, it was timid.

To summarize: It is difficult to make general statements about French Catholics in the Affair. There were Dreyfusard Catholics; there were ever so many more anti-Dreyfusard Catholics; and there were the vast majority of Catholics who, like the simple people of France of every opinion, remained completely outside the controversy. On the other hand, Catholics who made their views known and remained obdurate after the evidence was in, were articulate and numerous enough to bring reprisals on the whole Catholic body.

There are some lessons Catholics might learn from the Dreyfus Affair:

All must suffer for the indiscretion of the few, unless the fanatics and extremists, who are never lacking in a social body, are *explicitly* repudiated. Silence will not do when moral issues are involved.

Catholic journals should review their positions critically from time to time. This was Abbé Pichot's warning when he pointed out that the attitude of *La Croix* might have been defensible at the beginning of the Affair, but should be re-examined in the light of the new revelations. If the paper had proofs of Dreyfus's guilt unknown to others, it had an obligation, Pichot reasoned, to make them known.[34]

An innocent man must never be sacrificed for the supposed national interest, even though an apparent case might be made along lines of national safety. Péguy saw this clearly at the time of the Affair;[35] others did not then, and do not now.

33. *Op. cit.*, pp. 243–246.
34. Pichot, *op. cit.*, p. 20. The newspaperman's obligation toward truth in matters great and small has been a frequent concern of Pius XII. "To ascertain truth and to be fearlessly faithful to truth in all that you write and speak is not an easy task," the Pope said in one of his many addresses to journalists, "but it is a precious service as well as a bounden duty." See *The Pope Speaks*, II, 1 (First Quarter 1955), pp. 71–72.
35. "In reality the true position of the people who opposed us was, for a long time, not to say and to believe Dreyfus guilty, but to believe and to say that innocent or guilty, the life and salvation of a people, the enormous salvation of a people could not be troubled, could not be upset, could not be compromised, could

The existence of enemies of the Church on one side should not, of itself, persuade Catholics to choose the other. This most frequent logical fallacy played an important role in the disaster suffered by French Catholics at the turn of the century.

The Catholic press is a necessity, but, since it speaks in the Catholic name, it has a frightening responsibility. The Affair reminds us that the Catholic press can err, and err gravely. It must seek the truth in fear and trembling.

Above all, the Affair reminds Catholics that anti-Semitism is a betrayal of the very heart of their faith, and that it is at the same time a real and concrete danger to the Church. We can rejoice that French Catholics have learned this lesson, and have learned it marvelously well.

---

not be risked for one man, for a single man. Tacitly they meant: the temporal salvation. And precisely our Christian *mystique,* our Christian ideal, culminated so perfectly, so exactly with our French *mystique,* with our patriotic *mystique,* in our Dreyfusist *mystique* that what must clearly be recognized is that our point of view focused nothing less than the eternal salvation of France. What indeed was it that we said? Everything was against us, wisdom and law, I mean human wisdom, human law. What we did was in the order of folly or in the order of holiness, which are alike in so many ways, which have so many secret correspondences, in the eyes of human wisdom, underneath the human scrutiny. We moved, we went at odds with wisdom, with law; at odds with human wisdom, with human law. . . . We said that a single injustice, a single crime, a single illegality, particularly if it is officially recorded, confirmed, a single wrong to humanity, a single wrong to justice and to right, particularly if it is universally, legally, nationally, commodiously accepted, that a single crime shatters and is sufficient to shatter the whole social pact, the whole social contract, that a single legal crime, a single dishonorable act will bring about the loss of one's honor, the dishonor of a whole people. . . . Following a Christian tradition in the deepest, the liveliest, the most orthodox sense, situated in the center and in the heart of Christianity, we meant no less than to rise, I don't say to the conception, but to the passion, to the anxiety for eternal salvation, the eternal salvation of this people. . . . Quite at bottom we were the men of eternal salvation and our opponents were the men of temporal salvation. Such was the true, the real division in the Dreyfus case. Quite at bottom, we did not wish France to be constituted in a state of mortal sin" (*Cahiers de la Quinzaine,* Paris, 1900–14, XI, 12, pp. 208–212. These passages can also be found in the bilingual edition of excerpts from Péguy's works, translated by Anne and Julian Green under the title *Men and Saints,* New York: Pantheon, 1944, pp. 108–115).

PERSPECTIVES

Quentin Lauer, s.j.

THE GENIUS OF BIBLICAL THOUGHT

TO THOSE who wish to understand the Christian vision of the world, the distinctive qualities of Hebrew thought are of no little significance. True, Christianity is a faith, and faith is man's response to God revealing Himself. But for thousands of years the custodians of revelation were the Hebrews. This implies that revelation is in some sense bound up with the characteristic way of thinking of the people to whom it was first given, for in revealing Himself to man, God makes use of the thought-patterns peculiar to those men who are His instruments. Only if we enter sympathetically into the thought-world of those instruments can we hope to understand the message which God has sent through them to us.

Whether or not one wishes to attribute to the Hebrews a characteristic metaphysics is unimportant (it is clear enough that they have bequeathed to us no metaphysics as a systematically formulated view of reality), but it is important that we recognize in the background of Hebrew thought an attitude toward being, against which their expressed thought is to be interpreted. The purpose of the present study is to bring out the dynamic and existential character of Hebrew thought—as opposed, for example, to the static and essential character of Greek thought. ("Opposed" here does not mean "hostile," and to contrast Hebrew and Greek thought is not to slight the genius of Greece.) The dynamic character of Hebrew thought makes it ideal for the expression of a faith which, more than an intellectual assent to a set of propositions, is an active surrender of the whole human person to God; and this same dynamism gives Hebrew thought a certain similarity to contemporary thought with its concern for the concrete, the temporal, the historical, the evolving. Hebrew thought may not, perhaps, be suited to the kind of verification science demands, but neither is the supernatural with which it is concerned. It can, however, do what scientific thought cannot

do. It can courageously face mystery. It can even rejoice in the fact that
the relationship between God and man is mysterious.[1]

THE VISION OF A CREATED WORLD

IT HAS been said that, though the fact of creation is discoverable by
natural reason, in reality it is not known to have been discovered before
its revelation given in the first chapter of Genesis. This might be
amended to read that the fact is not known to have been discovered by
the logic of "Greek reason." [2] In any event, one of the most striking
characteristics of Hebrew thought, distinguishing it from all philosophical thought not dependent on it, is that it *begins* with a recognition that
the world is created. Whatever else can be said of biblical thought is
ultimately traceable to this recognition. Rather than starting with a
contemplation of the world and working up from it to a first principle,
it starts with God, the first principle, from which all else flows.[3]

While the Greeks speculated about God, the Jews accepted the God
revealed to them, their cast of thought making them ready for such an
acceptance—whatever their experience of His mighty acts told them
about Him they believed, for they did not distrust experience.[4] Homer

1. In the course of this study I shall have many occasions to refer to several
excellent works in French and German, to which I am indebted both for information and inspiration. They are: Claude Tresmontant, *Essai sur la pensée hébraïque*
(Paris: Editions du Cerf, 1953), referred to as *Pensée hébraïque;* Claude Tresmontant, *Etudes de métaphysique biblique* (Paris: Gabalda, 1955), referred to as
Métaphysique biblique; Thorleif Boman, *Das hebräische Denken im Vergleich mit
dem griechischen* (Göttingen: Vandenhoeck & Ruprecht, 1954); Johannes Hessen,
Platonismus und Prophetismus (Munich: Reinhardt, 1939); and Oscar Cullmann,
Christus und die Zeit, quoted here in its English translation by F. V. Filson, *Christ
and Time* (Philadelphia: Westminster Press, 1950).

2. It would, of course, be an oversimplification to say that all Greek thought was
dominated by logic; Heraclitus is an exception which immediately springs to mind.
Suffice it to say that, to the extent that Greek thought was dominated by logic, it did
not discover the fact of creation.

3. That God creates the world out of nothing, Hessen has reminded us, is the
scandal for all idealism, as Fichte's protest against "this Jewish superstition" shows
most clearly. And that He created the world by His word is the scandal for that
realism which conceives creation only according to the category of causality (*op.
cit.,* pp. 218–219).

4. It changes little if we call this difference between the Hebrew and the Greek
casts of thought a difference in "temperament," as Livingstone does: the result is
the same. The biblical writers, he says, "show a self-submission and self-abasement
to [God] which is quite un-Greek. They are obsessed with the sense of Him. He
is the inspiration of all that is great and memorable in their writings. . . . [The
books in the Old Testament] are continually occupied with the relations of God
to man; nineteen—the Book of Job, the Psalms, the prophetic books—have no

and Hesiod, on the other hand, described the deities the Greek spirit had made in the likeness of corruptible man. Seeing something wonderful in every impulse, aspiration, virtue, or whim, the Greeks called each one god. "Their God was too much the creation of his worshippers ever to become absolute. He was a constitutional monarch whose subjects never quite forgot that they had put him on his throne." [5]

But the God of Israel cannot be a human creation: He goes too much against the natural tendencies of human thought.[6] He is, it is true, a God with whom man can enter into dialogue, since He made him according to His image, an image to which freedom is essential, but in that dialogue man is never unaware of on which side dependence lies. We have but to page through the prophetic books of the Old Testament to recognize an awareness of God not equaled elsewhere in the world's literature. It is the consciousness that He works in and through His creatures, a consciousness which can be the result only of a vital experience, not of rational speculation. Read Isaiah's account of his calling by God (chap. 6) or Jeremiah's (chap. 1). No room there for asking questions, for "reasoning out" the situation—God has touched His prophet, and all that is left is to obey.

In the first verses of Genesis and throughout the Old and New Testa-

other subject. It is not so with Greek literature. There does not lie behind that, as an unchanging background, a struggle between the will of man and the will of God. It has no repeated protests against a backsliding people, whose ears continually wax dull and their hearts gross. And this is not due to an exceptional righteousness of the Greeks. Rather it is because religion was not the same thing for Homer or Aeschylus as for Moses or Isaiah. In their scheme of the world God was not everything. He was part of their life, an important part, but not more. He was there to lend His countenance to their occupations and interests, but not to direct, dominate, and override them. So it is even with the most religious Greeks. When Plato constructs his ideal city, the first word in his pages is not God, the first thought of the writer is not how he shall please Him. Much later in the treatise do we come to such considerations. Read the *Republic* by the side of one of the prophetic books, and the difference of temper is apparent" (R. W. Livingstone, *The Greek Genius and Its Meaning to Us,* London: Oxford University Press, 1924, pp. 58–59).

5. *Ibid.,* pp. 51–53. "If the Greek rejected magic, it was because he expected nothing from his gods; if the Israelite abhorred magic, it was because he expected everything from his God, trusted in Him for everything" (Hessen, *op. cit.,* p. 61).

6. "There is no chance that the biblical idea of God was fabricated by the hands or the thought of man. It contradicts, if one is to believe the history of philosophies, the natural tendencies of human metaphysics; it goes in an opposite direction, against the spontaneous intuitions recorded in the traditions of India and in Western thought. More than that, the biblical conception of God met with constant resistance among the people chosen to transmit it. Like all the other peoples of the world this people had only too strong a tendency to make itself a god 'which would go before it' " (Tresmontant, *Métaphysique biblique,* p. 182).

ments, one thing is clear: for biblical thought the world has a "beginning," and this is enough to characterize the whole biblical attitude toward the world and toward all that is in it. A world that has a beginning owes its very being to Him who is responsible for that beginning. To the Hebrew this was so evident that he felt no need to speculate on the inner principles which would explain the apparent contradictions in the world about him: its oneness and its diversity, its permanence and its constant changing. The problem itself was foreign to his way of thinking, as was the problem of reconciling sensible appearances with the rational essence behind those appearances. For a way of thinking like the Greeks', which sees perfection in unity and in multiplicity imperfection, the multiplication of beings involves a descent to imperfection, which an all-perfect being could scarcely will freely.[7] For the Hebrew, however, it was sufficient that God made things numerous and manifold and "saw that they were good"; he simply would not allow philosophical speculation to impose upon him a problem already invalidated by what his faith "knew" about God and His creation. The Hebrew adored God, not reason.

The first major heresies to threaten the Church were precisely those which found something essentially evil in creation itself, particularly in the creation of matter. To Manichaeism, for instance, matter was evil because it was the principle of multiplicity and hence of a falling away from the perfection of the One. This was, in a way, the outcome of the Greek approach, an outcome the Greek philosopher, however, could avoid, since for him matter was eternal, not needing to be created. But the Manichaean was faced with the problem of reconciling his view of matter with revelation—the result was heresy. The other great heresy of the first two centuries was Gnosticism, whose very name indicates pride in human reason as against the humility which accepts a world as it is revealed to be. Whereas biblical thought distinguished between creation and the fall, seeing in the one the excellence belonging to God's work and in the other the evil introduced by man's misuse of the freedom God had given him, the Gnostic saw in the fall not a sin but an indispensable element for the very genesis of the world and of history. To Manichaean and Gnostic alike, matter was the source of evil, but to the Hebrew, the greatest evil was sin and its source was in the spiritual

7. It is extremely doubtful whether one can read a will activity at all into the God of Greek speculation.

realm—its type was the lie.[8] The early Christian heresies, then, preferred to submit God to the measure of their own reasonings and to make of sin a defect inherent in the very concept of matter and multiplicity, but biblical thought dared to conceive God as creating a freedom capable of defying Him.

The Hebrew would never have belittled creatures in order to glorify their Maker; on the contrary, by recognizing their full dignity he exalted Him far more, since he was constantly aware that whatever exists does so because God created it. If he made any comparisons at all, it was the radical comparison of the mystic: God is all, the creature is nothing—but this mystical view never prevented him from taking the individual creature seriously. Again, aware that the world is created, the biblical writers did not have to speak of a duality of matter and form in order to explain finite being—why "explain" God's activity at all? Nor would it have ever occurred to them to look for an "explanation" of God's creative activity—creation out of nothing—in man's creative activity, which organizes a pre-existent material: the difference was too obvious.

When the pre-Socratic philosopher Parmenides looked at the material world around him, his experience told him that there is in it a multiplicity of beings and that these beings move, change, grow. But his reasoning was that all this was impossible: there was only one being, underived and unchangeable. *One,* for being could not be distinguished from being, since there was nothing in "beings" which was not being whereby they could be distinguished; *underived,* for there could not be any coming into being, since being could not come from nothing, from not-being; *unchangeable,* for change or growth would imply that what is, at the same time becomes. For the Greeks and those who follow their thought, this is the beginning of fruitful speculation on the nature of being, multiplicity, and change. But for the people of Israel, such speculation would simply have been time wasted; no "logic" could make them contradict what their faith knew, and their faith knew that God made and makes what was not before. Greek reason would call this impossible, or at least be concerned with finding out how it was possible. The Hebrew mind, however, was not concerned with how a creation from nothing was possible; it could not even ask itself the question as to whether what *is* is possible. For if one begins not with nothingness but with the fullness of being, then the existence of other

8. See Tresmontant, *Pensée hébraïque,* pp. 21–23.

beings, with their genesis, their growth and development, does not constitute a problem; it is simply a fact.[9]

Likewise, Hebrew thought was less concerned with analyzing the world into its "component elements" than it was with seeing in the functioning, growth, and development of all things an extension of God's creative activity. When Jesus said: "My Father works even until now" (Jn 5:17), His hearers had no trouble understanding Him. The world works, and since it does, God does; creation is, as it were, still going on. Matter, for the Hebrew, was not something inert; it was dynamic, because God made it so. The assertion of modern science that atoms and stars are ever coming into being, that matter is constantly in the state of genesis, would in no way have troubled him, for his confidence in God would have told him that this genesis was good. Nor would he have been troubled by the notion of evolution, since it could never have occurred to him that an evolving matter would detract in the slightest from God's creative activity. To seek to discover any special laws governing matter he would have considered superfluous; there was for him only one law ruling all finite beings, and that was the law of creation.[10]

Perhaps one of the most striking differences between Hebrew and Greek thought—and this too flows from Israel's faith in God the Creator—was in their attitudes toward sensible things. Whether with Plato, who saw in the things that strike the senses but defective imitations of eternal ideas, or with Aristotle, who saw true perfection in essences, universals, rather than in concrete and particular things, the Greek was inclined to stress not the individual being that exists but rather the ideal of which existing things are but particular examples. Because the Hebrew began with God rather than with the world, and because all that God does is good, he contemplated the perfection in things rather than their imperfection. He could dare to love the sensible world, because

9. "It is characteristic of Hebrew thought, as compared with Greek and Western philosophy, that it is not troubled by the negative ideas of nothingness and disorder. It is not haunted by the idea of an original nothingness which would be 'in the right' and which would have to be surmounted, or by a disorder, a chaos, which would have to be dominated and which would undermine the real with its menacing presence. The Hebrew does not begin with the empty to arrive at the full. It is not nothingness which by right is at the beginning. It is He whose name is: I am, Yahweh, the living God who created heaven and earth. 'In the beginning God . . .'" (*ibid.,* p. 55).

10. See Tresmontant, *Métaphysique biblique,* pp. 42–44.

the almighty word of God brought it into existence.[11] Nor did he feel constrained to reserve intelligibility to that which is either above, or abstracted from, the sensible. No dualist, he did not see in things a sensible element which is not intelligible and an intelligible element which is not sensible; he saw everything as a creature of God and as, by that very fact, intelligible. True, there were in his world angelic spirits, but he felt no need to speculate on their nature, being more concerned with their function as messengers of God.

On the other hand, and this may seem paradoxical, the people of Israel were not impressed by the beauty of sensible things in themselves. For them beauty was not something but Someone, and all things spoke to them of that Someone. Their hands have left us no paintings, no sculptures, no great monuments to admire; their one great work of art is their poetry, telling almost exclusively God's goodness toward His creatures. They had respect, no doubt, for His handiwork, but when they were in their right mind there was no danger of their becoming fascinated by it. To them things were real, but they were also signs, words, speaking of Him from whom they came.[12] Perhaps one can say that it was not the intelligibility of things they thought important, rather their transintelligibility, that is to say, He who is known through them.[13]

Yet in the Old Testament, all things point not only backward, as it were, to Him from whom they came, but also forward to Him whom they announced. From beginning to end the Bible is messianic; indeed, the whole Hebrew world of reality conspired to point toward a greater Reality to come. It is significant, too, that when the Holy One of God did come, He came as One who could be heard and looked upon, whom eyes could see and hands touch (1 Jn 1:1). True, "He came unto His own, and His own received Him not" (Jn 1:11), but their not receiving

11. "The Hebrew has the sense of the 'carnal' because in it he discerns its spiritual core. The biblical universe is the exact opposite of the Manichaean universe. To have a sense of the 'carnal,' a taste for the elemental, a sense of contemplation and of the spiritual, is all one from the biblical point of view, because the sensible world is language, it has been created by the word" (Tresmontant, *Pensée hébraïque*, p. 56).

12. Not that Israel was always faithful to the highest vision of its saints and prophets. Its history is so often a history of unfaithfulness: again and again kings and people set up an idol in place of the true God; but the genius of Hebrew thought, the supernatural inspiration of Israel's prophets, always recognized unfaithfulness for what it was.

13. See Tresmontant, *Pensée hébraïque*, p. 68; and Hessen, *op. cit.*, pp. 91–94.

Him cannot be ascribed to a faithfulness to the genius of their own thought. Those early heresies which, shocked at the thought of God in the *flesh,* denied the true humanity of Christ, were Greek, not Hebrew, in inspiration. Unwonted though this assertion may be, even contradicting so much that is said in this respect—that God should become incarnate in a sensible human nature was a logical scandal not to the Jews but to the Greeks. The great stumbling block to the Jews was the Crucifixion, not the Incarnation (see 1 Cor 1:23).

THE VISION OF MAN

IT IS the merit of Tresmontant to have pointed to creation as the great theme of Hebrew thought; he has likewise thrown new light on the biblical view of man. Because Israel believed in God the Creator—a faith so revolutionary in the pagan world—Israel could not but esteem all that God had made and could not but love man. It is biblical faith that God did not create because anything accrued to Him thereby; again, it is biblical faith that the Son did not become man for His own sake. The writers of the Bible had no doubt that God "works" for the benefit of man, and, because of this, their vision of man is important for our understanding of their world-view.

As I said before, the Hebrew felt no need to distinguish between the sensible and the intelligible elements in all that surrounded him. His was a childlike familiarity with being, coming from his initial certitude that saying "God created all" explained all. Like everything else man was created, but he was not seen in the Greek way as a "body informed by a soul"; he was simply a "living being" (Gen 2:7), living corporeally, sensibly. The Hebrew did not search for an intrinsic principle which would explain how one person could be distinguished from another: God created more than one, and that was enough for him.[14] Yet he knew too that man was not only a creature but an image of God and

---

14. In the biblical universe, the multiplicity of beings is no accident, nothing negative, but a sign of God's fruitful love and power. The multitude of creatures is willed, for there is excellence in their multitude and excellence in each of them. Hence it is the particular that is the existent; neither negligible nor insignificant, the particular is the bearer of meaning. God chose one particular people, for instance, to witness to His truth; to accomplish this, He chose one particular man, Abraham, at a particular time, at a particular place. And it is the biblical metaphysics of multiple and particular beings, created by a positive act of God intending their excellence, that is the foundation of Christian personalism. See Tresmontant, *Pensée hébraïque,* pp. 15–16, 69, 99; and Hessen, *op. cit.,* p. 20.

that, as such, he had a certain duality in him. This duality, however, was not so much the philosophical duality of the body and the soul that animates it, rather that of spirit and flesh.[15]

"Flesh," in biblical language, is simply man himself, with stress on the element of fragility essential to his earthly condition.[16] Yet for the Hebrew, this was no reason to wish to get rid of the flesh as of something embarrassing. The flesh, too, was the object of a positive act of creation, and God "saw that it was good." It is most meaningful that St. John chose this very word to tell the mystery of Christ: "The Word was made flesh" (1:14); and that Jesus Himself did not hesitate to say: "Unless you eat the flesh of the Son of Man . . . you shall not have life in you" (Jn 6:54).

One might venture to approximate the biblical dialectic of flesh and spirit to that of the natural and the supernatural. But neither Jew nor Christian needs to depreciate the natural in order to exalt the supernatural, nor did it occur to either (until the Greek influence made itself felt in early Christian heresies) to lay the blame for evil on the flesh because it was material. The true Judaeo-Christian tradition is not tempted to explain away evil by attributing it to matter; rather does it recognize evil—that is, in so far as it is sin—as belonging to the spiritual order. Only the spiritual in man can sin, and the spiritual in man is the "breath" God breathed into him (Gen 2:7). It is difficult enough to see how a Plato or an Aristotle could have understood a multiplicity of spirits without bodies,[17] but it is impossible to see how either could have looked upon an "evil spirit" as anything but sheer nonsense.[18]

Further, the Greeks would have writhed in agony at the thought of attributing corporeal passions to the soul or the soul's emotions to the body. But the sacred writers thought little of attributing weeping to the soul or joy to the bowels (Ps 118:28; Prov 23:16). It is not that they saw all things as one, that they were unaware of the distinction between the inanimate and the animate, or that they did not see the vital, biological aspect of man as different from that which transcends it. Once again, it is merely that the Hebrew felt no distrust of the sensible. Though he knew that man is different from all that is not man, he

15. See Tresmontant, *ibid.,* pp. 87, 109, 112.
16. *Ibid.,* p. 96.
17. Medieval Scholasticism also had its problems on this score.
18. See Tresmontant, *Pensée hébraïque,* p. 101.

saw no need of breaking man down into elements in order to explain the difference. Man was created by God as a sensible being, upon whose face the Hebrew could read anger, or fear, or joy; in whose clenched fists he could read pain or sorrow; in whose walk he could see consciousness of human dignity or despondency. Hence it was natural for him to say that a man's face was angry, that his eyes had seen the glory of the Lord, or that his soul thirsted.[19]

Yet Hebrew thought knew intimacy not only with the sensible world but also with the supra-sensible, the "world" of God and His ministering spirits. God walked in paradise and Adam conversed with Him; Moses stood in His presence, hearing Him and answering; Job could reproach Him with the way he had been treated (Gen 3:8–12; Ex 3:4—4:17; Job 23 and 24). The Hebrew was on familiar ground, therefore, when speaking of the spirit, the higher and altogether new dimension in man (new, that is, in the realm of living creatures on earth); and therefore too his thought was a remarkable preparation for the Christian theology of grace, of man's union with God, his participation in that which is proper to God Himself. The word the biblical writers used to express this supra-sensible dimension was taken, however, from the sensible world: *ruaḥ,* "breath." "And God breathed into his nostrils the breath of life, and man became a living being" (Gen 2:7). The spirit, the breath of life in man, is not supernatural in the strict sense, but it is that which makes possible supernatural life in him, possible the encounter of his spirit with the Spirit of God. For God Himself is Spirit, and that He can dwell in man, as the biblical message proclaims, is because of the spirit He created in him. Thus God's coming into man is not like the intrusion of a stranger but is desired, and it is prepared for by the creation of the human spirit, an embassy, as it were, in the land of man.[20]

Of the spirit there was no psychology, as there was of the soul among the Greeks—no more than there is, in Christian theology, a psychology of the theological virtues of faith, hope, and charity. It is not to be expected in Hebrew thought, and yet there is a sense in which psychology can be of help, by enumerating all the things which the spirit is not. By so doing, psychology liberates the spiritual, as it were, somewhat as photography liberated art by doing better all those things

19. See *ibid.,* pp. 102–104.
20. See *ibid.,* pp. 107–110.

which are not properly the function of art.[21] There is in the Bible not the least attempt to present a systematic psychology; what it does offer is an anthropology, an understanding of man. For the biblical writers this was necessarily the understanding of man as a person, as a spiritual being who, in his relations to God, can rise to the heights of faithfulness or sink to the depths of unfaithfulness. Not even of cognition is there any psychology in the Bible, since knowledge was for the Hebrew not the act of any distinct faculty but the activity of the whole man. Knowledge was not seen as distinct from action—it was action, and man as a totality was wrapped up in it; it was a special sort of relation with man, with things, or with God. To the Hebrew mind, then, the most intimate of human relations, the conjugal act, was the exemplar of knowledge, for nothing is known that is not loved. So we read that Adam "knew Eve his wife" (Gen 4:1).[22] Thus there was nothing strange to the Hebrew when he heard the supreme unfaithfulness to God, which is idolatry—not-*knowing* God and turning to other gods— denounced by his prophets as "fornication." But to know God was to love Him, to pray to Him, to address Him as "thou"; it was to respond to Him who had spoken first.

THE VISION OF TIME

THE "creational view" which marks Hebrew thought carries with it a unique appreciation of time. The first words of Genesis are usually translated: "In the beginning God created the heavens and the earth." But they can also be translated: "In *a* beginning God created heaven and earth."[23] Now, a beginning must be the beginning of something; and anything that begins is a process. It can be said that time is a required condition for process, since process implies continuous succession, and succession presupposes time. Yet it can also be said that process is a condition for time, since where there is no process there is no succession properly speaking, and where there is no succession there is no time. Again, there can be no beginning unless there be a process of

21. One is reminded of the kind of hagiography which Ida Görres has given us of St. Thérèse of Lisieux in *Das verborgene Antlitz*. In it she has turned the lens of psychology on all that could possibly be explained naturally, so that the supernatural stands out all the more sharply.
22. See Tresmontant, *Pensée hébraïque*, pp. 105–106.
23. See Tresmontant, *Métaphysique biblique*, p. 255.

which it is a beginning; and, conversely, there can be no process unless there be a beginning. This is the point at which all materialistic philosophies are forced to be irrational. They cannot admit a beginning, since a beginning implies something, or rather Someone, on whom the beginning depends. At the same time, they cannot deny process, since their materialism was designed precisely to explain process. They can and do speak of a "cyclic" process, but that is merely a mental construction devised to get them out of an embarrassing situation and having no reference to reality as we know it. Or they can say that there is no logical necessity for process to have a beginning, but this is the same as saying that according to a logic they have arbitrarily chosen, according to notions unrelated to reality, they *see* no need for a beginning. The Hebrew, however, never made the mistake of imposing his own notions on reality.

Even the language of the Bible shows that the people of Israel thought in a framework of movement, action, growth, process.[24] The static, obviously, needs to be expressed, but the Hebrew language does so in verbs of action. It uses the same verb to express position, such as standing or lying, as it does to express the action of getting up or laying oneself down. But how is this possible? Does one and the same word have two different, and almost contradictory, meanings? Or has it not rather one fundamental meaning from which various shades of meaning spring? Thus, Hebrew uses the same verb for "to stand up" and "to stand (in a spot)," for "to place oneself" and "to stand." "To lie down to rest" is the same as "to rest," "to seat oneself" the same as "to sit" or "to dwell." Examples could be multiplied almost indefinitely to illustrate this one point: the Hebrew thought of "being in a position" in terms of action, of doing something, of putting himself in that position.[25]

For us, to be still and to move are somehow opposites, as the inactive is to the active; for the Hebrew, they were so closely related as to form

---

24. One need not be a linguistic expert to know that the language of a people reveals a great deal about its soul. "The character of a people or of a family of peoples, a race, finds its expression in its language. This is particularly true in regard to a people less developed culturally, the inner logic of whose language, and hence its connection with the psychology of the people, is easier to penetrate. In any case the Hebrew language, which to our way of thinking and feeling is most distinctive, betrays from many points of view the character of the Israelite psyche" (Boman, *op. cit.,* p. 18).

25. *Ibid.,* p. 19.

a unity.[26] He found an absolutely motionless state of being impossible to conceive, not because he had the scientific knowledge that matter and motion are inseparable, but because of his metaphysical view: for him "not to move" was "not to be." The Hebrew was concerned primarily neither with being (as a state) nor with becoming (as a coming into being), but with the subject of whom being or becoming is predicated; and since it is the nature of a subject to act, it was characteristic of the Hebrew that he conceived whatever could be said of a subject in terms of action. Even in so simple a thing as a comparison, what English expresses by the static "than," Hebrew expresses by the dynamic "away from": Saul was not merely a head taller than the rest of the people; he was (literally translated) "from his shoulders and upward high away from the rest of the people" (1 Kg 9:2). Most strikingly, "silence" is understood, not in our way as an absence of speaking, but as an active "keeping oneself silent," as "an activity of the subject, emerging from within." [27]

Like Russian, for instance, the Hebrew language usually dispenses with "to be" as a copula, since it can be expressed adequately by juxtaposition alone. What we translate as "The Lord is my shepherd" is in Hebrew "The Lord my shepherd." When "to be" is used, it functions as a verb much more distinctly than it does for us: "to be" means to become, to exist, to act, and somehow expresses all these at once. Since "to be" is to become something or to do something, being in its full sense is the being of a person.[28] And Israel's awareness of God was always of Him as a Person. Whereas a typical Greek conception of God was the motionless perfection of being, the people of Israel knew Him as the God who acts, for to be is to act, and not to act is not to be. Israel's God, then, is the Creator; the Greek God is an object of contemplation.[29] For the Greek, God was an object attained at the end of a train of rational speculation; for the Hebrew, He was a Person, whom from the beginning he experienced as dynamic, as One who wills, who is

26. This recalls Alfred North Whitehead's definition of rest as motion of zero velocity: "Rest is merely a particular case of such motion [uniform rectilinear motion], merely when the velocity is and remains zero" (*An Introduction to Mathematics,* New York: Henry Holt, 1911, p. 44).

27. Boman, *op. cit.,* p. 24; see pp. 20 and 143.

28. See *ibid.,* pp. 29–30, 34–35.

29. Significant here is a contrast: when Socrates was in the grip of a problem, he stood motionless for hours; when the orthodox Jew prays, his awe and devotion make him active, make him sway his whole body to and fro (see *ibid.,* p. 166).

infinite love.[30] Even the attributes of God were for him active, vital attributes. He could find no better words to describe God than "the living God." [31]

Once more the difference between the static and the dynamic conceptions of reality is clear: it might be said, then, that Greek thought moves in a spatial framework, while Hebrew thought moves in a temporal framework. There seems little doubt that modern man knows he is living in a world that is not ahistorical, that the world is temporal because it is moving forward and not in a circle. In this, at least, he manifests more affinity with Hebrew than with Greek thought; and, whether he be Jew or Christian, believer or non-believer, modern man cannot simply disregard the biblical outlook on being—he has been conditioned by it. This much is clear: the world in which man lives is temporal, and its temporality is irreversible. In other words, the present is not a repetition of the past, nor will the future be a repetition of the past or present; the world of today is not the world of yesterday, no more than a man can remain a child, for man and world alike have grown and cannot go back to what they were. But if man's world is temporal, it is more than a world that changes; it is a world of constant novelty, and novelty bespeaks not merely change but creation. Thus, though it is certainly true to say that the world was created, it might also be said that, in a way, the world is being created and will be created. More than he realizes, modern man is the debtor to Hebrew thought, which gave us the good news of creation, for it is only in the light of creation that time, history, newness, make sense.

Henri Bergson has aroused us to the realization that time cannot be caught in the concepts of scientific analysis.[32] Moreover, he showed that process, of which time is the "measure," is not to be grasped in terms of Darwinian or Lamarckian evolution, which have process governed by a "law of survival." He saw that the only law of process must be a law of creation, and in so doing he returned by "intuition" to the "creational vision" which the writers of the Bible had attained by faith.[33]

30. See Hessen, *op. cit.,* p. 77; Max Scheler, *Vom Umsturz der Werte* (Leipzig: Der Neue Geist Verlag, 1923), II, 109ff.

31. See Hessen, *op. cit.,* p. 68.

32. Is there something more than coincidence in the fact that Bergson was a Jew?

33. One has the impression sometimes that Bergson is describing time as he found it—unformulated—in the Bible: see, for example, *Creative Evolution,* trans. A. Mitchell (New York: Modern Library, 1944), pp. 14, 180–181, 374; *The*

It is only where the idea of growth involves something more than the idea of change that time is seen as a constant forward movement, a movement which can be analyzed into concepts only if it is stopped, thereby ceasing to be what it is. Thus, apart from the development of the universe itself, in which God's creative work continues ("My Father is at work until now"), the production of any living being is creation, since it always involves more than the mere organization of matter— the beginning of *new* being.[34]

Inseparable indeed are time and creation, in the sense that we could not speak of time in any meaningful way if there were no creation, no beginning. The biblical consciousness of time, however, would seem to tend even further and to suggest that without time there would be no creation, in the sense that one condition of creation as such is that it be in time, that it be continuous.[35] It might, of course, be argued that, absolutely speaking, God could have created everything at once, but there is really not much point in speaking of absolute possibilities, since that always implies our knowing more about possibility than we do; an "absolute possibility" is what we can think of, not necessarily what can be. Might we perhaps say, then, with Tresmontant, that "time enters as a determining factor into the very logic of the real"; that time is needed for the world of finite beings to move from the pre-living to the living, from the pre-conscious to the conscious; that certain physico-chemical conditions on our planet had to exist before life could appear; that the earth had to be readied before man was made? [36] Since God's ultimate purpose in creating is to communicate Himself to His creatures, not only to spirits but to spirits-in-flesh, might there not be a "logic" of communication demanding that God, though He communicate Himself with sovereign freedom, does so to a creature of flesh only after He has progressively rendered it capable of receiving that communication, which at the highest level is a participation in the divine life itself? In any case, even though the last word on the evolution of creatures has not been said and may not be for a long time, a vision of God's creative

Creative Mind, trans. M. L. Andison (New York: Philosophical Library, 1946), p. 17; *Time and Free Will,* trans. F. L. Pogson (New York: Macmillan, 1910), p. 98.

34. See Tresmontant, *Métaphysique biblique,* pp. 79–81.

35. The Hebrew did not "argue" rationally to the necessity of God's "causality" in all that takes place in the world; he was simply vividly aware of God's presence in every event, every word, every thought.

36. *Ibid.,* pp. 121–122.

work which embraces the idea of non-mechanical evolution, far from "diminishing" His sovereignty, is rather its sublime unfolding.

Never forgetting that time implies creation, that it too is God's creature, I have asked if the creative action is itself somehow temporally conditioned. Whether or not such a relation can be proved, it seems at least to be the tacit presupposition of much of biblical writing, and this precisely because the Bible is conceived throughout in the framework of the supernatural, which means ultimately a supernatural communication of God to His creatures. For the Hebrew, history is God's work; it is creation, it is revelation: there is no separating history, creation, revelation.[37] Hence, in the light of biblical history—which in the Old Testament points toward a future event, the advent of the Messiah, and which in the New Testament goes out from that same event—is it possible to speak of time as purely incidental to creation? There can be no question, however, that the work of salvation, which crowns that of creation, involves time, as man passes from fall to redemption, from sin to glory. Surely the biblical concept of *kairos,* the God-given moment, the time, or period of time, appointed and designed by God for any salvific event (be it the witness of God's love on the cross or the final reaping of the good sown by the faithful, be it God's promise come true in the Apostle's preaching or the beginning of God's judgment— 1 Tim 2:6; Gal 6:9; Tit 1:3; 1 Pet 4:17), surely this concept seems to imply that one time prepares for another, and this again for another.[38]

There is one more feature in the Hebrew view of time which separates it from both the Greek and the scientific concepts of time and likens it to the Bergsonian view. For the Hebrew, the tripartite division of time into past, present, and future could not be represented by a line on which the present is a *point* separating past and future. The notion of a mathematical instant had no meaning for him, since an instant is not time nor a part of time but an abstraction, an assigned division between times, one of which is no longer and the other of which is not yet. The "dimensionless instant" raised for the Greeks, very much as it does for scientists and all abstract thinkers, many interesting problems, problems

37. See Hessen, *op. cit.,* pp. 94–96.
38. Tresmontant, *Métaphysique biblique,* pp. 127–130. It should be remembered that biblical history has a sense which "scientific" history cannot have; it is essentially a "history of salvation," which is primarily concerned with the passage from the fall to the participation in divine life.

which did not exist for the biblical mind. In the Bible the present is that which is actual, that which is acting, whether the period of acting be short or long. Hence original sin is said to be still present, because it is still acting. The past is that which is no longer acting; the future is that which is not yet acting. God is the eternal present, because He is ever-present act; all times are before His eyes at once, and a thousand years in His sight are like a watch in the night or like one day, and one day is like a thousand years (Ps 89:4; 2 Pet 3:8).[39]

Linguistically speaking, Hebrew does not have past and future tenses properly so called; there is simply action, which from the point of view of the speaker can be looked on as complete or incomplete. It might be said that there is only one time, that this time is continuous, and that there are aspects of it which are relative to persons, whether to the speaker or to the one with whom the narrative is concerned. In order to understand this view, we have to realize that, unlike Western thought, to which space is primary and time is conceived according to movement in space, the Hebrew conceived time vitally and personally, in relation to a subject. No abstraction, biblical time is identical with that which happens in time. Thus day and night are not conceived cyclically but according to a subjective experience. Day is light, night is darkness; the sun, moon, and stars are not "heavenly bodies" but "lights," the sun ruling the day, the moon and stars ruling the night (Gen 1:5, 16).

Time is continuous; hence, Boman explains, the life of the people of Israel, though it lasts for hundreds and thousands of years, is one life. Thus the poem which describes the lot of Jacob's sons speaks of them now as persons, now as tribes (Gen 49). And the prophets view patriarch and people together as one; the people is simply called "Jacob" (Is 41:8; Os 12:2). No less is it a wholly Hebrew way of thinking when St. Paul sees the turning to Christ of a future generation of Israel as the salvation of all Israel (Rom 11:26).[40] Time is continuous, but it does not last forever. A man's years are as brief as a sigh; all flesh is grass, and grass withers; heaven and earth will pass away (Ps 89:9; Is 40:6-7; Mt 24:35). But this knowledge brought no gloom to the people of Israel, for they knew that the word of Yahweh shall stand forever, that He is an everlasting Rock, the Creator of the ends of the earth, who does not faint or weary (Is 40:8; 26:4; 40:28).

39. See *ibid.*, pp. 139–140.
40. See Boman, *op. cit.*, pp. 111, 118–120.

THE GOSPEL AND TIME

THERE seems to be an anomaly in the New Testament's having come down to us in Greek. St. Luke excepted, of course, it was written by Jews who thought as Jews and who, save for St. Paul, had not been to any great extent "hellenized." On the other hand, the anomaly is providential. As, in our times, the Church may well be destined to assimilate Eastern thought, so she was destined to assimilate Greek, and then Roman, thought; and the language of the New Testament was, as it were, a first step in this direction. Still, it is Hebrew thought that dominates the writings of the evangelists and apostles, a fact well illustrated in the New Testament attitude toward time.

God is the eternal present, which is to say He is "outside" time. And outside history He remained, in a sense, throughout the Old Testament, directing it by His providence, though even in the days of old, by revealing Himself, by calling patriarchs and prophets, by acting in the life of the people of Israel, God entered into history by His word. In the Incarnation, however, God entered into time in a way altogether new, taking upon Himself a history and identifying Himself with His own creation. Both His revelation and His entrance into history became more "tangible," for here it was the substantial Word of God which became His living revelation and, in becoming incarnate, became historical. Yet God's entry into history is not an event like other events in the over-all history of the world. Redemptive history, of which Jesus Christ is at once the central figure and the central event, is not properly speaking a "part" of general history; rather is it that which gives to general history its ultimate significance.[41]

Fundamentally, the temporal line of redemptive history is one and the same in New and Old Testaments, beginning with the first going forth of creatures from the hand of God and ending with the return of creatures to God. Creation itself is historical, but it is revelation which gives to this history a specific structure. According to that structure history is a continuous line of events, but, unlike a history conceived apart

41. The birth, life, and death of Jesus of Nazareth are events in time, which historical method can verify. That Jesus of Nazareth was the Word-made-flesh can be verified only by faith—historical method can say nothing for or against it. Thus, in so far as the events of Jesus' life on earth are historically verifiable, they are a part of general history. In so far as they have a significance which transcends the "scientifically" verifiable, they belong to a history which is unique.

from the divine plan of salvation, it is a continuous line which has a "mid-point," one central event, from which all other events, before and after, derive their significance. In the Old Testament, that event is the coming of the One who is to come; in the New, it is the coming of Him who is come—the Incarnation which has taken place,[42] or, in a phrase of Cullmann's, "the Christ-event." [43]

For Jew and Christian alike, all creation prior to the coming of the Messiah leads up to this event and is conceived in terms of it; all creation after the event flows, and derives its significance, from it. The Jew looks forward to it with hope, but for the Christian, the hope is already fulfilled, the event has taken place and is ever present to his faith. Not that he is without expectation, for he hopes in the future glory. But his life is not centered there; though the end is still to come, the center has been reached. To use Cullmann's illustration, the decisive battle of a war may have been won early in the war, and yet the war goes on. The crucifixion and the resurrection were that decisive battle, that center. Thus creation itself is a revelation leading up to the concrete presence of the Word and continuing as an unfolding of that presence. The world is at once a continuous creation and a continuous revelation, and as both it is temporal, historical.[44]

For both Jew and Christian the Bible is something more than a recorded history; it is a prophetic revelation about history.[45] Hence more than the historian's eye—faith is needed to assent to the central affirmation of biblical history, that Jesus Christ is the Son of God. And once redemptive history is seen as a supernatural revelation, the manner in which Old and New Testaments are integrated becomes clear. In no way did the significance of the Old cease with the coming of the New, for as St. Paul says, the Old Testament was written *for us,* "for our

42. When I speak of "Incarnation" in this context, I have in mind not merely "And the Word was made flesh," rather the whole context: "And the Word was made flesh, and dwelt among us." Hence the Incarnation here is the *presence* of the Word of God in the flesh, which is also the total event constituting the presence of the Word of God in history.

43. See Cullmann, *op. cit.,* pp. 90, 107–114.

44. See *ibid.,* p. 84. "The Word, the Logos, is God in His revelatory action. Nowhere, however, is God's action revealed more concretely than in the history which, to speak theologically, presents in its innermost nature the revelation of God to men" (*ibid.,* p. 24).

45. See *ibid.,* p. 98. Unfortunately the English language has only one word, "history," to express two concepts: the actual process of events or the "organic" growth of the world, and the record in language of that process. In German the first of these is expressed by the term *Geschichte;* the second by the term *Historie.*

instruction" (Rom 15:4).[46] It tended toward the New, though it was only the New that revealed this, its splendor. Its witness remains, that is to say, the Old and the New are not contemporaneous.

The Old Testament offers another part of the redemptive history than does the New. It is itself first of all a unique story of what once happened. But its meaning for redemptive history is recognized only when this entire section of time is placed in relation with the unique, once-for-all event of the mid-point, and this relation may be understood only as a relationship conceived in a strict time sense, between *preparation* and *fulfillment*. To find the witness to Christ in the Old Testament does not mean, then, to find the Incarnation of Jesus in the Old Testament. It means rather to learn, upon the basis of our knowledge concerning the incarnate and crucified Christ, how to understand the past events of redemptive history as preparation for the Incarnation and the Cross.[47]

Paradoxically enough, distinguishing the Old and New Testaments this way permits us to unify them most profoundly. It is not a unity of an artificial identification; rather is it the unity of integration into one historical process, into one total and progressive revelation. Thus, the history of creation and the history of redemption are united into one indivisible whole, because creation and redemption form one line of divine action flowing from God's goodness, through God's Word. "From Him, and through Him, and unto Him are all things" (Rom 11:36).

All dualism between creation and redemption is here excluded. In the New Testament there cannot be, in addition to the Christ-line of redemption, another and separate God-line of creation. Rather, the redemptive process receives its world-wide significance not only from the broad base of departure and the broad final goal, but also from the universal outreach of the event at the mid-point, the event in which the narrowing reaches its climax precisely for the sake of the redemption of all. For primitive Christianity, there is only the one line of divine activity; it is that one of which it is said from beginning to end: everything *from* God and *to* God, and everything *through* Christ, through the Word, "through Him."[48]

Thus the good news of creation is taken up into the good news of redemption. There can therefore be no place in the spiritual life of a Christian for a flight from the world as from something evil. The God who

46. See also Rom 4:24; I Cor 9:10; 10:11.
47. Cullmann, *op. cit.*, p. 135.
48. *Ibid.*, pp. 178–179.

"saw that all He had made was very good" (Gen 1:31) is the same
God who became man "that they may have life, and have it more abundantly" (Jn 10:10). With reverence, then, can the Christian look at
the world. He embraces it because in it God has revealed Himself; he
embraces it because it has "already been drawn into the redemptive
process"; [49] he embraces it as a historical world, which has "a beginning" and continuously tends toward an end, which end is glory in God.
But his affirmation of the world remains always guarded. For men are
free, so that the world in its tending to God can become disoriented. To
this extent the Christian remains critical in regard to the world, not to
the world as God's work, which is good, but to the world, in so far as it
contains deviations from the one unique line running from creation,
through redemption, to its final goal "in Him." Never can the Christian
forget that, if this world, if history, has a beginning, it will have an
end, and that his destiny is not to end with it.

49. *Ibid.*, p. 212.

Kathryn Sullivan, R.S.C.J.

PRO PERFIDIS JUDAEIS

MAN'S redemption is a mystery of love: love seeking, love faithful even were rejected, love oblative. The mystery was accomplished in the place and at the moment chosen by God, that is, in Jerusalem during the paschal solemnities of almost two thousand years ago. This yearly feast recalled miracles of divine tenderness for a people long sought, sometimes unfaithful, often afflicted, but always privileged to have God's ministers, Moses, Joshua, and all the other prophets, to recall it when unfaithful, to console it when afflicted. Out of Egypt God brought His people. At Sinai He bound Himself to it, asking in return its love and worship. In the desert He fashioned it for forty years. To its own land He guided it. There it was to prepare for another exodus, the exodus of the Anointed One, the Redeemer who was to fulfill all the vast promises of the prophets, to undo the ancient wrong, and to die a salvific death for all men.[1] The pasch was, therefore, memorial and prophecy. To Jews it remains a sacred commemoration of their marvelous deliverance from the Egypt of bondage and idolatry. To Christians it is the quickening rite which reveals again and again mankind's deliverance from the death which is sin, and its entrance into life. The Christian pasch unfolds in a succession of sacred days that bring to an intense conclusion and mighty climax the purifying work of Lent.[2]

The General Decree of the Sacred Congregation of Rites in 1955

1. Louis Bouyer, Orat., *The Paschal Mystery* (Chicago: Regnery, 1950), p. 58. Jean Daniélou, S.J., describes the typology of the exodus in the Old and New Testaments in *Sacramentum Futuri* (Paris: Beauchesne, 1950), pp. 131–200. See also Barnabas M. Ahern, C.P., "The Exodus, Then and Now," *The Bridge,* I, 53–74. "All in all, the story of Christ as told in the Gospels is best understood when it is read in the biblical context of Israel's exodus" (*ibid.,* p. 66).

2. The biblical theology of the paschal mystery is analyzed by Jean Daniélou, S.J., in *Bible et Liturgie* (Paris: Les Editions du Cerf, 1951), pp. 388–408. The author's theme is succinctly stated in the first sentence: "The paschal mystery is in a sense the whole Christian mystery." On the climactic quality of the paschal feast, see Dom Jean Gaillard's *Holy Week and Easter,* trans. by William Busch (Collegeville, Minn.: The Liturgical Press, 1954).

renewed the order of these richly powerful days so that in the twentieth century, as in the first centuries, these solemn rites commemorating the crucified, buried, and risen Christ are celebrated as nearly as possible on the same days of the week and at the same hours of the day that the sacred mysteries occurred.[3] Thus on Thursday evening, the solemn Mass of the Lord's Supper recalls the institution of the Blessed Eucharist, for it was "when evening arrived [that] He reclined at table with the twelve disciples" (Mt 26:20). On Friday afternoon, a deeply significant ceremony commemorates His Passion, for it was "from the sixth hour [that] there was darkness over the whole land until the ninth hour" (Mt 27:45). And a solemn vigil, beginning on Holy Saturday night, leads to the joy of the resurrection on Easter Sunday morning, for it was "late in the night of the Sabbath, as it began to dawn towards the first day of the week, [that] Mary Magdalene and the other Mary came to see the sepulchre" (Mt 28:1). The days of this sacred triduum are closely linked. Jesus' voluntary act of oblation in the eucharistic banquet on Holy Thursday was completed by His sacrificial death on Good Friday in His life-giving immolation on the cross. After the silence of the Great Sabbath, in the early hours of the first day of the new week, He rose from the dead, glorious and immortal, reconciling all things unto Himself (Col 1:20).

The importance of the Good Friday service in this life-bringing sequence has been reverently acknowledged through the centuries. The words of the 1955 decree sharpen the focus:

The faithful should be trained to gain a right understanding of the unique liturgical services of this day. In these services, after the sacred reading and prayers, the Passion of our Lord is sung solemnly, prayers are offered for the needs of the entire Church and of the human race, and the Holy Cross, the memorial of our redemption, is devoutly adored by the Christian family, the clergy and the people. Finally, according to the rubrics of the restored Ordo, and as was the custom for many cen-

3. The new ordinal of Holy Week (*Ordo Hebdomadae Sanctae Instauratus*) whose use was made preceptive for the Roman rite by the decree of the Sacred Congregation of Rites *Maxima redemptionis nostrae* and the instruction *Cum propositum,* which were published in *L'Osservatore Romano* on November 27, 1955, together with an authoritative article by an eminent Roman liturgist, Ferdinando Antonelli, O.F.M., explaining the pastoral importance of the restored rite. The official text of the two documents, dated November 16, 1955, was published in the *Acta Apostolicae Sedis,* 47 (December 23, 1955), pp. 838–847. See also John J. Danagher, C.M., "The Ordinal of Holy Week," *Homiletic and Pastoral Review,* LVI, 6 (1956), pp. 466–475.

turies, all who wish to do so and who are properly prepared can go to Holy Communion, so that, devoutly receiving the Lord's Body which was given for all men on this day, they may receive richer fruits of the redemption.[4]

The service, then, consists of four parts: Scripture reading, intercessory prayers, adoration of the cross, and holy Communion. It is of the intercessory prayers that I wish now to speak.

INTERCESSORY PRAYERS

AFTER the reading of the Passion, the story of Love's oblation, which is retold for no other reason than to arouse our answering love and to remind us who hear it of the words of the risen Christ, "Be not unbelieving, but believing" (Jn 20:27), there follow nine solemn prayers. In a cosmic sweep, disregarding limitations of space and time or distinctions of origin, embracing all, those inside and outside the Church, we ask for peace, for the unity and protection of God's holy Church, for the well-being of the Pope, for the loyal service of the Church's entire body, for wise governing by those in authority, for the spiritual needs of those about to be baptized, for the comfort of those in distress, for the return of those separated from the Church's unity, for the turning to Christ of the children of Israel, and for the enlightenment of pagans and unbelievers. These nine petitions, which go back to the early days of the liturgy, are no less than an expression of the great longings that filled the soul of Jesus as He hung dying on the cross. Perhaps this is why they are retained in the Good Friday service. Once explicit in every Mass, their daily recitation had ceased by the time of St. Gregory the Great, but, of course, they are still implicit in the Church's prayer, implicit in every Mass, when Christ's sacrificial death is sacramentally renewed.[5]

4. "General Decree by which the Liturgical Order of Holy Week Is Renewed" (an English translation and a commentary), *American Ecclesiastical Review*, 134 (January 1956), pp. 51–62. The publication of the decree and the instruction was the occasion of many commentaries. P. Doncoeur, "Chronique de liturgie: Ordo de la Semaine Sainte," *Etudes*, 288 (January 1956), pp. 94–100. G. Ellard, S.J., "Easter, Holy Week Rites Revised," *America*, 94 (December 17, 1955), p. 319. J. Löw, "New Holy Week Liturgy, A Pastoral Opportunity," *Worship*, 30 (January 1956), pp. 94–113. G. Montague, "Reform of the Holy Week Ceremonies," *Irish Ecclesiastical Review*, 85 (January 1956), pp. 58–64.

5. M. Andrieu, *Les Ordines Romani* (Louvain, 1948), p. 351. See A. Bugnini, C.M., "Una Particolarità del Messale da Rivedere," *Miscellanea Giulio Belvederi* (Rome: Pontificio Instituto di Archeologia Cristiana, 1954), p. 119.

Scholars have singled out one of these prayers for special study: the eighth, the prayer for the children of Israel. What gives more than an antiquarian interest to their findings is the fact that they have shaped two recent decrees of the Holy See. A point of translation was clarified in 1948,[6] and a practice that was dropped a thousand years before was restored by the decree of 1955. Who were the scholars whose inquiries preluded the statement of 1948 and the modified rubric of 1955? The list is long, so that only a selective answer can be given here. The origin of the prayer was examined by Cappuyns.[7] Its historical development was traced by Canet[8] and Neut.[9] Its position in the liturgy was clarified by Guéranger,[10] Schuster,[11] Parsch,[12] and Bouyer.[13] Philological difficulties were the object of the perceptive studies of Peterson,[14] Oesterreicher,[15] and Blumenkranz.[16] A final summation was made by Bugnini.[17]

The prayer so exhaustively studied belongs to the golden age of liturgical formulae. It is a tender plea that those who, for so long, guarded the light of truth will come to see the full brightness of what they preserved for other men. It distinguishes between the people loved so faithfully by God and the strange paradox of its not recognizing His love's greatest Gift. It crowns the liturgy's pleading for the Jews, which may be said to have begun with the introit of the first Sunday of Advent, to have been heard with mounting insistence during the weeks of

6. *Acta Apostolicae Sedis*, 40 (1948), p. 342.

7. Maïeul Cappuyns, "Les '*Orationes solemnes*' de Vendredi Saint," *Les Questions Liturgiques et Paroisielles*, 23 (1938), pp. 18–31. See "L'Office du vendredi saint," *ibid.* (1930), p. 74.

8. Louis Canet, "La Prière '*pro Iudaeis*' de la liturgie catholique romaine," *Revue des Etudes Juives*, 56, 122 (April 1911), pp. 211–221.

9. E. Neut, "La Prière pour les Juifs," *Bulletin des Missions*, 8 (1927), pp. 245–248.

10. Prosper Guéranger, O.S.B., *The Liturgical Year* (Dublin: James Duffy, 1875), VI, 484.

11. Ildefons A. Schuster, *The Sacramentary* (New York: Benziger Brothers, 1925), II, 212.

12. Pius Parsch, *The Church's Year of Grace* (Collegeville, Minn.: The Liturgical Press, 1953), I, 334.

13. Louis Bouyer, Orat., *op. cit.*, p. 226.

14. Erik Peterson, "Perfidia iudaica," *Ephemerides Liturgicae*, 50 (1936), pp. 296–311. See his *Le Mystère des Juifs et des Gentils dans l'Eglise* (Paris, 1935).

15. John M. Oesterreicher, "Pro Perfidis Judaeis." *Theological Studies*, 8 (March 1947), pp. 80–96. The same article appeared in French in *Cahiers Sioniens*, I (1947), pp. 85–101.

16. B. Blumenkranz, "Perfidia," *Archivum Latinitatio Medii Aevi*, 22 (1951–52), pp. 137–170.

17. *Op. cit.*, pp. 117–132.

Lent, and now to find gentle, forthright expression in the Good Friday synaxis:

Let us pray for the unbelieving Jews that our God and Lord withdraw the veil from their hearts, so that they too may acknowledge our Lord Jesus Christ.

Almighty, everlasting God, who dost not withhold thy mercy even from Jewish unbelief, hear the prayers we offer for the blindness of that people, that, acknowledging the light of thy truth, which is Christ, they may be delivered from their darkness. Through our Lord Jesus Christ thy Son, who is God, living and reigning with thee in the unity of the Holy Spirit, forever and ever. Amen.

PERFIDIA

IN THIS prayer, so often misunderstood, the Church sorrows that Israel still disbelieves; she grieves that so many of the sons of Abraham, "the father of those who believe," have failed to see Christ as the Revelation of revelation. Yet this sense of sorrow born of affection has, at least in the past, often been missing in translations of the missal. The key words of the text, *perfidia* and *perfidus*, "unbelief" and "unbelieving," have at times appeared in some pejorative form: in English "unfaithful," "faithless," or even "perfidious"; in French *perfide*; in German *treulos* or *untreu*; in Dutch *trouweloos*; in Italian *perfidi*; etc.[18]

Questioning that these translations indicated a moral judgment, unusual in the liturgy, scholars examined *perfidus* and *perfidia* to see whether philology supported these indictments of Jewish "treachery" or "wickedness." Their conclusions were unanimous. I list some. One of the first of these philological studies was made by Félix Vernet. Examining the works of St. Ambrose and of St. Gregory the Great, the *Decretum Gratiani,* and other texts, he concludes that in the official language of the Church *perfidia Judaica* seems to mean the "error" or the "unbelief of the Jews."[19] Erik Peterson in his brilliant analysis likewise proves that *perfidia* is to be equated with "unbelief." He shows that the Jews are not the only ones charged with it, but that it is also to be found in here-

18. Father Oesterreicher, in *Theological Studies,* 8 (1947), p. 80, gives examples of translations of *perfidia.* I am happy to note here that an examination of recently published Holy Week books shows most of them to have accepted the correct translation.

19. "Juifs et Chrétiens," *Dictionnaire apologétique de la foi catholique* (1915), II, 1733f.

tics, schismatics, and *lapsi*. He finds support for his thesis in the works of St. Ambrose, St. Isidor of Seville, and St. Leo the Great.[20]

A similar investigation has been carried out by Bernhard Blumen-kranz. He does not limit his inquiries to the present text of the Good Friday service but examines earlier editions, those of Amalarius of Metz, Rabanus Maurus, and the Pseudo-Alcuin.[21] Then he studies the word as it is used by twenty-six representative authors from the fifth through the eleventh centuries. His conclusion is a model of clarity. Though *perfidia* may at times refer to the lapse of a convert or may mean "false belief," "erroneous belief," "the refusal to believe," "lack of confidence," most of the time, Blumenkranz finds, *perfidia* and *perfidus* have a religious and not a moral sense. They are used as antonyms of *fides* by Leo the Great, Gregory the Great, Rabanus Maurus, Remy of Auxerre, Paschasius Radbertus, and Ratramnus; of *credulitas* by Bruno of Würzburg; of *fidelis* by Maximus of Turin; of *credere* by Gregory the Great, Rabanus Maurus, Remy of Auxerre; or as synonyms of *incredulus, impius, infidelitas, incredulitas,* or *impietas.* Among Blumenkranz's many interesting observations is his statement that *perfidia* is conspicuously absent from texts on the betrayal of Judas.[22] Hence his study corroborates the equation of *perfidia* in the Good Friday prayer with "unbelief."

The language of the Good Friday prayer is examined in the light of the liturgy itself by Father Oesterreicher.[23] Quotations from the Leonian

20. *Ephemerides Liturgicae,* 50 (1936), p. 296. Cf. St. Ambrose, *Ad Psalmum 43* (PL 14:1171); St. Isidor of Seville, *De fide catholica contra Judaeos* (PL 83:450); and St. Leo the Great, *Sermo LXX* (PL 54:381).

21. Blumenkranz, *op. cit.,* p. 159, makes the apposite suggestion that Amalarius's words: *Oremus et pro haereticis perfidisque Iudaeis* (PL 105:1027) should be translated: "Let us pray for heretics and for [those among] the Jews who persist in their refusal of belief." Cf. Rabanus Maurus (PL 107:349) and Pseudo-Alcuin (PL 101:1210).

22. The following partial list gives some indication of the documentation of this article: Peter Chrysologus (PL 52:485), Arnobius (PL 53:322), Leo the Great (PL 54:381), Maximus of Turin (PL 57:721), Avitus of Vienna (PL 59:207), Cassiodorus (PL 70:400, 596, 744), Gregory the Great (PL 75:772, 783; 76:69, 108, 509, 541, 764, 920; 77:694, 1053), Isidor of Seville (PL 83:450, 460), Quiricus (PL 96:193), Ildefonsus of Toledo (PL 96:68), Julianus of Toledo (PL 96:540), Idalius of Barcelona (PL 96:816), Adamnanus (PL 88:785, 787), Bede the Venerable (PL 94:247), Pseudo-Bede (PL 92:659), Alcuin (PL 100:436), Paulinus of Aquilea (PL 99:363), Ratramnus (PL 121:20), Remy of Auxerre (PL 117:442; 118:445, 598; cf. 117:442), Bruno of Würzburg (PL 142:67, 82, 191, 195, 217), etc.

23. *Theological Studies* 8 (1947), pp. 83–85. He reaches this conclusion: "What we implore for [the Jews] is enlightenment, the gift of faith; lacking it, their state

Sacramentary and the Ambrosian liturgy are in accord with the findings of Vernet, Peterson, and Blumenkranz. Particularly cogent is the use of the word *perfidia* in the Rite of Baptism for Adults. Having first bid the catechumen to profess his belief in Father, Son, and Holy Spirit, Creator, Redeemer, and Sanctifier, the priest admonishes him, if he is an idolator or heathen, to abhor idols and reject images. If a Moslem desires the sacrament, he is told to turn away from "Moslem unbelief" (*Mahumeticam perfidiam*). And if he is a Jew, he is enjoined to turn away from "Jewish unbelief" (*Judaicam perfidiam*). In each case, this plea, this command, is followed by a solemn entreaty to worship God the Father and Jesus Christ His only Son. The absence of any reference to morals in this last entreaty, the earlier inquiry into the catechumen's faith, the demand that he reject false or incomplete beliefs and cults, the use of *perfidia* for both Moslems and Jews—all these clearly indicate that the convert from Judaism is not told by the Church to abandon the "perfidious ways" of his "treacherous and deceitful brethren" but to abandon their unbelief in Christ, their failure to acknowledge Him.

All these studies of *perfidia* show that there is no doubt in the minds of scholars about the meaning of the word. There is, however, less agreement about the history of the rubric which for centuries, till Easter 1956, prefaced the Church's Good Friday intercession for the children of Israel.

THE RUBRIC

ALL stand, while the priest summarizes or "collects" the individual prayers into the official collect. The same procedure of kneeling and praying silently and then rising, at the priest's (or deacon's) invitation, is repeated in all the following prayers.[24]

This new rubric has put an end to a centuries-old anomaly. Before the decree of 1955, the ritual for the eighth prayer, the prayer for the Jews, differed from all the others in that it prescribed the omission of *Oremus*, "Let us pray"; *Flectamus genua*, "Let us bend our knees"; and

---

is unbelief. The words of the Church echo the bewilderment of the Apostle that the people of the revelation, who had watched through the night and witnessed the dawn, should, as a whole, have failed to see the day. And she employs his gentle image for their ignorance—the veil with which Moses covered the radiance of his face is now upon their hearts . . ." (p. 86).

24. Godfrey L. Diekmann, O.S.B., *The Masses of Holy Week and the Easter Vigil* (Collegeville, Minn.: The Liturgical Press, 1956), p. 110.

Levate, "Arise." The reason so often given since medieval days was that the invitation to prayer and the genuflection were here omitted so as not to repeat the gesture with which, at His scourging, the Jews dishonored Jesus on this day.[25]

On two counts this statement may be challenged: it is logically and historically untenable. Why, we cannot help asking ourselves, is it fitting that we stand? Should we not rather kneel in humble reparation for the derisive genuflections made before Christ? Why not repeat the gesture without the irreverence? Why not bow down in adoration in order that the outward and inward act may proclaim the majesty of the God once so outraged by knees bent in scorn? In doing so we should be following the example of St. Stephen recorded in the Acts. Standing, he prayed for himself: "Lord Jesus, receive my spirit," and then, kneeling down, he prayed for those who were about to put him to death: "Lord, do not lay this sin against them" (7:59–60). But there is a more serious objection to this once so common interpretation of the rubric than its illogicality. A simple reading of the Gospels shows that those who clothed Christ in a bright robe, placed a crown of thorns upon His head, and knelt before Him in a derisive act of homage were Roman soldiers, not Jews.[26] These legionaries were ridiculing not only Jesus but the messianic expectation of Israel; their contempt was not only for the Man who claimed to be King but for the people who hoped for the King-Messiah.

Not all medieval authors were satisfied with the explanation of the old rubric in terms of Jewish contempt for Christ. Joannes Beleth, for example, admitted that the scornful treatment Jesus received was not the work of the Jews, but contended that they were responsible for it because they were responsible for His death.[27] Sicardus of Cremona begins with the usual explanation that "we do not bend the knee for the Jews, so

---

25. Guéranger, *op. cit.,* p. 484; Parsch, *op. cit.,* p. 334.
26. *Cambridge Ancient History* (Cambridge: Cambridge University Press, 1934), X, 851: "If the procurators could not hide their antipathy in their daily contacts with their subjects, far less could their underlings and the soldiers drawn from the non-Jewish population of Palestine." M.-J. Lagrange, O.P., writes in *The Gospel of Jesus Christ* (London: Burns Oates, 1938), II, 259: "What a stroke of good luck to have Him at their mercy, the mercy of these Roman soldiers who scorned all kings and held the Jews in contempt." F. Didon, O.P., writes in *Jesus Christ* (English trans.; New York: D. Appleton and Co., 1891), II, 343: "What caprice of cruelty were these soldiers obeying? Why this detestable and vulgar mockery? The Roman soldiers entertained an intense hatred of the Jews and the condemned man who was delivered to them was made the victim of this hatred."
27. *Rationale Divinorum Officium,* 98 (PL 202:102).

that we may avoid their deceit, who derisively genuflected before God";
then he offers this not too convincing explanation:

> Since the blindness that befalls Israel cannot be dispelled as long as the
> Gentiles have not yet entered [the Church], intensive prayer must not
> be offered for them, nor should a genuflection be made. But it is right
> to pray, since He who was lifted upon the cross will draw all things to
> Himself and will one day dispel this blindness.[28]

There is no need to point out the weakness of the positions so ingeniously
and so feebly defended by Joannes Beleth and Sicardus. There is not a
shred of evidence that they represent the mind of the Church.

While admitting that the old rubric lacked intrinsic logic—is it possible to show that it enshrined an old and universally observed custom
which could be traced back to the earliest centuries? Pioneer studies suggest that the answer is no. Though extant sources are so few that this
conclusion cannot be absolutely certain, it remains highly probable.
Manuscripts available indicate that until the ninth century, a silent
prayer, with clergy and people kneeling, was said at the intercession for
the Jews as at all the others. From the ninth to the close of the sixteenth
century, the silent prayer was said but no genuflection was made. From
1570, in the pontificate of Pius V, until the decree of Pius XII in 1955,
both silent prayer and genuflection were omitted, and in all missals the
following rubric preceded the preface and the prayer for the Jews:
"*Amen* is not said, nor *Oremus,* nor *Flectamus genua,* nor *Levate,* but the
priest says immediately, 'Almighty, everlasting God.'" Let us examine
each part of these omissions.

The injunction to omit the *Amen* is not an expression of hostility to
the Jews. It is merely a useful reminder that the words soon to be said:
Jesum Christum Dominum nostrum, mark not, as so often, the end of a
prayer but the end of a preface, to which it is not customary to add
Amen. As a matter of fact, none of the prefaces of the nine intercessory
prayers of Good Friday have, or could have, an *Amer.*[29] Durand of
Mende took the trouble to record that some considered this omission
particularly appropriate in the case of the Jews and of the pagans who,
being outside the Church, deserved no sign of affection (needless to say,

28. *Mitrale,* 6 (PL 213:317). See Rupertus the Abbot, *De Divinis Officius,*
6, 18 (PL 170:163–164).
29. Bugnini, *op. cit.,* pp. 124–130.

an attitude totally opposed to the spirit of the crucified Jesus, with His arms outstretched for all); but he went on to give the real reason for the omission, which was that these prefaces, like the prefaces of the Mass, are never followed by *Amen*.[30]

The *Oremus* and the *Flectamus genua* have different histories. In the ancient discipline of the Church, all nine prayers seem to have included silent prayer and genuflection. The *Sacramentarium Gelasianum* (Cod. Vatican. Reg. 316), which may have been written for the Abbey of Saint Denis at the end of the seventh or the beginning of the eighth century, makes no distinction in the rubric for any of the solemn prayers. This is corroborated by the eighth-century *Ordo Romanus* of Saint-Amand (Paris, cat. 974) and the *Ordo Romanus* of Einsiedeln (326).[31] The *Oremus* introducing the Church's prayer for the Jewish people is found also in missals like the *Missale Gallicanum vetus* in the eighth century and the missal of Jumièges in the eleventh century. Durand of Mende attests its use in the thirteenth century, and it is still retained in sixteenth-century French missals. But after 1570 it rarely appears.[32]

Much earlier than this, the *Flectamus genua* had been dropped. The first indication of a change is found in the *Ordo Romanus I,* where it is expressly enjoined that no genuflection be made before the prayer for the Jews. This innovation seems to have come from the Franks and soon took its place in most missals and sacramentaries, so that, from the ninth century on, the deacon's injunction to bend the knee was suppressed in almost all liturgical books. On this statement most liturgists agree, but as to the cause of the change there is less unanimity. Some forty years ago, Louis Canet discovered an interesting marginal note in the tenth-century Sacramentary of Saint Vast: "None of us [priests] is allowed to bend his body on account of the fault and madness of the people." If, as Canet believes, "people" refers to Christians who, imagining themselves animated by "pious indignation," stoned the houses of Jews during Holy Week, then it was the "fault and madness" of the faithful that forced the hand of the Church. The people's unholy wrath might, he thinks, have resisted the liturgy's impassioned appeal for the Jews, so that the Church (if Canet is right) may have altered the rubric simply as a record of the popular usage. This thesis is supported by such scholars

30. *Rationale,* 6, 77.
31. Oesterreicher, *op. cit.,* p. 91.
32. Canet, *op. cit.,* p. 219.

as Félix Vernet [33] and Dom Henri Leclercq, O.S.B.[34] It is contested by
Dom G. Morin, O.S.B., who considers the omission akin to the subtle
and delicate omission of the Kiss of Peace on Maundy Thursday and of
the *Gloria* and *Alleluia* on the feast of the Holy Innocents.[35] Another
Catholic scholar, Peterson, likewise disagrees with Canet's interpretation
of the marginal note on the Saint Vast Sacramentary. He asks whether
"people" might not refer to the Jews who were thought to be guilty of
"the fault and madness" of mocking Christ. He goes on to suggest that
oriental drama and not anti-Jewish prejudice may have been responsible
for the omission of the genuflection. The dramatic Reproaches of Good
Friday, brought to the Franks from Syria in the tenth century, started a
trend alien to the dignified restraint characteristic of the Roman liturgy,
so that those to whom the Reproaches appealed, with their ardent dialogue between God and man, might have wanted to introduce into the
liturgy some dramatic touches of their own.[36]

Until further evidence is available, here arguments on the suppression
of the genuflection must rest. But it is good to know, indeed it is a joy,
that the Church, after a thousand years, has re-established the old order,
and that on Good Friday *Oremus, Flectamus genua,* and *Levate* are said
at each of the solemn intercessions when she prays for all men, with none
excepted, with all included in her love.

CONCLUSION

THE discussion of the meaning of *perfidia* and of the former rubric has
come to a close with the new decrees. One last question remains: What is
the nature of that "Jewish unbelief" the Church yearns to see ended and
for the ending of which she bids all her members to pray? Does "unbelief," as used in her intercession, imply *stubborn* resistance and *will-
ful* blindness to the reality of Jesus? I think not. We must always distinguish between the act and the state, or, to speak with Monsignor
Journet, between the sin and the heritage of unbelief. For no matter how
grievous the sin of those who once, in the house of the high priest and
before the governor's seat, rejected Jesus, today the unbelief of Jews is

33. *Op. cit.,* col. 1715.
34. "Judaïsme," *Dictionnaire d'archéologie chrétienne et de la liturgie* (1928),
VIII/1, col. 181.
35. "De quelques publications liturgiques récentes," *Revue Bénédictine,* 30
(Maredsous, 1913), pp. 122–123.
36. Peterson, *op. cit.,* p. 310.

an inculpable patrimony. So says Monsignor Journet in his masterful work on the Church. Consequently, in Judaism there are welded together into a single block divine truths and human deviations from the truth.[37] And without guilt in the original act of denial of the Christ, Jews down to this very day, when reading Moses, have a veil covering their hearts (2 Cor 3:15)—a veil which keeps them from seeing Him, who wants to be seen by them.[38]

Love, nothing but love, compels the Church to pray for His kinsmen, and love must compel us. Without the least haughtiness, rather with humble awareness of our own often faltering belief, we who enjoy the fulfillment of the promises of old must pray for those who guarded them for us during the long hours of the Advent. They were watching for the dawn but they failed to see the Sun of Justice because of the veil over their eyes. Yet, St. Paul assures us, "the veil shall be taken away" (2 Cor 3:16). This, then, is the petition of the eighth intercessory prayer: that Israel may see; that the mystery of redemption, the mystery of Love crucified and risen, may find in it an echo that will make earth and heaven resound.

37. Charles Journet, *L'Eglise du Verbe incarné* (Paris: Desclée de Brouwer, 1951), II, 815.

38. A further distinction, in addition to that of Monsignor Journet, must be made. As Father Oesterreicher, in *The Elder Brother: The Prayer of the Church for Israel* (Newark, N. J.: The Institute of Judaeo-Christian Studies, 1951), p. 21, has pointed out, the Church does not pray: "God, who dost not withhold thy mercy even from the unbelieving Jews," but rather: "from Jewish unbelief." He calls it a momentous, indeed a divine, distinction. It is God Himself, and the Church as His voice, who distinguish between the *sin* of those who resisted the work of redemption and the *people* of Israel, "which remains, in spite of it, the object of His lasting love."

Mary Ruth Bede

THE BLESSINGS OF THE
JEWISH PRAYER BOOK

ONE hundred times a day the observing Jew is bound to bless God. The ancient rabbis had many ingenious ways of accounting for this rule. Rabbi Meïr, for instance, used to say: "It is written: 'And now, Israel, *what* does the Lord, your God, ask of you?' (Deut 10:12)," interpreting this text as if it read: "And now, Israel, *one hundred* does the Lord, your God, ask of you." [1] Or, as a profound legend has it, when a plague came upon the people as a punishment for David's sin (2 Kg 24:10–15) and one hundred youths a day died, the king ordained one hundred blessings to be recited daily, and the Lord was appeased. [2] But whatever the origin of the rule of one hundred—whether it is really concealed in Scripture; whether it was really established by the repentant David; or

---

1. Men. 43b; cf. *The Babylonian Talmud,* ed. I. Epstein (London: Soncino, 1948), *Menaḥoth,* pp. 263–264. When the consonants alone are written, as is usual in Hebrew, *mah,* "what," differs from *me'ah,* "one hundred," only by a single silent letter. An even subtler explanation of the rule of a hundred daily blessings was claimed in 2 Kg 23:1, which, according to the Hebrew, says of David that he was raised on high, "on high" in Hebrew being *'al.* Now, an ancient rabbinical commentary reads instead: "*'al* was established," and then goes on to link *'al* with "one hundred" by the methods of *gemaṭria.* This word (derived, most likely, from the same Greek source as is our English word "geometry") refers to the rabbis' exegetical numerology, that is, their attempts to uncover concealed meanings in Scripture by manipulating the arithmetical values of the Hebrew letters. For, as do a good many languages, Hebrew traditionally employs the alphabet in lieu of numerals. The first nine letters provide for 1 through 9, and the next nine for 10 through 90; the remaining four letters, together with the "final forms" of those five letters which change their shape at the end of a word, stand for 100 through 900. In our example of *'al,* for instance, the letter *'ayin* represents 70 and the letter *lamed* 30. Consequently, the rabbis considered "one hundred was established" to be a hidden sense of 2 Kg 23:1, and the rule of one hundred daily blessings was thus thought of as confirmed in Scripture (Num. R. 18:21; cf. *Midrash Rabbah,* ed. H. Freedman and M. Simon, London: Soncino, 1939, VI, 737).

2. Louis Ginzberg, *The Legends of the Jews,* trans. H. Szold (Philadelphia: Jewish Publication Society of America, 1939), VI, 270–271.

whether it took its start with the men of the Great Assembly (who, it is said, instituted blessings and sanctifications for the people[3]), and then grew to the present number in the course of generations of Jewish piety —in any case, by the second century after Christ the rule was already fixed, and to this day it remains one of the most characteristic and beautiful features of orthodox Jewish life.

Baruk attah Adonay Elohenu Melek ha-ʿolam, "Blessed art thou, O Lord our God, King of the universe." So each benediction, each *berakah,* begins. What is the meaning of *baruk attah,* "blessed art thou"? For it must be kept in mind that these benedictions are not the blessings God bestows on man nor the blessings our love begs from Him for our fellow men. Indeed, some prayer books avoid the word "blessed" and render *baruk attah* as "praised be thou." But this is no more than side-stepping the question, since there are other verbs in Hebrew much closer to our English "praise." An appealing, though unconvincing, etymology would like to link *baruk* to *berekah,* "a pool of water," so that *baruk attah* would suggest that God is the pool of living waters in the midst of life's desert.[4] It may be that the prayer book's use of *baruk* has no explanation in the science of words. But it does show something of the bent of the Jewish mind, for which "to bless" a thing and "to give thanks" to God for it are synonymous. "In Jewish practice one only blessed a thing *by* giving thanks to God for it before using it."[5] Similarly, in a way, God is called blessed because He is thanked. Not least among the gifts from the Giver of all good things are a mind and a heart that can be thankful. Hence to thank and bless Him is Israel's duty, teaches the Jewish Morning Service:

It is . . . our duty to thank, praise and glorify thee, to bless, to sanctify and to offer praise and thanksgiving unto thy name. Happy are we!

3. In the middle of the fifth century B.C., after the return to Jerusalem from the Babylonian Captivity, the leaders of the Jews, under Ezra and Nehemiah, pledged themselves anew to observe the Torah (Neh 9:38). This body of men is known as the Great Assembly. See Ber. 33a; cf. *B. Talmud,* Soncino ed., *Berakoth,* p. 205.
4. Gen. R. 39:11; cf. *Midrash Rabbah,* Soncino ed., I, 322. A more exact etymology relates *baruk* to *borak,* "to fall on one's knees, to kneel, to worship"— interesting when one remembers that kneeling at prayer is rare indeed among contemporary Jews, but was a frequent posture of the Jewish worshipper in times past (see, for example, Ber. 34b; cf. *B. Talmud,* Soncino ed., *Berakoth,* pp. 213–214). Rabbi Bernard J. Bamberger, in "Baruch," *Judaism,* V, 2 (Spring 1956), pp. 167–168, gives an account of the deep devotional meaning of *baruk.*
5. Gregory Dix, *The Shape of the Liturgy* (Westminster: Dacre Press, 1945), p. 79.

how goodly is our portion, how pleasant our lot, and how beautiful our heritage! [6]

THE EIGHTEEN BENEDICTIONS

OF ALL the benedictions which grace the *Siddur,* the Jewish prayer book, the most solemn and elaborate are the "Eighteen," the *Shemoneh 'Esreh,* recited in the Morning, Afternoon, and Evening Services.[7] Known also as the *Tefillah,* simply *the* prayer, it is prayed standing, which gives it yet another name, the *'Amidah.* When prayed congregationally, it is first said by each in silence and then aloud by one for all. On a weekday morning, when it is at its most typical, it opens with three blessings of praise, continues with twelve blessings which petition,[8] and closes with three blessings of thanksgiving.

The very first of the Eighteen Benedictions acclaims God as the God of history:

Blessed art thou, O Lord our God and God of our fathers, God of Abraham, God of Isaac, and God of Jacob, the great, mighty and revered God, the most high God, who bestowest lovingkindnesses, and art Master of all things; who rememberest the pious deeds of the patriarchs, and in love wilt bring a redeemer to their children's children, for thy name's sake.[9]

The second benediction, of the God of nature, of the God who supports, heals, and frees, makes a profound transition from adoring Him as the One who "causes the wind to blow and the rain to fall" to adoring Him

6. *The Authorised Daily Prayer Book,* trans. and ed. J. H. Hertz (New York: Bloch Publishing Co., 1952), p. 29.

7. The sacrifices of the Temple being no more, the ancient rabbis teach that the "Eighteen" take the place of the daily sacrifices, morning, afternoon, and evening. They stress, however, that fixed though the hours of prayer are, "if a man makes his prayers a fixed task, it is not a [genuine] supplication," for prayer ought not to be like a heavy burden. Interesting is the thought of Rabbi Eleazar, who laments that since the day the Temple was destroyed, an iron wall has come between Israel and its Father in heaven and the gates of prayer have been closed; but he adds that what are still open are the gates of weeping (Ber. 26b, 28b, 29b, 32b; cf. B. *Talmud,* Soncino ed., *Berakoth,* pp. 160, 174, 179–180, 199–200).

8. These twelve are really thirteen because of the added prayer discussed in note 10.

9. *The Authorised Daily Prayer Book,* ed. Hertz, p. 131. In this edition of the prayer book, the Eighteen Benedictions will be found on pp. 130–160. The entire tractate *Berakoth* of the Babylonian Talmud is concerned with blessings, while the *Jewish Encyclopedia,* in its article on *"Shemoneh 'Esreh"* (XI, 270–282), gives the talmudic and scriptural sources of the Eighteen.

as the One who "causes salvation to spring forth" and who "revives the dead." In the third, Israel's praise is joined and likened to that of the seraphim who, with their threefold "Holy," hallow God's name in gladness and awe.

The intermediate benedictions, begging God's favors, are divided into prayers for individual well-being and prayers for the whole people of Israel. Since the life of goodness requires understanding, they begin by imploring "the gracious Giver of knowledge" for spiritual insight. As the soul needs wisdom, so too it stands in need of repentance and God's forgiveness. For what is the soul without *teshubah,* the turning from its crooked way to the straight, from sin to the fear of God; and without *selihah,* God's pardon, which crowns repentance? Hence the next two benedictions:

Cause us to return, O our Father, unto thy Torah; draw us near, O our King, unto thy service, and bring us back in perfect repentance unto thy presence. Blessed art thou, O Lord, who delightest in repentance.

Forgive us, O our Father, for we have sinned; pardon us, O our King, for we have transgressed; for thou dost pardon and forgive. Blessed art thou, O Lord, who art gracious, and dost abundantly forgive.

Only having prayed thus does the Jewish worshipper venture to ask for earthly blessings: for deliverance from affliction, for healing and recovery from illness, for rescue from want. "Give a blessing upon the face of the earth," this, the ninth of the benedictions, closes: "O satisfy us with thy goodness, and bless our year like other good years. Blessed art thou, O Lord, who blessest the years."

The petitions that follow, those for the people as a whole, are for the ingathering of the exiles; for the restoration of justice, the restoration of the social order Israel knew of old; for the punishment of slanderers; [10]

10. This prayer "against slanderers" (the twelfth benediction), seems to have been inserted into the Eighteen Benedictions after the destruction of the Second Temple by Titus, thus making them in reality nineteen. It was, at the beginning, clearly directed against Jewish Christians, and it is perhaps important to note that it was not introduced without opposition. Since that time, it has undergone many modifications and has acquired a more general character. In its most widely used form today, it reads, in Rabbi Hertz's translation: "And for slanderers let there be no hope, and let all wickedness perish as in a moment; let all thine enemies be speedily cut off, and the dominion of arrogance do thou uproot and crush, cast down and humble speedily in our days. Blessed art thou, O Lord, who breakest the enemies and humblest the arrogant" (*op. cit.,* pp. 143–145). Particularly

for God's tender mercies toward His faithful; for the rebuilding of Jerusalem as an everlasting city; and for the coming of the King-Messiah, the offspring of David. Then there is the last of the intermediate petitions, utterly convinced that God listens and hears, for He knows the heart He made.

From thy presence, O our King, turn us not empty away; for thou hearkenest in mercy to the prayer of thy people Israel. Blessed art thou, O Lord, who hearkenest unto prayer.

The three closing benedictions are called thanksgivings although only the middle one is explicitly of gratitude, the first pleading again for the return to Zion and the last for God's peace on Israel.[11] The middle of the three, a veritable anthem, acknowledges God's mercies:

We give thanks unto thee, for thou art the Lord our God and the God of our fathers forever and ever; thou art the Rock of our lives, the Shield of our salvation through every generation. We will give thanks unto thee and declare thy praise for our lives which are committed unto thy hand, and for our souls which are in thy charge, and for thy miracles, which are daily with us, and for thy wonders and thy benefits, which are wrought at all times, evening, morn and noon. . . .

While the reader who speaks in the name of all prays these words aloud, the congregation recites in an undertone a similar prayer, whose closing words beautifully express the spirit of this and of all the blessings of the prayer book. "Blessed be the God to whom thanksgivings are due," all the worshippers say, or, in another translation, which gives God a lovely and unexpected name: "Blessed be the God of thanks."[12]

its opening words are, to put it mildly, harsh to the ear. Still, it is only fair to record Rabbi Hertz's emphatic statement that the prayer calls not for the wicked to perish but for wickedness, and that in it modern Jews do not utter an imprecation against those of another faith (*ibid.*, pp. 143–145, 588). It may be fruitful to compare with the Jewish prayer "against slanderers" the Church's collect from the Mass for Protection Against the Heathens: "Almighty, everlasting God, in whose hand are the powers and the rights of all kingdoms: look to the help of Christians, that the heathen nations, who trust in their own fierceness, may be crushed by the power of thy right arm."

11. "The character of this group of Berachoth is not disturbed by the inclusion of these requests," Rabbi Elie Munk feels, quoting Rabbi Zilkiah ben Abraham ha-Rofe, "the Physician": "The greatest homage paid to God is when the entire nation turns to Him for help." See his *The World of Prayer*, trans. H. Biberfeld and L. Oschry (New York: Philipp Feldheim, 1954), p. 149.

12. Lewis N. Dembitz, *Jewish Services in Synagogue and Home* (Philadelphia: Jewish Publication Society of America, 1898), p. 396, note 8. Similarly, a talmudic

THE DUTIES OF THE DAY

THERE are still other blessings that are part of the sacred services in the synagogue. No act of piety is sufficient to itself; indeed, precisely those actions which bring the Jewish worshipper nearest to God demand most imperatively that he praise the One who lets such marvels be. Hence the study or reading of Scripture, the performance of any of the works of the Law, call especially for a blessing of God:

Blessed art thou, O Lord our God, King of the universe, who hast hallowed us by thy commandments, and commanded us to occupy ourselves with the words of the Torah.[13]

Nor does one step aside after reading from Scripture as if one had not been in close audience with the Almighty:

Blessed art thou, O Lord our God, King of the universe, who hast given us the Torah of truth, and hast planted everlasting life in our midst.[14]

If the Scripture read is from the prophets, special thanks is offered beforehand to Him "who has chosen good prophets, and has found pleasure in their words which were spoken in truth." When the reading is over, He is thanked again:

Blessed art thou, O Lord our God, King of the universe, Rock of all worlds, righteous through all generations, O faithful God, who sayest and doest, who speakest and fulfillest, all whose words are truth and righteousness. Faithful art thou, O Lord our God, and faithful are thy words, and not one of thy words shall return void. . . .[15]

No feast of the Jewish calendar arrives but is greeted as coming from Him "who has kept us in life, and has preserved us, and enabled us to

commentary on the eighteenth benediction reads: "We give thanks unto thee, O Lord our God, because we are able to give thee thanks" (Soṭ. 40a; cf. *B. Talmud,* Soncino ed., *Soṭah,* p. 197).

13. *The Authorised Daily Prayer Book,* ed. Hertz, p. 13. Blessings following this pattern are recited on many occasions: "Blessed art thou, O Lord our God, who has hallowed us by thy commandments, and hast given us command concerning the circumcision . . . concerning the redemption of the firstborn son . . . who commanded us to kindle the light of Chanukah, etc." For a summary of all the blessings, together with their talmudic sources, see "Benedictions," *Jewish Encyclopedia,* III, 8–12.

14. *The Authorised Daily Prayer Book,* ed. Hertz, p. 191.

15. *Ibid.,* pp. 495–497.

reach this season." [16] And week by week, the Sabbath is ushered in with a blessing of Him "who commanded us to kindle the Sabbath light." [17] "In love and favor thou hast given us thy holy Sabbath as an inheritance," another blessing tells, "as a memorial of the creation . . . and in remembrance of the departure from Egypt." [18] Not man but God's goodness "hallows the Sabbath." Hence a blessing at the Evening Service for Sabbaths begs: "Purify our hearts to serve thee in truth; and in thy love and favor, O Lord our God, let us inherit thy holy Sabbath. . . ." [19] Again, before Aaron's blessing is solemnly pronounced over the people, the congregation which is to receive it is cautioned that it comes ultimately from Him "whom alone it serves in awe," and those who pronounce it give thanks that He has commanded them "to bless His people Israel in love." [20]

The day of a pious Jew finds no occupation, religious in itself or not, unheralded by a "Blessed art thou, O Lord our God, King of the universe." Just as, in the desert, the Lord commanded that His priests wash their hands before undertaking any ministry (Ex 30:19–21), so every observing Jew approaches God only with hands purified, purified by water and by prayer:

Blessed art thou, O Lord our God, King of the universe, who hast hallowed us by thy commandments, and given us command concerning the washing of the hands. [21]

Engagingly, the Hebrew idiom for the washing of the hands is *netilat yadayim,* "lifting up the hands." This may be derived simply from the physical act of raising the hands in order that water may be poured over them, but in all likelihood it is linked with the psalm verse which, at one time, was recited while the hands were cleansed: "Lift up your hands toward the sanctuary, and bless the Lord" (Ps 133:2). [22]

Then there are the blessings of the early morning, said nowadays, however, not at the appropriate moments but as a preliminary to the Morning Service in the synagogue. The first is for awakening from sleep:

16. *Ibid.,* p. 797 and elsewhere.
17. *Ibid.,* p. 345.
18. *Ibid.,* p. 395.
19. *Ibid.,* p. 383.
20. *Ibid.,* pp. 835–837.
21. *Ibid.,* pp. 9, 11. It should be noted that "command" in this benediction refers to a rabbinical rather than a biblical instruction.
22. *Ibid.,* p. 963. See "Ablution" in the *Jewish Encyclopedia,* I, 68–71.

So long as the soul is within me, I will give thanks unto thee, O Lord my God and God of my fathers, Sovereign of all works, Lord of all souls! Blessed art thou, O Lord, who restorest souls unto the dead.[23]

The wonder of restored consciousness is not casually accepted but is related to the mighty promise of the wakening of the dead. Likewise, God is blessed for the gift of sight, for strength and clothing, for firm ground under foot:

Blessed art thou, O Lord our God, King of the universe, who openest the eyes of the blind.
Blessed art thou, O Lord our God, King of the universe, who clothest the naked.
Blessed art thou, O Lord our God, King of the universe, who settest free them that are bound.
Blessed art thou, O Lord our God, King of the universe, who raisest up them that are bowed down.
Blessed art thou, O Lord our God, King of the universe, who spreadest forth the earth above the waters.
Blessed art thou, O Lord our God, King of the universe, who providest my every want.
Blessed art thou, O Lord our God, King of the universe, who hast made firm the steps of man.

Thus each moment of the morning is experienced not as routine but as a new mercy: the opening of one's eyes, dressing oneself, stretching one's limbs, standing upright, stepping on the ground, putting on one's shoes, setting forth to walk—things so common, so disregarded—are related to the Author of all and in Him receive a higher significance.[24]

Of the blessings for the early morning—for there are still others— one group of three must be dealt with explicitly. A man is ordered to pray: "Blessed art thou, O Lord our God, King of the universe, who hast not made me a heathen . . . who hast not made me a woman . . . who hast not made me a bondman," while a woman is simply to

23. *The Authorised Daily Prayer Book,* ed. Hertz, pp. 19–23, where this and the other early-morning blessings will be found.
24. Bamberger (*loc. cit.,* p. 168) sums up the purpose of these blessings: "One who is thus made aware of the divine Reality and nearness amid his daily experiences and affairs will react not only with awe and with a sense of responsibility, but also with gratitude and thanksgiving." Rabbi Bamberger comes, therefore, to the conclusion that whatever the literal meaning of *baruk attah,* discussed in the opening paragraphs of this paper, its inner meaning is: "I rejoice and am grateful because God is accessible to me."

declare: "Blessed art thou, O Lord our God, King of the universe, who hast made me according to thy will." The three benedictions to be recited by a man hardly breathe the humble spirit of so many other of the blessings; they seem to reflect a human, rather than a divine, order of things, and modern Jews have often strenuously objected to them.[25] Orthodox rabbis, however, are at pains to defend them, claiming that here men thank God not for any privileges but for the burden of the Law, many precepts of which are not binding on women, for instance. Hence these blessings, Rabbi Munk declares, well up from "the joy in the special task allotted to [the free men of Israel]."[26] Again, in defense of these blessings many rabbis have appealed to the words of an ancient teacher: "I call heaven and earth to witness that, whether it be Jew or heathen, man or woman, free or bondman—only according to their acts does the divine Spirit rest upon them."[27]

The prayer a devout Jew says before sleep contains various psalm verses, verses full of confidence: "He that dwelleth in the shelter of the Most High, abideth under the shadow of the Almighty" (90:1); "I lay me down and sleep; I awake, for the Lord sustaineth me" (3:6); "Behold, He that guardeth Israel will neither slumber nor sleep" (120:4); and "Into thy hand I commend my spirit; thou hast redeemed me, O Lord, God of truth" (30:6). It contains, too, a remembrance of the command: "Thou shalt love the Lord thy God with all thy heart, and with all thy soul, and with all thy might" (Deut 6:5). But the Jewish prayer book would not deem even so loving a prayer complete were it not prefaced by a *berakah:*

Blessed art thou, O Lord our God, King of the universe, who makest the bands of sleep to fall upon mine eyes, and slumber upon mine eyelids. . . . O lighten mine eyes, lest I sleep the sleep of death, for it is thou who givest light to the apple of the eye. Blessed art thou, O Lord, who givest light to the whole world in thy glory.[28]

Many are the opportunities the observing Jew finds and seeks throughout the day to bless his Maker, and many are the opportunities of lifting daily events into the sphere of holiness, as when, through the

25. For a vigorous expression of this attitude, see Mordecai M. Kaplan, *The Future of the American Jew* (New York: Macmillan, 1948), pp. 402–412.

26. Munk, *op. cit.,* p. 27.

27. *Yalkut* to Judges IV, 4; cited by Munk, *op. cit.,* p. 28, and Hertz, *op. cit.,* p. 21.

28. *The Authorised Daily Prayer Book,* ed. Hertz, p. 997.

saying of grace, "the family table becomes the family altar."[29] To it, as to all worship, the Jew approaches only with hands washed.

Blessed art thou, O Lord our God, King of the universe, who bringest forth bread from the earth,

is *the* prayer before meals. But the man of thanks, always content with God's good providence, is never content with his own gratitude, so the observing Jew has a blessing for wine, for fruits that spring from the ground or grow on a tree, for foods other than bread but made from grain, and for anything to eat or drink not included in these categories:

Blessed art thou, O Lord our God, King of the universe, who createst the fruit of the vine.

Blessed art thou, O Lord our God, King of the universe, who createst the fruit of the earth.

Blessed art thou, O Lord our God, King of the universe, who createst the fruit of the tree.

Blessed art thou, O Lord our God, King of the universe, who createst various kinds of food.

Blessed art thou, O Lord our God, King of the universe, by whose word all things exist.[30]

Grace after meals is most elaborate, and varies in form depending on how many men over the age of thirteen are present.[31] No selfish thanks, the grace sings God's giving unto all:

Blessed art thou, O Lord our God, King of the universe, who feedest the whole world with thy goodness, with grace, with lovingkindness and tender mercy; thou givest food to all flesh, for thy lovingkindness en-

29. *Ibid.,* pp. 962–963, 984–989.
30. The Talmud declares that if two or more eat together and do not speak words of Torah, they are sitting in the company of the insolent (Ps 1:1); they are like idolators and their table is "full of filth" (Is 28:8). But when those dining together do exchange words of Torah, the Shekinah, the divine Presence, is in their midst; it is as if they had eaten at God's table (Abot III, 2, 3; cf. *B. Talmud,* Soncino ed., *Aboth,* pp. 27–28). Since "holy conversation" at table is thus a religious duty, it is customary to recite or sing a psalm, such as: "The Lord is my shepherd; I shall not want," or "By the streams of Babylon we sat and wept," or "When the Lord brought back the captives of Zion, we were like men dreaming" (Pss 22, 136, 125).
31. For food eaten outside of mealtime, a shorter grace is provided, which sums up the longer prayer, and the Talmud tells of one Benjamin the Shepherd who, having "made a sandwich and said, Blessed be the Master of this bread," was deemed to have fulfilled his obligation of thanks (Ber. 40b; cf. *B. Talmud,* Soncino ed., *Berakoth,* pp. 249–250).

dureth forever. Through thy great goodness food hath never failed us: O
may it not fail us forever and ever for thy great name's sake, since thou
nourishest and sustainest all beings, and doest good unto all, and providest
food for all thy creatures whom thou hast created. Blessed art thou, O
Lord, who givest food unto all.[32]

Then thanks is given for the deliverance from Egypt, for the Covenant
and the Law, and Zion and the house of David are remembered, lest
material benefits loom too large. Under a series of impassioned invoca-
tions, the great Giver is praised, and begged to give again:

Blessed art thou, O Lord our God, King of the universe, O God, our
Father, our King, our Mighty One, the Holy One of Jacob, our Shepherd,
the Shepherd of Israel, O King, who art kind and dealest kindly with all,
day by day thou hast dealt kindly, dost deal kindly, and wilt deal kindly
with us; thou hast bestowed, thou dost bestow, thou wilt ever bestow
benefits upon us, yielding us grace, lovingkindness, mercy and relief, deliverance and prosperity, blessing and salvation, consolation, sustenance
and support, mercy, life, peace and all good: of no manner of good let us
be in want.

In the concluding prayer, one of the mighty favors asked is: "May the
All-merciful make us worthy of the days of the Messiah and of the life
of the world to come."

One more *berakah* in regard to food must be mentioned, because of
its signal universality. After eating herbs, eggs, or cheese, for instance,
or after any drink other than wine, the devout Jew says:

Blessed art thou, O Lord our God, King of the universe, who createst
innumerable living beings with their wants. We thank thee for all the
means that thou hast created wherewith to sustain the life of each of them.
Blessed art thou who art the Life of all worlds.[33]

Here animals and, though the one who prays it may not be aware of it,
even plants are drawn into the orb of prayer. Are not all beings, all
creatures, all realms, known and unknown, remembered when God is
addressed as *Hey ha-ʿolamim,* "Life of [all] worlds"?

VARIOUS OCCASIONS

THE orthodox life is often dismissed as repressive. But is there not poetry
in giving thanks to God for fragrant barks, plants, fruits, spices, and oil?

32. *The Authorised Daily Prayer Book,* ed. Hertz, pp. 964–981.
33. *Ibid.,* p. 989.

"Blessed art thou, O Lord our God, King of the universe, who createst fragrant woods . . . who createst fragrant plants . . . who givest a goodly scent to fruits . . . who createst divers kinds of spices . . . who createst fragrant oil." [34] Sights and sounds are also drawn into the sphere of religious awe. Lightning, falling stars, lofty mountains, great deserts, or the sky in splendor, remind the observing Jew of God, King of the universe, "who wrought the work of creation." Thunder, earthquake, and hurricane speak of Him "whose strength and might fill the world." Blessed too is He "who made the great sea." Beautiful persons, animals, or trees call forth a breathless thanks to the Lord "who has such as these in His world." The first blossoming of the year evokes these words:

Blessed art thou, O Lord our God, King of the universe, who hast made thy world lacking in nought, but hast produced therein goodly creatures and goodly trees wherewith to give delight unto the children of men.

That the band of colors produced when the sun's rays are broken by prisms of water should be so gratuitously lovely does indeed show God to be the Lord of generosity and beauty. But to the devout Jew, the rainbow is a sign of the God of fidelity, "who remembers His covenant and fulfills His word."

What might be just common curiosity can become wonder, can be raised to the height of gratitude. To be in the presence of a man learned in the Torah is to bless God for "imparting of His wisdom to them that revere Him." Subtly different is the blessing on seeing a man distinguished for other than sacred knowledge; here God is spoken of as the One who "has given of His wisdom to flesh and blood." The splendor of a king and his court ought not to be witnessed without praise of Him who "has given of His glory to mortals." And there is delicacy in the words said on meeting strangely formed persons, such as giants or dwarfs: "Blessed art thou, O Lord our God, King of the universe, who variest the forms of thy creatures."

The gathering together of many people is to be hallowed by a "Blessed be He who knows the secret thoughts of all these." A devout Jew meets a friend after long separation with thoughts of the Reviver of the dead, and he greets a man recovered from grave illness with thanks to "the Merciful who gave thee back to us and not to the earth."

34. *Ibid.*, pp. 989–995, for all the "Blessings on Various Occasions."

If he himself recovers from an illness or is rescued when in peril of his life, he publicly confesses:

Blessed art thou, O Lord our God, King of the universe, who doest good unto the undeserving, and who hast dealt kindly with me.[35]

Good tidings or the sight of joy make the heart sing to the Lord "who is good and dispenses good," while sad news or the sight of illness or of a holy place in desolation prompt praise of "the true Judge." Time, all time, and particularly the landmarks of joy, need hallowing. Hence the blessing which marks the start of each festive season is used also for any new and joyous event, such as tasting any fruit for the first time in the year, entering a new house, or wearing new clothes for the first time:

Blessed art thou, O Lord our God, King of the universe, who hast kept us in life, and hast preserved us, and hast enabled us to reach this season.

Places too are occasions for blessings. There are those offered over a spot renowned for wonders of old, over a holy place restored after long desolation, or over a place from which idolatry has been removed, hailing Him who performed miracles for the fathers, who re-establishes the border of the widow (that is, Jerusalem), and who wipes out idolatry. Moving are the words prescribed on seeing a statue of Hermes, once the most common heathen image, or any place where idolatry is practiced:

Blessed art thou, O Lord our God, King of the universe, who showest long-suffering to those who transgress thy will.[36]

35. *Ibid.*, p. 193. The one who wishes to fulfill his duty of thanksgiving for recovery from grave illness or for escape from the dangers of desert or sea is called forward to read a portion of the Pentateuch. Then, after the usual benediction which closes such readings, he pronounces the blessing given above, the *Gomel Benshen*. The word *benshen* appears also in the invitation to recite grace after meals as it was often said in Yiddish by Jews from central and east Europe: *Rabosai, mir wellen benshen*, "Gentlemen, let us say grace." This affords a striking sidelight on the cultural interrelations that must have existed centuries ago between the Jewish and the Catholic communities, for *benshen* clearly comes from the Latin *benedicere*, "to bless."

36. There are other rabbinical sayings on the habitations of heathens which have not this same spirit. Moreover, when an orthodox Jew sees a place where idolatry has been uprooted within Palestine, he is to say: "Blessed be He who uprooted idolatry from our land; and as it has been uprooted from this place, so may it be uprooted from all places belonging to Israel; and do thou turn the heart of those that serve [idols] to serve thee" (Ber. 57b; cf. *B. Talmud*, Soncino ed., *Berakoth*, p. 358). Maurice Simon, in his notes to *Berakoth*, identifies "those that serve them" as renegade Israelites. These "renegade Israelites" may well be Jewish Chris-

In sum, the rabbis teach that "if anyone enjoys anything of this world without a benediction, he commits sacrilege. . . . [It] is like making personal use of things consecrated to heaven . . . like robbing the Holy One, blessed be He," for "the Lord's are the earth and its fullness" (Ps 23:1).[37]

CONCLUSION

THE hundred daily blessings have been likened to the hundred sockets of silver which once supported the sanctuary of the desert (Ex 38:27), for they support, Rabbi Munk says, the sanctuary of Jewish life.[38] True, the number "one hundred" may at times become almost an end in itself. Such a temptation is the orthodox Jew's as it is every religious man's; indeed, all men, in all too many of their strivings, are inclined to forget the goal and linger with the means. Hence a hasidic rabbi taught that the Jewish worshipper is to say "Blessed," the first word of each benediction, with his whole strength, leaving no strength for the rest of the prayer. For if he is mindful of the verse: "They that wait for the Lord shall renew their strength" (Is 40:31), he will utter his "Blessed" as if to say: "Our Father in heaven, I am giving you all the strength that is within me in that very first word; now will you, in exchange, give me an abundance of new strength, so that I can go on with my prayer." [39]

The biblical spirit of thanksgiving which pervades the ancient blessings of the Jewish prayer book marvelously marks the liturgical books of the Catholic Church. Such hymns of grateful joy as the *Magnificat:* "My soul magnifies the Lord . . . because He . . . has done great things for me . . . He has given help to Israel . . . as He spoke to our fathers" (Lk 1:46–55); the *Te Deum:* "We praise you, we acclaim you Lord and Master. . . . We will confess and glorify your holy name"; or the *Benedictus,* whose opening words are: "Blessed be the Lord, the God of Israel" (Lk 1:68)—such hymns as these, rich in

tians. Now, the Jewish Christian must realize that this and similar prayers were uttered in zeal for God (see Rom 10:2). That he knows this zeal to be mistaken must not lead him to meet bitterness with bitterness; in no way does it absolve him from responding to it in patient love.

37. Ber. 35ab; cf. *B. Talmud,* Soncino ed., *Berakoth,* p. 220.
38. Munk, *op. cit.,* pp. 15–16.
39. Martin Buber, *Ten Rungs* (New York: Schocken Books, 1947), p. 29.

memories of the Old Testament, are recited day after day as part of the Church's official prayer. Indeed, the heart of Catholic worship, the Eucharist, takes its very name from *berakah,* blessing and thanksgiving.

More than the name, "the pattern of the Christian Eucharist, not only as a whole but in all its organic details, developed from the pattern of the Jewish eucharist." [40] The telling, for instance, in grace after meals, of God's mighty acts of deliverance has its counterpart and climax in the Eucharistic Prayer of all Catholic Liturgies, as in the Preface of the Roman Rite. And the *berakah* over bread, the *berakah* over the cup, have become the glorious consecration of bread and wine. Hence it might be said that, as thanksgiving binds together the Old Dispensation and the New, so, however much separates them, the two voices of prayer, the Christian and the Jewish, are still kindred voices because of their giving of thanks.

40. Louis Bouyer, Cong. Orat., *Liturgical Piety* (Notre Dame, Ind.: University of Notre Dame Press, 1955), p. 126.

Richard J. Schoeck

CHAUCER'S PRIORESS:
MERCY AND TENDER HEART

IT IS, of course, a shallow, schoolboy enterprise to read attitudes of later ages back into one's interpretation of history or to read literature of the past with modern lenses: this we all recognize. No one today would seriously propose a criticism of the poetry of Provence of the twelfth century because it is not the Whitmanesque singing of a democracy. But modern readers must continually be on guard against the assumption that medieval men and women always shared our twentieth-century notions of gentleness and our abhorrence of physical cruelty. On the other hand, kindness is no modern discovery, and charity has been practiced for many centuries.

I want to reconsider the conventional reading of the cruelty of the Prioress's Tale in Chaucer's *Canterbury Tales.* There is now, I take it, general acceptance of some irony in Chaucer's portrayal of the Prioress in the General Prologue to the *Tales,* though not yet universal agreement on how critical our view of her is to be. Curiously, however, there seems to be a widespread reading of her Tale itself as sincere, devout, and univocal. I should like to suggest another reading of the Prioress and her Tale, and to examine the complex of attitudes toward Jews and toward Christian-Jewish relations that is embodied in Chaucer's poem.

THE CANTERBURY TALES

LET us begin by reminding ourselves of the essential characteristics and qualities of Chaucer's great poem. In the Prologue, the pilgrims gather together to form their company for the journey to Canterbury,

> *from every shire's end*
> *In England, down to Canterbury they wend*
> *To seek the holy blissful martyr, quick*
> *In giving help to them when they were sick.*
> (p. 25; Prologue, lines 15–18)[1]

1. The page reference is to Nevill Coghill's modernization of *The Canterbury Tales* (Baltimore: Penguin Books, 1952). The line reference is to F. M. Robinson's edition of *The Complete Works of Geoffrey Chaucer* (Boston: Houghton Mifflin, 1933).

Sundry folk they are, some nine and twenty that fall into their fellowship for their long ride to Canterbury. Their companionship is one of
the essential keys to understanding the *Canterbury Tales:* an enduring
part of the appeal of this work resides in the sense of interpersonal relationships—the attitudes of the other pilgrims toward the Knight, for
example, or the humor of the rivalry of the Miller and the Reeve, or the
bitter clash of Summoner and Friar. This company forms and devises a
plan (left incomplete by the poet's failure to carry it to fulfillment)
for the telling of tales both going to and returning from Canterbury.
Lots are drawn for the order of the stories, the Prologue ends, and the
pilgrimage is under way.

    This, we recall, is the general plan and procedure of the *Tales.* But
no such bald summary can do justice to the rich sense of person that
Chaucer develops within his characterizations of types, to the subtle
nuance of attitude (of which I shall say more), and to the overwhelming feeling of reality. There are breaks in the continuity of social scal-
ing, but the sense of the wholeness of the society projected is very
strong. In a few words, "it is the concise portrait of an entire nation,"
and the stories "exemplify the whole range of contemporary European
imagination." [2]

    Even if Chaucer had completed the massive structure of his projected
Tales (some hundred and twenty were planned, of which we have less
than a quarter), we may be sure that no explicit moral would have in-
truded upon the poem as a whole. Still, Chaucer's poetry has its own
kind of high seriousness, and many of the individual Tales end with an
expression of proverbial wisdom; indeed, the last of the Tales in the
order in which they have come down to us, the Parson's, is overtly di-
dactic. Chaucer's work has so profound a relationship to our own life
today that we cannot afford to ignore it or, worse, to dismiss it as "mere
poetry," nor can we on the other hand read his poetry as though it had
no significant relationship with ideas and problems of his own times.

    Another essential point about Chaucer's style and poetic attitude
must still be made. This is his

perfect *tact* towards the idea he is presenting. This enables him to express
opposite attitudes to the same theme—such a theme, for instance, as the
relation between a man and his wife—with equal sympathy and under-

    2. Coghill, *ibid.,* p. 15.

standing. These opposite opinions are entertained and made credible, though seeming to come in all sincerity from the same mind, in virtue of Chaucer's variable manner or tone of voice, varied as it were by a kind of poetical politeness of a very wide range that is nevertheless always within the scope of a single master style.[3]

Respect for the idea, tact in handling the attitudes involved—these qualities mirror the most conspicuous characteristic of all: compassion. Not a compassion which brims over and sentimentalizes, but a tremendously open-eyed feeling for the "typical sorrows of ordinary human beings . . . the common human joys"[4]—a compassion for the individual as a unique person that is rare enough in our own times.

Thus Chaucer the poet. But his times were an extraordinarily complex compounding of gentleness and cruelty, of understanding and prejudice. This explains, in part, why generations of readers have apparently taken with little questioning the picture he gives of hatred of Jews.[5]

JEWS IN CHAUCERIAN ENGLAND

THERE is no need to document the sad lot of the Jews in medieval England and western Europe during the thirteenth and fourteenth centuries. European Jews were in effect excluded from Christian society. Viewed from within, their refusal to accept the Cross was a challenge to the growing sense of the essential unity of Christendom: no other group, in fact, posed so special a challenge to the Christian revelation. Viewed from without, theirs was the unfortunate fate of an enclave in an otherwise homogeneous culture. But however they are viewed, the Jews were allowed no place in Christendom in the late thirteenth and the fourteenth centuries; under Innocent III it was made clear that their place was outside the pale, and their exclusion was marked by the Badge.[6]

3. *Ibid.,* p. 19. One contemporary critical survey of Chaucer's poetry which, on the whole, gives evidence of awareness of this range of voice, is John Speirs, *Chaucer the Maker* (London: Faber and Faber, 1951).

4. Joan Bennett, *George Eliot* (Cambridge: Cambridge University Press, 1954), p. 180.

5. The exceptions are few: Alois Brandl many years ago, in Paul's *Grundriss der Germanischen Philologie* (Strassburg, 1889–93), II, i, 680, expressed the opinion that Chaucer meant the Prioress's Tale as a satire on childish legends, but in his authoritative edition Professor Robinson comments that this opinion was "certainly mistaken" (*op. cit.,* p. 840).

6. For the nadir, the half-century from 1198 to 1254, one may see the documents in S. Grayzel, *The Church and the Jews in the XIIIth Century* (Philadelphia:

But can this be the full explanation of the Prioress's cruelly anti-Semitic Tale within Chaucer's Canterbury framework? Can the reader close his eyes to the unmistakable reality of the anti-Jewish theme and concern himself only with the literary form in which that theme finds expression? Can he be content with analyzing the twenty-seven and more analogues of the miracle of the Virgin as a literary type,[7] or with performing similar functions of literary analysis, necessary, but meaningless when divorced from life? I think not. The interpretation which I am about to suggest is that in the Tale which Chaucer assigned to the Prioress, the widely circulated ritual murder legend is held up for implicit condemnation as vicious and hypocritical.

THE PRIORESS

WE MUST begin with the teller of the Tale, the Prioress herself, and look with some care at Chaucer's portraiture of her. One recent commentator has declared that the mere fact that she "is one of the Canterbury pilgrims is the first point of satire in a portrait that is satiric,"[8] for prohibitions of nuns' going on pilgrimage were frequent. Of course, as a prioress, the head of her house, she would have found that a great deal of business took her outside the nunnery.[9]

Dropsie College, 1933), which prints the papal letters and conciliar decrees of the period. But there is a broader view in *The Jew in the Medieval World,* ed. by J. R. Marcus (Cincinnati: Sinai Press, 1938), and closer historical treatment in Cecil Roth, *History of Jews in England* (London: Oxford University Press, 1941). Finally there is the work of Peter Browe, S.J., on *Die Judenmission im Mittelalter und die Päpste* ("Miscellanea Historiae Pontificiae," VI, 8; Rome: Pontificiae Universitatis Gregorianae, 1942).

7. This analysis—by Carleton Brown in *Sources and Analogues of Chaucer's Canterbury Tales,* ed. by W. F. Bryan and Germaine Dempster (Chicago: University of Chicago Press, 1941), pp. 447–485, and by Margaret H. Statler, "The Analogues of Chaucer's *Prioress' Tale:* The Relation of Group C to Group A," *Publications of the Modern Language Association,* LXV (Sept. 1950), pp. 896–910—is painstaking and necessary scholarship: I do not mean to condemn it in itself. From his study of the analogues, Carleton Brown attributes the detail of making the child a seven-year-old to Chaucer: aside from obvious significations of the age, it is well worth noting how heavily Chaucer stresses the diminutive throughout the Prioress's Tale (" a little school," "her little boy," "his little book," "his little body," and so on)—this is consonant with the Prioress's excessive and false charity over her "little dogs."

8. Muriel Bowden, in her *Commentary on the General Prologue to The Canterbury Tales* (New York: Macmillan, 1948), p. 93.

9. Consider the view developed by Eileen Power in her *Medieval People* (Baltimore: Penguin Books, 1951), pp. 92–94; and in her *Mediaeval English Nunneries* (Cambridge: Cambridge University Press, 1922), *passim.* However, it must be pointed out that a rather different interpretation is offered by Sister Madeleva in

A gentlewoman by birth, yet there is a sense of straining in her manner

> *To counterfeit a courtly kind of grace,*
> *A stately bearing fitting to her place,*
> *And to seem dignified in all her dealings.*
> (p. 29; Prologue, lines 139–41)

Much of the phraseology that colors her portrait is taken deliberately from the medieval romance, particularly when she is said to be "simple and coy." Years ago Professor Lowes pointed out that this phrase set the stage for the many secularizing nuances of the Prioress which four-teenth-century readers "must have been quick to gather." Then her very name, Eglantyne, "exquisitely incongruous," for in each of the romances known to the century, "the lady bearing the name of Chaucer's Prioress is a beautiful, romantically worldly figure far removed from a nun." Her sparkling eyes, her small soft mouth, her beautifully broad fore-head, her shapely nose—all these attributes are conventional in the cata-loguing descriptions of medieval heroines.[10] The point is double: not merely that she is physically attractive, but that the reader should be cognizant of that attraction. The Prioress could not help being beautiful, but the reader is being shown her attractiveness in the mode of the me-dieval romance with all its worldliness and sentimentalizing falseness of values.

Her manners are carefully those of polite society, and to the attentive fourteenth-century listener there was subtle but effective irony in Chau-cer's evocation, for the manners described are taken from a famous ac-count in the *Roman de la Rose* of what wiles a woman is to use to attract and hold her lover. But what is perhaps the most ironic touch of all, richly ambiguous and controversial, is the brooch whose significance is still debated by some Chaucerians. Hanging from her rosary, it is of

Chaucer's Nuns and Other Essays (New York: Appleton, 1925); she (in Robin-son's words, *op. cit.*, p. 755) "takes issue not only with the critics who have seen moral disparagement in Chaucer's portrayal of the Prioress, but even with Professor Lowes in his more sympathetic interpretation of the character" [cited in note 10].

10. John Livingston Lowes, "Simple and Coy," *Anglia Zeitschrift für Englische Philologie*, XXXIII (1910), pp. 440–451; and in his *Convention and Revolt in Poetry* (Boston: Houghton Mifflin, 1919), pp. 60–65. It must be remarked that Chaucer with great tact refrains from the exhaustive cataloguing of the conven-tional description—see D. S. Brewer, "The Ideal of Feminine Beauty in Medieval Literature, Especially 'Harley Lyrics,' Chaucer, and Some Elizabethans," *Modern Language Review*, L (July 1955), pp. 247–269.

shining gold, engraved with a crowned A and the motto *Amor Vincit Omnia.* In the earlier Middle Ages, this originally profane motto had been endowed with a connotation of sacred love, but by the fourteenth century the motto was again employed in its original sense—while of course the sacred connotation was still current. Lowes's questioning of the meaning of this brooch is justly famous:

> Now is it earthly love which conquers all, now heavenly; the phrase plays back and forth between the two. And it is precisely that happy ambiguity of the convention—itself the result of an earlier transfer—which makes Chaucer's use of it here, as a final summarizing touch, a master stroke. Which of the two loves does "amor" mean to the Prioress? I do not know; but I think she thought she meant love celestial.[11]

One may wish to be chivalrous to the Prioress, but (and this is really the issue) how did Chaucer's audience see her? At the moment of their first viewing her in the dramatic narrative there was no certitude but only ambiguity: from the first hint in "simple and coy" of the discord between the woman and the nun so subtly suggested by the two contradictory sets of associations to the summarizing touch of the magnificently ambiguous brooch, we have a nun who is something less than the fulfillment of the spiritual ideal.

One final point:

> *As for her sympathies and tender feelings,*
> *She was so charitably solicitous*
> *She used to weep if she but saw a mouse*
> *Caught in a trap, if it were dead or bleeding.*
> *And she had little dogs she would be feeding*
> *With roasted flesh, or milk, or fine white bread.*
> *Sorely she wept if one of them were dead*
> *Or someone took a stick and made it smart;*
> *She was all sentiment and tender heart.*
>
> (p. 29; Prologue, lines 142–50)

What Coghill renders as "her sympathies and tender feelings" is in Chaucer "hir conscience." In Middle English, conscience had our primary denotation (the faculty which pronounces upon the moral quality of one's actions or motives), but also the secondary meaning, now

---

11. *Convention and Revolt in Poetry,* p. 66. Even if one conjectures a secular lady as the original owner, the force of the ambiguity remains.

largely lost, of "tenderness of feeling": both meanings are bound up in Chaucer's use of the word here. "To speken of hir conscience," "to speak of her conscience," Chaucer says—but we get nothing of her moral faculty, only her emotional tenderness. Moreover, the object of that tenderness, of her "charitable" nature, is not the neighbor but pets; and there seems little disputing that it was contrary to ecclesiastical regulations for a nun to have such pets as the Prioress's "little dogs" [12] (though earlier, to be sure, such religious as those addressed in the *Ancrene Riwle* were permitted them). The Dominican Bromyard, late fourteenth-century theologian of Cambridge, thundered from his pulpit against the wealthy who indulged themselves in pampered pets, especially at a time when food was scarce.[13] One may well ask what kind of "charity" it is that Chaucer chose to describe as lavished on animals. The point is not (as one scholar has suggested recently) that this is "the sort of woman who would weep even over a dead mouse or a whipped dog"; [14] it is that she weeps only over such sentimentalized suffering and apparently ignores the human suffering so prevalent around her. It is that warped quality, as we shall see, which dominates her Tale.

Only this far does Chaucer go in the General Prologue, but with superbly controlled irony and devastating tact he has contrived to leave shadows of doubts, several kinds of uncertainty, and some strong implications about the Prioress in the mind of his audience. Beyond that, at this stage of Chaucer's developing portrait of this religious woman, we cannot declare.

THE PRIORESS'S TALE

PRECEDING the Prioress's Tale is a Prologue which, in Professor Robinson's words, "contains many ideas and expressions drawn from the

12. See Power, *Mediaeval English Nunneries*, pp. 305–309, and Note E ("Convent Pets in Literature"); also her *Medieval People*, pp. 90–91, 194. There are further references in E. P. Kuhl, "Notes on Chaucer's Prioress," *Philological Quarterly*, II (1923), pp. 302–309. J. M. Manly, in his edition of the *Canterbury Tales* (New York: Henry Holt, 1928, p. 506), cites an order of 1345 quoted in William Dugdale's *Monasticon Angelicanum* (II, p. 619, no. xi) : "Also we command that neither birds [perhaps falcons] nor dogs nor little birds be kept by any abbess or nun within the walls of the abbey or within the choir, especially while they should be engaged in divine services."

13. Quoted by G. R. Owst in *Literature and Pulpit in Medieval England* (Cambridge: Cambridge University Press, 1933), p. 327.

14. Charles W. Dunn, *Chaucer Reader* (New York: Harcourt Brace, 1952), p. 41.

Scriptures, the services of the Church, and other religious poetry." As would be most appropriate to the Prioress, it recalls in particular certain passages of the Office of the Blessed Virgin; "it was a regular literary convention to prefix to a miracle or saint's legend an invocation to Christ or the Blessed Virgin." [15] A carefully wrought prayer, this Prologue of hers, and rich in symbolism; the attentive reader may well be struck by the irony of having an anti-Semitic legend prefaced by a prayer rich in images from the Old Testament. The Prioress invokes Christ:

> *in honor of Thee, as best I can,*
> *Of Thee and of that whitest lily-flower*
> *That bare Thee, all without the touch of man,*
> *I tell my tale and will put forth my power.*

Then she calls Mary:

> *O mother-maid, maid-mother, chaste and free!*
> *O bush unburnt, burning in Moses' sight,*

and implores her:

> *help me to tell my story*
> *In reverence of thee and of thy glory!*
> (p. 193; lines B 1650–3,
> 1657–8, 1663) [16]

Against this note of seeming sincerity and the subtly suggested background of the Old Testament roots of the Christian faith, we hear the Prioress's Tale: how the "wicked Jews" slew a happy child for no reason other than his joyful singing of the praise of Mary, and how the murder was revealed when, from the privy drain into which he had been cast,

> *This gem of chastity, this emerald,*
> *This jewel of martyrdom and ruby bright,*
> *Lying with carven throat and out of sight,*
> *Began to sing* O Alma *from the ground*
> *Till all the place was ringing with the sound.*
> (p. 197; lines B 1799–1803)

15. Robinson, *op. cit.,* p. 840.
16. It is likely that a great many of Chaucer's audience were not aware that the titles given here to Mary are taken from the Old Testament, the "Burning Bush" from Exodus, the "Lily" from the Song of Songs.

Having expanded on this "miracle" with great unction, the Prioress gratuitously links it with the thirteenth-century legend of the choir-boy Hugh of Lincoln:

> *O Hugh of Lincoln, likewise murdered so*
> *By cursed Jews, as is notorious,*
> *(For it was but a little time ago) . . .*
>   (p. 199; lines B 1874-6)

It has long been remarked that her Tale displays a "fierce bigotry" (as Wordsworth put it). This is how she begins:

> *In Asia once there was a christian town*
> *In which, long since, a Ghetto used to be*
> *Where there were Jews, supported by the Crown*
> *For the foul lucre of their usury,*
> *Hateful to Christ and all his company.*
>   (pp. 193-194; lines B 1678-82)

And this is how she accounts for the alleged murder of a Christian child by Jews:

> *First of our foes, the Serpent Satan shook*
> *Those Jewish hearts that are his waspish nest . . .*
>   (p. 196; lines B 1748-9)

That the Prioress's own words should convict her of bigotry is not enough; they must be seen as a clear contradiction of the mind of the Church, and to this end Dunn's comments in his *Chaucer Reader* can be of help:

Her tale is derived from a vague but ancient and widespread libel, already current in England before Chaucer was born, that Jews were accustomed to murder Christian children for ritualistic purposes. She does not, it is true, claim any firsthand acquaintance with the Jews and is, in fact, unlikely to have had it, for they were expelled from England in 1290 and were not readmitted until the seventeenth century; and she sets the scene of action in an unidentified part of distant Asia. But she accepts without question the validity of the legend underlying her tale and, in her epilogue, quite gratuitously cites an equally legendary English story of the boy named Hugh of Lincoln, who was reported in the thirteenth century to have been murdered by the Jews . . .[17]

17. Dunn. *op. cit.*, pp. 41-42.

Let us single out these points for emphasis, so that later reference can easily be made to them: (1) the vague but widespread belief that Jews were accustomed to murder Christian children for ritualistic purposes; (2) the acceptance of the validity of the report without question, and the retelling of this report or legend; (3) implicit approval of the action taken against the Jews; and (4) the continuing or stirring up of old prejudices.

These points are specifically covered by several popes in bulls condemning the ritual murder libel and offering to the Jews the protection of the Holy See.[18] I should like to quote here passages from that of Gregory X in 1272, not in the order in which they appear in the original but in accordance with the four points.

Point 1:

It sometimes happens that certain Christians lose their Christian children. The charge is then made against the Jews by their enemies that they have stolen and slain these children in secret, and have sacrificed the heart and blood. The fathers of the said children, or other Christians who are envious of the Jews, even hide their children in order to have a pre-

18. One of the earliest and most weighty papal condemnations of the blood accusation was addressed by Innocent IV to the Archbishops and Bishops of Germany in 1247: "We have received a mournful complaint from the Jews of Germany, telling how some princes, both ecclesiastical and lay, together with other nobles and powerful persons in your cities and dioceses, devise evil plans against them and invent various pretexts in order to rob them unjustly of their goods, and gain possession thereof. This they do without stopping to consider prudently that it is from the archives of the Jews, so to speak, that the testimonies of the Christian faith came forth. Holy Scripture pronounces among other injunctions of the Law 'Thou shalt not kill,' forbidding them when they celebrate the Passover even to touch any dead body. Nevertheless, they are falsely accused that, in that same solemnity, they make communion with the heart of a slain child. This is alleged to be enjoined by the Law, whereas in fact such an act is manifestly contrary to it. Moreover, if the body of a dead man is by chance found anywhere, [some nobles and powerful persons] maliciously ascribe the cause of death to the action of the Jews. On this, and many other fictitious pretexts, they rage against the Jews and despoil them of their possessions, against God and Justice and the privileges mercifully granted to them by the Holy See; notwithstanding that they have never been tried for these crimes and have never confessed them and have never been convicted of them. By starvation, imprisonment and many heavy persecutions and oppressions [some nobles and powerful persons] harass them, inflicting upon them divers kinds of punishment, and condemning large numbers to a most shameful death. Hence the Jews, who are under the power of the aforesaid nobles, lords and princes, are in a worse condition than were their fathers in Egypt, and are compelled to go into exile from localities where they and their ancestors have dwelt from time immemorial." Quoted by Cecil Roth, *The Ritual Murder Libel and the Jew* (London: Woburn Press, n.d.), pp. 97–98.

text to molest the Jews, and to extort money from them so as to pay their dues. They assert thereupon, most falsely, that the Jews have taken away these children and slain them, and have sacrificed the heart and blood. Yet their Law expressly forbids the Jews to sacrifice or to eat or to drink blood: even though it be of animals which have the hoof cloven. This has been confirmed in our *curia* on many occasions by Jews converted to the Christian faith. Nonetheless, on this pretext many Jews have frequently been seized and detained, against all justice.

Point 2:

Inasmuch as the Jews are not able to bear witness against the Christians, we decree furthermore that the testimony of Christians against Jews shall not be valid unless there is among these Christians some Jew who is there for the purpose of offering testimony.

Point 3:

No Christian shall presume to seize, imprison, wound, torture, mutilate, kill, or inflict violence on [the Jews]; furthermore, no one shall presume, except by judicial action of the authorities of the country, to change the good customs in the land where they live for the purpose of taking their money or goods from them or from others.

Point 4:

We decree that no Christian shall stir up anything new against [the Jews].

Moreover, if any one, after having known the content of this decree, should—which we hope will not happen—attempt audaciously to act contrary to it, then let him suffer punishment in his rank and position, or let him be punished by the penalty of excommunication, unless he makes amends for his boldness by proper recompense.[19]

At the end of the thirteenth and during the fourteenth centuries, the charge of ritual murder became more frequent; yet the popes had proclaimed the truth and set up an ideal against which these excesses and

19. For Point 1, see *ibid.,* pp. 21–22. Points 2, 3 and 4 are quoted from *The Jew in the Medieval World,* ed. by J. R. Marcus, pp. 151–154. Regarding such a decree there is always the twofold question of how effective it is and how generally known. The bull quoted could not have been very widely effective, and it may well be that the Prioress had not seen this bull; it was not her office to. Nor is it likely that Chaucer's listening audience would have had firsthand experience with a document like this, for it was the direct concern of ecclesiastical chanceries. But the view expressed was doubtless known.

tortures and false charges should have been seen for what they were.

Doubtless most of the company hearing Madame Eglantyne's Tale would not have seen a Jew in England—the situation is very much like that of the Shakespearean audience and Shylock [20]—but most of them would have traveled in France, some of them perhaps as widely in Europe as Chaucer had traveled on the king's business, and the likelihood of acquaintance or contact with Jews would be correspondingly greater, for in England it seems fairly certain that only the smallest pockets of Jews were left after their expulsion in 1290.

By such a sophisticated court audience the disparity between the Prioress's professed devotion and her bigotry could doubtless have been more easily seen than by a county audience, less traveled, and therefore of narrower views. While not all could have measured the great distance of that disparity, surely readers have always recognized that other Tales (like the Pardoner's) present hypocrisy, or (like the Shipman's) knavery and deceit. For those who did discern the pious hypocrisy of the Prioress, there is a level of irony in the symbolism that reinforces this startling incongruity and develops the irony of her portrait in the Prologue. There is for example her reference to Rachel:

> *His mother, swooning as they went along*
> *Beside the bier, could not be reconciled,*
> *A Second Rachel weeping for her child.*
>   (p. 197; lines B 1815–17)

The allusion is to the weeping of Rachel for her children—the sons of Jacob in captivity (Jer 31:15)—, used by the Prioress, we may be sure, as a conventional figure of lamentation and weeping. There is deep meaning in the fact that the First Nocturn of Matins on the feast of the Holy Innocents gives Jeremiah's poetical representation of Rachel, with its magnificent consolation in a bitter time: "Let thy voice cease from weeping and thy eyes from tears" (31:16). But this (like the Old Testament symbolism in the Prologue to her Tale, of which she is, I take it, unaware) is lost on the Prioress and is without influence on her conscience or charity. There is even more. Rachel's weeping is interpreted in the New Testament (Mt 2:18) as a prophetic parallel to the lamentation of the mothers whose children were slain at the com-

20. See Barry Ulanov, "Shylock: The Quality of Justice," *The Bridge*, I, 266–279.

mand of Herod the Great. The Third Nocturn on this day is a homily by St. Jerome:

When he took the Child and His mother, and fled into Egypt, he took them by night, and in darkness. And that darkness signified the night of ignorance in which he left the unbelievers from whom he fled. But when he returned into Judaea, the Gospel makes no mention of night or darkness; for at the end of the world the Jews shall be enlightened, and shall receive the faith again as once they received Christ returning from Egypt.[21]

In all this evocation of Old and New Testaments there is a compassion beyond the Prioress's reach of soul: bland and unmoved, indeed with merciless satisfaction in "the evils they deserve," she tells of the torturing of the Jews, how they were drawn apart by wild horses and then hanged (p. 198; lines B 1822–4). The culminating irony of her last lines is the echoing of her petition for a mercy of which she is herself incapable:

> *Pray mercy on our faltering steps, that thus*
> *Merciful God reach mercy down to us,*
> *Though we be so unstable . . .*
> (p. 199; lines B 1877–9)

One more point. The Prioress's bearing and Tale are not only opposed to the authentic mind of the Church; they also seem to be in contrast with much else in the *Canterbury Tales.* Though I do not wish to make too much of it, the Prioress's story is followed by Chaucer's own story of Sir Topaz, the *Tales'* one unmistakable burlesque, a satiric jousting with decadent knight-errantry of late medieval romances. Perhaps it is introduced in order to clear the air: the Prioress's Tale had left the company "sobered" for a moment, but then the Host began to "japen," he "again began his jokes" (p. 200; lines B 1881–3). There might well be more than one reason for him to feel that the company should be cheered

---

21. *Comm. Matth.* 2 and *Gloss.* (cf. PL 26:27). In connection with the kind of scriptural interpretation used here by St. Jerome, see D. W. Robertson, Jr., and Bernard F. Huppé, *Piers Plowman and Scriptural Tradition* (Princeton: Princeton University Press, 1951); and my review of it in *Thought,* XXVII (Winter 1952– 53), pp. 582–586. For an application of this method to one of the poems of the *Canterbury Tales,* see R. P. Miller, "Chaucer's Pardoner, the Scriptural Eunuch, and the Pardoner's Tale," *Speculum,* XXX (April 1955), pp. 180–199.

up at once. In any case, his reaction to the Prioress's story is most ambiguous.[22]

Within the larger framework of the *Tales* one has only to look to the Plowman for a true model of the Christian, for here is one who follows Christ in loving, in true charity:

> *Loving God best with all his heart and mind*
> *And then his neighbor as himself, repined*
> *At no misfortune, slackened for no content,*
> *For steadily about his work he went*
> *To thrash his corn, to dig or to manure*
> *Or make a ditch; and he would help the poor*
> *For love of Christ and never take a penny*
> *If he could help it . . .*
>
> (p. 39; Prologue, lines 533–8)

Or take his brother, the Parson:

> *He was a shepherd and no mercenary.*
> *Holy and virtuous he was, but then*
> *Never contemptuous of sinful men,*
> *Never disdainful, never too proud or fine,*
> *But was discreet in teaching and benign.*
> *His business was to show a fair behavior*
> *And draw men thus to Heaven and their Saviour.*
>
> (p. 39; Prologue, lines 514–20)

There are, then, within the poem models of right conscience, true charity, and proper tenderness to human needs and suffering.

JEWS AND THE FOURTEENTH-CENTURY MIND

IT MIGHT be objected that Chaucer was a man of the fourteenth century and shared its limitations: how could we expect him to transcend them, to shatter the wall of prejudice?

I do not know what most Englishmen of the century thought about Jews. The answer may well be that for them there could be only "Jews!," not a Jew, and that they were to be found in unidentified distant re-

22. Chaucer's reference to Sir Topaz's hauberk (p. 205; line B 2053) as "Jewish work" has been interpreted by Kölbing and Brusendorff as used by Chaucer in ridicule (see Robinson, *op. cit.,* p. 845), but it seems more likely that Chaucer is here simply reflecting conventional attitudes, as Langland does in speaking of the Jews as usurers. The Jews were in fact famous armorers.

gions or, as the Prioress places them, in the past. But certainly, there were those who did not hate them; there was at least one honest chronicler, William of Newburgh, who saw two sides to the slaughter of the Jews in York, and he was not afraid to speak the truth as he saw it.[23] Converted Jews like the fourteenth-century Strassburg banker Merswin followed Nicholas of Lyra in pleading that Jews could be saved.[24] On the other hand, Mannyng, an Austin canon of Bourne, complains in his early fourteenth-century *Handlyng Synne,* a realistic picture of medieval living, rich in its detailing of virtues and vices, that not only some of the "lewd folk" but even some priests say of the Jews that "we wot not whether they be saved or no." He attempts to controvert this, for "certes," he writes, "they are all in error." [25] Mannyng would doubtless not have charged as he did that the layfolk and priests erred in supposing it possible for Jews to be saved if there had not been quite a few who thought so.[26]

In Langland's *Piers Plowman* later in the century, we find the thought defended that there must somehow be a place in heaven for the good Jew and for the good pagan, for if there is truth in a man, "the true God would never allow His truth to be dishonored." Along with such passing allusions as suggest the conventional ideas about Jews as usurers, at times connected with the Lombards, we see Langland holding up their kindness to each other as a measure against which he can charge his fellow Christians with lack of charity, speaking of the Jews as our "lores-men," our teachers. Deeper still:

23. Verification of his account (the Chronicles are to be found in volume I of the Rolls Series) is seen by H. M. Colvin, in *The White Canons in England* (Oxford: Clarendon Press, 1951), pp. 165–166.

24. Doubtless we must look behind Nicholas of Lyra (the Franciscan biblical scholar and commentator who died at about the time Chaucer was born) to the influential work of the Premonstratensian order and their preaching (see Petit François, *La Spiritualité des Prémontrés,* Paris: Vrin, 1947). At present, one can only speculate on how much the conversion of individuals like Merswin was due to the preaching of Nicholas and the Premonstratensians. Certainly relevant is the seminal work of Andrew of St. Victor who drew not only on traditional Christian, but also on Jewish, exegesis (see B. Smalley, *The Study of the Bible in the Middle Ages,* Oxford: Blackwell, 1952, pp. 166–185), for English mysticism of the fourteenth century learned a great deal from the Victorine tradition.

25. *Handlyng Synne,* Early English Text Society, 119 (1901), p. 298—its title suggests its purpose as a manual of sins.

26. That this thought was not rare in medieval England is supported by a passage in Matthew Paris (R.S. 57, vol. V, p. 546), and in Burton Chronicle (R.S. 36, vol. I, p. 346), to which my colleague, Professor M. A. Donovan, has called my attention.

> *The Jews live in the law that our Lord wrote himself*
> *In stone, for it was steadfast and should stand forever;*
> *Love God and love thy neighbor is the law of the Hebrews.*
> *He took it to Moses, its teacher till the coming of the*
> *Messiah.*
> *And they live still in that law and believe it the best.*

True, they rejected the Messiah,

> *But Pharisees and Saracens, Scribes and Greeks*
> *Are folk of one faith and hold the Father in honor.*
> *And since the Saracens as well as the Hebrews*
> *Know the first clause of our creed,* Credo in Deum
> patrem omnipotentem,
> *Prelates of Christian provinces if possible should teach*
> *them*
> *Little by little* et in Jesum Christum filium,
> *Till they can speak and spell* et in Spiritum Sanctum,
> *And render it and remember it, with* remissionem
> peccatorum,
> Carnis resurrectionem et vitam eternam. Amen.

But that Jews and Moslems, that all may so spell, Christian leaders, Langland pleads time and again, must "live as they teach us" and "every Christian creature should be kind to others." [27]

There was not only Langland but also the quiet current of mysticism and scriptural study that was somehow indebted to the rabbinical tradition. (Though this influence would seem to have been strongest in the thirteenth century, there is much evidence of its continuing through the fourteenth.) When we look over the theological work of the Victorine school, and against the evidence of Mannyng's *Handlyng Synne,* read the pleadings of Langland (and on the Continent, of Merswin and others) for a more tolerant, a more loving, view of the Jews, and add to all this the work of the Premonstratensians—then the view I am suggesting as the implicit framework within which the Prioress and her Tale are fitted is, I think, not implausible.

A fourteenth-century Englishman such as Chaucer or Langland could

27. The reference to Jews as our "lores-men" is from B, IX, 83–87. Other quotations are from Henry W. Wells's translation of *The Vision of Piers Plowman* (New York: Sheed and Ward, 1935), pp. 161, 212–214, 206, 124 (XII, 299; XV, 622–626, 647–655, 420; X, 384).

scarcely have questioned the laws and social forces that had excluded the medieval Jew from Christian society. Nor had the time yet come to condemn anti-Semitism the way Pius XI was to do when he reminded us that our faith, and hence our civilization, were born with Abraham's loving sacrifice and that, in the spirit, Abraham is every Christian's father. But there is in Chaucer's treatment of the Prioress a clear-eyed recognition of the inhumanity of her Tale, its violation of the deepest sense of charity which fourteen centuries of Christianity had been laboring to develop, and its failure to carry the burden of charity which is enjoined on all Christians but especially on religious. The Prioress is not condemned, however; rather is the poem's objective view one of understanding pity of her: further than this all of Chaucer's compassion could not go.

But how great a thing it was in such a complex social and cultural environment for a poet to insist that anti-Semitism could be viewed through the recognizable frame of such a woman as the Prioress, one who succumbed too easily to the worldly concern with things and manners, and whose charity was too much of this world.

Friedrich E. Pater

THE BEASTS AND THE EVERLASTING LOVE

INTRODUCTION

IN THE spring of 1954, a letter reached me from Haifa, Israel, telling me that its writer had found my *Walls Are Crumbling* a source of delight. He enclosed with his letter a manuscript—a series of what he called "modest meditations on a sublime text"—asking if it could appear in *The Bridge,* asking, too, if I could give hospitality to his unpublished papers, which he had been forced to leave behind in his native country. Before I could make any decision, I learned that the author had died. Decades ago, he and I had lived in the same city but had never met. Now that the written word had brought us together for so short a time, an obligation seemed to rest on me to make at least his meditations known, as a kind of testament and as a memorial.

Friedrich Emanuel Pater was born of Jewish parents on January 7, 1891, in Olmütz, Austria, later Czechoslovakia. Having studied law and philosophy in Prague, he won his doctorate with *One and All: A Theory of the Comical.* This dissertation was dedicated to his teacher, Christian von Ehrenfels, who introduced the concept of *Gestalt* into modern thinking. Among those Pater was fortunate enough to know was Adolf Loos, a father of modern architecture, who boldly used new materials, new lines, new forms, without feeling it necessary to cut all ties with the past. Pater was also drawn to Karl Kraus, the intrepid critic of all he thought hollow and untrue in public life, literature, and journalism. Having learned from Kraus awe for the word and responsibility as response to meaning, Pater—not surprisingly—came in later years to look on Theodor Haecker, the German Catholic thinker of the late '20s and early '30s, as a spiritual guide.

In 1954, Pater published in *Der Brenner* an essay, "On Mount Carmel: Meditations on Beauty," which revolves around the sentence: *Hässlichkeit kommt von Hassen, wie Schönheit von Lieben,* "Ugliness comes from hate, as loveliness from love," the Love which made the world. He asks, for instance: "Whence comes the virginal, unapproachable beauty of the lily, its white and gold, with the green of its leaves, making so kingly a triad?" Answering with the Gospel that God so clothes it, he continues that He has done so "out of love, for loveliness comes from love, from the great love of the Creator." God, who makes beautiful all He loves, his essay ends, delights not in our possessions, our "ornaments and precious stones, not in images, not even in those of artists and philosophers. They are for men, for minds richly endowed, whereas it is poverty in spirit alone we need to enter heaven. For God has revealed Himself that we may all follow Him, all, great minds and little."

As these meditations on beauty breathe an evangelical spirit, so do the present meditations on Mk 1:13. In a few instances, Pater's language here is not so exact, so severe, as it might be and as, I am sure, he would have liked it to be. Hence, being unable to ask him to elucidate his words, I have added a few notes of my own. In any case, his meditations are without doubt a profession of Christ, and, written as they were shortly before his death on June 27, 1954, they are a testament.

Friedrich Pater's meditations echo, I think, the compassion of great Catholic mystics like Blessed Henry Suso, who confessed that the wants of all the creatures on the earth went to his heart and that, when he himself could not help them, he begged the kind God to do so; or St. Gertrude the Great, of whom it is said that she felt with all dumb creatures in whatever befell them and held their miseries up to God, mindful that the dignity even of beasts has received new nobility through Christ.

There is, it seems to me, something of St. Francis' spirit in Pater's meditations, which, unknown to him, were a kind of farewell. I mean that spirit which once made Francis of Assisi, feeling that death was not too far off, take loving leave of his hermitage, of the rock that had sheltered him, and of the bird that had given him joy when it awakened him for his morning prayer: *Io mi parto, a Dio, a Dio, a Dio tutti! A Dio, monte santo, a Dio, monte Alverna, a Dio, monte d'Angeli! A Dio, carissimo fratello falcone . . . !* "I am departing. Good-bye, good-bye, good-bye all of you! Good-bye, holy mountain; good-bye, Mount Alverna; good-bye, mount of the angels! Good-bye, dearest brother falcon; I thank you for the love you have shown me! Good-bye, good-bye, lofty rock; never again shall I visit you! Good-bye, rock that took me into your bosom, making a fool of the devil; never again shall we see each other!"

No more than was St. Francis' was Pater's a hopeless farewell. The last line of his meditations suggests that the air of Mount Carmel made there grow in him the faith of an Ambrose that in Christ risen the whole universe is risen, heaven and earth, for heaven and earth will be made new (PL 16:1403). So he looked for the Day to come, the Lord's day, when, an old lenten hymn says, all will bloom anew:

Dies venit, dies tua
In qua reflorent omnia.

JOHN M. OESTERREICHER

AND immediately the Spirit drove Him forth into the desert," it is written in the Gospel according to St. Mark. "And He was in the desert forty days and forty nights, being tempted the while by Satan, and was with the wild beasts, and the angels ministered to Him" (1:12–13). In the other two Gospel accounts of Jesus' stay in the desert (Mt 4:1–2; Lk 4:1–2), the words, "and was with the wild beasts," are missing; they are St. Mark's alone.

This is the picture evoked: the desert beyond the Jordan, under the harsh southern sun, before which Jesus may have been wont to withdraw into the hollow of a rock. There, in that solitude, He was tempted by Satan, then served by angels. And there, with no other earthly creature near Him, beasts were His company. This is so significant, its implications are so many, that one does not know which to follow first.

I

SINCE the Gospels portray Jesus throughout as truly man, lacking no human quality, we will not err if we see His life within a truly human frame. Thus regarded, His stay in the desert, along with the fasting which Matthew and Luke stress, appears like a final preparing for a hard mission, like the final gathering of mind and strength of one who knows what awaits him. He was about to go to men; they alone were to be the concern of His labors, of His striving and His patience. He would speak to them in their language, and in the language of Scripture, as man among men. May it not have been, then, that before all this Christ wished once more to see the beasts, for which He would later have no time? For His saving work was not merely for man but for all creatures, which He willed to redeem together with man their head.[1]

The beasts of the desert are the lion, the panther, the vulture, also the

---

1. "Redeem" is not used here in the strict sense of redemption from sin; however, all things are sanctified by Christ. [Editor.]

serpent, the scorpion, the hyena, and the jackal. Since there, as in the ocean depths, hardly any plants grow, the animals are almost all beasts of prey. It is by them we ought to picture Jesus surrounded, in the heat of day and in the coolness of night, under a sky alight with stars.

We dare not say as certain what can only be divined. But this much is sure. None of the beasts that are thought of as wild and dangerous hurt Him; unharmed, He returned from the desert to men—so that He might die at their hands. All else about His dwelling among the desert beasts is conjecture. Later He was to make His entry into Jerusalem on a donkey. He bid the demons of the two possessed go into a herd of swine. "Brood of vipers," He rebuked the Pharisees. He recalled the foxes that have their dens and the birds that have their nests, the birds that do not toil but are provided for. Not even the sparrows, He taught, are unknown to God. He Himself was the Lamb of God, and repeatedly He spoke of shepherd and flock. But otherwise there is little in the Gospels about the beasts and nothing about man's relationship to them. It seems, then, that His stay in the desert was like a leave-taking, as if, before setting out on His hard road, He took leave of the mute and innocent creation, of all the world other than man, of nature's beauty and grandeur.

This is perhaps the first meaning of the sentence, "Christ was with the wild beasts."

II

THERE were with Jesus in the wilderness Satan, the angels, and no other creatures but the beasts.

At this sublime moment in Christ's earthly life, when spirits approached and conversed with Him, only the beasts were worthy to draw near and—we would fain assume—with love to surround Him. When the princes and the mighty of the earth whisper to one another of closely guarded secrets, no courtier or nobleman may be present; only the servants are admitted. Though belonging to another and lower class, they are members of the household. Likewise, no men, only beasts, witnessed the high things that took place in the desert. Because of their unmixed nature, beasts are, in their own, lower way, peers of angels and demons, peers of the creatures who are not of earth. No man may be present when such beings settle accounts.

Once man too was in the same, or rather, in a similar situation: conversing with angels and with the evil one, dwelling in the midst of nature, above all in the midst of the beasts, whose language he understood. He was in paradise. Commentaries duly underline this parallel. Take Clarke's, for instance: "The wilderness was the abode of evil spirits. This very short account perhaps suggests that the second Adam, like the first, was with animals, and met the tempter, but unlike Adam vanquished him. Like Elijah miraculously fed, angels cared for Him."

Christ in the wilderness: here again is man's paradisal situation. But with what a difference! Even the contrast in landscape makes clear that it is a similarity of opposites. There the paradisal fullness of the Garden of Eden; here the emptiness of the waste. There man was placed in the center of the Garden to be joyful and glad; here the Spirit of God had brought Jesus that He might prepare for the sacrifice He had chosen. But again angels are close and the tempter draws near. There are again the beasts, the very beasts that are part of our own world, whereas we meet angels and the devil only in the shape of men—men who are, as it were, their deputies, playing their roles among us, for they are not real angels and devils, only men like ourselves.

It is rooted in the incomprehensibly double nature of Christ [2] that, while living here on earth, He lived also in the world of spirits, who for us are invisible but with whom He conversed. This is never so clearly stated as in this passage of Scripture. There in the desert, there was the place: there Christ, even as man, lived in a world inaccessible to us, from which He had come and to which He was going, or rather, through which He was to go into one still higher [3]—He lived in the world where angels and Satan themselves appear.

The events in that middle realm of spirits—to which we are linked,

2. Friedrich Pater's phrase, *die auf unbegreifliche Art doppelte Natur Christi,* "the incomprehensibly double nature of Christ," strikes me as saying the very same thing as Catholic doctrine does of Jesus. However, the Catholic uses a more precise language to express the mystery of Him who, like a mighty arch, spans the divine and the human. With the Church he says that in Jesus there is one person, the divine person of the Word; but that there are in Him two natures, one divine, one human. In other words, the Son, the eternal Word of God, took to Himself a human nature and made it so entirely His own that it is He who gives it existence; still—impossible though it is for us to fathom this union—Jesus' thinking, willing, and speaking are, in the fullest and truest sense, human. [Editor.]

3. This "still higher" realm is, of course, the infinite light in which God dwells. That Christ ascended into that realm comes here as an afterthought, as a correction of what is said immediately before. But though the correction covers explicitly only the one clause, "and to which He was going," the whole essay seems to me to imply that had Friedrich Pater looked back to the clause just preceding, he would have

as it were, by the beasts in the desert—have come down to us as re-corded by Matthew and Luke; and the very words exchanged between Christ and the tempter are known. This exchange, these words, are not fantastic; they are not speeches made beautiful and impressive by the imagery of a rich imagination, as poetic speeches may be beautiful and meaningful. These words, which issue from a realm that is a middle realm between heaven and earth, are unforgettably simple and deep; above all they are true, indeed sheer truth, since He who spoke them was the Truth, in whose mouth the words of Scripture were made once more new and true. Hence they are, like all things that come from par-adise, beautiful.

In His combat with the tempter, Jesus used as His one weapon words of Scripture, or, to be explicit, words from the fifth book of Moses. With this weapon alone He conquered the adversary, the prince of this world. Words in which such power dwells cannot but be lofty. In this they match the hour of their use, the dignity of Him who used them, the dig-nity also of him against whom they were directed, and the greatness of the stakes.

Now, here there is given us, in the margin as it were, insight into an ancient problem. What took place in the desert was, of course, a much deeper mystery than the ontological or aesthetic question of how truth and beauty are related; but when deepest mysteries are offered us, such questions, to which the Evangelist never gave a thought, are solved in passing. For they are, if at all matter for systematic treatment, sooner the object of theology illumined by faith than of ontology and aesthet-ics—of theology, which is richer and deeper, by a whole dimension, than those philosophical disciplines.

As the lofty, as the sublime, springs from God's majesty and omnipo-tence, so the beautiful from His love. And since He is at once Truth and Love, therefore "beauty is truth, truth beauty—that is all ye know on earth, and all ye need to know," that is the whole of aesthetics and on-tology, Keats had a right to assert. Wherever a man believes, faith solves such problems at a single stroke. Haecker, however, was right too when, with profound discernment, he said that beauty is partly more and partly less than truth.[4] What else can this mean if not that

corrected it too and have said that the same infinite light was the realm from which Christ had descended. [Editor.]

4. Theodor Haecker's exact words are: "The beautiful seems to be at once more and less than the true and the good." His explanation is this: The beautiful is what is pleasing to the eye, the eye of the body, the eye of the soul. Now, it seems

truth and beauty are like two equal leaves which have shifted; the upper edge of the one projects as does the lower edge of the other, while in their main parts the two leaves are identical, *sola ratione differentes.* This is said, of course, only of that beauty which truth, like a seer, sees and experiences in reality, not of that beauty which is merely dreamt of.

Thus it becomes clear why the artist—maker of the beautiful, who, when he creates from things given, in his own way imitates creation from nothing—must reach into a higher world from which he brings down the beautiful. To that realm man is not admitted, for it is the realm of innocence; the child, however, *is* admitted, and the artist, the everlasting child, and also the beasts, but Satan too, at God's express bidding and for the single purpose of temptation.

Obviously, ever since man was expelled from that world, which is the world of paradise, he cannot enter there. With innocence gone, the oneness of love and thought is no more. The adult man is divided: there is in him appetite and thought, and this twainness is ever tempted, in freedom wavering between truth and error. Only in love and in faith—for truth has been announced to man—can he find his way back from this uncertain duality to the original oneness and surety. The beasts have never lost their oneness; in their strength and charm they are as they were created and as they were in paradise. Therefore *they* were with Jesus in the desert, but no man.

This is a second meditation on these six words.

III

FROM philosophical speculation our thoughts return to the picture of Christ in the desert. The Spirit drove Him there that He might prepare Himself: to this the fasting points, for always, before grave decisions, fasting serves to cleanse the body and the soul and to bring the faculties

to be *more* than the true and the good because it is grasped, enjoyed, with immediacy and without effort. It seems more because it is a free gift, given without regard to merit, and in this is like grace. Truly, the graceful is an image of the grace-full. Yet the beautiful seems to be *less* than the true and the good because it speaks exclusively of the Creator's giving love, the torrential overflow of His being, and because it sovereignly bars—or at least appears to ignore—the merit of the creature, indeed of all creation. It seems less because it ignores the use of freedom. For no matter how much toil, indispensable toil, goes into a work of beauty, beauty is not the reward of toil. Toil is the mark of man the pilgrim, but beauty is the anticipation of that heavenly life which is love. See Haecker, *Schönheit: Ein Versuch* (Leipzig: Verlag Jakob Hegner, 1936), pp. 39–59. [Editor.]

to their keenest. And He was led there also to be tempted; this too was planned—as were all things in His life. Hence it cannot have been accidental, nor can it have been incidental, when Mark wrote that "He was with the beasts," and not that "the beasts were with Him." He was with them, as if He had sought them out, as if such was His purpose.

What Jesus meditated on and how He spent His solitude we cannot even surmise unless it is told us. But this we may assume: that there were hours of rest from inward effort, since His was a human nature too, with all its needs. We may picture, then, how He relaxed mind and heart in the company of the beasts and found joy in their trusting love, how they must have pressed around Him, how they may have warmed Him at night.

After all, this would not be without precedent. Of Elijah it is written that ravens fed him while he was hiding near the torrent Cherith (3 Kg 17:3–6). Jonah was swallowed by a great fish and then vomited out on dry land (Jon 2).[5] And no harm came to Daniel from the lions when he was thrown into their pit (Dan 6:16–23). But with Christ there begins a beautiful line of animals close to the saints and, as it were, part of them: the fish that listened to the sermon of St. Anthony of Padua, the unicorn of St. Justina, and, above all, St. Francis' brother ass, brother ox, and brother dog, to which he was tender with a tenderness embracing the entire world of beasts and plants, the whole of creation. It is a new language that is spoken here, and it has its start with the words: "And He was with the beasts."

The Old Testament contains a number of precepts for the protection of animals, and later interpretation has underlined them. Still, there is no doubt that the orthodox Jew, today as in the past, keeps animals at a distance, like something unclean, and that he feels them utterly alien to himself. The Christian mind here is quite different from the Jewish,

---

5. The story of Jonah and the great fish makes the modern reader either smile condescendingly or squirm in embarrassment. There is no need for either attitude. Without pausing to discuss the arguments of those commentators who consider the story "inspired fiction," much like Christ's parables, it should be noted first of all that many writers on whaling are loath to discard it as an impossibility. A sperm whale, such as is to be found in the Mediterranean, can swallow whole a shark far larger than a man, they claim, and give instances in point. Moreover, a case has been recorded of a sailor lost overboard and found alive the next day in the stomach of a captured sperm whale. Still it remains wondrous how Jonah, a prophet fleeing the burden of his mission, was heard in his affliction and preserved for his prophetic destiny: first to preach God's justice to the Ninevites and then, reluctant again, to learn the "evangelical" lesson of His mercy. [Editor.]

that is, from the orthodox Jewish. In every creature, the Christian sees
not only a special idea embodied but a God-made fellow creature entrusted to him to guard.[6]

True, the Egyptians worshipped gods in animal form, or later, gods
with human bodies and animal heads. But these were terrifying gods,
in no way close: they embodied the alien in the beast. The Greeks had
their gods, Zeus above all, assume various animal shapes, and gave each
god and goddess an animal companion. But these animals were mythi-
cal, not real. Man's simple, matter-of-fact relationship to the beast, not
as to a fabulous being but as to a co-creature, a member of that creation
which he lovingly embraces in its entirety, has appeared only in the
Christian world. It was this Christian world—was it not?—that abolished slavery. And just as every kind of slavery is growing more and
more intolerable to our feelings, so this open relationship to creation
conforms to them ever more nearly as time passes: one is closely linked
to the other.

It is not too much to say that Western man's feeling for nature has
its pattern in St. Mark's account: Jesus, while making decisions of greatest import, is with spirits, beings of the higher order of creation, and yet,
at the same time, dwells with its lower realm, embodied in the beasts.
Here is only a hint. Christ's teaching is more explicit and more easily
understood when we hear His own words, particularly when He says:
"Look at the birds of the air: they do not sow, or reap, or gather into
barns; yet your heavenly Father feeds them. Are not you of much more

6. Though a certain remoteness from animals may be part of the *Weltgefühl*
of orthodox Jewry, Friedrich Pater's statement seems too sweeping when one remembers, for instance, that Jewish legend has the animals eat from the hands of
Adam and Eve. As they were tame before the fall of man, so, tradition holds,
they will be tame again in messianic times. Further, since it is Jewish belief that
the universe was created for the glory of God, legend endows the beasts with the
power to sing His praise. The cock, for example, is made to crow seven times,
each time reciting a verse such as these: "Lift up, ye everlasting doors, and the
King of glory shall come in," or: "I have waited for thy salvation, O Lord," or:
"How long wilt thou sleep, O sluggard?" and finally: "It is time to work for the
Lord, for they have made void thy law." The lion is said to roar: "The Lord shall
go forth as a mighty man," and the fox to cry woe to those that build their house
on injustice. Even the mute fish proclaims that the voice of the Lord is upon the
waters. While the mouse sees itself as the image of the wicked and praises the
justice of God's punishment, the cat sings: "Let everything that hath breath praise
the Lord. Praise ye the Lord." (See Louis Ginzberg, *The Legends of the Jews*,
trans. H. Szold, Philadelphia: Jewish Publication Society of America, 1942, I, 44–
46.) To be sure, this does not prove that orthodox Jews look on animals as loved
and loving *companions;* the fact, however, that sacred words are put into their
mouths shows that they are not considered irrelevant to God's plan for man.
[Editor.]

value than they?" (Mt 6:26). And again: "Are not two sparrows sold for a farthing? And yet not one of them will fall to the ground without your Father's leave. But as for you, the very hairs of your head are all numbered. Therefore do not be afraid; you are of more value than many sparrows" (Mt 10:29–31).

What clearly marks off the Western way of looking at the world from the Eastern, above all from Hinduism—so often proposed to us as a tutor—is measure and order. It is they that distinguish the West from the East with its exuberance and its lack of limits. The sparrows are, as we are, creatures of God; they are borne up, as we are, by His love, and kept from falling. But there is a hierarchical order of being, and man is the head of earthly creation, of more value than the beasts. There can be no doubt about it: as his fellow creatures, they are not unclean to him; but in rank they are beneath him and, like the whole earth, given into his charge.

The Western spirit is thus equally removed from the two attitudes of which we have spoken: the estrangement from nature of orthodox Judaism, and the exuberance of the East, which sees all creatures as peers among peers and would like to see them vanish in the allness of nature. Distinction and order are the marks of that spirit which, in love, embraces nature but which knows man to be separate from it and superior to it by reason of the mind that dwells in him. While for the East man must dissolve and become one with the All, for the West man must find himself; and it is just by giving himself to his neighbor, to concrete concerns, that he becomes himself, the irreplaceable personality, the one who is truly the image of his one and only Creator.

From the difference between these two frames of mind there can be derived and explained, I think, the difference between Western architecture and sculpture and its Eastern counterpart, unrestrained and overladen. The Western cathedral, too, had affixed to its façade fabulous beasts and chimeras as waterspouts or ornaments. But they fit into a meaningful order as subordinate details, and, undistracted, the statues of angels and saints gazed beyond them.

IV

IT PROVES little against the truth of Christian principles that precisely the Western world has sinned grievously against animals and harmless primitive peoples, and that it has spread havoc among them that cannot be undone. On the contrary, are not the ever more bitter sufferings which have come as a judgment upon the white race like an avenging for these devastations, inevitably brought about by the disregard of those very principles? I found this thought well put in the greeting a cobbler in my dear home town sent to his friends one Christmas. Its Czech words are still in my memory; translated they might be something like this: "Not till men rank all living creatures, down to the last worm, among their relatives, will we be on the sure road to peace."

Indeed, what could bring men—above all, what could bring children—closer to all creation, and what could teach them more effectively to be considerate and peaceful, than companionship with defenseless beasts? For the abyss between us and the rest of creation is bridged over by our feeling for domestic animals, which are constantly around us and which, time and again, astonish us by their good nature and their helpfulness to one another. How impoverished we should be if these companions of our workaday life and of our leisure did not speak to our hearts except through that usefulness without which no member can fill its place in a community!

I should like to bring this meditation to a close with a very personal memory. Though it is something that is not uncommon and may seem hardly worth telling, it meant much to me, for it disclosed to me the meaning of those six words of St. Mark which, before, I had simply passed over, as do so many others. It all started when the big gray cat which had made our house and garden in Haifa her hunting ground searched on our balcony for a place for her kittening. In a little while, six kittens were looking timidly up out of a cardboard carton from behind the shelter of their mother. Bravely and devotedly she brought them up, though a little white one got lost, and another, a blue-gray, turned out to be stunted in its growth. Otherwise it seemed normal, and we soon made it our pet, feeding it the best bits from our table. It became very friendly and delighted us with its graceful ways, so that we took it to our hearts.

But every day, the symptoms of an inner disorder became more visible, and it was clear that the little animal would not live long. It began to refuse even the tastiest bits of food, and grew apathetic, while its belly swelled more and more. But its head, with its great yellow eyes, still looked grave and precocious, as the faces of dwarfs often do. Indeed, we called it "Dwarf" or "Bat," for it was no bigger than a bat.

Once, when it had grown very weak, our little kitten tried to jump as usual onto a kitchen chair. It failed, fell to the floor, and stayed there for a long time, trembling. This must have been a critical point in its brief life. A little later—it was our first clear day after a long siege of rain—I took it out into the sunshine, where it liked to warm itself. It looked at me searchingly, as if to ask whether I was going to catch it and take it into the house, as I usually did. But I felt it had something in mind, and so waited to see where it would turn. Sure enough, it picked itself up and walked with quick unswerving steps to a low wall of earth and rocks, crudely built by Arabs a long time ago. This garden wall was full of holes, and the kitten, going straight to one of them, tried to squeeze inside. However, the opening was not quite big enough for the swollen body to follow the head and shoulders. So with its frail legs braced against the ground, the kitten forced its way into the wall—the hole must have been larger inside than it appeared. I watched in silence. I knew this was the last time I should see the kitten alive; and the other little cats seemed to feel the same, for they looked on as motionless as I. Respecting the kitten's decision, I let it do as it wanted. We never saw it again.

Now, I had heard that animals about to die seek out inaccessible places in which to hide and perish, and that therefore one sees so few animal bodies in the open. This may explain, but it in no way degrades, the incident—no, the action—of the little animal, which went to its death with firmness and dignity.

How great must be the glory of God if even the gentle gleam it sheds on a poor cat is so majestic! How great His dignity if even its faintest reflection in a little beast keeps us at a distance and in awe! How great His goodness if it gives us such joy through an animal so ordinary, so lavishly prolific!

No king entering his mausoleum has ever gathered his mantle about himself with better bearing. Not even the Hasmonean Berenice, daughter and granddaughter of queens, whose walk was the enchantment of the world—when she descended the staircase of the palace, the people burst into jubilant cries, as if applauding an artist—not even Berenice was more beautiful than this wretched beast. Straining its feeble limbs, it withdrew into a stony wall that it might die in solitude, return its little body—hide, hair, and dimmed eyes—to the bosom of the earth, and enter the great darkness of the night.

From there may God's voice one day call us all, all, back into His presence. Amen.

SURVEYS

Edward H. Flannery

HOPE AND DESPAIR AT EVANSTON

ON AUGUST 27, 1954, at Evanston, Illinois, the Second Assembly of the World Council of Churches voted 195 to 150 to strike from a statement on "Christ—the Hope of the World" any reference to Israel's part in Christian hope. This, the most turbulent session of the seventeen-day Assembly, was, at the same time, one of the most important, for it represented a great ecumenical victory in that 162 denominations from forty-two countries succeeded in affirming in theological terms their unity in Christ as the sole hope of mankind. It was also the session that witnessed the sharpest divisions and educed the strongest negative emotions. Strangely, the reef on which the concord of the Assembly was shaken was the people of Israel.

The conflict was largely unforeseen and came as a painful revelation to most of the 1,242 delegates and participants. There was rapid fire from several quarters against affirming a special connection between the destiny of the people of Israel and the fulfillment of the Christian hope, as well as against affirming any special obligation to bring the gospel to Israel. Political, sociological, and scriptural issues were raised, and soon the discussion became hopelessly ensnarled. The vote was taken, the references scotched, and the question recommended for further study. Two days later the Second Assembly closed, with little prospect of an early resolution of the problem that had so shaken it.

It will not be unprofitable, nor ungracious I trust, for a Catholic to study this failure of the World Council to resolve a question which tests the metal of our theologies, of our moral attitudes, and of much of our thinking.

THE MAIN THEME

A FIFTY-PAGE Report on the Assembly's Main Theme, "Christ—the Hope of the World," was presented at Evanston as the fruit of three years of study by an Advisory Commission, made up of some thirty theologians and churchmen of high rank, such as Karl Barth, Emil Brunner, Reinhold Niebuhr, and Charles Malik. The Commission had met in three major sessions to draft a "common word on the Christian Hope as the result of genuinely ecumenical encounter." [1] Its first efforts were marked by extensive disagreement, yet in the end a Report signed by all members was handed over to the Executive Committee of the World Council.

On August 15, the first Sunday of the Assembly, the Report, published four months previously, was formally presented to the plenary body by Edmund Schlink, rector of the University of Heidelberg, and Professor Robert L. Calhoun of Yale, both members of the Advisory Commission. Their addresses offered interesting contrasts. The standpoint of the Continental theologian was frankly biblical and eschatological: "Christ is the end of the world," he said. He is our hope because He liberates us from all binding ties to it. Christian hope begins where human hope leaves off, in His second coming. Speaking for those for whom earthly hope had failed, mostly Europeans who had seen Nazism and Communism at work, Professor Schlink told his listeners that the apocalyptic passages of the New Testament "illuminate the whole of human life and the situation of the Christian in the world and become a definite stronghold, by means of which God makes it possible for man to live, to suffer and to die joyfully." Professor Calhoun, a Congregationalist, spoke rather of temporal hope, of the gospel as "a word for this world." He was the spokesman for those of "activist" temper, mostly Americans influenced by the "social gospel," with its emphasis on the value of the human person, on the brotherhood of men, and on love as a social force. "We must conceive of Christian hope," he declared, "primarily as assurance that our best efforts will succeed, with God's help." [2] Here was the tension that had marked the discussions of the Advisory Commission and that would mark the deliberations of the Committees and the sessions of the Assembly.

For the most part, reaction was in Professor Calhoun's favor. Evanston, obviously, was too thriving an American community to serve as a setting for Professor Schlink's eschatological message. Already it was

1. "Report of the Advisory Commission on the Main Theme," p. v; in *The Christian Hope and the Task of the Church* (New York: Harper, 1954).

2. See *The Christian Century*, August 25, 1954, pp. 1004, 1006; *Time*, August 30, 1954, p. 64.

clear that the Assembly's mood was optimistic and somehow modernist, suited rather to the temperament of many of the Americans and Anglo-Saxons present than to the more somber view of the Continentals, and in a way foretelling the vote the Assembly would take on Israel.

The Report on the Main Theme is a lengthy statement, rhetorical in style and homiletic in genre. Divided into three sections, "Christ Our Hope," "Christ and His People," and "Christ and the World," it makes these chief points:

1. Christian hope is centered in Christ crucified and risen, in Him who has "overcome the world," all the powers of evil, sin, and death. It cannot be spoken of unless judgment and repentance are spoken of too, for it stands under the sign of the Cross. No mere extension or reaffirmation of human desires, it looks forward to where human hopes end—to the end of this world and to the kingdom to come.

The story of Christian hope is told in the Scriptures. The Old Testament recounts its coming forth from God the Creator and its growth in Israel. Men gripped by God's promise and possessed by His Spirit foretold that the Messiah would come to redeem mankind from sin; and none of Israel's failings could deter God from His plan. The New Testament announces that the promised Deliverer has come, whose life, death, and resurrection have brought a new life, a new community, and a new hope.

In one sense, Christian hope has already been fulfilled. In Christ, history is transfigured; a new humanity and a new age, the reign of the Spirit, has begun. By the power of the Spirit, the Christian can surmount suffering and triumph over evil. His hope, then, is fulfilled, but not fully; it is a having and a hoping.

A pilgrim, he must carry on the warfare of the flesh and the spirit. Hence a twofold temptation assails him: to give too much attention to this life or to stand aloof from it. It is by faith and fellowship that he shall be victorious. "A true index of our having and hoping is given to us in the sacrament which under various names—Lord's Supper, Holy Communion, Eucharist, Mass—is common to the whole Church." [3]

Fulfilled and yet expectant, the Christian's hope looks to the future. He knows that the pure in heart shall see God as He is, that in a new heaven and a new earth the dead shall rise, and that the holy city shall appear. But he does not know at what moment his hope shall be realized, so he must watch and pray. To hope for the coming Day is

3. Here, as all through the Report, it is the voice of Protestant theologians that is heard. For the Catholic, the difference is greater than one of name.

not to say that earthly endeavors and hope are vain. The consummation of all things "means neither that the history of this world will be swept aside as irrelevant, nor that our efforts will be finally crowned with success."

2. The one concrete result in history of the tremendous Event comprising the incarnation, ministry, death, and resurrection of Jesus Christ, is the Christian Church, which bears responsibility for the world for which Christ died. A historical society, living among other societies in the world, the Church is yet not of the world. By proclaiming the gospel, by worship and sacraments, by its fellowship in the Holy Spirit, it carries on the work of Christ. Its members are members of Him and yet frail, ignorant, and sinful men. For this reason it ever stands under the judgment of God and in need of forgiveness. It fails particularly when its members are self-righteous or arrogate to themselves the things that await them only at the end of the way. Its task is to preach the gospel to all men without exception, and its mission, therefore, is "the most important thing that is happening in history."

The Church is essentially one, and yet its unity is concealed, even mocked, by the many divisions between and within the various Christian communions. A scandal, the divided state of the Church hinders its missionary effort to gather all men into unity. Hence each denomination must examine itself to find what steps could be taken toward greater unity. The Church is also holy, but, always tempted to settle down among secular societies, it must live in humility and penitence and be constantly renewed in Christ until the final victory.[4]

3. A divine purpose overarches the whole of the world's history, and because God is its Lord, Christians must reject the doctrines of automatic progress or of fated decline. But though God is history's Lord, human responsibility has a part to play, and human misuse of knowledge and power complicate the flow of history. Men have their own hopes and plans, which do not always take the divine plan into account, and in so far as they do not, they are deceptive and misleading. It is the task of the Church to sift what is truth from what is deception in them.

In this age of encircling despair, there are many hopes around which

4. This, the best of modern Protestant thinking on the Church, does not square at every point with the Catholic vision of the Church. A Catholic would never say that the Church is under the judgment of God, even though he is painfully aware that he and his fellow members are. Nor would he, in his sorrow over the divisions among Christians, declare that Christian unity is hidden. To him it is manifest in the Catholic Church. On these points, see the statement by Catholic theologians quoted in the closing section of this survey, "Catholic Response."

men rally, but four of them seem to be representative. Democratic human-ism, scientific humanism, Marxism, and Nationalism hold out glowing promises. All such secular hopes doubtlessly include partial truths and possibilities, yet, promising too much, they are interlarded with illusion and evil. To those in their grip, the Church must demonstrate that the gospel alone can conserve what is best in them and add what is lack-ing. "The Church needs to be warned against clouding its witness and neglecting its present duty by a disproportionate emphasis on other-worldly hopes."

To those who have abandoned hope and become embittered by in-justice and suffering, as to the atheistic "existentialists," who have re-nounced hope in favor of despair, the answer is the same: Jesus Christ, who "has plumbed the depths of human existence as no one else, [who has] passed through the darkest night of the human soul . . . before rising victorious," is the hope of all without exception. Hence the Chris-tian, in his daily work, in social and political action, is to bring this hope to all, especially to those lacking the necessities of life, to the ignorant, to the godless. Serving Christ in serving them, he will strive to bring them justice, freedom, truth, and peace. "The life of service lived in Christ is therefore a life of unquenchable hope." [5]

Such is the Christian hope as described in the Report on the Main Theme. Immediately after its presentation to the Assembly, the Report was handed over for study and criticism to the delegates, divided into fifteen study groups, which discussed it in four two-hour sessions during the following several days. After this it was passed on to a Co-ordinat-ing Committee, made up of the secretaries and chairmen of the study groups, who brought with them the recommendations of their respec-tive groups. From these recommendations, the Co-ordinating Commit-tee, under the chairmanship of Bishop Hanns Lilje of Hanover, evolved a Statement designed to serve as an introduction and a corrective to the Report on its final trip to the floor of the Assembly and from there to the member churches themselves.

In the hands of the study groups the Report met with considerable criticism. Few rejected or accepted it in its entirety. Many felt that a "note of joyous affirmation and radiant expectancy" was missing. Some wished that a strong solidarity toward non-Christian religions had been

5. This condensation of the Report uses, as far as sentence structure allows, the words of the Report itself, whose complete text may be found in *The Christian Hope and the Task of the Church.*

emphasized; others did not. Again, some found too sharp a distinction drawn between the Church and the world. But the brunt of the criticism bore on the failure of the Report to include Israel in the perspective of Christian hope. To understand what happened in the study groups and on the floor of the Assembly on this subject, we must retrace our steps.

THE DEBATE ON ISRAEL

THE debate on Israel's destiny at the Plenary Session of the Assembly was not planned but adventitious. Yet from the time that the World Council of Churches first met at Amsterdam in 1948, a series of events converged on Evanston, in such manner, we now see in retrospect, as to render the flare-up on the floor of the Assembly all but inevitable.

FORESHADOWS

At Amsterdam, the World Council had received—but not adopted—a pronouncement on Israel which recommended that the member churches include the Jewish people in their evangelistic work, and which told of the need to study the causes of and remedies for anti-Semitism, the opportunities to co-operate with Jews in social and civic affairs, and the many questions raised by the creation of the new state of Israel.[6] The Council resolved that "the Assembly recognizes the need for more detailed study . . . of the many complex problems which exist in the field of relations between Christians and Jews."[7]

The Assembly's resolution found echo in several quarters of the Protestant ecumenical world. Without delay the Committee on the Christian Approach to the Jews, a branch of the International Missionary Council of the World Council, set to work on a symposium on the relations of Judaism and Christianity. The results were published in 1954 in *The Church and the Jewish People,* under the editorship of Göte Hedenquist, a Lutheran pastor, director of this Committee. It was an important pioneering effort. Not only did its authors fulfill the directives of Amsterdam but they probed some of the deeper theological prob-

6. The complete text of the Amsterdam "Report on the Christian Approach to the Jews," of which these recommendations are a part, can be found in *The Church and the Jewish People,* ed. by Göte Hedenquist (London: Edinburgh House Press, 1954), pp. 201–205.

7. *Ibid.,* p. 5.

lems binding and separating Israel and Christianity. It was their hope
that their reflections would offer a stimulus to discussion at the oncoming
Evanston Assembly.

From 1951 to 1953, the Advisory Commission on the Main Theme
and the various Preparatory Commissions [8] drafted their reports and surveys. None of them came to grips with the question of Israel in any
form whatever. The Commission on the Main Theme, we have seen,
was content to allude to Israel's function in preparing the path for the
Gospel by Law and Prophets, but made no reference to its possible
relation to the Christian future, to Christian hope. So also the Committee on Intergroup Relations, which acknowledged Israel's place of
privilege under the Old Covenant but emphasized rather the oneness of
the human race in the New Dispensation, in which "there is neither Jew
nor Greek." [9] In its Survey, this Commission specifically excluded an
"explicit treatment of anti-Semitism, principally because this question
involves other issues of such depth and scope as to place a full consideration of it outside the bounds of a discussion on race." [10] In its Resolutions, however, this Commission did affirm its opposition to anti-
Semitic prejudice as "incompatible with Christian faith," and recommended to the Central Committee that study of the problem be pressed
forward in conjunction with the Committee on the Christian Approach
to the Jews.[11] At one moment during the deliberations of the Commission on Evangelism, the possibility of making special mention of Israel
was entertained, but it was then abandoned as a problem too special for
its survey. The other Commissions maintained a hands-off policy on
the subject.

Some efforts were made to combat this timidity toward the question of
Israel's hope. Most notable was doubtless that of a group of students working under Karl Barth, theologian of Basel and member of the
Advisory Commission on the Main Theme; their memorandum was
circulated among the delegates at Evanston but, it seems, never published. Entitled "The Hope of Israel," it deals with the problem under

8. The Preparatory Commissions dealt with the six topics planned for consideration, other than the Main Theme: Faith and Order, Evangelism, Social Questions, International Affairs, Intergroup Relations, The Laity.

9. "Intergroup Relations," pp. 25–33; in *The Christian Hope and the Task of
the Church.*

10. *Ibid.,* p. 2.

11. *The Evanston Report,* ed. by W. A. Visser 't Hooft (New York: Harper,
1955), p. 159.

six points. The first three see Israel as the people of hope: It is messianic hope, the expectation of the kingdom, that is the life of Israel,
that gives unity and meaning to its history, that yields the secret of its
preservation. In spite of their purely political origin, Zionism and the
state of Israel must be taken as a sign of the vitality of this hope in our
day. The Messiah has come, and with Him, the memorandum continues
in the fourth point, the pardon, the peace, and the kingdom of God.
But He was rejected and crucified by His people. (It is disappointing
to note that here the Barthian memorandum seems to place the responsibility on all Jews, past and present.) Because of the sin of rejection,
the promise of God has been transferred to the Church. Still, Israel's
election remains, and if the Church is to be alive to its own hope, it
must keep alive its interest in the Jewish people. This is the fifth point,
while the last shows that Christian hope cannot find its fulfillment unless Israel returns to Christ. Hence the Church must announce its hope
to the Jews and, by its whole existence, bear witness to it. Yet their
coming into the Church will be the work of none other than Christ
Himself.[12]

The points of this memorandum were amplified by Göte Hedenquist,
who gave a précis of Barth's views on Israel as contained in his Dogmatic Theology. What follows here is extracted from this précis, aided
by reference to Barth's own text.

There is only one, everlasting Israel in the Old and in the New Testaments, one Israel with one Lord. The people of Israel, before and after
the birth of Christ, and the Christian Church, become visible on Pentecost, are two forms, two aspects, of the one, inseparable communion in
which Jesus Christ has His existence in earthly history. Jesus is in one
person Israel's crucified Messiah (and as such the hidden Lord of the
Church) and also the risen Lord of the Church (and as such no other
than the revealed Messiah of Israel). Though the old and the new Is-
raels are two aspects, two "economies," of the one grace of God, there
is only one history, beginning in the old, having its center in Jesus
Christ, and hastening toward its goal in the new. Israel, as the chosen
people of God, is potentially also the Church for the world, as the
Christian Church of Jews and of Gentiles is still only a little Israel surrounded by the nations of the world.

From the days of the apostles, the Church has understood itself as a

12. See Paul Démann, N.D.S., "Israël à Evanston," *Cahiers Sioniens*, IX, 1
(March 1955), p. 63.

Church of Jews and Gentiles, and as the "Israel of God" (Gal 6:16). Were one to deny this unity, one would deny Jesus Christ Himself. The very existence of the Synagogue alongside the Church is an ontological impossibility, a wound, indeed a void, in the Body of Christ, which is utterly intolerable. Does this create a "Jewish question"? Does it not rather pose a question to Christians? Can they rest as long as an estranged, opposite Israel faces the Church? "Jewish missions" is really not the right word for the call to abolish the separation, a call which, without ceasing, ought to go forth from the Church to those brethren not yet recognizing their unity with it.[13]

Pastor Hedenquist's summary was part of an address given on August 8, just a few days before the Evanston Assembly. This was the opening day of a four-day conference at Lake Geneva, Wisconsin, which the American branch of the Committee on the Christian Approach to the Jews had convoked with a view to studying the problem of Israel's hope in the light of the Evanston Main Theme, "Christ—the Hope of the World." The proceedings of this Conference were the furthest evolved position Protestant theology had taken on the question of Israel. Two excerpts from addresses by the German-born Franz von Hammerstein and the Austrian-born Dr. Frederick Neumann, both engaged in pastoral work in the United States, elucidate the position taken:

Israel has a special place in God's Revelation. Even today it keeps this place. There is no final hope for the Church without the Jews, without Israel. Therefore we should not only love Israel, but know it and try to understand it better than we do.[14]

Our destiny as a Church is in a mysterious way bound up with the destiny of God's Old Covenant people. Before the full number of Jewish musicians have joined in, the eternal kingdom orchestra cannot start performing the jubilant symphony of the love of God in Christ, the Redeemer of all. It can only do some rehearsing.[15]

The Conference concluded by issuing a set of resolutions which summarized its findings and was distributed among the participants in the Evanston Assembly four days later. It read in part:

13. This summary is drawn from Hedenquist in *The Christian Approach to the Jews,* Addresses Delivered at the Pre-Evanston Conference (New York: National Council of the Churches of Christ in the U.S.A., 1954), pp. 4–5; and from Karl Barth, *Die Kirchliche Dogmatik,* IV/1 (Zurich: Evangelischer Verlag, 1953), pp. 747–749.
14. *The Christian Approach to the Jews,* p. 31.
15. *Ibid.,* p. 92.

The Christian hope cannot be fully comprehended without relation to the hope of Israel, manifested not only in the Old Testament, but also in God's continuous dealings with the Jewish people. The existence of the Synagogue and of the Jewish witness to the God of Abraham after two thousand years of Christian history is a challenge to the Church. The Church cannot rest until the title of Christ to the Kingdom is recognized by His own people according to the flesh.[16]

This Conference recognizes the urgent and imperative need for a united work of Christian witness in the new State of Israel, calls the attention of the Churches in the United States and Canada to the immediate opportunity for evangelism in this new State.[17]

Amsterdam to Evanston, then, was not a path of rectilinear progress toward a clear and common formulation of Israel's place in Christian hope. Contrariwise, the seeds of conflict were unwittingly being sown. On one side, the Preparatory Commissions were markedly reluctant to include the people of Israel in their Reports and Surveys; on the other, the Committee on the Christian Approach to the Jews and the followers of Karl Barth called vigorously and insistently for Israel's inclusion. The lines seemed drawn. But no one as yet suspected the troubles ahead.

DEBATE ON THE FLOOR

Acting on complaints made in the fifteen study groups that the Report on the Main Theme did not allude to Israel's hope—complaints inspired by the findings of the Lake Geneva conference and by the Barthian memorandum—the Co-ordinating Committee, under Bishop Lilje, suggested two references to the people of Israel. The first spoke of the need for a "statement of the New Testament concept of the ultimate fulfillment of God's promises to the people of ancient Israel and the consequent special responsibility of the Christian Church for the proclamation of the hope in Christ to the Jews." The second declared: "The Christian concern for the Jewish people, scattered over the whole world, is a sign of hope. It was the hope of ancient Israel which was fulfilled in the coming of Christ. His Church cannot rest until the title of Christ to the kingdom is recognized by the people among whom He came in the flesh." [18]

16. *Ibid.,* p. 127.
17. *Ibid.,* p. 128.
18. See Robert Smith, "Israel at Evanston," *The International Review of Missions,* XLIV, 174 (April 1955), p. 200.

On August 25, in his presentation to the plenary Assembly of the Report on the Main Theme, Bishop Lilje emphasized that in asserting the Christian hope, there must not be left unmentioned the biblical witness to the bond between Israel's fate and the consummation of that hope. Nevertheless, it was not long before a barrage of criticism came down on the two rather timid references to Israel. The first to speak was Bishop W. H. Stewart, a Church of England prelate from the Old City of Jerusalem, who charged that they were superfluous, since by His death Christ was the hope of the whole world without distinction. After him, Dr. Aziz Sorial Atiya, president of the Higher Institute for Coptic Studies in Cairo, took the floor and pleaded with the Assembly to strike them out, for fear that they might be interpreted as an approval of the new state of Israel. Bishop Lilje answered that, while political interpretations must be avoided, the issue was too important to be omitted. A resolution was passed to amend the Statement and present it again to the Assembly on Friday, the 27th.

For a nonparticipant, the sequence of events on Friday is hard to follow. Two exciting sessions were held, one in the afternoon, one in the evening. In general, those opposing any reference to Israel were divided into two camps. Arab Christians, including the Coptic Orthodox churches, the Orthodox Patriarchate of Antioch, and the evangelical churches of Syria and Lebanon, fearing political implications in the references, wanted them dropped in their entirety. They were joined by Charles P. Taft, mayor of Cincinnati and one of the most outstanding Protestant laymen in the United States. In the spirit of the "good will" movement, he called for the deletion of the second half of the first reference: ". . . the consequent special responsibility of the Christian Church for the proclamation of the hope in Christ to the Jews." "I think," he said, "it would jeopardize my friendships and my relations with my Jewish friends." [19] Bishop Angus Dun, an American Episcopalian prelate, sided with Charles Taft.

The situation was not without its touch of irony. Orthodox and fundamentalist Arab Christians struggled side by side with American "activists" in an effort to prevent European eschatologists from affirming Israel's place in Christian hope. Philo-Semites, anxious not to offend Jews, worked hand in hand with anti-Zionists who, more than anything else, feared giving help to the new state of Israel. The alliance was an uneasy one, yet effective and marked for success.

19. See *Time*, September 6, 1954, p. 42.

Tense moments were not the scarcest commodity at the Friday sessions. Dr. Farid Audeh of Beirut, president of the Council of the Evangelical Churches of Syria, pleaded with the Assembly not to aggravate the difficulties of Christians in the Near East, and had some hard words for the state of Israel which put the entire body ill at ease. A cablegram from Dr. Charles Malik, Lebanese ambassador to the United Nations, sent after his departure from Evanston, had a strong effect on everyone. In what seems a misreading of the text and tenor of the references, a misapprehension probably engendered by the third point of the Barthian memorandum, he declared in part that while there undoubtedly was in the Bible a profound aspiration to see the Jews return to the Cross and to recognize Jesus as the Messiah, this authentic aspiration did not have the least relevance to the state of Israel or the return of the Jews to Palestine.[20] A second talk by Bishop Stewart, who resides in the Kingdom of Jordan, had an anti-Israel flavor, disturbing to many. A calmer address by Dr. Atiya had a quietening influence; it was, nonetheless, a very effective plea for deletion of the references.

There was little doubt at this point where matters stood. The opponents of the references had drawn considerable applause. Many neutral delegates, especially Americans, were swayed by the violence of the opposition; rather than chance a rift in the Assembly, they threw their support against retaining the references. Those who favored them, mostly Continental churchmen with their grieved memories of Hitler's persecution of the Jews, were thunderstruck. Unaccustomed to the political view taken in the Assembly, they saw in it a new form of anti-Semitism; not having counted on this turn of events, they seemed at a loss as to what to do. They appeared as if hypnotized, it was said; [21] actually, they were scandalized, but were unable to find a foothold against the wave of opposition rapidly assuming tidal dimensions. At last, Dr. H. Berkhof, a Dutch Reformed pastor, took the stand and explained that the question was not political but biblical and was based on St. Paul's Epistle to the Romans. The people of Israel, he declared, has not been finally rejected by God. Robert Smith, editor of the *Quarterly News Sheet of the Christian Approach to the Jews,* spoke in the same vein. Applause rose from the German, French, and Swiss sections.

20. See Démann, *loc. cit.,* p. 66.
21. *Quarterly News Sheet of the Christian Approach to the Jews,* XXIV, 4 (December 1954), p. 4.

The moment for a ballot had arrived. Votes were cast in an over-charged atmosphere and had to be counted three times, so great was the confusion. The result was clear, however: by a vote of 195 to 150 the Assembly had repudiated the allusions to Israel's part in Christian hope. Immediately after the vote Dr. Franklin Clark Fry, sensing the confusion of many delegates, called, in the name of a group of Lutheran delegates, "for further study and ecumenical conversations" on the issue. Bishop Stewart objected to this motion, but it was carried anyway—a poor consolation for the defeated forces.

The last word had not yet been spoken. On Saturday morning, some of the delegates who had been in favor of the references gathered to draft a minority declaration. That evening, before the plenary Assembly, Dr. Joseph Sittler of the Lutheran seminary at Maywood, Illinois, read their declaration, which bore the signatures of twenty-four outstanding theologians from England, Scotland, France, Holland, Norway, Germany, Austria, Hungary, Switzerland, Canada, and the United States— it is perhaps not unimportant to note that six of them were from this country. The signers stated that their concern was wholly biblical and should not be confused with any political position taken toward the state of Israel, and then continued:

We believe that Jesus Christ is the Saviour of all mankind. In Him there is neither Jew nor Greek; but we also believe that God elected Israel for the carrying out of His saving purpose. Jesus Christ as Man was a Jew. The Church of Jesus Christ is built upon the foundation of the Apostles and Prophets, all of whom were Jews, so that to be a member of the Christian Church is to be involved with the Jews in our one indivisible hope in Jesus Christ. . . . Whether we are scandalized or not . . . we are grafted into the old tree of Israel (Rom 11:24), so that the people of the New Covenant cannot be separated from the people of the Old Covenant. . . . Our hope in Christ's coming victory includes our hope for Israel in Christ, in His victory over the blindness of His own people. To expect Jesus Christ means to hope for the conversion of the Jewish people, and to love Him means to love the people of God's promise. In view of the grievous guilt of Christian people towards the Jews throughout the history of the Church, we are certain that: "The Church cannot rest until the title of Christ to the Kingdom is recognized by His own people according to the flesh." [22]

22. *The Evanston Report*, pp. 327–328. The quotation which closes this excerpt is from the Findings of the Pre-Evanston Conference.

AFTERMATH

Reaction to the Assembly's vote was widespread and varied. Some critics were optimistic and tended to make light of it; others were bitter and aggrieved. Generally, the decision was not considered a repudiation of the stand taken at Amsterdam; it was clear indication, however, that little progress had been made since then. The *Quarterly News Sheet* advised against interpreting the vote as a denial of the biblical basis of Israel's hope, preferring to see it as the result of a failure to recognize what was at stake. But the same magazine termed the event a "false compromise." [23] Both anti-Semites and philo-Semites fail to understand the mystery of Israel and the hope of Israel; for both, Israel is a worldly power, Pastor Berkhof charged. But he too warned against reading too much into the vote, deeming that some progress had been made in the very fact that the issue had become a major one on the Assembly's agenda.[24] Hendrik van Oyen, a Calvinist theologian of Basel, was not so content with what had happened: he described the debate as a significant defeat, a grave defection, and a sad page in contemporary religious history which fills one with shame.[25]

THE SOURCES OF DESPAIR

THESE comments lead us to inquire into why Evanston despaired of coming to a full affirmation of Israel's part in Christian hope. But first a word of warning. There is no reason for a Catholic to be complacent about Evanston's failure.[26] Were a group of Catholics to convene in order to discuss Israel's hope, there might be similar oppositions and embarrassments, nor would they be immune to political passions or emotional influences. Yet we have all reason to assume that in the end a Catholic gathering would decide the issue on a biblical and theological basis; that the "mystery of Israel" would take precedence over political, social, practical considerations.

23. *Quarterly News Sheet*, XXIV, 3 (November 1954), pp. 6–10.
24. *Ibid.*, December 1954, pp. 6–7.
25. See Démann, *loc. cit.*, p. 71.
26. Father C. J. Dumont, in an article in the French Catholic quarterly *Istina*, warns against this course: "Let us not smile too quickly at the difficulties which our non-Catholic brethren meet in an area where we ourselves find it so difficult to rise above similar opposing tendencies" (as reported in *The Ecumenical Review*, VII, 3, April 1955, p. 278).

Though not a defined dogma, the doctrine of Israel's final return to Christ is theologically certain, for it is most firmly anchored in the sources of the Catholic faith. It is the promise of the New Testament as it is the teaching of tradition. St. Thomas gives witness to this when he writes in his Commentary on the Epistle to the Romans:

If God for the benefit of the whole world has permitted the misstep and the dispossession of the Jews, how much more generously will He restore their ruins for the advantage of the whole world. . . . And what will be the effects of their reintegration, if not to call back to life the Gentiles, that is to say the lukewarm faithful, when on account of the progress of iniquity, the charity of a great number shall have waxed cold (Mt 24:12).[27]

It was left to Luther to strike the first discordant note in the harmony of Christian teaching on Israel. In violently anti-Semitic terms he contradicted the belief in its final turning to Christ and dubbed it "foolish" and "groundless." [28]

Yet it was not Luther's deviation which governed the Assembly; indeed, Lutheran theologians were conspicuous among the signers of the minority declaration. This is not to say that theology played no part in the Assembly's decision. True, there can be no question that political considerations were a powerful factor; some think them to have been the most powerful, overriding all others. But this, I fear, is an oversimplification, for, underneath the political lines, the deeper and less visible theological lines were drawn. There were in the main three factions to share the stage. First, there was the Near Eastern bloc, comprising Arab Christians, who adopted a point of view exclusively political and in opposition to the state of Israel. Next, there were the mainly, though by no means exclusively, Continental theologians, who adopted a wholly theological and biblical stand. Lastly, there were the neutrals, mostly Americans and Anglo-Saxons, potential candidates for either of the other factions. This last was the decisive faction, for neither the first nor the

27. *Comm. in Ep. ad Romanos,* xi, 2; as quoted by Jacques Maritain, *The Living Thoughts of St. Paul* (New York: Longmans Green, 1941), pp. 83–84.

28. "A Jew," he wrote, "or a Jewish heart, is as hard as wood, stone, or iron, as hard in fact as the devil himself, and hence cannot be moved by any means. . . . They are young imps condemned to Hell. . . . Those who conclude from the eleventh chapter of St. Paul's Epistle to the Romans that the Jews will all be converted toward the end of the world, are foolish and their opinion is groundless" (*Sämtliche Werke,* Jena ed., VIII, 109; as quoted in Pohle-Preuss, *Dogmatic Theology,* Vol. XII, *Eschatology,* St. Louis: Herder, 1917, p. 106).

second was able by itself to muster sufficient votes for a majority. Two groups made up this neutral faction. The first sided with the Arab Christians through sympathy or fear—fear of causing a split in the Assembly. The second, headed by Charles Taft, was devoted to "good will" as a principle and refused to single out the Jews in any theological context. Both groups combined to throw their weight with the Christians of the Near East to eliminate the references to Israel. It was against this alliance that the terms "compromise" and "opportunism" were hurled by some Protestant critics.

How are we to explain a neutrality which permitted considerations of "good will" or of harmony in the Assembly to overrule all scriptural and theological claims of Israel's hope? Such a neutrality is obviously not a surface manifestation; rather it has its roots in certain modern Protestant theological thinking. To focus our attention only on one school, influential in the United States, that of neo-Reformation theology: such thinkers as Paul Tillich, Reinhold Niebuhr, and H. Richard Niebuhr have molded the outlook of many American Protestants. The point of interest here is what these men think of the nature of Christianity, of the Church, and of Scripture. If I may summarize their common thought in the simplest of terms, I should say that, partly under the influence of Emil Brunner and Karl Barth, they have come to believe in the "total otherness" of God and the radical relativity of everything else, including Christ, the Church, and the Bible. An earlier Protestant liberalism had subjectivized God, and religion generally, reducing Christianity to a mere ethics. In a strong reaction against this kind of liberalism, these thinkers, seeking an absolute objectivity on which to found faith, have swung to the opposite extreme. They have posited this absolute objectivity in God, but in such a way as to declare relative everything else, even everything Christian. Declaring it idolatrous to see in the Church or in the Bible the voice of Truth, they are forced to deny "that the 'Christian religion' is somehow 'true' in an ultimate fashion, somehow less involved in relativism than the 'Jewish religion' "—not to speak of other religions. H. Richard Niebuhr is but being consistent when he draws this inference:

Our problem is one of *conversion* from all the finites in which we believe, of turning from all the idols we worship. . . . When we look at the Jews we cannot desire that they should be converted to our point of view but only that they should be delivered from their idolatries and reconciled to God. . . . The question is one of conversion to God, not to Christianity or to Judaism. Hence our fundamental attitudes with respect to the Jews must be of gratitude, of intercession for them that their faith fail not, of community—of offering them in our confession not the "truth" that Christ is the Messiah, but the statement that Jesus Christ is the one who is reconciling us to God and that it is he whom we expect to triumph, not over Jews so much as over ourselves.[29]

The fate of Scripture in this new relativism is not hard to surmise. Since the Bible must not be "absolutized" as a source of universal and timeless truths, its interpretation must be given a new turn. Its words must not be understood as the Christian past has understood them, but in a way that makes them "meaningful to the man of our age." For Scripture speaks to us in symbols, says Tillich, or, according to Bultmann, in myths. With Rudolf Bultmann, theologian of Marburg, and his demand for *die Entmythologisierung,* the "demythologization" of the Christian faith, the nadir has been reached. For he deprives the sacred text of all real meaning and the revealed word of all objective truth. The New Testament, he tells us, is a product of its time and speaks the language of mythology, unacceptable to our scientific world-view. "Myth" is what he calls the mysteries of Christ's pre-existence, of His virgin birth, of His miracles, of His resurrection, ascension, and return; "myth" too the mysteries of original sin, of redemption through Christ's vicarious sacrifice, of baptism and Eucharist as the means of bringing Christ's saving deed to man. All these, then, have to go. What is left is Jesus' historic existence (and it is little enough that can be known of it, for the sources are choked with legend); His death (no more than a prophet's martyrdom); and faith (which, together with love, is simply native to man, his natural attitude). It is by "faith" that man can escape the world of transitoriness, anguish, and death, by faith in Christ, in whom he encounters the all-embracing love of God. But this Christ is not the Christ of history, the living Christ, only the Christ of "faith." [30]

The neo-Reformation theologians in the United States are certainly not so radical as Bultmann; nonetheless, one finds in them a tending to-

29. From a letter by H. Richard Niebuhr; quoted in A. Roy Eckardt, *Christianity and the Children of Israel* (New York: King's Crown Press, 1948), pp. 130–131.

30. For an exposition of Bultmann's views and a critical evaluation of them from a Catholic standpoint, see, among others, Fritz Hofmann, "Theologie der Entmythologisierung—Ausweg oder Irrweg?", *Theologie und Glaube,* XLIII, 5 (1953), pp. 321–347.

ward his position. But whatever Bultmann's influence may be in Europe or here, and no matter how much weight the theology of Tillich and the Niebuhrs may have carried with the "neutrals" at the Assembly, the new relativism found response among them. Having inquired into representative American Protestant opinion on the problem that so agitated the Assembly, Dr. F. Ernest Johnson reports that there are those "who find in Rom 9–11 a permanent, normative principle that should govern the Christian attitude toward the Jews as a people." The majority, however, seem to consider this position a "narrow biblicism," not meaningful to our day. Some typical comments are:

> [St. Paul's epistles] afford no sound basis upon which to erect a theory of the Church which gives it any such continuity with the Abrahamic covenant as to make the conversion of the 20th-century Jews any more important in the eyes of God than the conversion of Hindus, Chinese—or Anglo-Saxon Americans.

> As I read Romans 11 it is a message of hope for Israel, but I doubt that it ever would have occurred to Paul that Christians centuries later could read his words as guaranteeing the salvation of Israel or placing the Jews' conversion in a different category from that of the Gentiles.

> It is difficult for me to understand the reality of the position based upon Romans. To me the only basis of this point of view must be either Biblical fundamentalism or a sort of ivory tower theology which is removed from the practicalities and exigencies of today. St. Paul faced a definite and practical situation in his day and therefore met it head on. We are faced in our generation with our own situation and cannot find the answer by adopting the answer given many centuries ago.[31]

Here the new relativism has come down to the level of mere practicality. Am I wrong when I conclude that Evanston's failure to speak of hope for Israel in a statement of Christian hope was a failure of Christian hope itself, and at bottom a failure of Christian faith, as it needs must be? For faith is "the substance of things to be hoped for" (Heb 11:1), and hope, conversely, the reflection of the substance of faith. Never can it go beyond the truths that support it. The despair of the

---

31. "The Jewish Question as an Ecumenical Problem," *The Ecumenical Review,* April 1955, pp. 225–231. For a further analysis, see Harold Floreen, "Attitudes in American Churches Towards the Christian Approach to the Jews," *Quarterly News Sheet.* XXVI, 2 (June 1956), pp. 1–8.

Assembly to solve its problem seems to have sprung from a weakened and divided faith in the nature of the Church and of Scripture. And it is not without significance that it was over the people of Israel that the Assembly experienced its division.

CATHOLIC RESPONSE

CATHOLIC theologians, in their comments on the deliberations and reports of the Evanston Assembly, have generally been sympathetic. In *Unitas,* an international review devoted, as its title indicates, to the spiritual union of all men, especially of Christians, Father Charles Boyer, S.J., its editor, though regretting that a subject had been chosen which deflected the Assembly from seeking doctrinal unity, was "agreeably surprised." "We had expected nothing so positive," he said.[32] *Istina,* a French quarterly which, from the stand of the Catholic faith, interprets all efforts to restore unity among Christians, confessed, in advance of the Assembly, "its unfeigned respect for the loftiness of thought and the properly Christian inspiration" of the Preparatory Reports.[33] As, before the publication of the Report on the Main Theme, Father Boyer had limned in broad strokes the Catholic concept of hope,[34] so, after its appearance, a group of European Catholic theologians produced a lengthy corporate effort in *Istina* on "Christ, the Church and Grace in the Economy of Christian Hope," laying special stress on what they felt lacking in the Report. They emphasized that they offered their statement not in any polemical spirit but with the wish that it might "perhaps prove a useful—and discreet—contribution to the deliberations occasioned by the Evanston Assembly." There is no room here to consider all its rich content, but a single excerpt will suffice to show its tenor:

Without the slightest doubt the sign—and a sign *in se* absolutely compelling—that salvation is come, "That they may be one in us; that the world may believe that thou hast sent me" (Jn 17:21), has been given basically in the essential, indestructible unity of the Church, unshakably founded on the rock of Peter; but in the eyes of men a shadow has been thrown over the brightness of its shining owing to the divisions which exist among Christians. These divisions hamper immensely

32. *Unitas,* VI, 4 (Winter 1954), p. 228.
33. "Christ, the Church and Grace in the Economy of Christian Hope," p. 1, an English offprint from *Istina,* April–June 1954.
34. *Unitas,* VI, 1 (Spring 1954), pp. 3–6.

the proclamation of the message of hope. . . . This invites us Catholics to weigh our responsibilities carefully, whether for the past, for the present, or for the future. . . . The charity of Christ compels us to acknowledge the mistakes of those who have gone before us, not in order to judge them, but in order to diminish the gravity of the results which have followed. However, because the Church is for us infinitely greater than and vastly different from the sum of her individual members—for she is the sum of realities and facts through which and in which Christ Himself is made present to us, communicating to us His life—, we refuse, just as our Orthodox brethren refuse, to proclaim the defection of the Church herself. She is the Body of Christ and His Bride. As such she has not fallen away and she cannot fall away. But alas! we, her members, do sin. . . . Our penitence must be deep, sincere and active; but rather than in the grandiloquent proclamation of a repentance of little practical effect, it will consist in the really hard, patient and courageous work of changing our own sinful lives, of healing the wounds caused by our separations, of doing all we possibly can, with God, to put an end to our separations themselves.[35]

To this study were appended a number of weighty theses by Dr. Karl Thieme of the University of Mainz, set forth because, as the author says, the theme of Christian hope cannot be discussed unless the hope of the Jewish people is expressly considered. Speaking in the name of "Catholics of Gentile stock" (cf. Ac 15:19; 21:25), he declares—though with much fuller texture than can be given here: We hope, in common with our separated "elder brethren" of the stem of Abraham, for the day of the Lord, which will surely come. But, in still irreconcilable contrast with them, we hope for that day to be the glorious enthronement of Him who began His kingship in the obscurity of His cross and resurrection: the returning Jesus of Nazareth. We believe, in common with our "elder brethren," that the living God revealed Himself first to the patriarchs and then at Sinai to the entire chosen people, and that His promise of mercy to them will never be broken. But, in still irreconcilable contrast with them, we believe that redemption has come to fallen mankind in Jesus, God-made-man, and that the fulfillment of our hope is attained by our sharing in Jesus' saving work, through the sacraments. Finally, God's love binds us indissolubly to our "elder brethren" through the revealed truth of the Scriptures of the Old Covenant and also through our sure confidence in their future ingathering and thus

---

35. *Istina* offprint, pp. 21–22.

our union with them; but it still separates us from them because we see in Simon bar-Jonah and his successors the foundation stone of the renewed people of God, because we see him who sits on the seat of Peter seated also on the seat of Moses. Further, God's love obliges us not to conceal from our "elder brethren" our differences and their salvific importance, rather to tell them of them in a brotherly exchange till the day comes when there will be "one fold and one shepherd" (Jn 10:16) and when all will call upon the name of the Lord and will serve Him with one consent (Soph 3:9).[36]

Eager for opinions on his theses, Dr. Thieme approached, among others, Father Oesterreicher, who wondered whether certain thoughts should not have been expressed with a little more precision. He suggested, for instance, that it might have been better to call the Jews instead of our *elder* brethren, just our brethren, separated because of Christ, and yet loved in Christ, very much as St. Catherine of Siena greeted the Jew Consiglio as *O carissimo fratello in Cristo Gesù,* "Dearest brother in Christ Jesus." For, he said, Israel is truly the "elder brother," the worker first called to the vineyard, only in relation to the Gentiles (see Lk 15:11–32; Mt 20:1–16). On the other hand, God's universal covenant with all men not only excels His particular covenant with the people of Israel, but the New is in a way before the Old. *Quod ultimum est in executione, primum est in intentione;* the last in accomplishment is the first in design. Israel's singling out was as a trustee of universality; from its first breath it was a prophet of catholicity. Hence when Abraham was blessed, his blessing was to redound over all the world. And before Israel's Scriptures tell of Abraham, they speak of Adam, the father of all men, to which Jewish legend adds that when God gathered clay for Adam's body, He took it from the four corners of the earth.

His raising this or similar points, Father Oesterreicher stressed, must not cloud his warm agreement with Dr. Thieme's theses and concern. Israel, people of tears, of Christ's tears and of so many of its own, is forever chained to expectation, he said, and on this note I should like to end my survey. There is no more startling title given to Israel in all of Scripture than Zechariah's "prisoners of hope" (9:12).[37]

36. *Ibid.,* pp. 30–32.
37. For the full text of Father Oesterreicher's comments and Dr. Thieme's reply to them, see *Freiburger Rundbrief: Beiträge zur Förderung der Freundschaft zwischen dem Alten und dem Neuen Gottesvolk im Geiste beider Testamente,* VII, 25/28 (September 1954), pp. 28–30.

William Keller

ANTI-SEMITISM IN THE SOVIET UNION

I

THE spring of 1917 was a time of joyful anticipation for the Jews of Russia: the apparent beginning of a "brave new world" which would bring all their dreams and aspirations to a satisfying reality. For a century and a half they had suffered the rigorous restrictions and intermittent persecutions of the Czarist regime; [1] but this regime had now been overthrown, and a democratic Provisional Government formed. The Jews, together with all the many peoples of the former Russian Empire, found themselves emerging for the first time into the full, blinding light of freedom.

Russian Jewry was by no means united within itself as to its future plans. There was first the vast body of Orthodox Jews, living a life apart. Then there were the Zionists and the nationalists, insisting that the Jews were a completely separate nation and culture. Others, the liberals, favored assimilation in all except religious practice, while the socialist labor group, Marxist and anti-religious, opposed national separatism but backed the development of a national culture, at least as a temporary measure. [2]

The most vocal Jewish organization in the years before the Revolution was the General Jewish Workers Alliance, the so-called Bund. As early as 1901, this group had affirmed that the concept of "nation" was applicable to the Jews. It was only natural that even a Marxist

1. For a more detailed account of the position of Russian Jews from medieval times to the Revolution, see Léon Poliakov, *Histoire de l'Antisémitisme,* Vol. I, *Du Christ aux Juifs de cour* (Paris: Calmann-Lévy, 1955), pp. 297–304.
2. Solomon M. Schwarz's *The Jews in the Soviet Union* (Syracuse: Syracuse University Press, 1951) is the best scholarly treatment in English of the relations of Russian Jews with the Soviet state. See pp. 3–23 for a description of the political movements in the Jewish community in the years immediately prior to the Revolution.

organization like this should think of Judaism in national terms, for the Jews in eastern Europe, unlike their brethren in the West, had always been, first perforce and later not unwillingly, a closed society.

In 1903, the Russian Social Democratic Workers Party, which included the Jewish Bund, declared its approval of the right of self-determination for all nations in the state. On this occasion, Vladimir Medem proposed on behalf of the Bund an amendment which would permit the various national minorities to establish institutions for the development of their own culture. This proposal was defeated, largely by Lenin's group, and the Bund withdrew from the Social Democratic Workers Party. From that time on, Lenin's followers, now known as the Bolsheviki, that is, the Party of the Majority, became more influential in Russian radical circles. Opposing the notion of a federal union of nations within the state, they canonized, from the very start, the principle of centralization. Lenin saw "self-determination" solely as the right of the various nations to secede if they wished. But a true merger could be formed only if they chose not to do so. Hence he urged his followers to take the lead in the various nationalist movements, but to work against the use of the right to secede. Any aspirations toward national culture were simply regarded as inspired by "clerical or bourgeois fraud."

II

THE Revolution of March 1917 brought the various radical groups down from the ivory tower of theory into the market place of reality. The national question was vitally pressing and required some immediate solution, for the huge Russian Empire, far from being a melting pot, had been a vast conglomeration of races, peoples and tribes, existing on every historical and cultural level. Each group, with the exception of the Jews, had its own territory. While more numerous in the Ukraine and White Russia than elsewhere, nowhere did the Jews form any extensive territorial majority. As a result, they posed a problem even more difficult of solution than that of the other national groups.

When, in November 1917, the Bolshevists took control of the Revolution, their emphasis on centralization and their interpretation of "self-determination" began to prevail. Every effort was made to prevent the nationalities from choosing to secede. The brief attempts in the Ukraine, Georgia, and Armenia to establish democratic institutions were criticized as "outdated bourgeois parliamentarianism." In 1921, Stalin went so far as to declare that once the national groups elected to join the Russian Soviet Federated Socialist Republic, they permanently renounced their right to secede.

Once the "merger" had taken place, it became necessary to harmonize in some way the widely varying groups that made up the new state. At that point there was an apparent change in Bolshevist policy, with Stalin even defending the right of national minorities to free national development. But this was no real doctrinal change, rather a temporary tactical compromise. National cultures were encouraged in order to bring them all up to a level where fusion could take place. Significantly, no national culture was permitted to develop a content in any way separate from Soviet culture; the only real difference allowed was a difference of language. Stalin prophesied that some nationalities might, and even certainly would, undergo a process of assimilation. But which nations he had in mind, he did not say.

Back in April 1917, the Provisional Government had achieved the goal long sought by all the oppressed peoples of Russia: all religious and national restrictions were repealed. The Jews immediately began organizing themselves along democratic lines. No opposition was given by the government, for all parties except the Bolshevists favored the establishment of autonomous national-cultural groups. When, in the fall of the same year, the Bolshevists secured full control, it became uncertain whether these autonomous developments would continue. Jews well remembered the words of Lenin: "The idea of a separate Jewish people, which is utterly untenable scientifically, is reactionary in its political implications." The Jews were neither a nation nor a nationality but a caste, he taught, and castes were not to be tolerated.[3] It was the Communist conviction that the repeal of restrictions, which had taken place in April 1917, would, by an irresistible sociological process, lead to complete assimilation of peoples.

III

IN JANUARY 1918, a Commissariat for Jewish Affairs was established as part of the People's Commissariat for National Affairs, which was

3. Quoted *ibid.,* pp. 50–53.

under Stalin's direction. The Commissariat organized subordinate provincial Jewish Commissariats, administrative in purpose, and Jewish Sections, intended as means of winning the Jewish people to the Communist Party. However, great difficulties were encountered in the organization of these groups, for hardly any practicing Jews had been members of the Bolshevist Party in its early days. While quite a few party members were of Jewish parentage, they were estranged from their origins and were not even familiar with Yiddish, the language then spoken by the overwhelming majority of Jews.

As Solomon Schwarz points out, the Commissariat-Section plan "implied the establishment of extra-territorial organs for the administration of Jewish affairs, thus virtually subscribing to that principle of national-cultural autonomy which the Bolsheviks abhorred."[4] But these were only temporary concessions, meant to win over the reluctant Jews to Communism. In July 1918 all non-Communist elements were eliminated from these groups, all autonomous tendencies were uprooted, and the Sections were wholly subordinated to the Communist Party. Furthermore, these agencies were appointive rather than elective, thus giving the Party greater control over the Jewish minority.

At first, Jewish reactions to the Communist campaign were unfavorable, for the Party threatened the newly found independence of the Jewish community. But the early reluctance was soon overcome, not so much by Communist concessions as by the anti-Semitism of those who fought the Soviets in the Civil War of late 1918. The cruel pogroms and the looting of Jewish property by the counter-revolutionaries literally forced the Jews to a position of greater co-operation with the Communists. Yet almost immediately the Communists began to show less interest in the Jews: in 1920 the Jewish Commissariat was reduced to a mere department, and in the following year all Jewish parties were finally liquidated. The administration of Jews would be dealt with locally by the provincial, district, and municipal Soviet authorities, not by any separate administrative body. For a few more years, the Sections were permitted to exist in ever decreasing importance, being finally dissolved in 1930. Since their disappearance, "no political, administrative, or cultural organization representing the Jewish minority as a distinct national or ethnic group has existed in

4. *Ibid.*, p. 96.

the Soviet Union." [5] Although some Sections lingered on for another decade, it was evident as early as 1921 that the first step in the Communist campaign against the aspirations of the Jewish community had been accomplished: all democratic Jewish institutions had been destroyed, and any future concessions would be nothing but the freely bestowed favors of the Communist Party.

IV

THE policy of the Soviet government toward the Jews in the years between the wars may seem erratic at first glance. But only at first glance: advancing and withdrawing time and again, its ultimate object was to detach the Jews from their ancient loyalties, national, cultural, and religious. To a considerable extent this policy was successful; those who failed to be absorbed were to be dealt with in later years by sterner measures.

An examination of various aspects of Jewish life may serve to bring these statements into sharper relief. As far as organized religious life was concerned, the Jews suffered along with all Christian bodies, for in a regime whose philosophy is built on the "dogma" that God does not exist, religion is at best barely tolerated and at worst openly persecuted. Hence the Soviet government suppressed all churches and synagogues; though groups of fifty or more citizens could be licensed to form private religious associations, they were subjected to oppressive surveillance. Religious instruction of youth was punishable by law; in fact, any form of religious activity put those engaged under the suspicion of being "counter-revolutionary." Those who were known to persevere in their faith were victimized in their livelihood. The result for the Jewish community was that membership in the synagogues drastically declined in the '20s. In spite of this considerable leakage, many—of whom the statistics will never be learned—secretly continued in their faith.

At the very beginning of the Revolution, the Bolshevists had agreed that minority groups could use their native tongues in the state schools. Yet here again the teaching was to differ "in language only, not in content." For all the ardent desire of the Jews to implant the seeds of their ancient heritage in their children, the schools were de-

5. *Ibid.*, p. 103.

liberately fashioned as a weapon to achieve just the opposite. In every state school for Jewish children, classes were conducted on the Sabbath, and neither Hebrew nor the national literature and history was taught; it was just another anti-religious Soviet school, but one which used Yiddish as its language. To thwart the religious influence of the privately conducted *ḥeder* (the centuries-old Jewish elementary school usually held in the teacher's own home), all Jewish children were forced to attend the Yiddish state school, at least in White Russia and the Ukraine. But in the late '20s Soviet interest in the Yiddish school fell off, as a passing stress by the government on things Ukrainian (not to speak of its ever present urge to increase Russian cultural influence), together with the moving of many Jews from the old ghetto areas, combined to reduce the number and influence of this type of school.

The same trend was observable in other cultural areas. In the last Czarist generation, the Jewish press had grown by 1914 to a peak of thirteen daily newspapers in Yiddish and two in Hebrew. After the Revolution, the increase in the number of periodicals was at first phenomenal: in 1917–18 there were 171 newspapers and periodicals being issued for the Jews in Yiddish, Hebrew, and Russian. But after 1921, the disappearance of all non-Communist papers brought a swift decline: in 1935 only four or five dailies remained, and in 1939 only three. A like trend occurred in non-daily periodicals. Scholars and scientific workers produced very little during these years. As the "party line" changed, they were frequently forced to renounce and "correct" their own work to bring it into accord with the latest shift. They were also forced into the repellent position of "exposing" all pre-Revolutionary and non-Soviet scholarship. But the Jewish theater movement saw rapid growth. This aspect of Jewish life, since it was wholly secular in origin, received considerable government support from the mid-'20s on. It flourished in some twenty companies during these years, only to fall a victim in the time of the political purges of the late '30s.

While minority self-government for the Jews was effectively quashed in the first years after the Revolution, a certain measure of autonomy was extended in some areas where Jews were numerous, principally in the Ukraine. These local Soviets were first organized in the late '20s; no figures on them have been released since 1933, however, when they began to decline. For they had been established in the hope that the young people, indoctrinated in the Soviet schools, would take the lead in their communities; but this was just the group that emigrated elsewhere into industry or agriculture, leaving dominant the older generation, tainted, as the Communists saw it, with "counter-revolutionary influences of clericalism."

Soviet law gives every citizen the right to the use of his native tongue in court, even supplying interpreters where needed. In Jewish districts, special Jewish courts were erected, mainly with the purpose of undermining religion by displacing the old form of justice meted out by the rabbi. On this court system, Solomon Schwarz quotes Soviet writer Yakov Kantor: "The national court divisions have made an important contribution to the eradication of pernicious attitudes, superstitions, and anachronistic religious survivals within the Jewish population; they have driven out the rabbinical practice of justice so widespread in the Jewish *shtetl*." [6] Once organized Jewish religious life was done away with, the government began to abandon the Jewish courts, only a few still existing at the last count in the late '30s.

V

THE complete reorganization of every department of Russian life effected by the Communist Party brought about a total alteration of the national economy. In Czarist times, the Jews had been kept off the soil and hemmed in by numerous other restrictions, with the result that most of them were small traders or merchants.[7] Under the new, state-organized economy, there was no longer room for private enterprise of this type, and thousands of city- and town-dwelling Jews were on the verge of destitution. To solve this problem, another apparent concession was offered by the government: Jews were to be given a territory of their own in Siberia—a plan first thought of, incidentally, by the government of Czar Nicholas I. Only Jews would be admitted to Birobidzhan, the territory selected by the Soviet government, and

6. *Ibid.*, p. 157.
7. Harry Schwartz, in "Has Russia Solved the Jewish Problem?," *Commentary*, V, 2 (February 1948), pp. 128–136, gives some interesting comparative statistics on the occupations of Jews in the Czarist and Soviet periods: in 1897 more than one-half were small businessmen or traders, 30 per cent artisans and handicrafters, with only 4 per cent engaged in industry and 2 in agriculture; in 1939 almost one-half were professional or white-collar workers, about 20 per cent artisans, roughly 25 per cent engaged in industry, with almost 6 per cent in agricultural work.

the immigrants would be divided between communal agricultural projects on the land and industry in the urban areas.

Birobidzhan seemed at first like all Jewish dreams of the past come true. But soon enough it became evident that the Soviet government had not undergone any real change of heart. Not only would the plan remove large numbers of Jews from the steadily progressing areas of western Russia; it might finally give, the Soviets hoped, the *coup de grâce* to what they liked to call the "internationalist" visions of the Zionists. But above all, and this was the reason for haste in getting the project under way, the Soviets feared the infiltration of the Chinese into Asiatic Russia, as well as its military vulnerability because of underpopulation.

It was in 1926 that the Soviets devised the Birobidzhan plan; in the years immediately following, emigrants from the West gradually moved in, and in 1934, the region, roughly the size of Connecticut and Massachusetts combined, was erected as a Jewish autonomous district. Even then the Jews constituted less than 20 per cent of the total population. The incoming Jews soon discovered that what was held out to them as a promised land was a wilderness of forests and swamps. Most of the emigrants, traditionally urban dwellers, found themselves unfit for the work and climate of their new home. Further, there had been no surveys or allotments of land by the central government. The result was that many returned to the West.

Voluntary colonization was obviously a failure, so after 1934 a new plan was tried, of more or less compulsory recruitment by the government, not of the destitute, rather of those Jews already active in industry and agriculture. But of the fifty thousand families expected in Birobidzhan during the next three years, only twenty thousand arrived. Less was now heard of Jewish autonomy, which had patently been a mere inducement to entice emigrants; indeed, the year 1937 saw the purging of the entire administration of the Jewish Autonomous *Oblast*. Though no exact statistics are available for the years following the purge, we know that immigration ceased or was reduced after the Soviet pact with Hitler in 1939, and that it was resumed after the war, many thousands—including ex-servicemen, evacuees, and slave laborers—entering without official authorization. In mid-1948, Birobidzhan was mysteriously cut off from the outside world, and since then there has been almost no contact with it.

However, the Tel Aviv *Haaretz* is quoted by Solomon Schwarz as stating on March 29, 1951, that in 1949–50 a further purge of leaders took place in Birobidzhan, whose population then was 130,000 and almost 30 per cent Jewish. Jews were constantly being charged with the crimes of "Jewish nationalism" and "cosmopolitanism," and only regard for world opinion prevented the official liquidation of Birobidzhan as a Jewish district.[8] Another break in the official silence was the permission granted the *New York Times* correspondent Harrison Salisbury to enter Birobidzhan in the summer of 1953. He reported that almost the only vestiges of Jewish culture were street signs in Russian *and* Yiddish, and one small newspaper, the *Birobidzhaner Shtern.* The whole district had become part of the Siberian slave-labor territory under the rule of the secret police. Mr. Salisbury even found a slave-labor camp adjoining the principal street of the capital.[9]

VI

IN EXAMINING the relations between the Soviet state and Russian Jews in the period from the Revolution to the mid-'30s, we have not noted any sign of official anti-Semitism. To the Party the Jews represented an obstacle, but this obstacle was regarded as one that could be eliminated in time by clever strategy. As we have seen, the strategy was to a great measure successful, for Jews gradually became assimilated to Soviet society or at least took on the protective coloring of their surroundings. This does not mean, however, that anti-Semitism was nonexistent during this period. But it was a popular mood, a mood at first opposed by the state as contrary to Marxist principles, later tolerated, and finally, in the period just before World War II and up to recently, taken over and used as a definite instrument of policy.

I have already mentioned the anti-Semitism manifested in the Civil War of 1918. This hatred was no doubt a carry-over of the anti-Jewish feeling of Czarist days, which the upper and middle classes had copied from the imperial house. In July 1918, the Soviet government took immediate action against it, and anti-Semitism was outlawed.

8. *Op. cit.*, pp. 193–194.
9. *The New York Times*, September 29, 1954; see also *American Jewish Year Book, 1955* (New York: American Jewish Committee, 1955), pp. 407–408.

Oddly enough, though the upper and middle classes were completely crushed in the following years, anti-Semitism did not die out. In the mid-'20s a whispering campaign accusing the Jews of flocking to the larger cities, especially the capital, and of taking "Soviet jobs," soon developed into open violence. Numerous anti-Semitic incidents were related in Soviet newspapers, while many others doubtless remained unmentioned. This new anti-Semitism seemed to flourish even among Party members, although the government tried to pretend that non-Communists were responsible. Schwarz declares:

Jew-baiting and anti-Semitic violence, it is plain, were not confined to backward regions, to the "non-proletarian" countryside or to the traditionally anti-Semitic Ukraine. All incidents reported by the Soviet press took place in industrial plants, with Young Communists—"even active members"—again and again singled out as having initiated or encouraged the persecution of their Jewish fellow workers.[10]

Though officially condemned by the government, this attitude made its appearance in industry and the universities; it even led to the mistreatment of Jewish invalids in rest homes. Local Communist authorities often ignored the law in their treatment of the Jewish populace: discrimination was shown by the discharge of Jewish employees, in the distribution of living quarters, and in tax assessments. A popular slogan of this period was "Kill the kikes, save White Russia," and once again the ancient lie was spread that at Passover time the Jews kidnap Christian children to make matzoth out of their blood.[11] In the Dagestan Republic, the local Communist officials not only tolerated anti-Semitism but even took an active part in it, supporting "our own people" against the Jewish "strangers." Anti-Semitism in this region was uninterrupted from the early '20s, and yet the frequent complaints of the Jews to the central government—which was ostensibly opposed to, and working against, anti-Semitism—were met with indifference. In 1928 an investigation of the charges was finally made, they were admitted to be true; still, no action was taken.

Much of the antagonism was due to the belief that Jews were coming to the cities in disproportionate numbers, taking jobs and living quarters from non-Jews. There was jealousy, too, since it was thought

10. S. M. Schwarz, *op. cit.,* p. 247.
11. See *ibid.,* p. 253.

that Jews had too large a share of the official positions. These charges are easily refuted by the official statistics which show that, while the general urban population was increasing between 1926 and 1939, the Jewish urban population declined from 8.2 per cent to 4.7 per cent; likewise there is no basis in fact to the charge that the Jews were monopolizing official posts.

When anti-Semitism manifested itself, first in 1917–18 and again in the mid-'20s, the government attempted to repress it by legal and educational means. *Izvestia* of July 27, 1918, contained an official order which declared pogroms a crime. "There is no place," it read, "for national oppression. The Jewish bourgeois is our enemy, not as he is a Jew, but as he is a bourgeois. The Jewish worker is our brother . . . Incitement to hatred of any nation whatever is intolerable, shameful, and criminal." [12] A further statute was promulgated on February 25, 1927, during the second wave of anti-Semitism. More precise definitions of racial hatred were given; the possible punishments, in time of war or popular disturbance, ranged from loss of freedom for two years, through forfeiture of part or all of one's property, to death together with such forfeiture. Severe in its threats, this law was rarely invoked. The government's plans for political re-education of the people were not much more effective. Schemes were outlined for the use of the various media of radio, press, stage, and screen to diffuse constructive propaganda, but little was actually attempted even in the peak period of anti-Semitism, 1926–30.

VII

THE millions of new jobs created by the Five Year Plans did far more to kill anti-Semitism than did the half-hearted legal and educational methods of the government. In the years 1930–36 the traditional anti-Semitism seemed completely dead, when suddenly, in the summer of 1936, Russia and the world were startled with the news of the Great Purge. The Communist Party as it had come down from the days of the Revolution was almost totally destroyed, and so were its leaders. The "old guard"—many of whom were Jews, such as Trotsky, Zinoviev, Kamenev, and Radek—were charged with treason and espionage, and their alleged plot was made to appear the work

12. Quoted *ibid.*, p. 274.

of "Jewish internationalism." Jews in minor positions suffered also, to such an extent that "the Great Purge virtually terminated the organized life of the Jewish group as a recognized cultural and ethnic minority." [13] After the Purge, anti-Semitism remained prohibited on the books, but no longer was there any official disapproval of it shown.

When, three years later, the Hitler-Stalin pact was signed, the Soviet government kept silent about Nazi anti-Semitism. This policy of silence proved utterly disastrous to Russian Jews when, in 1941, war suddenly broke out between the two countries. The Russian Jews had been kept in utter ignorance of the Nazi persecutions and were thus totally unaware of the mortal danger coming upon them as the German army invaded. The pogrom the Nazis released on those Jews who remained in their path was true to the literal meaning of the word—devastation.

The German press strove to give the impression that the Russian people shared the Nazis' hatred of the Jews in their midst. While such statements can obviously not be depended on, there are strong indications of apathy on the part of most Russians. Some efforts by civilians to rescue Jews from the Nazi onslaught were later publicized by the Soviet press, but the number of such incidents is surprisingly small in comparison with the many rescues in traditionally anti-Semitic Poland. One explanation, surely, is the virtue of practical Christian charity, which certainly should be more in evidence in a nation professedly Christian than in one officially atheist. Another explanation might be that the Russian people, so long accustomed to totalitarian rule, were completely unused to opposing the powers that be, however much they may have disliked their policy. In addition, there were many, particularly in the Ukraine, either neutral or openly collaborationist.

Harrison Salisbury, in his series of articles "Russia Reviewed," has this to say on the first anti-Semitic outbreak in nonoccupied Russia shortly after the beginning of the war:

Its most spectacular manifestation was the circulation in Moscow of rumors that "the Jews are deserting Moscow." It was said that rich Jews had bought places on the evacuation trains and fled to the East. The

13. *Ibid.*, p. 298.

truth was that the Government itself had evacuated a number of "rich Jews"—artists, singers and writers—in a general organized movement of certain classes of intelligentsia. The rumors actually had been started by the Government in order to divert the resentment of the vast majority of Muscovites, who were being left behind. Possibly to the surprise of the Government, the anti-Semitic reports snowballed to such an extent that many department chiefs began to discharge all Jews from their staffs. Professors were relieved of their university posts. Many Jews lost their deferred status and were inducted into the Soviet Army. Apparently this anti-Semitic outbreak served some obscure Government purpose, because it was allowed to mushroom without interference for more than a year. Finally it was brought to a summary end by the propaganda chief of the Communist party, the late Alexander Shcherbakov. He called in the Moscow party leaders and bluntly told them that the Government was against anti-Semitism and that the whole thing had been started by "German propaganda leaflets." No one but Shcherbakov, it would appear, had ever seen these leaflets.[14]

In complete contradiction to what the Soviet constitution avowed, but not to the real spirit that animated the government, the Soviet press made almost no mention of the Nazi atrocities against Jews, maintaining the same sphinx-like silence it had begun in the days of the Hitler pact. The fact that Jews were the prime target of Nazi wrath was passed over, all the emphasis being placed on attacks on "Soviet citizens." When the great Jewish centers of Kiev and Odessa were attacked, no mention of Jewish victims was made. Only toward the end of 1944 were a few anti-Jewish incidents reported. But shortly after, a *Pravda* report on the Auschwitz concentration camp, where over four millions, the overwhelming majority of whom were Jewish, met cruelest deaths, did not so much as refer to the Jews.[15]

The Nazi persecution of the Jews influenced, directly and indirectly, Soviet anti-Semitism. Very great, especially among the Soviet army, was the effect of German propaganda. Prisoners and slave laborers returning to Russia at the war's conclusion were gravely infected by it. And the wholly negative attitude of the official press permitted their hatred, already nourished by the anti-Jewish feeling inculcated by the pre-war purges, to continue its growth.

14. *The New York Times,* September 29, 1954.
15. *Pravda,* May 7, 1945; quoted by S. M. Schwarz, *op. cit.,* p. 341.

VIII

AFTER the war, the Soviet government permitted Polish Jews who
had fled into Russia before the Nazi armies to remain as Soviet citizens. But their awareness of the threat of anti-Semitism was no doubt
at least partly responsible for their almost unanimous decision to return to the new Poland.[16] Likewise, the few and utterly impoverished
Jewish survivors of central Europe naturally expected, on their return
to their old homes after the dread war years, to receive restitution of,
or compensation for, the property stripped from them by the Nazis.
But they were bitterly disappointed to find their small factories, their
shops, their very homes, occupied, and to find themselves regarded as
"Jewish intruders," "looters of national property," and supporters of
"capitalist restoration." Moreover, perhaps because the new possessors
were so many, the post-war Communist bureaucracies took no action
on behalf of the Jews, with the result that many sought to emigrate
to Israel. But even this door was soon closed to them when emigra-
tion was prohibited.[17]

In the Soviet Union itself, little active anti-Semitism was observable in the years after the war, except that Jews appeared to play a
constantly smaller role in official life. The emphasis on nationalism,
evident from 1949 on, carried with it a corresponding anti-Semitic
spirit. In 1948, Stalin, who before had always stressed the international aspect of Communism, now conferred special praise on the
Russian nationality as opposed to less advanced groups within the
state. The corollary of the new nationalism was a vigorous campaign
against the "cosmopolitans," a euphemism for the Jews, with their
family and cultural ties in western Europe, America, and Israel. The
extensive purge which followed, while never admitted to have been
anti-Jewish, was waged largely against people with Jewish names.
The implications were obvious to all.

Beginning in January 1949, the Soviet press suddenly "discovered"
and "exposed" that notable figures in the literary world, especially
critics, were using "aliases," hiding their Jewish origin behind non-
committal or Russian-appearing pen names. The fact that Lenin and

16. See H. Schwartz, *loc. cit.*
17. See Peter Meyer, "The Jewish Purge in the Satellite Countries," *Commentary,*
XIV, 3 (September 1952), pp. 212–218.

Stalin and many other non-Jewish Russian leaders had also used aliases was of course ignored. Jews, now generally suspected of "cosmopolitanism," of "American imperialism," of "subversive and treasonable connections" with "world Jewry," completely disappeared from the Soviet foreign service. In almost every phase of life, anti-Jewish discrimination was making its advances.

The inner insecurity of the post-war Soviet government was first visible to the outside world in a series of purges, both in Russia and in the satellite countries, beginning in 1948 and continuing intermittently under various forms. The years 1948–51 saw the removal of many satellite officials who were accused of nationalist tendencies. It was feared that the Tito rebellion might be repeated unless the least deviation was immediately uprooted. Although numerous Jews were the victims of these purges, little public emphasis was placed on their origin. Only in 1951 did anti-Semitism raise its head again when Vaclav Kopecky, Czechoslovak Minister of Information, accused several Jews, including Otto Sling, a Party secretary, of "cosmopolitanism." Kopecky's campaign—he liked to call Jews "scum" or "bearded Solomons"—soon resulted in the overthrow of Rudolf Slansky, the Secretary General, and in a general purge of Jews in public office and in nationalized industry.

To trace the purges and persecutions of the Jews in the satellite lands is outside the province of the present paper. Suffice it to mention the removal of Ana Pauker in Rumania, the execution of Slansky in Czechoslovakia, the many arrests, trials, deportations that followed in Hungary, Poland, and, to a lesser extent, in East Germany. The multiplicity of these Jewish "plots," allegedly inspired by a world Jewish conspiracy and controlled by the Jews of America and Israel, set the stage for the infamous "doctors' plot," first "revealed" in *Pravda* on January 13, 1953. Charges were made that nine physicians (six of them Jews) had deliberately killed the Soviet leaders Zhdanov and Shcherbakov, and also had attempted to undermine the health of many military leaders, including three marshals, one general, and one admiral. It is interesting to note, since Zhdanov's death was the principal one listed, that he had died at the end of August 1948; at that time *Pravda* published his death certificate, which indicated a natural decease and was signed by five doctors, none of them Jewish. Actually, Zhdanov had become too popular for his own good and had been officially liquidated. Four years later when scapegoats had to be found for failures of the administration, Zhdanov's death was made to appear the focal point of an international Jewish-British-American conspiracy. Here are a few excerpts from the *Pravda* article—they speak for themselves:

Some time ago agencies of state security discovered a terrorist group of doctors who made it their aim to cut short the lives of active public figures of the Soviet Union through the sabotage of medical treatment. . . . Among the participants in this terrorist group there proved to be: Prof. M. S. Vovsi, therapeutist; Prof. V. N. Vinogradov, therapeutist; Prof. M. B. Kogan, therapeutist; Prof. B. B. Kogan, therapeutist; Prof. P. I. Yegorov, therapeutist; Prof. A. I. Feldman, otolaryngologist; Prof. Ya. G. Etinger, therapeutist; Prof. A. M. Grinshtein, neuropathologist; G. I. Maiorov, therapeutist.

All these murderer-doctors, who had become monsters in human form, trampling the sacred banner of science and desecrating the honor of scientists, were enrolled by foreign intelligence services as hired agents.

Most of the members of the terrorist group . . . were bought by the American intelligence service. They were recruited by a branch of American intelligence, the international Jewish bourgeois nationalist organization Joint [the American Joint Distribution Committee]. The dirty face of this Zionist espionage organization, concealing its foul work under a mask of charity, has been completely exposed. Relying on a group of depraved Jewish bourgeois nationalists, the professional spies and terrorists of the Joint spread their subversive activity to the territory of the Soviet Union. . . . Exposure of the band of poisoner-doctors is a blow at the international Jewish Zionist organizations. Now all can see what "charitable friends of peace" are hiding behind the Joint letterhead.[18]

The "doctors' plot" was only the beginning, however. Except for Lazar M. Kaganovich (who, it has often been said, is the brother of Stalin's second wife), no Jew was left in high political office: those who were not arrested and put on trial on trumped-up charges were dismissed or demoted. Jewish professors were purged from the Kiev Medical Institute because of "sabotage, malfeasance, and nepotism."

18. *American Jewish Year Book, 1954* (New York: American Jewish Committee, 1954), pp. 273–274; see also Peter Meyer, "Soviet Anti-Semitism in High Gear," *Commentary*, XV, 2 (February 1953), pp. 115–120.

The American Jewish Year Book for 1953 records a "continuous purge" during 1952 of so-called "cosmopolitans" and "petty-bourgeois nationalists," convenient synonyms, recognized by all, for Jews.[19] Deportations of Jews without trial "for their own security" took place on a large scale from the Ukraine and White Russia; at most one or two days' notice was given, and sometimes the victims were deported at once following midnight raids of their homes. They were sent to Georgia and Dagestan, later to Siberia and Central Asia. Some were given a modicum of independence with the title of "free settlers," while the rest, the "politically suspect," were delivered over to slave-labor camps. Birobidzhan, once offered to the Russian Jews as another promised land, now became a vast Jewish concentration camp.[20]

The bitter anti-Jewish campaign in Russia and the satellites was reflected in an unfortunate incident: on February 9, 1953, Israeli extremists, members of an illegal organization, exploded a bomb in the Soviet legation in Tel Aviv. Although the Israeli government apologized and promised punishment of the offenders, Russia broke off diplomatic relations, which were resumed only in August 1953, after the death of Stalin.

IX

AFTER the dictator's death in March 1953, the charges against the "murderer-doctors" were retracted, and further rehabilitation of all the other victims of the anti-Semitic campaign was expected. This was not the case, however, and in the satellite nations, at least, open persecution continued. As proof that the change in leadership did not mean any change in basic policy, a new anti-religious campaign was inaugurated in the summer of 1954. So bitter were the attacks against religious "superstitions" that *Pravda,* on November 11, 1954, had to call for restraint; propaganda was to continue but on a "scientific" basis and with moderation. Judaism, while not singled out, was of course included in the general attack.

In 1955, after having long kept aloof from the Middle East, Rus-

19. *American Jewish Year Book, 1953* (New York: American Jewish Committee, 1953), p. 330.
20. *American Jewish Year Book, 1955,* pp. 407–408.

sia began to take great interest in it. Denunciations by the press of the Egyptian government were suddenly reversed, and Gamal Abdel Nasser was praised for his stand against the West. An arms agreement was made with Egypt, and other Arab states were approached by Soviet diplomats. Little was said about Israel in the Soviet press; only in one *Pravda* article, on November 5, 1955, was Israel openly denounced as an aggressor. While the new Soviet friendship with the Arab states may possibly be viewed as a further manifestation of anti-Semitic policy—after all, the state of Israel is a perpetual irritant to the Soviet leaders, implying as it does that Communism's claim to end the sufferings of Jews, indeed of all minorities, is vain—another explanation may well be the consistent Communist policy of exploiting in its own interests all conflicts, no matter who the antagonists may be.[21]

During the last year there has been no overt anti-Semitism on the part of the Soviet government. Time alone can tell whether the let-up is to be permanent or temporary. The sudden attack on Stalin's reputation which astonished world opinion in March of 1956 might indicate some possibility of change. But a true change of heart appears unlikely when it is recalled that Lenin himself, now the lone idol of the Communists, could see no place whatever for the Jews as a group in the Communist scheme of things. Communism is by its very nature "anti-Semitic"; even were the Soviet leaders to refrain from ever again persecuting the Jews, Communism works toward, and aims at, the complete disappearance of Jews and of all things Jewish.

A true change of heart appears unlikely, for up to this moment—the summer of 1956—no Soviet leader has clearly denounced the former violence against Jews. It is only the Warsaw Yiddish-language newspaper *Folksshtime* which has spoken out against the anti-Semitic purges of the recent past, publishing a long list of victims: scholars, writers, critics, actors. The fact moved the *Daily Worker* to the following editorial complaint:

We also express our concern that, in the long list of crimes mentioned in the speech [by Nikita S. Khrushchev before the Twentieth Communist Party Congress in Moscow on February 24 and 25, 1956], there was silence on those committed against Jewish culture and Jewish cultural

21. Walter Z. Laqueur, "Soviet Russia and the Arabs," *Midstream*, II, 1 (Winter 1956), pp. 24–38.

leaders. To date, this series of outrages has not been publicized in the
Socialist countries except in the columns of a Jewish-language paper in
Warsaw.[22]

All that has been heard from Khrushchev about the persecution of
the Jews are some remarks made to a delegation of French Socialists
in May 1956 to the effect that, in the years just after the Revolution,
Jews held an unduly high number of important posts because Russia
had too few trained people, but that now, with many Russians suitable for such positions, the former proportion of Jews is no longer
needed—which amounts almost to a justification of discharges, de-
motions, and purges.[23]

Everything I have stated about the dealings of the Soviet state and
so many of its citizens with the Jews is in complete contrast with the
official version of these relations. According to the "party line," there
is no land where the situation of the Jews is more blessed: anti-Semitism has been illegal since the early days, all religious and racial discrimination are barred by the very constitution; Jews are free in all
aspects of life and their culture is flourishing. Giving Communism its
due, an objective analyst must agree that in the Soviet Union, Jews
have the same rights as all other citizens; they also have the same restrictions and limitations. In the words of one writer: "Where political liberty is dead, as in the USSR, cultural autonomy becomes little
more than the right to sing the praises of the existing regime in Yiddish or Armenian as well as in Russian."[24] Jews also are subject to
the same atheistic propaganda as their fellow Russians. And, while
anti-Semitism is not tolerated in law, it is evident that there is a
strong, constant current of anti-Semitism existing among the people;
that, from time to time, this feeling has been, in the most cynical way,
tolerated, directed, and used to secure the ultimate ends of Soviet ideology; and that all this can happen again. As Harrison Salisbury puts
it:

The soil is always prepared for anti-Semitism if, in fear or to inspire
fear, a Soviet Government wishes to make use of it. The anti-Semitic
feeling aroused by the "doctors' plot" spread like wildfire—so much so,
that when, after Stalin's death, it was announced that the case had been

22. As quoted by *The New York Times,* June 6, 1956.
23. *The New York Times,* June 10, 1956.
24. H. Schwartz, *loc. cit.*

reversed and the doctors freed, two in the small circle of ordinary Russians with whom I had conversational contact expressed frank and open regret. "They should not have turned them loose," one Russian said. "I do not care what they say about their being innocent. You cannot trust the Jews." [25]

X

HAVING given what I hope is a sober analysis of the facts, I think I may now record a passionate Catholic statement of 1953, signed by Abbot Baldwin Dworschak, O.S.B., of St. John's Abbey; Father Laurence J. McGinley, S.J., president of Fordham University; Father Thomas A. Meehan, president of the Catholic Press Association; Father John LaFarge, S.J., associate editor of *America;* Sister Mary Madeleva, C.S.C., president of St. Mary's College; George N. Shuster, president of Hunter College; Clare Boothe Luce, then Ambassador-Designate to Italy; Senators John F. Kennedy and James E. Murray; Representative Eugene J. McCarthy; General William J. Donovan; the poet Alan Tate; the playwright Emmet Lavery; the drama critic Walter Kerr; and many others. Published in *The Commonweal* of February 20, 1953, it was introduced by an editorial, saying in part: "When Jews are threatened, we are threatened; just as the arrests of

25. *The New York Times,* September 29, 1954. In recent months new evidence of the Soviet attitude toward the Jews has come to light. Khrushchev is reported to have said, during a visit to Warsaw in March 1956: "Even a second-rate Kowalski is more useful than a first-rate Rosenblum," and: "You have too many Abrahamoviches here" (C. L. Sulzberger in *The New York Times,* July 9, 1956). Again, several United States rabbis, delegates of two rabbinical organizations, declared on their return from a study-tour of the Soviet Union that they "found the major institutions of Jewish religion and culture 'all but vanished, leaving a Judaism that is anemic and moribund.'" A series of articles by one delegate, Rabbi Morris N. Kertzer, has brought out a number of interesting points. First, Stalin is referred to by the Jews of Russia never by name but always as "the Terrible One." Second, though religious education and Hebrew language lessons are denied to Jews, as are other privileges accorded various nationality groups, every Jew bears on all his documents, even on his school diploma, the label "Jew." Third, while the rector of Leningrad's Russian Orthodox cathedral learned from Nazism that "anti-Semitism is always linked with the denial of God," the government persists in this denial. From his experiences at the Museum of Religion and Atheism, whose visitors are mostly impressionable adolescents, Rabbi Kertzer "left the Soviet Union with the unhappy feeling that it was almost impossible, in this cunningly devised battleground, for religious forces to withstand the assaults of godlessness. All the machinery of state, the educational institutions, the mass media, the arts and literature are arrayed against religion." (*The New York Times,* July 13, 30, 31; August 1, 1956).

priests and the subversion of Catholic churches behind the Iron Curtain cast a shadow of threat on the Jews, the next group with independent allegiance and a devotion to something beyond Caesar." This was the statement:

We call upon the conscience of the world through governments and the United Nations to protest against the outrageous new Anti-Semitism of the Communist world, and in David's words we pray that God will deliver the Jews from the hands of their enemies and from those who persecute them. Having seen our fellow Catholics persecuted by the Soviets, we offer special sympathy to Jews in their new trial, in this latest threat of genocide in our time.

BOOKS

Joseph Klausner: THE MESSIANIC IDEA IN ISRAEL *

JOSEPH KLAUSNER is among the best known of contemporary Jewish scholars. Any book of his is sure to command interest and attention,
but a book of his on *The Messianic Idea in Israel* no other scholar,
Christian or Jew, can afford to ignore. Indeed, we must be grateful that
it has finally been made available in an effortless English translation by
W. F. Stinespring of Duke University. Like Dr. Klausner's other writings, this book shows his great learning and wide familiarity with his
field. He brings to his work a manifest reverence for his topic; if his
method is scientific, his attitude is worshipful. For him the messianic
idea in Israel is not just an intellectual or emotional phenomenon in
the history of his people; it is a hope and a dream that he shares with
them and their forefathers from generation to generation.

For all that is admirable in it, Dr. Klausner's book cannot be said to
fulfill every demand of objective study. Occasionally he appears to be
guilty of unrealized contradictions, and throughout the book there is no
really fair consideration given to Christian exegesis. No one can expect
Dr. Klausner to agree with the Christian interpretation of the messianic
prophecies, but one has a right—has one not?—to expect him to acknowledge that interpretation rather than, for the most part, ignoring
it as though it did not merit attention. I fear, also, that Dr. Klausner at
times misunderstands Christian theology. Whenever he presents Christian beliefs or discusses Christian exegesis, it is quite apparent that the
teachings of liberal Protestantism are his concern—but its voice is not
that of the teaching Church. It is always the "rationalistic" approach of
the Christian to the Scriptures that he deplores and it is the "individualistic" approach of the Christian to his salvation that he finds incompatible with Old Testament revelation. Yet these are not characteristics
of Catholic Christianity, the only Christianity that Judaism knew for
fifteen hundred years; they are, the one an outgrowth, and the other a
mark, of the Reformation. Whoever looks to the Reformation, and,
more especially, to some of its modern corollaries, for a full and correct

* New York: Macmillan Co., 1955.

understanding of Christian doctrine will naturally fail to see the
Church's continuity with the thought and institutions of the ancient
Israel. I am sure that Dr. Klausner's failure to come to grips with Catholic teaching is not intentional, yet this is a not uncommon mistake
among Jewish thinkers, perhaps going back to Judaism's conflict with
medieval Christendom and a resultant tension. The unfortunate consequence is that even today, when old hostilities are dead, Catholic tradition is passed over, leaving vast areas unexplored or misunderstood.

Dr. Klausner's justified impatience with Christian scholars who are
"rationalistic theologians from the soles of their feet to the tops of their
heads" (p. 145) is an illustration in point. He condemns the widespread tendency to cut up the prophetic books and assign to them a
multiplicity of authors, blaming it on a lack of imagination. "These
scholars," he writes, "cannot imagine that some prophet might have
lived a long time, with the content and even the style, of his prophecies
changing in the course of time" (p. 200). But he shows no awareness
that Catholic exegetes hold a position similar to his own. Ten years ago
a Catholic scholar, approaching the problem of the "Deutero-Isaiah,"
voiced almost these same sentiments, and, in doing so, clearly expressed
the Catholic attitude which, without ever wavering in its belief in the
supernatural character of Scripture, seeks to meet the difficulties of
Higher Criticism. Father W. McClellan, S.J., suggested that chapters
40–66 of Isaiah were "the fruit of enforced retirement after 698 . . .
a transition from tongue to pen . . . the visions of a recluse who was
no longer a public orator" (*Catholic Biblical Quarterly*, October 1945,
p. 468), thereby accounting for the difference of style and content between the first and second halves of this great prophetical book. Father
McClellan is not singled out here because his suggestion is in any way
final, rather because his position closely parallels that of Dr. Klausner.

Again, one suspects that Dr. Klausner's insistence on the "other-
worldliness" of Christian messianism is chiefly due to his tacit identification of the Christian Church with the Protestant body, so largely and
deliberately individualistic. Stressing what he calls the ethical, idealistic,
and exalted but always terrestrial character of the Jewish messianic
world, he writes: "The Kingdom of Heaven of the Jewish Messiah is
not only within the soul of man, but also upon the earth" (p. 10), as if
this last were no part of Christian doctrine. Luther's interpretation of
Christ's saying that "the kingdom of God is within you," that is, within

your reach or among you, as if it meant that the kingdom of God is in souls alone, was born of his protest against the Catholic Church and of his attempt to find scriptural evidence for his "invisible Church." But any such misunderstanding is outside the mainstream of Catholic thought and practice. It is true, Christians have all too often forgotten—and alas! will forget—their social responsibility, though their Master clearly stated that they will be judged on whether or not they have fed Him in the hungry, refreshed Him in the thirsty, received Him in the stranger . . . (Mt 25:31–40). All too often Christians forget how James spoke out against those who live a life of glitter built on the sweat of men they have defrauded of their wages, and against those who scrape before the finely dressed while they scorn the ill clad (Jas 5:1–6; 2:1–13); how John warned that he who hates his neighbor is a murderer, and that he who says "I love God" but does not love his brother is a liar (1 Jn 3:15; 4:20). But when Christians forget their social responsibility, they forget Christ's kingdom too.

Further, despite Dr. Klausner's dislike of rationalistic criticism he is not altogether above falling into it himself. When discussing the Seventy Weeks prophecy of Daniel, he concludes that "the author . . . erred, therefore, by about seventy years" (p. 233), and he comes to this conclusion because the historical interpretation he, with many others, wishes to give the prophecy will not otherwise commend itself chronologically. The particular passage in Daniel (9:24–27) is admittedly difficult. But could it not be—as is the opinion of such Catholic scholars as Lagrange, Ceuppens, Chaine, and Saydon—that Daniel's figures, though not without reference to history, are largely symbolical; that he predicted a sequence of events and not their precise dates; and that there are in this prophecy, as in many others, more than one perspective? In it, there seem combined into one vision the Maccabean, the messianic, and the eschatological perspectives. Israel's oppression in the days of the Maccabees will lead to the new era of the messianic kingdom; this kingdom too will be oppressed, yet its sufferings will end in triumph and heavenly glory. No need, then, to place in doubt the inspired character of this prophecy by assuming Daniel to be in error.

When discussing the "Servant of Yahweh" prophecy in Isaiah 53, Dr. Klausner acknowledges that it was realized at least to some extent in the person of Jesus. He writes first that "the early Christians, from Paul the Apostle (Ac 8:32–35) onward, saw in [it] a reference to the suffer-

ings and death of Jesus of Nazareth," then admits that "as a matter of
fact, some of his career did resemble what is described in Chapter 53,"
only to lessen the impact of this admission by going on: "The rest of his
career is *intentionally* portrayed in the Gospels in such a manner that
the events appear to have happened in fulfillment of the words in this
chapter" (p. 162). Apart from the fact that this is the approach of rationalistic critics, Dr. Klausner offers no proof—and would, of course,
be hard put to it to offer any—of this his assertion. He insists that the
Messiah described in the Servant-Songs is not just an individual but even
more the nation, the best of the people of Israel. "Thus," he says, "the
whole people Israel in the form of the elect of the nation gradually became the Messiah of the world, the redeemer of mankind" (p. 163).
But nowhere does Isaiah or any other prophet, nowhere do the saints and
servants of old, claim so exalted an office as "redeemer of mankind." Do
they not rather all say with John the Baptist: "I am not the Christ," "One
mightier than I is coming, the strap of whose sandals I am not worthy to
loose" (Jn 1:20; Lk 3:16)? Dr. Klausner's interpretation of the "Servant" as a collective body is not new, nor restricted to Jewish exegetes,
but our ever growing knowledge of Semitic thought and language continually reduces its acceptability. A recent study of V. DeLeeuw's (in
L'Attente du Messie, L. Cerfaux, ed., Paris, 1954, pp. 51–56), by analyzing the various words used to describe the person or activity of the
Servant, demonstrates that, although he evidences certain prophetic
traits, he is primarily and undeniably a king, and if a king, "undoubtedly he belongs to that dynasty alone which the prophets regarded as
legitimate—the house of David." If the Servant is a collective body in
any sense, it can only be in the same way that every prince or king
represents his people.

  Does not Dr. Klausner walk on vulnerable ground also when he so
firmly asserts that Judaism never took the step of postulating a divine
Messiah (p. 24)? Toward the end of his book, he is forced to modify
this claim by admitting that "of the divine nature of the Messiah, there
are perhaps certain indications in the later Midrashim" (p. 466), but explains them as an indirect and unconscious borrowing from Christianity.
Would it not be more logical and in better historic perspective to assume
that they are survivals of ancient glimpses? Would it not be much more
in accordance with the data we have to regard the divinity of the Messiah
as something sensed and implied by the prophets and developed in later

apocryphal literature, well before there could have been any "Christian influence"? In chapter 9 (verse 6 of the Douay version, verse 5 of the Hebrew Bible), Isaiah says of the Messiah that His name shall be called "Wonderful, Counsellor, God the mighty, the Father of the world to come, the Prince of peace." I do not wish to suggest that the prophet and his hearers fully realized the tremendous implications of his foretelling. But does not Dr. Klausner sidestep these when he transfers the content of these stupendous names from the Messiah, the son promised, to God Himself, and adopts the translation used in the Bible of the Jewish Publication Society of America: "And his name shall be called: Wonderful in counsel is God the Mighty, the Everlasting Father, the Ruler of peace" (p. 64). This translation does not seem very convincing; but, apart from that, there can be no doubt that the names are meant to describe the Messiah Himself, for in the next verse the prophet shows how these qualities will be reflected in His reign, and in chapter 11 he continues his description of this Messiah by endowing Him again with attributes reminiscent of the names in chapter 9. I cannot help fearing that Dr. Klausner avoids the challenge of Isaiah's prophecy. For did not a dark and yet luminous prophetic perception that fused the Messiah with Yahweh, a prophetic perception that saw Yahweh at work in the Messiah and the Messiah in Yahweh, dominate all of Isaiah's visions?

Similarly, are not the words of Micah that the origins of the King-Messiah are from of old, from ancient days (5:2 Douay, 5:1 Hebrew), deprived of all significance when Dr. Klausner says that they "indicate only the antiquity of his origin . . . but nothing more" (p. 77), and that this antiquity is His Davidic descent? It is hard to see how this could have been the prophet's meaning, since the house of David was not distinguished by its antiquity. All the Israelite tribes and families were equally ancient, and the house of David was not even the first to occupy the throne. On the other hand, in Scripture "of old" refers to God's doings in the times of the exodus (Is 51:9; 63:9), or—and this is really pertinent here—to the hidden depth of eternity: "From of old [wisdom] was poured forth, at the first, before the earth" (Prov 8:23).

The great reluctance of any Jewish scholar, theologian, historian, or philosopher, to see divine traits in the revealed delineation of the Messiah is based upon his fervent and admirable devotion to God's unity. Anything that might suggest a duality or trinity of persons in the divine nature is, to the Jew, anathema. He does not see how it can be reconciled with the Oneness of God. Here we are at the center of a paradox, for the Jews have, through the centuries, accused Christians of rationalizing the biblical faith, of robbing it of its warmth and beauty by reducing it to the logic of Greek metaphysics. In Dr. Klausner's own words: "The prophet is not a philosopher of logic, but a philosopher of emotion . . . it is necessary to remember always that certain variations and inconsistencies are inevitable" (pp. 55–56). Yet it is the Christian who, sharing Israel's fervor for the one God of Abraham, Isaac, and Jacob, asserts that God is One, yet Three, only to find the Jew accusing him of illogic! It was Tertullian, a *Latin* Christian, who, faced with the tremendous mystery of the Incarnation, could write that just that which made it seem outrageous to human ears, fantastic to the "logical" mind, or simply impossible—that it was just that which gave him the confidence of faith: "The Son of God was born: I am not ashamed of it, precisely because it is scandalous. The Son of God died: I believe it utterly, because it is absurd. And He was buried and rose again: I am certain of it, because it is impossible" (PL 2:761).

Just as Dr. Klausner will not allow a divine Messiah, neither will he acknowledge a Messiah whose kingdom is "not of this world." Although we have already disproved the notion that the messianic kingdom of Jesus makes no claim on man's social life, it is nevertheless true that the Church seeks no material kingdom. Yet here again the paradox returns; for Dr. Klausner says with sadness: "Alas! it is not the Hebraic, the prophetic, the Messianic-Israelitic social conception which has become a basis for bringing about redemption in the land of vision and promise, but a foreign social conception, linked up with economic and historical materialism, to which the prophetic idealism is a mockery" (p. x). When he says that the state of Israel must be guided by "prophetic idealism," no God-fearing man will contradict him. But is "prophetic idealism" so far removed from the "other-worldliness" of Christ's kingdom? The economic and historical materialism he condemns is such because it sees human life altogether grounded in this world, and because in this world alone it places all its hopes and seeks all its means. The prophetic ideal is to bring peace and love and godliness through an inner change of the whole man which makes him seek his strength in God and not in himself or the things of this world. To which of these two ways does the teaching of Jesus adhere? Dare I say that if Dr. Klausner followed his deepest inspirations, he would find the difference between the true Jewish and the Christian concepts of the Messiah not quite so great as he thinks (p. 529)? For it is not a prince of this world who will overcome the evil fruit which the world itself has produced.

J. EDGAR BRUNS

Jacob B. Agus: GUIDEPOSTS IN MODERN JUDAISM *

JEWISH survival in America may not be taken for granted." This is the
warning of Rabbi Jacob B. Agus in his *Guideposts,* a volume of his essays collected for the American Jewish Tercentenary in 1954. He feels,
therefore, the need to outline the attitudes he thinks should shape the
American Jewish community in years to come. It is as a man at home
both with the language of rabbinic culture and the hardly less formalized
idiom of contemporary philosophy that he, a leading Conservative rabbi
of Baltimore, writes. His tool is reason, operating in the open forum of
universal experience; neither "illumination" nor "mystical wonderment"
seem to him suitable for marshaling the forces which will secure the
Jewish future. But before looking to the future, he sketches American
Judaism as it is today, and in this performs a service so useful, at least to
the non-Jewish reader, that I think I should be reporter before I turn
reviewer, difficult though it is further to compress some 120 tightly
packed pages.

If any section of Jewish life might be expected by a Christian to be
a uniform block, surely it is the Orthodox. Yet Rabbi Agus has to dif-
ferentiate, within the "Orthodox stream," four main currents, each patient
of infinite subdivision, and each represented in the United States. There
is the *musar* movement. When *haskalah,* the secularistic Enlightenment
of the last century, and with it revolutionary enthusiasms, began making
serious inroads among Jewish intellectuals of eastern Europe, the ideal
of a "holy community" seemed shattered. In reaction to this breakdown,
the *musar* movement aimed at the formation of an elite of learned and
saintly individuals by persistent ethical self-criticism. Not reason, not the
triumphant dialectic of the apologete, but awe and love are the sources
of the religious energy of the *musar*-man, the "disciplined," "ethical"
man. In the presence of the Holy One, the original *musar*-man trembles,
mindful of his sins and failures, mindful of judgment. "You are young
men, and you have felt perplexed only for a short time," said the aged
Rabbi Blaser to a group of rabbinical students. "I have been lost for a
long, long time. Let us cry together. Perhaps the Almighty will help us."

* New York: Bloch Publishing Co., 1954.

Another tendency in the *musar* movement, to become more influential than the first in the United States, relies on the more benign dynamism of love and aspiration to produce a man of serene perfection rather than his trembling and anxious brother. It teaches peace and imperturbability of spirit, to be attained by constant reflection, "the key to wisdom, the focus of all the faculties." This stress on reflection has led to metaphysical speculation, not in terms of contemporary secularized philosophy, but in the framework of the Kabbalah, the system of theosophy which sees the world as an emanation from God and sensible realities as but shadows of higher realities, and which therefore regards every word, letter, number, and accent of holy Scripture as filled with hidden meaning. In the universe of the Kabbalah, no frontier divides the natural from the supernatural, miracles are routine, and the past is idealized to such an extent that its ordinary men and women are imagined to have known the mystical links between the lower and higher worlds.

Between the *musar* movement, so radically other-worldly, and an Orthodoxy which has achieved a maximum accommodation to Western speculation may be located two other currents: the complex of ideas promulgated by Rabbi Kuk, the late Chief Rabbi of Palestine, and that expounded by Rabbi Soloveitchik, professor of Talmud and Religious Philosophy at Yeshiva University, New York. Rabbi Kuk, whom Dr. Agus considers the real heir of the great mystical tradition of Hasidism, derived from his own mystical experiences, the author tells us, the conception that the world, although one, presents two faces to man. There is the happy side of the universe, God-centered and beneficently ordered by Torah: it is the side of faith. But doubt sees a melancholy side, the side of moral disorder, of meaninglessness, of frustration. Through this contradiction the mystic penetrates; he is joyously lifted by the love that comes from God, so that he glimpses the truth in its depth and healing power; his is "the view of all things together." Kabbalah had its role in the development of Rabbi Kuk's ideas, but he did not reject the conceptions of a more secular philosophy nor the literally down-to-earth ideals of Zionism. Indeed, he "advanced at times," in Rabbi Agus's revealing phrase, to the intellectual position of Conservatism, as when he found that even the secular achievements of the Jewish people constituted Torah, holy teaching.

For Rabbi Soloveitchik, *halakah,* traditional Jewish Law, corresponds to the fundamental structure of man. Founded on revelation, the Law needs no secular scaffolding, no validation from outside. Kierkegaard is right about Abraham, he holds: not even the best ordered reason has anything to tell the man of true faith. Abraham's trial on Mount Moriah

was not to teach him that God desired no human sacrifice (the general
Jewish interpretation), but that God's thought and will are incommen-
surate with man's. All of the Law—that given on Sinai and that ham-
mered out in later ages—is of divine origin. There is no room in the
life of the Halakist, we are told, for anxieties, for warfare against the
flesh, for the vagaries of religious "feeling." The Law gives him mas-
tery over all these. Restrained though the man of *halakah* is, nonetheless, in the words of Rabbi Soloveitchik, "every person is called upon
to renew his being in accord with the ideal pattern of the prophet" in
order that the divine Presence may rest upon him.

The fourth grouping within American Orthodox opinion (small at
present but likely to grow in numbers and importance) proceeds under
the sign of an alliance with Western intellectual influences. In it there
is no longer to be found that unsophisticated, spontaneous devotion
which marks the Orthodoxy rooted in the East. Sometimes termed Jewish "neo-Orthodoxy," it must not be likened to Protestant neo-orthodox
opinion; it is as fundamentalist as the other Orthodox traditions. The
most recent expression of this type of Orthodoxy is Isaak Breuer's *Der
Neue Kusari,* an effort, on the eve of the Nazi deluge, to synthesize
three elements: a profound conviction of the inadequacy of mere human reason, the idealism classic in certain German philosophic circles,
and the persuasion that the Law is the only salvation for mankind. The
surging, restless world of experience, the physical world of inexorable
causal relations, is a construct, Breuer contends. It is the product of the
noumenal realm (which he calls "meta-physical"), but only as ordered
by a subconscious will, common to all men (which he terms the "meta-
ethical" aspect of the human personality). Inaccessible to rational analysis, the "meta-ethical" is manifested both in our anxiety and in the decision which alone conquers anxiety. Hence ultimate knowledge is not the
business of intellect but of the inner will of man, and the ultimate
truth which is Torah cannot be submitted to the methods of rational
demonstration. And the Jewish people? They are the "meta-historical"
reality. As the "meta-physical" and the "meta-ethical" constitute the really
real behind all phenomena, so it is the role of the authentic Jew, says
Breuer, to stand beyond the aspirations for power and the groping wisdom of the nations, beyond their ever frustrated efforts to conquer evil.
His role is to show all mankind the ultimate answer to the tragedy of
human living. That answer is detailed, concrete, precise: it is Torah, the
pattern of the kingdom of God. If the Jewish people are a minority,
scattered among the nations, this is because their destiny makes them
"the people of peoples," men who "learn to love and cherish the pe-

culiar characteristics of each nation." It goes without saying that, in this perspective, Zionism is a betrayal of, a rebellion against, the "meta-historical" function which is the duty and the glory of the Jew, a deliberate reduction of what ought to stand beyond the shifting façade of history to the status of another temporal nation: competing, unstable, merely equal.

If Orthodoxy in every form dramatically emphasizes the separation of Jew from non-Jew, another tendency in American Judaism has been to attempt a reconciliation with the spirit of time and place as thoroughgoing as possible—indeed its critics will complain that it goes beyond what is possible. This is the Reform movement, with its Central Conference of American Rabbis, its Union of American Hebrew Congregations, and its Hebrew Union College. Originating especially in Germany and Hungary, where a strong effort was made to weld together progressive cultural elements with whatever must be retained if Judaism is to be an intelligible reality, this movement was peculiarly well adapted to certain requirements of the American scene during the second half of the nineteenth century. To begin with, it provided the more cosmopolitan Jews of German and Hungarian origin with an ideological and even a theological basis for their very real cultural difference from the Orthodox Polish and Russian immigrants who were so little at home in the new world. Second, in a century when necessary progress enjoyed the status of a self-evident truth, Reform theology was ready to explain that Judaism is an essentially progressive religion, able and even eager to jettison whatever might be found inconsistent with the spirit of the times. It was eager (in the days of its youth) to transfer the Sabbath services to Sunday, to replace Bar Mitzvah by "Confirmation," to have a Jewish school give lessons in German but abandon Hebrew. The Reform leaders looked on themselves as the vanguard of the entire Jewish community and firmly hoped that their program would become *"minhag America,"* "the American form of Judaism." Although the Mosaic Law is considered by Reform theology to express perennial moral values, traditional ceremonies are retained only on condition that they conform to contemporary habits and aspirations. Judaism, in short, is, to the Reform rabbis, what some liberal Protestant theologians had reproached it for failing to be: a religion of progressive perfection, careless of ritualistic law, dedicated to making this world a better place, burdened with no degrading dependence on hell and paradise to buttress the conviction that virtue is its own reward and that the human spirit is immortal because it is "divine." Though during the nineteenth century Zionism was an eminently academic issue, Reform Judaism roundly condemned it as a survival of unprogressive nationalism—this, at any rate, was the Reform Judaism of the celebrated "Pittsburgh Platform" of 1885.

And today? The "Columbus Platform of Guiding Principles" adopted in 1937 made some adjustments to the spirit of still another time. While not urging American Jews to settle in Palestine, it affirmed the "obligation of all Jewry" to aid in the building of a homeland. Furthermore, the Columbus Conference marked an attempt to emphasize the continuity of Jewish tradition by searching in the medieval literature of *halakah* for the sources of present-day practice. However, this practice varies so much from congregation to congregation that it is impossible to record it here. At Columbus, the "progressive" character of Reform Judaism was maintained, while avoiding the brutal rupture with past ages implied in the sweeping disclaimers of the Pittsburgh Platform. Perhaps no one has better expressed the religious philosophy of Reform than the venerable survivor of Theresienstadt, Rabbi Leo S. Baeck, who calls the essence of Judaism an "ethical dynamism." The divine challenge "thou shalt," he says, is the full and fundamental reality, the great hope. Revelation, moral duty, and promise are here one; this is "the Torah, which, according to ancient simile, was 'before the creation of the world.'"

A third major grouping within the framework of Jewish faith and practice in the United States is the Conservative movement. It is to be understood, Rabbi Agus tells us, as a kind of golden mean between two extremes: the fundamentalism and literalism of all forms of Orthodoxy, and the willingness of Reform to sacrifice the integrity of *halakah* to the exigencies of time and place. Rejecting the intransigent devotion of Orthodoxy to the interpretations of the Law made by the courts and rabbis of the past, a Conservative thinker defends rather the authority of the rabbi or court of our own day: else, he fears, law and life will lose their dynamic contact. For him, the ultimate authority shifts from the dead letter to the living people. The people speaks, for the Conservative ideology, through a Committee on Jewish Law and Standards. In this way, the Conservative reasons, a chaotic, every-man-for-himself subjectivism is avoided, but so is rigidity and standstill. In the interest of "strengthening the faith," therefore, the letter of the Law may undergo progressive modification—the dietary laws be obligatory, for example, only at public synagogue functions, and literal Sabbath observances modified as necessity may dictate. The Bas Mitzvah for girls complementing the Bar Mitzvah for boys, and a Consecration ceremony for children about to enter Hebrew school, are instances of "the search for new vehicles of religious expression." Yet the Conservative is committed to the whole Jewish tradition. Rabbi Agus is fond of quoting the paraphrase "nothing

Jewish is alien to me." Hence the tendency, indeed the policy, of Reform to dispense with those practices and beliefs which single out the Jews: to drop Hebrew, in the name of a shallow rationalism to maintain only the moral prescriptions of the Mosaic code, and to make no room for mysticism—all this seems to the Conservative a wanton squandering of riches amassed through centuries of creative effort.

The mediating character of Conservatism is exhibited also in its genesis. Although the movement was already well defined in Europe before it appeared on the American scene, here it only reluctantly disassociated itself from Reform. Its original intention had been to heal the wounds of disunity which divided American Judaism into an Orthodoxy represented chiefly by new immigrants from eastern Europe and the Reform movement based on the more urbane representatives of German and central European Judaism. The Conservative thinkers had consequently set themselves a double task: to bring to the Orthodox a "culture" which would complement their religious devotion and at the same time to provide the Reform movement with a demonstration of fidelity to the integral tradition of *halakah* without the sacrifice of legitimate cultural aspirations. But the Orthodox are still Orthodox, and the Pittsburgh Platform revealed what an abyss separates Reform from Conservative ideology. Hence an effort to transcend sectarian division has resulted in the formation of a third force with its own explanations and its own institutions— chief among these last the Jewish Theological Seminary, the United Synagogue, and the Rabbinical Assembly.

No narrow set of principles, Conservatism is nonetheless fairly easy to identify. A merely literal interpretation of revelation is rejected. Revelation is continuous, containing the eternal under a temporal, human envelope; the continuing task of Judaism is to disengage one from the other and to pay divine honors only to the former. The past is not to be worshipped, but its achievements are to be preserved with humility and love; the present is the extension of that past, and Torah is still in the making. Ritual and symbol, so little valued by Reform, truly "strengthen the faith," and the insights of depth psychology and social anthropology are considered to confirm the practice of the Conservative synagogue. Both rationalism and mysticism find their place in this "open" conception of Judaism, for rationalism alone is incapable of a full appreciation of the holy, but it plays an indispensable role in the bewilderingly exact network of reasoned interpretation which adjusts the ancient formulae of the Law to each new ethical problem and circumstance. The Law itself, in its exquisite balance, justifies the rational, the sober, the measured. Even for the Conservative thinker, who does not regard Sinai as a "once-for-all" revelation of an eternally fixed law, Judaism remains a religion which necessarily tends to lawfulness as its final goal. But lest a spirit of mere legalism vitiate faith, the values of mysticism are welcomed and cultivated. It is enough to mention the names of Martin Buber and Abraham Heschel to realize what place of honor the traditions of mystical piety hold within the Conservative pattern.

Contemporary "existentialism" has found a place in this mosaic. Judaism is to be reduced neither to a system of abstract thought, nor to a blueprint of legal prescriptions, nor to Zionist patriotism: it is, for the Jewish existentialist, the vital and dynamic contact between God and the human person. The two meet in the context of space and time, a phantasmagoria which masks three ultimate realities: God, man, world. The contact of God and man is revelation; of God and the world, creation; of man and the world, redemption. On the part of God, the act of grace; on the part of man, the leap of faith; the whole people of Israel owes its entity to such a temporal-eternal experience with God, and this is revelation.

Within the framework of Conservatism, the Reconstructionist Fellowship is a kind of "left wing." This movement hopes to "reconstruct" the divisions of American Jewry into an "organic community," a unity in diversity comparable to that which has succeeded so brilliantly in certain modern nations. It would be the maximum development of the "people" in the Conservative triad: God, Torah, and People. Faith is pre-eminent in the ethos of this people, but it is only one of many cultural elements which conspire in its formation, and the exponents of Reconstruction have not always spoken of Judaism as a *religious* civilization. The intention of this tendency within the Conservative movement is to bring to full fruition the dynamics implicit in the "we-feeling" of the Jewish people, and it is maintained that religion is a consequence rather than a cause of that fundamental group-consciousness. The theology of Reconstructionism is liberal to the extreme. The ineffable God is conceived as "a process that makes for salvation" rather than as a Person; He becomes "what the world means to the man who believes in the possibility of maximum life and strives for it." This, it must be noted, is not the dominant view of Conservatives; characteristic of them, Rabbi Agus holds, is faith in a personal God and the ineluctable belief that the Jewish people is in a unique way the carrier of revelation through its total tradition.

Such is American Judaism in the view of a distinguished Conservative rabbi, who is convinced that it is something new—more, that its history is only now beginning. In this fluid situation he sees both dangers and opportunities; a future of unsuspected achievement or one of profound disappointment may flow from the choices made by this generation. By his *Guideposts,* Rabbi Agus hopes to help guide that choosing.

Perhaps because Rabbi Agus is not only a rabbi, but also a trained philosopher, he has presented his problem as a search for unity in diversity. According to him, Judaism, with perhaps one exception at the end of the Middle Ages, has never been "monolithic in thought" (p. 349). On the contrary, it is extremely varied; it carries in its sweep the debris of many storms, the flotsam of the centuries; a random wealth eddies on its surface. And yet, for him, Judaism in its deepest reality is *one* thing; he will not refuse to propose *the* Jewish solution to the problems of the immediate future. If this requires that he speak out roundly against competing Jewish solutions, his love for everything Jewish does not deter him from that duty. He is sure the Orthodox are wrong: to him they are "literalists" (p. 322). This does not mean that the men of Reform fare any better. They are wrong to propose a "mission" theory— that the Jews have been dispersed all over the earth to diffuse the principles of "ethical monotheism"—as justification for efforts to guarantee Jewish survival and as a consolation for the diaspora (p. 150). Rabbi Agus has other goals for Judaism:

> While the first approach subjects the living Jews of today to the mores of the past, the second approach is a frank acceptance of the caprices and confusions of the momentary present, "the idols of the market-place." Our own approach is to orient Jewish life in terms of the future—the state of affairs we should like to bring about. Accordingly, our basic question is: What can Judaism do for the individual Jew of the future? Or, what function can it fulfill in his life? (p. 158)

Thus, to Rabbi Agus in one mood, at least, Judaism seems to have no goal other than the Jew. Faith itself is measured by the requirements of the individual:

> Faith in God is sterile if it is not conceived in terms of faith in man. Religious Jews cannot succumb to a paganism that exalts God in the heavens but conceives man on earth as little better than the beasts of the field. If we failed to build our lives on the cornerstone of faith in our fellowmen, we would deny ourself [*sic*] as both Jews and Americans (p. 170).

The paganism at issue here is not, of course, one dedicated to Odin or to Aphrodite. "From the Jewish viewpoint, Christianity partakes of the qualities of paganism and mythology" (p. 422), writes Dr. Agus. Apart from the disappointment at seeing so learned a rabbi confuse mystery with myth, I cannot help the marginal comment that the characteristic pagan attitude would seem to be that which makes man the measure of all things, makes of religion a device for human purposes, creates a divinity designed to reflect man's aspirations. Would it not seem, then, that Rabbi Agus's concept of Judaism, rather than Christianity, partakes of pagan qualities?

But no matter how much religion may be centered on man and his needs, religion bespeaks a conception of God, and to explore it is, for Rabbi Agus, the task of one of the two pillars of Judaism, reason or revelation. His choice is made without hesitation: it is reason, "the only highway of progress open to man" (p. 231), which must guide us to God, and logical reason at that, although he will not deny a role to what Lévy-Bruhl would term the "pre-logical" approaches of aesthetic and moral feeling. Hence his appeal to what he terms the "most fundamental principles of thought, as these have been formulated in our time" (p. 229): the principle of causality and the principle of polarity. Morris R. Cohen's theory of polarity, which Rabbi Agus follows, is this: The universe is a tension of opposites, of "poles," which are directions rather than states or qualities, so that "the whole is mind as well as matter; purposiveness . . . as well as mechanism . . . ; life as well as death; God as well as nature" (p. 240). Moreover, the poles of any given relation are not homogeneous to each other: one functions as a "point" and the other as a "field"—the pattern of infinite relations to which every point is subject. Neither point nor field exist in themselves, but every existent is an expression of a polar tension between some point and its field. Now, each field in turn can be considered a point with respect to the greater field within which it is located. Scientific experience with lesser relations encourages us to extrapolate to infinity this rising scale of being.

Space forbids the discussion of this theory, as it forbids me to discuss, among other things, Rabbi Agus's interpretation of Kant (pp. 255–256) or of Simone Weil (p. 422), or what he calls "the creative orchestration of Jewish and Christian traditions" (p. 222). But I have to draw attention to the result of his use of the theory of polarity. The personal God who is both immanent and transcendent, both near and far (p. 269), receives new names. The Ineffable has become the "Self of the Universe" (p. 254), the "Field-Builder" (p. 252), the "Divine Pole of being" (p. 256). I shall not be thought irreverent if I suggest that the new divine names would not demand that the high priest enter solemnly, once yearly, into the Holy of Holies before he pronounces them. Indeed, I wonder whether Rabbi Agus expresses an authentic conception of the God who is personal, the God of Abraham, Isaac, and Jacob, when he says: "In our view, God is conceived as the Pole of Absolute, Ideal Personality in the back and forth flux of the multiple processes of reality, and the love of Him as the highest peak of the Divine process in the heart of man" (p. 334).

In the presence of this account of contemporary American Judaism and of what one Conservative rabbi would like it to become, it is clear that its unity is rather tenuous. If their present situation finds American Jews without a sure road, will Rabbi Agus's "guideposts" safeguard them on their journey? The Torah is described by him as a law because human beings have bound themselves to accept it (p. 134). But, surely, it is the Jewish way to say "Amen" to nothing but the Law that is God's. And the God of Torah—He told the Jews of old His mysterious name, and that name has been the object of a loving and reverent speculation from that day to this. Philosophers have been persuaded that in this revelation they had a hint as to the rational analysis of all that is real; prophets and saints have found in it an enduring food for their souls. While I must grant that it is "modern" to call God the "Field-Builder," I cannot think that Exodus 3:14 is obsolete. I find it hard to escape the painful impression that although Dr. Agus has mastered the language of contemporary philosophy, somehow the accents of biblical faith are missing. But the affection I have for him as a Jew and the respect I gladly owe him as a rabbi make me pray that my impression is wrong.

EDWARD A. SYNAN

Jacob Epstein: AN AUTOBIOGRAPHY *

THIS revised and extended edition of Sir Jacob Epstein's *Let There Be Sculpture* could well be subtitled: The Story of an Embattled Artist. His own aim in his work was lofty. "The sculptor with his vision, planning, working, laying loving hands upon the willing and love-returning stone, the creation of a work, the form embodying the idea, strange copulation of spirit and matter, the intellect dominating hammer and chisel—the conception that at last becomes a piece of sculpture. This seems to me fit work for a man" (p. 153). But the world did not agree with him about the nature of his art. One viewer cried out: "I should like to take Epstein out to a butcher's shop and have his hands chopped off" (p. 106).

Born in New York in 1880, Epstein went to Paris at the age of twenty-two and to London at twenty-five, where he settled and married a "Scottish lady," who has since died. Recently he was married again, to his secretary, known to the art world by his study "Girl with the Gardenias." He remarks of his youth that he was a "tremendous reader" and that he would go off to Central Park and there give himself up to solitary reading, "coming back home burnt by the sun and filled with ideas from Dostoyevsky's *Brothers Karamazov,* or Tolstoy's novels. Also I absorbed the New Testament and Whitman's *Leaves of Grass*" (p. 5). When he arrived in London in 1905, he haunted the British Museum, studying the Elgin Marbles, Greek sculpture generally, and "the Egyptian rooms and the vast and wonderful collections from Polynesia and Africa" (p. 20).

Three years later he received his first major commission: to decorate the new British Medical Association building in the Strand. With these Strand Statues—representing man and woman in all their various stages from birth to old age, "a primitive, but in no way a bizarre program," he remarks—the saga of the "Epstein scandal" began. The statues were attacked and their removal demanded, even before the scaffolding had been entirely taken down. Father Bernard Vaughan, fearing that many

* New York: E. P. Dutton & Co., Inc., 1955.

of the public might not look upon the nude figures with the temperament of the artist but with the hunger of sensualists, joined in the demand: "Let us teach self-reverence and self-respect, and not convert London into a Fiji Island, where there may be some excuse for want of drapery" (p. 240). Others defended the statues, while Epstein himself wrote: "I wished to create noble and heroic forms to embody in sculpture the great primal facts of man and woman . . . figures joyous, energetic, and mystical . . . [having] an ideal aspect, and . . . possessed of an inner life" (p. 245). For thirty years the controversy did not die down till, in 1937, the statues were in large part demolished because of deterioration of the stone and an alleged danger of falling fragments. In the meantime, however, the artist had gone on to new and mightier battles.

These battles had the fervor of religious wars. What impresses us in Epstein's autobiography is the struggle of an artist who wishes to communicate his own religious feelings through human forms that challenge conventional notions, ingrained preconceptions, of how the human figure ought to be portrayed. Had he projected his religious feelings in abstractions; or, at least, had the religious promptings to which he was impelled to give form been a vague religiosity embracing everything and nothing, shunning the real, the historic, Christ as the heretic shuns the rack, he might have avoided his "rack." But with a kind of essential realism, Epstein hurled himself into the very heart of the matter: from 1917 to 1920, he did his first statue of Christ, and followed it with many others on Christian themes.

His "Christ" had been preceded by work on a number of portrait busts, and it was from a portrait in clay that his first inspiration for the Christ-figure came. We must note, at this point, the respect, the deep, almost reverent, concern for the human personality his portrait busts reveal. Speaking of Franz Hals, he observes that "his outlook on humanity is cold and detached . . . human beings [his sitters] evidently aroused in him no feeling of sympathy, and he turned to their clothes with greater pleasure than he got from their faces." But of his beloved Rembrandt, he says: "His great heart seemed to warm towards the men and women who sat for him, and he seemed to penetrate into their inner selves, and reveal their very souls" (p. 70). Similarly, Epstein's portrait busts of Joseph Conrad, T. S. Eliot, and Ernest Bloch, among others, disclose a sharp sensitivity to the human condition.

While working on a mask of Bernard Van Dieren, a gravely ill friend, Epstein felt that his head was "so spiritual and worn with suffering," his face "so noble and [having] such a high quality of intellectual life, I thought of him as the suffering Christ, and developed the mask into a head, then into a bust with arms, and extended it again, and so made my first image of Christ in bronze" (pp. 101, 79). So intense was Epstein's feeling that this face with "its pitying accusing eyes" *was* "the Christ head" that he compares his experience of recognition with one recorded by Turgeniev, "how, standing in the crowd somewhere, he instantly felt, in some man beside him, the presence of the Christ Himself and the awe that overcame him" (p. 101). To see, as Epstein did, the pain of Christ reflected in the pain of a neighbor, to be reminded by some present sorrow of the past and ever present sorrow of Christ—this is an experience that can be had only by one who has had a genuine glimpse of the Redeemer.

Yet when the statue was exhibited, it was assailed. John Galsworthy left it with "clenched fists and an angry, furious face" (p. 106). Father Vaughan leaped again to the attack:

I have studied the unshapely head, the receding brow, the thick lips, the untipped nose, the uncanny eyes, the poorly built body, with its ugly feet and uglier hands, till I felt ready to cry out with indignation that in this Christian England there should be exhibited the figure of a Christ which suggested to me some degraded Chaldean or African, which wore the appearance of an Asiatic-American or Hun-Jew, which reminded me of some emaciated Hindu, or a badly grown Egyptian swathed in the cerements of the grave. I call it positively wicked and insulting to perpetrate such a travesty of the Risen Christ and to invite a Christian people, to whom the Founder of Christianity is the Man-God, to come and admire it (pp. 103–104).

How beside himself with anger Father Vaughan must have been to forget that Chaldean and African, not only European, features are made in the likeness of God; that not only an English gentleman, but also an "Asiatic-American" or a "Hun-Jew," is shaped in His image; and that none of them is foreign to Him who is the Saviour of them all. One is thankful that God in His mercy does not permit our anger to kindle His. For it would have been terrible had Father Vaughan's words been challenged by a glimpse of Christ as He was seen by Isaiah: "Unregarded as brushwood shoot, as a plant in waterless soil; no stateliness here, no majesty, no beauty, as we gaze upon Him" (53:2; Knox trans.). A suggestion of this may well be in Epstein's vision, seeing Christ as he did at once in His passion and in His rising. "The statue rose swathed in clothes," he tells, "a pillar firmly set on the two naked feet—Christ risen supernatural, a portent for all time" (p. 101).

This is how some of the friendly critics saw the statue:

Epstein's conception of Christ—a strong, stern, ascetic young Christ—is not an ordinary one (p. 261).

Mr. Epstein has made his Christ before all things powerful. . . . Power is in every line; the flat crown of the head; the shoulders; the defiant chin; the intellectual brows; the immense hands and feet; by all such means the artist shows that for him Christ is not the gentle and passive being of Christian art [more accurately, of a great deal of conventional Christian art—C. and I. S.], but the fierce and even violent leader of men. There is an absence of charm; clearly there is no beauty that man should desire Him; He looks stern and austere, and yet terrible in His intensity of passion. . . . This may have been the Christ of whom men said: "Elijah is returned." This may have been the Christ who strode ahead of His disciples towards the city, and they were afraid of Him. This Christ might have cleansed the Temple and cursed the fig-tree. It is as though the artist has personified this aspect of the historical Christ (pp. 261–262).

Epstein's own feelings about his statue are deeply sincere; one cannot doubt the purity of his intention. As we have seen, his first inspiration for the figure came while he was at the bedside of a dying friend. It was a work of love and grief, and the artist knew it to be so:

I must maintain that my statue of Christ still stands for what I intended it to be. It stands and accuses the world for its grossness, inhumanity, cruelty, and beastliness. . . . How prophetic a figure! Not the early Evangelical Christ of Byzantium and Rome, nor the condemning Apollonian Christ of Michelangelo, or the sweet rising and blessing Christ of Raphael, but the modern living Christ, compassionate and accusing at the same time. I should like to remodel this "Christ." I should like to make it hundreds of feet high, and set it up on some high place where all could see it, and where it would give out its warning, its mighty symbolic warning to all lands. The Jew—the Galilean—condemns our wars, and warns us that "Shalom, Shalom," must be still the watchword between man and man (p. 102).

This indignant, almost flaunting faith in his work, in the validity of his vision, has given many the feeling that Epstein lacks humility. But he is a man who has had to fight for his work against a fiercely hostile public; if he has gone to an extreme in praising his own work while defending it, one is surely required, in all charity, to remember his embattled position. He is fighting not just for his work but for the religious impulses he has expressed through his work. But what are Epstein's religious impulses, what his beliefs? To what is he giving form? Here is an artist, a Jew, who has sculptured some of the most arousing Christian statues. In speaking of his "Christ," he calls Him "the Jew," "the Galilean." Does he think of Him as God incarnate? Or as a great man? It is impossible for us to answer, and yet we must not overlook that he speaks of the "living Christ," that for him Christ lives.

First of all, in what sense can Jacob Epstein be named a Jew? Just as little as he thinks of his work "as peculiarly of London or of [his] time" (p. 115), so he is "most often annoyed rather than flattered to be told that [he is] the best or foremost Jewish artist" (p. 198). And as little interest as he shows in British politics, or in the London weather for that matter (p. 140), so little does he have in Jewish affairs—which has not endeared him to some Jewish critics. Once, arriving in New York, he was asked his attitude toward Zionism. When he replied that he had none, the reporter warned: "We will want to know your attitude, make no mistake about it." But Epstein did not care, and left him (p. 124). He seems to have cared even less for the religious faith and practice of his boyhood home:

Saturday in the synagogue was a place of ennui for me, and the wailing prayers would get on my nerves, and my one desire would be to make excuses to get away. The picturesque shawls with the strange faces underneath only held my attention for a short while; then the tedium of the interminable services would drown every other emotion. Certainly I had no devotional feelings, and later, with my reading and free-thinking ideas, I dropped all practice of ceremonial forms, and as my parents were only conventionally interested in religion, they did not insist (pp. 6–7).

On the other hand, he recalls his grandparents and their blessing hands most tenderly:

My grandparents on my mother's side were a dear old couple, whose kindness and patriarchal simplicity I remember well. Every Friday evening the children would go to them to get their blessing. Before the Sabbath candles they would take our heads in their hands and pronounce a blessing on each one of us in turn. Then followed gifts of fruit and sweets (p. 6).

That Epstein came from an Orthodox Jewish background and tradition is almost all one can say about his Jewishness. Yet despite his reading in Christian literature, and despite his habits, studies, friendships, in no way different from those of any non-Jewish artist, he carries deep in his being the stamp of his childhood. He himself writes:

I saw a great deal of Jewish orthodox life, traditional and narrow. As my thoughts were elsewhere, this did not greatly influence me, but I imagine that the feeling I have for expressing a human point of view, giving human rather than abstract implications to my work, comes from these early formation years (p. 9).

When he looks at Rembrandt's Jews, he recognizes them as a child recognizes his father in the dark. Doubtless the sufferings of the Jewish people awaken in him an empathic understanding. He tells us also that he has painted and sketched Jews of New York's lower East Side, European Jews (and, much later, Old Testament figures). It must have been more than the plastic beauty of these subjects which called to him; it must have been a voice from his early years. The connecting link between these drawings and the figures he has made of Christ and Mary, whether or not he is conscious of it, is worth thinking about. But in no way does it explain them.

It would be gratifying if somewhere in this autobiography one could point to an explicit statement by Jacob Epstein on why he, a Jew, has turned with passionate absorption to Christian subjects. But ever since he chose as a motto, "I rest silent in my work" (p. 100), he has demanded that his work speak for him. There is a striking pattern in it: he perpetuates in stone what for want of a better word we might call essential moments of Jesus' life, moments which are living Catholic belief. He feels deeply about them, so deeply that, in defending them, he seems again and again to overstep the bounds between self-defense and self-praise. He does not seem to be defending himself. He seems to be defending these moments and what they mean to him. Of his "Visitation" (1926), he says: "This figure stands with folded hands, and expresses a humility so profound as to shame the beholder who comes to my sculpture expecting rhetoric or splendor of gesture" (p. 112). Indeed, so tender is his feeling about this bronze figure of Mary that he could not bear the thought of controversy over it, and hence, when it was first exhibited, called it simply "A Study." He offers yet another name for it, "Charity," perhaps the sweetest title that could be given to Mary.

Again, while some repudiated his "Behold the Man" (1935) as "debased," "ugly and vile," "an outrage," "an Asiatic monstrosity" (p. 147), and others spoke of its "Romanesque affinities," its "austere pattern," and saw in it "a caryatid of suffering," conveying, it seems, "the idea of the unending sorrows of the Master whose teachings were denied by the world every day and of that cumulative denial crushing down upon him" (p. 148), to Epstein this statue in Subiaco marble is "a symbol of man, bound, crowned with thorns and facing with a relentless and over-mastering gaze of pity and prescience our unhappy world" (p. 145).

His "Consummatum Est" (1937), which aroused the same bitter protests, was conceived by the artist during a transporting experience —the "Credo" of Bach's *B minor Mass:*

I have been listening to Bach's *B minor Mass.* In the section, Crucifixus, I have a feeling of tremendous quiet, of awe. The music comes from a great distance and in this mood I conceive my "Consummatum Est." I see the figure complete as a whole. I see immediately the upturned hands, with the wounds in the feet, stark, crude, with the stigmata. I even imagine the setting for the finished figure, a dim crypt, with a subdued light on the semi-transparent alabaster (p. 152).

With all his heart, Epstein longed to see his religious works placed in churches or monasteries. For many years his wish remained unfulfilled, but eventually one of his works found its proper home. A few years ago his "Lazarus" (1948)—still in the bands of death but ready to be awakened and waiting for the word "Come forth!"—a statue which proclaims as loudly as stone can that death's Master is in our midst, was installed in the New College chapel at Oxford. He thought it miraculous how its stone harmonized with the ancient stone walls. An even greater victory and joy came to him when the London Convent of the Holy Child Jesus commissioned a "Madonna and Child." Thirteen and a half feet high, and placed above an arch connecting two Palladian-style buildings on Cavendish Square, it was unveiled in May 1952 by the Chancellor of the Exchequer—a ceremony that "seemed to reach back to the days of the Renaissance when the appearance of a new religious work was the occasion for public rejoicing" (p. 236). Happily he recounts how the work absorbed him for over six months and how the Mother Superior came with another Sister to view it. "They immediately showed the warmest interest in the work and asked to be allowed to contemplate it quietly and alone for some time" (p. 235).

"The modern sculptor without religion, without direction, tradition, and stability, is at a terrible disadvantage compared with the sculptors of previous periods" (p. 192), Epstein writes, but he never analyzes his interest in Christ and Mary. Despite his verbal inexplicitness, his inner inclination is made quite clear, not only through his work, but through his "loves." Outside of sculpture his major love is religious music:

We crowd into the hall to listen to Beethoven's *Mass in D,* as in other periods worshippers devoutly made their way into cathedrals to attend Holy Mass. . . . Powerful massive chords lead to the majestic choral outburst of the "Kyrie Eleison" and then on to the triumphant "Gloria in Excelsis Deo." With dramatic suddenness comes the contrasting "Et in terra pax." The music now is hushed and filled with divine peace. Soon, to the words "Pater omnipotens," there comes the magnificent outburst of chorus with orchestra and organ. The slow prayer, "Qui tollis peccata mundi," rising and falling, male and female voices alternating, pleading, and supplicating, die mysteriously away. Then distant drums announcing the "Quoniam Tu Solus Sanctus" growing in glory, ending with the majestic fugue. . . . The "Credo" begins. A song of divine praise, until the sudden change of key and mood with the words "descendit de coelis." The hushed mystery of the section "et incarnatus est" is sung by the solo quartet. The throbbing passionate statement of the tenor declaims "Et Homo Factus Est" rising to a culminating ecstasy. The solemn tragedy of the Crucifixion, the dramatic resurrection at the end with the great fugue "Et Vitam Venturi". . . . The "Agnus Dei" begins with a solemn prayer from the bass voice answered by a chorus of male voices, and this final movement is pierced through and through by a poignant female cry, as if it were the voice of Eve, as in Michelangelo's "Last Judgment," where Eve lifts her hands to the enthroned figure pleading for her children (pp. 205–206).

Whether this awed experience remains for Epstein within the realm of music, or takes him into the realm of truth and worship, we do not know. One is driven to ask: Are his sculptures of Christ and Mary merely concepts, immense concepts, but concepts only?

Christ, the Word made flesh, demands that the world follow Him, and that, to be His disciple, a man leave, if need be, his father, mother, or wife, and always himself. This is not a "concept." This is an "either-or" demand. So to believe in Him as to follow Him, to let Him redeem us —this is what He asks of us, what He asked two thousand years ago, asks today, will ask tomorrow, unto the Last Judgment. We do not know how much of this Epstein acknowledges. Nor do we know how deeply he, the inner man, is committed. We know only his work.

There is his "Genesis" (1931), the mother of the human race. He tells that he deliberately carved this Seravezza marble "without the trappings and charm of what is known as feminine" so as to express "the profoundly elemental in motherhood" (p. 139). Here is the loving hand that protects the child to be born; here, the fruitfulness which gives an ever new chance to man; here, then, a glimpse of the Creator's blessing, "Be fruitful and multiply; fill the earth" (Gen 1:28). But one is taken aback to hear Epstein say that this Eve of his is "serene and majestic" when we rather find in it a sullen dignity; and again, that her expression is one of "calm, mindless wonder," as if all that mattered in motherhood were the elemental, the instinctive. Surely, the hope portrayed in this "Genesis" is altogether natural; she has not yet heard the first good tidings of the Redeemer.

As with all art that aspires to any degree of greatness, one finds implicit meanings in this Eve configuration that go beyond the artist's own words. Dorothy Sayers in her *Introductory Papers on Dante* speaks of the validity of the "reading-in" process (never violating the inner logic of the subject) and says in part: "If an image displays the universal pattern, it will display it at all levels and in all circumstances, whether the poet was or could have been conscious of these possible applications or not." So, in Epstein's "Genesis" one may discover implicit significances of great force. For this statue can be seen as Eve, at the instant after the fall, the anger of God having deprived her of

JACOB EPSTEIN: Madonna and Child (1952)

JACOB EPSTEIN: Madonna and Child (1926)

JACOB EPSTEIN: Madonna and Child (1926)

JACOB EPSTEIN: Madonna and Child (1952)

spiritual beauty: in this image of stricken resignation, pregnant with new life, and also with the sins that the world will be made to bear —some of the vast overtones of a true work of art disclose themselves to the wondering viewer.

Epstein's "Adam" (1939), carved in alabaster, is Adam after the fall. This is not the pure man made in God's image. This is Adam who has lost paradise and must go into the world, setting out on his task of fulfilling creation's purpose with the dignity and ferocity of the legendary bull who, with his broad back, tempted Europa and so founded a continent. Does he remember his sin and cry up to God for forgiveness? Is he listening for a voice which will announce the coming of another Adam? In any case, he is bound to earth and yet knows that the earth does not fulfill his destiny. While the massiveness of his body shows that it was made from what lies beneath its feet, the marked upward thrust of breast, hands, and head shows that he is made for God alone.

Whether or not this "Adam" is open to the promise of the new Adam, He has come, and, in order to come, He willed to need a mother. Epstein has spoken of Him and His mother in the "Madonna and Child" of 1926 and again in that of 1952. In the first, the Child leans against His mother; her hands embrace and yet barely hold Him, for He can stand on His own feet. More than that: He stands erect; though still a Child, He is conscious of His mission and so beckons all to come to Him. In the second, she is the handmaid: having borne Him for the world, she has no other life but His, that life He is ready to give so that His brethren may live. Could Epstein's bronze in Cavendish Square tell more clearly than it does that Christ has come to serve, to love, to heal?

In Epstein's "Lazarus," Christ is not visible, yet He is present as the Quickener, as the Death of death. He is the Quickener by His own suffering and dying, and Epstein's "Behold the Man" shows Him as wronged, crowned with thorns, grieved by mute hearts. Not only was He wronged, He emptied the cup of suffering; thus in Epstein's "Consummatum Est," His dead body is stretched out as if His passion had been in vain. Here Epstein seems to look at the Son of Man (he himself uses the title on page 153) very much the way the disciples did for a while. To him, *Consummatum est* seems to mean only "It is finished," and not also "It is fulfilled," the mandate of the Father carried out, the errand of mercy done. Still, in his "Christ" the Son of Man is risen. His face does not reveal His glory; but this is not surprising, for His glory was veiled from Mary Magdalene and from the disciples on the road to Emmaus. Accusingly He points to His wounds, for He is wronged again and again; and again this is not surprising, for He redeems *and* judges, precisely because He loves.

Ever since 1917, when he began work on his "Christ," Epstein has wrestled with religious themes. Does his powerful "Jacob and the Angel" (1941) tell his own story? All we have are his works. There can be no doubt that they, his works and his sculptor's heart and hands, are saying that Christ was born of Mary; that He wrought miracles, raised the dead; that He suffered under Pontius Pilate, was crucified, died, and was buried; that He arose from the dead. Though we would wish that the sculptor's was an ultimate commitment, this witness of bronze and stone is one the Christian cannot but be grateful for.

CORNELIA AND IRVING SÜSSMAN

John Beaty: THE IRON CURTAIN OVER AMERICA *

IN HIS *Orthodoxy,* G. K. Chesterton pointed out how pleasant it can be to explain the world's troubles as the result of conspiracy. For one thing, a theory of conspiracy permits us to blame all ills on others than ourselves. For another, it gives a feeling of superiority to our own elite group, which has uncovered the "truth" and is thus wiser than the duped masses. Third, such theories usually stand up well in argument, for their tight "circle" of causes and effects following so neatly on each other makes them difficult to disprove. When the world outside is disturbed, your armchair conspiracy expert can retire into a universe of innocence and smugness, immune to reality.

Thus, if a man should conclude that he was Napoleon, he would decide that his commitment to a mental hospital was a conspiracy of the Bourbons or the British. And the more his friends would argue that it was not so, the more reason he would have for considering them dupes or agents of that conspiracy. His whole world would be simplified by his mania. The stirring of every leaf would be the revelation of an ambush. Every ambiguous remark would be a signal. Every unfamiliar stranger would be an agent of the foe.

Even more than Chesterton's world of the turn of the century, our age is so complex and so full of impending tragedy that men yearn for easy explanations, preferably such as show them blameless for our ills. Hence the innumerable "Conspiracy!" schools flourishing around us. The good people are always ourselves, innocent (if naïve) red-blooded Americans. But the bad vary: Franklin D. Roosevelt, the Catholic hierarchy, the liberals, or the Jews; wittingly or not, they were, or are, supposed to be making us prey to Communism. Because the bad vary, there is political capital or publisher's royalties in raising a banner, mounting the rooftops, and analyzing *the* conspiracy.

The Iron Curtain Over America is but one of the current conspiracy tracts. The work of John Beaty of Dallas, who is a teacher at Southern Methodist University, a novelist, and the holder of a Co-

* Dallas: Wilkinson Publishing Co., 1951.

343

lumbia doctorate, it is, in its way, among the most successful of its kind, having passed through fourteen editions since its publication in 1951. It has uncovered a *new* secret vanguard of Communism, not simply the Jews but one particular group of Jews: the "Khazar Jews," who, according to Dr. Beaty, are not Semites, so that opposition to them is not anti-Semitism.

The Khazars, he tells us, originally a tribe from Asia, lived in south-central Russia. In the eighth or ninth century A.D., their king was converted to Judaism, leading his nobles and chiefs with him. Later conquered by the Russians to the north, the Khazars were, according to Dr. Beaty, dispersed throughout Europe and are now known as "Russian Jews" or "Judaized Khazars" or just "Khazars." Their religion, he continues, was ruled by the Babylonian Talmud, which, he quotes the Jewish historian Graetz as saying, contains "much that is frivolous," also "superstitious practices and views . . . which presume the efficacy of demoniacal medicines, of magic, incantations . . ." (p. 19).

All this is supposed to have prepared the "Khazars," centuries later, for the acceptance of Communism:

The Marxian program of drastic controls, so repugnant to the free western mind, was no obstacle to the acceptance of Marxism by many Khazar Jews, for the Babylonian Talmud under which they lived had taught them to accept authoritarian dictation on everything from their immorality to their trade practices. Since the Talmud contained over 12,000 controls, the regimentation of Marxism was acceptable—provided the Khazar politician, like the talmudic rabbi, exercised the power of the dictatorship (p. 27).

Dr. Beaty also discloses that various elements of the Khazars have nurtured through the centuries a determination to remain separated from other peoples, together with a fourfold aim: international Communism, control of Russia, Zionism, and migration to America (p. 25).

With the evil motives of the "Khazar Jews" thus set forth to Dr. Beaty's satisfaction, he moves on to a charge that they are essentially responsible for most of the ills twentieth-century flesh is heir to. There are no further details given on this doctrine, no restrictions upon its implications beyond the pious denial that individual Jews are evil, and no corroboration for it except the fact that the ills are with us and the doctrine seems to explain them to Dr. Beaty. It would aid our presentation of his theory if we could quote him at greater length, but he prefaces his book with a set of intricate rules on quotations from it; and I am quite sure he would not permit longer excerpts for inclusion in a book like *The Bridge*.

Catholics must see at once that a theory which postulates an affinity for Communism on the grounds of religious discipline can be used even more easily against themselves than against Jews. Indeed, the charge by anti-Catholic bigots that Communism and Catholicism are two forms of authoritarianism and thus akin antedates Dr. Beaty's theory and may be the basis of it. For the Talmud one could substitute some old books read by Catholics, books full of unverified legend. Nor must it be forgotten how, in ages past, Christians, Protestants and Catholics alike, were so ready to see witches everywhere. As for the alleged 12,000 "controls" enjoined by the Talmud on the Khazars, certainly an imposing number could be found in the works of moral theologians of the Catholic Church. Hence Dr. Beaty's reference to the Talmud proves nothing.

Not only could an anti-Catholic case be made out of Dr. Beaty's book by substituting "Catholic" for "Khazar," but the very method of his work is reminiscent of such established experts in the anti-Catholic world as Paul Blanshard. Like Blanshard, Beaty appears to prove his case by quoting his enemies. Blanshard quotes official Catholic sources; Beaty quotes approved Jewish sources. But, on analysis, we find that they both prove only part of their cases in this way—the final conclusion of hate, the charge of conspiracy, is out of whole cloth. Thus Blanshard, from the undoubted fact that the priest in the confessional acts as counselor and judge in moral matters, blithely assumes clerical dictatorship over Catholic lay activity. And thus Beaty quotes a Jewish historian on superstition in the Talmud; but its "immorality" is based on nothing, while the flight of fancy which makes the religiously disciplined mind fertile for Communism is an obvious absurdity.

Like Dr. Beaty, I was an army intelligence officer in World War II, and half my work was counter-intelligence on the Communist problem. Since then I have been, as a lawyer for labor unions, in very frequent contact with Communism in action. Lastly, I have been an active Democrat, a member of a party Dr. Beaty says is full of Khazars. In the first two activities, at least, I have known quite a few Jews with Communist leanings. No Jewish Communist I have ever known or heard of was at all religious. No religious Jew I have ever known or heard of was Communist. Marx himself was completely secularized, indeed opposed to all religion, and certainly not friendly toward the Jews when he declared that there could be no emancipation of Jews without the emancipation of society from Judaism, which he equated with commercialism—yet Dr. Beaty thinks he has said something relevant when he says Marx was of Jewish origin (pp. 26–27). Indeed, quite a respectable case could be made out for explaining whatever Communism there is among Jews as due to a lack of religious discipline, just as a case could be made out (as indicated in Pius XI's encyclical *Divini Redemptoris*) for explaining whatever Communism there is in Catholic countries as due in part to a failure to learn and practice social justice. Communism is not a religion, properly speaking, but it will rush in and fill the vacuum left in men who have lost religion.

However that may be, Dr. Beaty, having established to his own satisfaction a tendency of the Russian Jew to Communism because of his talmudic discipline, proceeds to enumerate the evils he alleges such Jews have done and are doing. Again like Blanshard, Dr. Beaty, having set forth his theory, does not blame each evil precisely on the Khazars. Occasionally the venom is spit only on Gentiles, like "the Truman-Acheson-Marshall clique" (p. 149). Often the blame is distributed, the rulers of Russia being divided between "renegade Russians" and "Judaized Khazars" (p. 227). Yet the general notion that we are caught in a Russian-Jewish conspiracy is constantly advanced. For this, race is sometimes blamed, only those Hitler would have called Aryans being judged capable of the American way (pp. 40–41). Sometimes the place from which people emigrate seems to poison them against us (pp. 57–59). But, in the end, the plot is detailed categorically, as in the title to Chapter III: "The Khazars Join the Democratic Party" (pp. 44–59).

The subjugation of the party of such Nordics as Andrew Jackson and Frank Hague came about through the immigration of Khazars. "Millions" of illegal immigrants were here in 1950, an unspecified number of them Khazars (p. 45). They were so numerous after

World War II that our returning heroes had few houses to live in. So numerous were the Khazars even before 1914 that they made a deal to join the Democratic minority party, thus making it the majority party. "Their price, carefully concealed from the American people . . . was the control of the foreign policy of the United States" (p. 51).

They were able, according to Dr. Beaty, to help get America into World War I. They prevented Hitler from destroying Communism (and note this mode of backhand praise of Der Führer) by having Franklin Roosevelt recognize Russia. By "some sinister underground deal [which] must have been consummated" (p. 64), they got the same Roosevelt to toughen his policy toward Germany, forcing England into World War II and maddening Hitler into a "deal" with Russia, resulting in our own entry, so that as many "Khazar-hated Aryans" as possible would be killed (p. 74). But that is not all: they "probably" were responsible for our over-rapid demobilization after World War II. (In his preface Dr. Beaty says he himself was discharged from the army in 1946, at his own request. He does not explain if in this he was a dupe of the Khazars or a co-conspirator with them.) The Khazar-controlled Democrats sacrificed China by "orders [to Chiang] to stop the mopping up of Communist forces" (p. 115). They aided in the creation of the state of Israel, which Dr. Beaty calls "extremely leftist—to say the least," because of communal farm methods (p. 127). Then the "leftist manipulators of the State Department" (p. 145) tried to have us defeated in Korea by sending too few troops. The Democrats were also responsible for "the black hood of censorship" (p. 80)—incidentally, Dr. Beaty manages to get himself into his own drama in the role of martyr: ". . . his book *Image of Life* . . . was granted, as far as he knows, not a single comment in a book review or a book column in New York" (p. x).

To cap the climax, upon the resignation of General Hurley as ambassador to China, our government's censors succeeded in canceling an interview of the General by Colonel Beaty, then a military intelligence interviewer (p. 86). Twenty-nine pages later this situation has worsened, and General Hurley "was not even allowed to visit the War Department . . . for an interview" (p. 115). Thus the Iron Curtain over America is finally all-pervading when the patriotic General and the patriotic Colonel are kept apart. One is left to conclude that Hurley and Beaty could not even meet for a chat over a short beer in Truman's Washington because of the lines of Khazar infantry drawn up on the White House lawn.

Enough. The list of Khazar crimes must be terminated, not because I have exhausted Dr. Beaty's supply, but because the list itself becomes exhausting. Even the unintended humor in Dr. Beaty's conceit wears thin when he speaks of the "alien minority" seeking to "own the coveted bodies of fair-haired girls and young men" of the East German Goths in Spain several hundred years ago (p. 196). His racism, thus revealed, is reminiscent of Streicher's infamous *Stürmer* of a little more than ten years ago.

But in kindling the fires of racism, Dr. Beaty is always careful not to exclude Catholics from his master race. As a former colonel, he knows it is best not to have two enemies at once. Even Catholic Slavs and Italians are part of his Indo-Germanic race, and he rejoices that they are being assimilated not only with the Irish but with the Anglo-American Catholics who, he is pleased to admit, have been here since before the Revolution. While claiming that East Germany is the home of Western Christian civilization, he is careful to have the Prussians fighting only Russians and never Poles. Hence when he cites a rather disquieting House report on the Immigration Act of 1924 as saying that "the basic strain of our population must be maintained" (p. 40), he does not mean to maintain it at the expense of Catholics, or maybe even Negroes. He means Jews. They are the people who form a nation within a nation, condemned by Dr. Beaty for refusing to be assimilated, even though he himself would object to assimilation as breaking down his own "basic strain."

On the other hand, Dr. Beaty does not limit his enemies to Democrats. Dulles he lumps with Truman, Acheson, and Hiss. Eisenhower he regards with pity and scorn because the Germans remember him in an unhappy light, and he cites an article from *Cosmopolitan* for July 1951 entitled "Truman's Plan to Make Eisenhower President," which may be intended to damn Eisenhower forever.

To vary his pattern of condemnation, Dr. Beaty sometimes singles out individual "Khazar-Jews" for special treatment. For example, Mrs. Anna M. Rosenberg, the first woman to hold a high position in our defense establishment, is accused of lowering the draft age for no other reason, so it seems, than that our soldiers would be more vulnerable to Khazar propaganda. But perhaps the most vicious of Dr. Beaty's individual character assassinations is that of the late Justice Brandeis, "Harvard Jew, of Prague Stock" (p. 47)—an excellent example of the conspiracy theory at its worst. Dr. Beaty quotes the *Universal Jewish Encyclopedia* as saying that Brandeis felt "that the Constitution must be given liberal construction," that he "probed the economics" of the problems presented to the Court, believing that "our individualistic philosophy could no longer furnish an adequate basis for dealing with modern economic life" (p. 48).

On reading this summary, any Catholic engaged in the social apostolate would be moved to praise. Not Dr. Beaty. To him it indicates that Brandeis fostered a philosophy of law which sponsored the movement to have courts assume judicial power over fields of government proper to the legislative authority, and thus to thwart the people's will. But let us contrast Dr. Beaty's wild theory with Justice Brandeis's own words, as he vainly pleads with six of his fellows (all Gentiles) in a famous dissent which is now the law: "The conditions developed in industry may be such that those engaged in it cannot continue their struggle [over the legality of a strike] without danger to the community. But it is not for judges to determine whether such conditions exist, nor is it their function to set the limits of permissible contest and to declare the duties which the new situation demands. This is the function of the legislature" (*Duplex Printing Press Co. v. Deering,* 254 US 443, 448). Thus Dr. Beaty has accused Brandeis of doing the opposite of what the record discloses. It is therefore not surprising that, in his next breath, he makes Brandeis the Zionist tool who caused Wilson to ask for a declaration of war against Germany in World War I. Dr. Beaty appears not to have heard about the U-boats which threatened Atlantic shipping: to the true conspiracy theoretician, facts which contradict his theory are ruled out of existence.

There are other "conclusions" in this book as much at variance with reality as those about Brandeis, but I must be content with some choice examples which reveal its main thesis. In unearthing that main thesis, however, a contradiction at once appears. Dr.

Beaty would seem to hold that race is the essential of American politics, religion, and culture. But he is altogether vague about the race of the Khazars and pinpoints their evils as the result of their religion. The wellspring of his antagonism would seem, then, to be the religious distinctiveness of the Jews. Like Blanshard, Dr. Beaty is at pains to divide good Jews from bad Jews so that he can rebut charges of bigotry; but in practice all Jews are bad. He makes no claim that Mrs. Rosenberg, Frankfurter, or Brandeis are Khazars; but they are Jews and they are bad. Their Jewishness is their crime. So it is their "talmudic discipline," rather than their blood, that adds a marked tendency to Communism to their other enormities.

It might thus be easy to accuse Dr. Beaty of being a religious bigot and to dismiss his book as the printed venom of that species. But there are flaws in such a theory. He is not a man of true religious concern, so far as one may judge from his *Iron Curtain*. His quotations from Scripture all seem afterthoughts at chapter ends. On the other hand, his background as a soldier, writer, and traveling scholar suggests the same type of unsuccessful dilettante as does Blanshard's. Both could have seized upon the theories which have brought them their brand of success merely as means to achieve that success. Hatred of Jews and Catholics may be inferred to be not so much their emotion as their business. If emotion be involved at all, it seems to be in the use of professionally held hates to escape their own apparent frustrations.

The theory about the Khazars, then, is not necessarily to be set down as religious bigotry. If it were, that is, if religious ideas seriously mattered to Dr. Beaty, we might hope to argue him into an admission, however reluctant, that the Jews, as a religious body, could be an aid in the spiritual war against godless Communism. Indeed, the very courage and cohesiveness of the Jewish community, in Israel and elsewhere, is a proof of the religious basis of culture and a denial of the Marxist claim that all human activity is basically economic. By lumping his half-mythical Khazars with the Jews of the Dispersion, Dr. Beaty implicitly confesses that faith, not race, makes a people or a nation or a civilization. But he no more admits this than Marx would. He bases our individuality on race, as Marx does on economic supply and demand. Frankly and parenthetically, Marx's theory is less repulsive.

But both Marx's and Beaty's theories are disproved by the very existence of "the Jews" as a separate or separable people. It is faith that has preserved and will preserve them as a group. Hence the state of Israel is a refutation of materialism, whether of breeding or of economics; and it is as ideologically embarrassing to the Soviet Union as it is at times politically embarrassing to our government. If Dr. Beaty were somewhat more objective, he might realize that communal farm methods no more make Israel "Communistic" than does common property make the religious orders "Communistic." This is not to say that a spiritual zeal animates all Israelis; but it is to say that even a faith as spent and as this-worldly as that of so many of them is still strong enough a force to bind them together.

In putting together as bedfellows the "Khazar Zionists" and the Communists, Dr. Beaty has lived up to still another mark of the conspiracy method, namely, to pick two pet hates and allege that they are conspiring against you jointly. Whenever the justified opposition to Communism is joined by another hatred—be it of the Catholic Church, Jews, Democrats, Negroes, or the British—then the mania has set in. Then the clear and present danger is parodied into "twenty years of treason" or "the plot of the Khazars," and all real problems are befogged in hate—hate made all the more detestable in this case by the author's conscious effort to enlist Catholics on the side of wrong.

I wonder whether Dr. Beaty is unaware that anti-Semitism hardly ever stops at hatred of Jews, but from there leads all too easily to hatred of the Old, and then the New, Testament, to rejection of Christ and the Church. For he is at pains to tell us that his "anti-Khazarism" does not reflect on the Bible and the Israel of old. He wants us to believe that as the Jews of old, through the house and family of David, brought Redemption into the world, so the Jews, through the conversion of the house and nation of Bulan, the Khazar king, brought Communism into the world. To the Catholic, salvation is of the Jews. To Dr. Beaty, damnation is of them also. Dr. Beaty's Christianity is not that of the One for whom it is named, as Hitler's swastika, according to Pius XI, was a cross that was not the cross of Christ.

Of the continued existence of the Khazars, Dr. Beaty offers no proof. Even the conversion to Judaism of any number of them other than the nobility he leaves uncertain; and he gives us no evidence of the converted gentry's steadfastness in that faith through the succeeding centuries. It is all bald assertion. He makes no claim of mutual exclusiveness between Khazar and non-Khazar Jews, so that the Khazars must by now be assimilated into the general Jewish body. To single them out as a conspiracy party is about as realistic as claiming that the Normans are ruining modern England or that the "Milesian party" is subverting Ireland. Of the theory that modern Jews coming from eastern Europe are descendants of the Khazars, D. M. Dunlop, in his *History of the Jewish Khazars* (Princeton University Press, 1954), says, with the scholarly caution so completely wanting in Dr. Beaty's book, that it "retains the character of a mere assumption" and goes "much beyond what our imperfect records allow" (pp. 261, 263).

Professor Dunlop also notes that the Khazars, prior to their king's conversion to Judaism, held back the Arabs from an attempted invasion of Europe by a route north of the Black Sea. He concludes that this military feat was scarcely less important to Christendom than the victory over the Arabs by Charles Martel at Tours in 732 (pp. ix, x). Hence those who Dr. Beaty says would destroy us today are descendants of those who saved us yesterday. But if good and evil may be descended from the same stock, then history is made by free will, and Dr. Beaty's theory of evil races is chased back into its sewer.

Thus the Khazars are a new dodge in an old game, that of baiting Jews, just as race is a new front for the attack on religion. It is therefore one of Dr. Beaty's crimes that he attacks a religion in the name of defense of religion, and seeks to create a spiritual civil war while the Communists camp at the gates. His attack on Jews is, in this sense, an attack on them where they are least vulnerable: in their spiritual discipline. This is not to say that I, as a Christian, find Jewish theology invulnerable. But it is vulnerable only theologically. And Dr. Beaty's book is anything but theological.

Jewish errors, whether in politics or in social or international relations, are, of course, open to a critical review, as are the errors of all men, of all groups. But Dr. Beaty gives us no such review. The very force of his attack forestalls any such review, obligating all men of good will to close ranks and defend the rights of Jews.

Those rights include the right to be Jewish in our society and the right to a good name. Dr. Beaty, who claims to be defending Western civilization, should certainly see that these rights and others are demanded by elementary justice. But logic and Dr. Beaty are friends only when the conclusion fits his predetermined desires. Otherwise, logic has nothing to do with the case, and, ultimately, hate or bigotry or monomania have everything to do with it.

To return to the Chesterton thesis with which I began, the conspiracy theorist transmutes any set of facts into his own proofs, until he thinks all the world is leagued against him, and the more one seeks to argue with him, the more reason he finds for linking his opponents to the plot. The devils who goad him are thus not subject to eviction by such a brief as this. That kind is not driven out but by prayer and fasting.

JOHN J. BRACKEN

NOTES AND ACKNOWLEDGMENTS

HOLY SCRIPTURE is generally quoted in accordance with the Confraternity version of the Bible or, in the case of the books not yet published in that version, in accordance with the Douay. Frequently, however, the divine Name, "Yahweh," is given where these two versions use "Lord" instead. The book of Isaiah is almost always quoted in Dr. Edward J. Kissane's translation (Dublin: Browne and Nolan, 1941–43). In quotations from Jewish authors, rabbinical texts, or the Jewish prayer book, their wording is retained.

No matter which translation of Scripture is used, chapter and verse are cited in accordance with the Confraternity version or, in lieu of it, with the Douay. The abbreviations of the titles of biblical books are those used by *A Catholic Commentary on Holy Scripture,* ed. B. Orchard, O.S.B. (London: Nelson, 1953). In transliterations of Hebrew and Greek, no attempt has been made to render all the complexities of the original. The system followed for Hebrew is, in general, that of the *Jewish Encyclopedia;* the system followed for Greek is, with minor modifications, that used by Webster's *New International Dictionary.* Biblical names are given in that English form most closely approximating the Hebrew.

Monsignor Journet's "The Mysterious Destinies of Israel" and Friedrich Pater's "The Beasts and the Everlasting Love" were translated by the Editor.

We acknowledge with thanks the gracious permission of the Viking Press to quote so extensively from Dr. Millar Burrows's translations in his book *The Dead Sea Scrolls;* of the editors of *Theological Studies* to quote from "Sectarian Psalms from the Dead Sea" by George S. Glanzman, S.J., in their issue of December 1952; of Miss Sally Ryan to reproduce the two photographs of Jacob Epstein's "Madonna and Child" (1926); of the Convent of the Holy Child, London, to reproduce one photograph of his "Madonna and Child" (1952); and of Maurice Lavanoux, secretary of the Liturgical Arts Society, to reproduce another view.

CONTRIBUTORS

Mary Ruth Bede, after undergraduate work in the natural sciences and graduate work in mathematics at New York University and Brooklyn College, turned to Judaeo-Christian studies. She is now assistant to the editor of THE BRIDGE.

John J. Bracken, a graduate of Seton Hall College and Rutgers Law School, is a practicing attorney and a teacher at the Institute of Industrial Relations of St. Peter's College, Jersey City. He is an oblate of Dormition Abbey in Jerusalem.

Father J. Edgar Bruns, holding an S.T.D. from the Gregorian University and an S.S.L. from the Pontifical Biblical Institute, has contributed to the *Catholic Biblical Quarterly* and to *Scripture*. A member of the Catholic Biblical Association, he was represented in Volume I by reviews of Buber, Dix, and Graves.

Father Edward H. Flannery, who studied theology in Paris, has translated works by Maritain and Mauriac, and undertook a survey of the Finaly case for Volume I. A member of the Catholic Theological Society and the Catholic Association for International Peace, he is assistant editor of the *Providence Visitor*.

Father Alexander Jones, S.T.L., L.S.S., is professor of Sacred Scripture and Hebrew at Upholland College in Lancashire, England. He is author of, among other things, *Unless Some Man Show Me* and the chapter on St. Matthew's Gospel in *A Catholic Commentary on Holy Scripture*.

Monsignor Charles Journet, professor of theology at the Grand Séminaire in Fribourg, Switzerland, is editor of *Nova et Vetera*. Among his many

355

works are *The Church of the Word Incarnate* and *Destinées d'Israël,* a fuller development of the theme he presents in this volume.

Father William Keller, S.T.L., assistant professor of social studies at Seton Hall University, is a member of the American Catholic Historical Association and the American Historical Association. He summarized for Volume I the fearful figures of the Nazi massacre of Jews.

Father Quentin Lauer, S.J., of Fordham University, earned his *Docteur ès Lettres* at the Sorbonne with *La Phénomenologie de Husserl.* His field is the whole range of modern philosophy. He is a member of the American Catholic Philosophical Association, the American Philosophical Association, and the Metaphysical Society of America.

Father Joseph N. Moody, PH.D., of Cathedral College, New York, is also chairman of the department of history and political science at the College of Notre Dame, Staten Island; vice-president of the Society for French Historical Study; and a member of the executive board of the Catholic Commission for Intellectual and Cultural Affairs. In 1937, he was awarded the B'nai B'rith citation "for services in defense of human rights."

Richard J. Schoeck, PH.D., studied at McGill and Princeton, taught at Cornell, and is now assistant professor of English at the University of Notre Dame. He has written widely for learned reviews, and is a member of the Mediaeval Academy of America and the Renaissance Society of America.

Mother Kathryn Sullivan, R.S.C.J., PH.D., research professor of Scripture and professor of history at Manhattanville College, Purchase, N. Y., is a member of the Catholic Biblical Association. Coauthor of the *Catholic Biblical Encyclopedia,* she contributes frequently to *Worship.*

Cornelia and Irving Süssman, who live in the Mojave Desert, have published in almost every genre. Volume I presented their analysis of "Marc Chagall: Painter of the Crucified." Their interest in art and artists is by no means academic, for Irving Süssman is himself a painter.

Father Edward A. Synan, S.T.L., L.M.S., PH.D., is chairman of the department of philosophy at Seton Hall University and a member of the American Catholic Philosophical Association. He examined an important figure of the contemporary Jewish religious scene in his essay "Abraham Heschel and Prayer" in Volume I.

Barry Ulanov, holding a PH.D. from Columbia, is assistant professor of English at Barnard College. A Renaissance scholar, a student of Christian humanism, a lecturer, and a music critic, he is vice-president of the Catholic Renascence Society. In Volume I he was represented by "Shylock: The Quality of Justice." He is associate editor of THE BRIDGE.